Empowered Families, Successful Children

Empowered Families, Successful Children

**Early
Intervention
Programs
That
Work**

**SUSAN EPPS
AND
BARBARA J. JACKSON**

American Psychological Association
Washington, DC

Published by
American Psychological Association
750 First Street, NE
Washington, DC 20002

Copies may be ordered from
APA Order Department
P.O. Box 92984
Washington, DC 20090-2984

In the United Kingdom, Europe, Africa, and the Middle East, copies may be ordered from
American Psychological Association
3 Henrietta Street
Covent Garden, London
WC2E 8LU England

Typeset in Century Schoolbook by EPS Group Inc., Easton, MD
Printer: United Book Press, Baltimore, MD
Cover Designer: Watermark Design Office, Alexandria, VA
Editor/Project Manager: Debbie Hardin, Reston, VA

The opinions and statements published are the responsibility of the authors, and such opinions and statements do not necessarily represent the policies of the APA.

Library of Congress Cataloging-in-Publication Data

Epps, Susan.
  Empowered families, successful children : early intervention programs that work/ Susan Epps and Barbara J. Jackson.
    p. cm.
  Includes bibliographical references and index.
  ISBN 1-55798-659-2 (alk. paper)
  1. Children—Counseling of. 2. Infants—Counseling of. 3. Counseling. I. Jackson, Barbara, 1952– II. Title.

  BF637.C6 E66 2000
  362.7—dc21
                                                                  99-086521

British Library Cataloguing-in-Publication Data
A CIP record is available from the British Library.

Printed in the United States of America
First Edition

In loving memory of our brothers:

Jones Newton Epps, Jr.
Joseph Eugene Epps

and

Steven Craig Sulley

Contents

Acknowledgments

We express our genuine appreciation to all the children and families over the years who have taught us how to reconfigure our relationships with them. The resolute support from our husbands, Rudy Forst and Joe Jackson, and urging from our children, Joshua, Leigh, and Joel, made this book possible. We are grateful to reviewers and indebted to Dr. Jan Hughes for her scholarly commentary. We also thank our colleagues who have helped us understand the true meaning of collaboration, celebration of the journey toward resilience-enhancing care, and reflective process as we all work together in organization change and development to infuse excellence into early childhood approaches.

Empowered Families, Successful Children

Introduction

Ms. Johnson, a psychologist for the community early intervention team, completes a developmental assessment with Adese, who is 3 years old. In interpreting the results of the assessment, Ms. Johnson identifies Adese's strengths in the area of communication. Adese understands many words and follows simple directions. Her less developed area is her limited expressive language. Adese only uses two to three words, both at home and at school. The early intervention team and Adese's family began to determine an intervention plan that included the services needed, with recommended duration and frequencies necessary to promote Adese's communication development. It was clear that speech/language therapy services were a priority. Together with Adese's family, the team recommended that she participate in a preschool program that was cotaught by a teacher and speech pathologist and that included typical 3- and 4-year-olds as language models. The plan identified the need to establish an augmentative communication approach that integrated symbolic aides (e.g., gestures and picture board) and teaching approaches that would enhance her communication. These strategies would be implemented across Adese's routines (e.g., pointing to pictures to request food choices at snack time) and her environment (e.g., home, preschool and childcare).

This example is one of many that describes a family-centered approach to early intervention based on the developmental concerns of children as well as their specific strengths and competencies. It also illustrates the principle of identifying environmental and family supports that shore up limitations in specific functional areas. In this book, a model for early childhood intervention is developed along these lines that also takes into account the diversity of young children and families and emphasizes integration with the community in which they live. The model is theory driven and empirically based and emphasizes a systems approach to service delivery.

Book's Audience

Those who work with children from birth to 5 years of age with developmental challenges or with children who are at risk for delays will find this book most useful, but the content can be generalized for those who work with older children as well. Psychologists, educators, social workers, program developers and administrators, and those providing specialized services to young at-risk populations are the target audience. Clinical child, developmental, pediatric, and school psychologists, as well as graduate students in these disciplines, should find the content particularly relevant to their work. Given the collaborative, transdisciplinary, and interagency nature of early childhood practice, however, we have geared the content to be broadly applicable to providers and service coordinators across disciplines and agencies. Professors, program administrators, and others in leadership positions in agencies will find the focus on professional development, administrative innovations, and systems change particularly relevant. Because of the heterogeneity of children who participate in early intervention programs (as well as children encountered in clinical practice), these providers and program administrators need a broad knowledge of a wide range of disabilities and risk conditions. They also must know how to develop strategies to gather information about new conditions that they encounter (Bailey & Wolery, 1992). This book provides this information.

This book draws from and integrates a diverse theoretical, empirical, and applied literature from psychology, early childhood education, early childhood special education, child development, maternal and child health, child life, neonatology, developmental and behavioral pediatrics, allied health and related services, bioethics, public policy, management, leadership, and organization development. The fundamental tenets of best practices in early intervention are interwoven throughout the chapters. Each chapter includes conceptual formulations, contextual factors, clinical and policy implications, and recommendations for empirical investigations. Numerous case studies and clinical scenarios also are presented to illustrate application and integration of concepts.

In the pages that follow, we describe the general principles on which the intervention model is based and outline the plan of the book. Although the chapters build on one another sequentially, the plan of the book is to enable readers to use the most relevant chapters for intensive study.

Five Key Principles

Five principles that are key to designing and implementing effective interventions for this population are interwoven throughout this book.

First, services are *family-centered*. This approach is built on the premise that families are active participants in all aspects of services for their children and for themselves. This partnership is built on trust, respect, and open communication. Family-centered services promote expansion of services that are exclusively directed toward the child to include support of the family by building on families' informal support systems rather than relying solely on professional services. (See chapter 4.)

Second, intervention needs to focus on *competence* and *resilience* of the child and family. (Refer to chapter 3.) Early intervention needs to identify family and child strengths. This emphasis on resilience represents a paradigm shift away from a needs-based model, which accentuates weaknesses and deficits, and toward a focus on child and family resilience, coping, and strengths (Epps, 1995).

Third, early intervention is part of an *integrated service delivery system* that occurs through a collaborative community-building process and prioritizes family and agency partnerships. (See chapter 4.) Family and agency partnerships occur when families have the opportunity to provide input at all levels of the service delivery system. Such input may include helping to identify and to plan their own family's intervention, serving on agency advisory boards, and reviewing materials developed and disseminated by a program. An integrated service delivery system is best defined from the perspective of the family. Services are comprehensive and accessible and address the priority concerns of the family in such a way that the family perceives the services as an organized whole (Illback, Cobb, & Joseph, 1997). In an integrated system, the family is central to the delivery system and the programs are committed to the full partnership and participation of the family. In addition, individual programs implement a team approach that integrates information across disciplines and agencies.

Fourth, a *systems approach* acknowledges the importance of examining individuals in relationship to others, to families, and to the organizations and communities in which they live and work. A systems approach reflects the dynamic nature of relationships. Influences at one level potentially have a ripple effect on others within their interrelated network. The child who becomes stressed when his or her primary child care provider changes certainly causes concern for a parent who may then be less effective in work, as she worries about her child's adjustment to a new caregiver.

Fifth is the need for early intervention to be *empirically driven*. Best practices are based on diverse theoretical perspectives and are grounded in research findings and applied literature. High-quality services are built from a strong theoretical foundation that are carefully considered and agreed on. Most flourishing programs are those that continually modify and improve their service delivery system based on information from empirical studies.

Incorporating these five principles into early intervention approaches is central to successful outcomes for children and families, and these themes are paramount throughout the following chapters.

Plan of the Book

In chapter 1 we trace the history of legislative programs that provide the political and economic support for many of the services that are provided to young children. We also review the diversity of children, families, and particular types of programs to serve them as they are most often configured today. Finally, we provide an overview of systems theory, which is the cornerstone of our approach to early intervention services.

In chapter 2 we describe the multiple pathways to eligibility for early childhood services. We define developmental delay as an eligibility category for early intervention, as well as the variations in its definition across states. We discuss diverse nosological systems used by service providers across agencies to promote an understanding of diagnostic processes. Next we describe a framework based on primary, secondary, and tertiary levels of prevention and explore its utility in early intervention. Finally, we introduce a model for conceptualizing risk in early childhood.

In chapter 3 we underscore the importance of examining child and family risk characteristics within an ecological context. Throughout the chapter, we advocate comprehensive screening paradigms that consider multiple risk factors and broad-based early childhood initiatives at various levels of the social ecology. We discuss at length the contextual view of development, with attention devoted to competence, protective factors, and the multiplicity of variables influencing risk. This chapter highlights the importance of understanding resilience to identify the characteristics of children, their environments, and their familial and social relationships that promote adaptive development under challenging conditions. We review the contexts of those living in poverty, young children of adolescent parents, growth deficiency, and maltreatment to illustrate implications for assessment and intervention when adopting a broad systems approach.

The cornerstone of an integrated service delivery system for early intervention is the aim of chapter 4—namely, family and community partnerships. The overall goal of this chapter is to provide information about promoting collaborative services that strengthen and support families. We provide concrete examples to clarify and to differentiate collaboration from coordinated and cooperative initiatives, and we explore the complex variables influencing collaboration between providers and families. Specifically, we describe skills related to family-centered practices and cultural competence. Case scenarios illustrate supportive relationship building with families and implementation of family-centered care.

In chapter 5 we discuss multiple factors that encompass the delivery of early intervention services. Effective planning, implementation, and monitoring are the cornerstones of early intervention services, with the family playing an integral role. The assumption is that an effective early childhood service delivery system must be fluid and dynamic, with opportunities for responding to changing family priorities and concerns. The goal is responsive and proactive systems of support that strengthen families and their natural support networks and provide proven child programs of high quality.

Chapter 6 allows us to highlight the dynamic nature of the developing parent–child relationship. Recognizing that early intervention needs to be more than a child-focused program, this chapter explores the insights from attachment and transactional theories and research related to early caregiver–child relationships. We explore the ecology of caregiver–child interaction in depth, as well as developmental and behavioral clinical implications, providing assessment and intervention strategies that facilitate caregiver–child interaction. The chapter also offers guidelines for supporting families with young children experiencing difficult behavioral patterns.

In chapter 7 we review ethical principles to provide a conceptual basis for ethical deliberation. Our contention is that ethics should be among the primary priorities in early intervention, including institutional policy. We provide examples to illustrate ethical deliberation by early intervention teams, and we explore professional codes of ethics and the need for reflection in ethical problem solving. Finally, we propose guidelines to enhance better-informed and broadly acceptable ethical decision making.

We argue for innovation and a substantive shift in priorities for professional development in chapter 8. We contend that it is the duty of professors and practitioners alike to provide those in training with an expanded array of expertise to establish effective alliances with families and other providers and to become agents of change. This chapter offers direction for the preparation of the next generation of early childhood psychologists and other early childhood providers who facilitate the development of young children, their families, and organizations. Rather than focusing exclusively on training activities for the direct service provider, this chapter addresses the entire spectrum of professional development, from preservice and inservice programs to supervision and mentorship. In addition to focusing on professional competencies, we address the processes of professional development activities, which adhere to tenets of early childhood best practices, including collaboration, family involvement, and relationship building. Extensive attention is devoted to cross-discipline training, collegial support, and reflective process.

We recognize that as programs begin to strive toward a new system of family-centered intervention, change is inevitable; we explore this change process in chapter 9. To be successful in confronting the many challenges inherent in change, we believe a framework that encompasses five primary activities is necessary. We present practical strategies to assist providers in adopting new programs and continually improving the quality of services and review the multiparadigmatic nature of leadership, with implications for early intervention systems change. A case study provides a comprehensive organizational and group analysis of a team in a community-based early intervention program, with recommendations for supporting change at both organization and group levels.

In chapter 10 we describe a multivariate evaluation framework, recognizing the interactive influence of program context, processes, and outcomes. It is essential that early intervention programs incorporate ongoing evaluation to facilitate program improvement and to examine the merit of their program. We present practical strategies for planning and implementing formative and outcome evaluation and discuss evaluating child and family outcomes. We also introduce result mapping, an innovative evaluation approach, as a mechanism to evaluate the complexity of early intervention through the analysis of program stories.

A Quest for Excellence

This book is about cultivating excellence in early intervention. We believe that the goal is ongoing evolution toward increasing concordance with best practices of cultural competency, family-centeredness, collaboration, and contextual and developmental appropriateness. Years of academic study offer the theoretical basis for early childhood constructs, and ongoing professional development entails lifelong endeavors to cultivate competence in integrating practice, research, and policy. Positive reframing is important. Rather than regarding one's own skills or the organization's practice as antithetical to contemporary thinking, we recommend viewing the process of change as a journey toward excellence. If institutions of higher education wish to prepare high-quality, early childhood personnel capable of responding to complex role requirements, they must move swiftly away from promulgating antiquated standards that benefit neither child nor society. Such a change requires innovation and a substantive shift in priorities. As Kramer and Epps remarked, "We can no longer blame schools, bemoan the intransigence of state departments of education, complain about the lack of appropriate practica and internship sites, nor deride unresponsive teachers" (1991, p. 453). Rather, our challenge is to support students and providers-in-training in developing and refining their skills through innovative educational approaches.

Psychology is at a pivotal juncture in its evolution toward early childhood best practices. As innovations in technology and provider role responsibilities, societal and economic forces, and legislative realities continue to transform the landscape of early childhood practice, it is important for those in the field to be courageous and flexible in responding to challenges. Visionary leadership is needed that transcends political interests, challenges taken-for-granted assumptions, and offers new directions in accelerating change. We advocate change efforts from a systems perspective in which the entire pattern of change is the focus rather than isolated portions of innovation. An alliance is needed among all players to enhance the scientific quality and community relevance of supports for young children and their families and to build harmony and common purpose from diverse resources.

The journey toward such revolutionary change requires rethinking and reframing throughout the assortment of professional activities. We must reduce paternalistic postures, renegotiate relationships with families and providers, and intertwine ethical principles at every phase of service delivery. In some cases, immense change is needed, relinquishing outdated, comfortable strategies and forging innovative approaches. As Gilkerson noted, "We must build around ourselves supportive processes as dependable as gravity, processes which hold and contain us, and which renew and launch us back again" (1992, p. 21). Infusing reflective process throughout professional practice is crucial given the complexity of early childhood contexts and the relationship-based, systems-oriented nature of early childhood supports. In all contexts, it is critical that professors, experienced practitioners, employers, professional associations, and even state certification boards, support psychologists and other providers as they expand their more traditional boundaries to the unique areas of early childhood practice. Strengthening relationships is the key to success for early intervention in the future. We need relationship building across agencies, relationships between families and providers, and relationships between families and their children.

Time and time again the literature has documented the importance of facilitating family–child interaction to build competence and to strengthen protective factors. We must appreciate the dynamic nature of the developing parent–child relationship and recognize that early intervention needs to be much more than child focused. Yet how often do early childhood programs really consider parent–child interaction? How many providers actually have the skills to support this complex relationship?

The current focus on cost containment, quality assurance, accountability, and documentation of effectiveness of programs has transformed our service delivery. Economic forces are exerting a profound impact on the practice of psychology—as it is on all education and health care services in the United States and beyond. Providers are experiencing reductions in reimbursement for psychological services and the growth of managed care in private payment systems and in the public sector (e.g., Medicaid). Hence the capitated environment compels all of us to consider judicious use of lower cost service extenders, which in turn highlights the importance of imaginative models of service provision. Effective early childhood service delivery must be fluid and dynamic, with opportunities for responding to changing family priorities and concerns. The goal is responsive and proactive systems of support that strengthen families and their natural support networks. Future policy development indeed may identify a multirisk definition of eligibility as an established condition (Federal Register, 1992), which then would enable comprehensive preventive interventions that enhance resilience. Rather than services exclusively for populations with identified delay or established conditions at risk for delay, we encourage expansion of early intervention to include prevention at multiple levels of the social ecology.

We face an enormous task and undoubtedly will encounter obstacles. However, there are heartening opportunities for creativity and innovation. We already have begun the trend toward better-informed policy decisions. The infusion of excellence into the full universe of early childhood services is the compass for future directions in ecologically appropriate, family-centered supports. Yet high expectations go hand in hand with the potential for disappointments. The challenge is to maintain our trajectory in the presence of significant barriers. Innovations cannot be achieved without energy, effort, and genuine commitment. They cannot be accomplished at all under an ideology unwilling to prepare for the future.

As service providers, our analysis, perseverance, reflection, and cognitive and emotional synthesis can catapult us into an enlightened and informed paradigm. We can do it. Let us begin our journey toward excellence in early childhood services.

Part I

Setting the Stage for Early Intervention

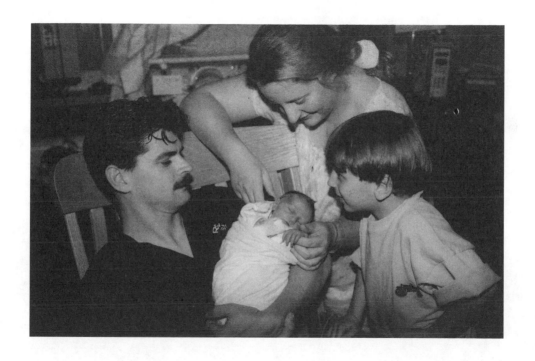

Early Childhood Programs: Models and Practices

The primary issues for early intervention now are ones of the political will to aid vulnerable children, the appropriate scale of resources needed to provide potentially effective interventions, and commitment to conducting rigorous research to move the field of early intervention forward. (Ramey & Ramey, 1998, p. 119)

This chapter begins with a review of some of the legislation that forms the political and economic basis for the existence of many of the services described in the book. In particular, the Education for the Handicapped Act Amendments, the Individuals With Disabilities Education Act Amendments, and maternal and child health legislation have led to a steep increase in the number of early intervention programs for young children and their families. An understanding of this material, although seemingly inaccessible and perhaps even dry, is absolutely necessary for those involved in the changing political and economic tides involving young children. Knowing the history of federal legislation provides a foundation for understanding additional legislation.

Following this review, we describe the diversity of children, settings, and families for whom this legislation was created. Finally, we provide an overview of systems theory, the theoretical cornerstone of our early intervention model.

Legislative Support for Early Intervention

The evolution of early intervention services is best understood by examining federal legislation and mandates. Legislative and judicial systems interpret and enforce public policy that guides service priorities and activities (Noonan & McCormick, 1993). State statutes, rules, and regulations influence the specific implementation of the essence of federal public policy and account for variability in services across states. Beginning in the mid-1960s there was an impressive history of increasing support for early childhood programs across federal agencies. Major legislation is summarized in Table 1.1. This legislation, resulting from research, public awareness, and advocacy efforts by family members and service providers,

Table 1.1. Prevention- and Disabilities-Related Legislation Influencing Early Intervention

Year	Legislation
1965	Elementary and Secondary Education Act (ESEA) of 1965 funded Head Start to support young preschool children who were environmentally at risk and their families.
1968	Public Law 90-538, the Handicapped Children's Early Education Assistance Act (HCEEAA), established the Handicapped Children's Early Education Program (HCEEP) that promoted development of model programs.
1972	Public Law 92-424 amended the Economic Opportunity Act to expand Head Start services to mandate inclusion of at least 10% of children with disabilities.
1975	Public Law 94-142, the Education for All Handicapped Children's Act (EHA), established the Preschool Incentive Grants and state grant awards that provided incentive money to promote early intervention.
1986	Public Law 99-457 amended Public Law 94-142 by extending the free and appropriate public education mandate to preschoolers with disabilities (Part B) and establishing a new discretionary program for infants, toddlers, and their families (Part H).
1990	Public Law 101-476 changed EHA to the Individuals With Disabilities Education Act (IDEA).
1991	Public Law 102-119, the Individuals With Disabilities Education Act amendments of 1991, amended the IDEA with a stronger emphasis on inclusion.
1992	Public Law 102-421, the Individuals With Disabilities Education Act amendments of 1992, amended the IDEA
1997	Public Law 105-17, the Individuals With Disabilities Education Act amendments of 1997, extended the use of "developmental delay" category for eligibility and extended authorization until 2002.

reflects the changing view of the child and the importance of early intervention in the lives of children who are at risk for or have disabilities. The following section reviews two decades of federal initiatives that have progressively broadened services for such young children (Hebbeler, Smith, & Black, 1991).

Prevention-Related Legislation: A Stepping Stone to Disability-Related Legislation

Early childhood special education has its roots in early childhood education and special education for school-aged children. The Elementary and Secondary Education Act (ESEA) of 1965 funded Head Start as a means of serving young children who were environmentally at risk (those living in poverty or with abusive or neglectful caregivers) and their families. Its passage was the first evidence of legislative concern for early education and marked the beginning of a national expansion of early intervention efforts (Noonan & McCormick, 1993). The overall purpose of the Head

Start legislation was to ameliorate the effects of poverty on children by providing support to both the child and family. In the United States the children's poverty level is twice as high as in most other industrialized nations (Danziger & Danziger, 1993). The Economic Opportunity amendments of 1972 (Public Law 92-424) expanded Head Start efforts to include children of all socioeconomic backgrounds with disabilities. This legislation required that Head Start programs reserve at least 10% of their enrollment for 3- to 5-year-olds with disabilities. The Head Start Act in 1994 created an umbrella of Head Start's programs for families with infants and toddlers, including comprehensive child development programs, parent–child centers, and migrant Head Start programs to provide more intensive support to children and their families at or below the poverty line (Advisory Committee on Services for Families with Infants and Toddlers, 1994). These Head Start initiatives served more than 17 million children and their families between 1965 and 1998 (U.S. Department of Health and Human Services, 1999).

Legislation Related to Early Childhood Disabilities

The Handicapped Children's Early Education Assistance Act of 1968 (Public Law 90-538) provided funding for short-term projects to identify effective procedures and models for serving young children with disabilities and their families. In 1991, the Individuals With Disabilities Education Act (Public Law 101-476) changed the name to Early Education Programs for Children With Disabilities. This legislation provided for the first federal special education programs targeted exclusively for young children with disabilities. These funded projects continue to provide an important resource to the field through the dissemination of effective data-based models of service delivery for young children with disabilities and their families.

Hallmark legislation for the rights of children with disabilities and their families occurred in 1975 through the Education for All Handicapped Children Act (EHA; Public Law 94-142), which mandated that if a state offered public education to children at any age, it could not exclude children with disabilities of the same age from a free and appropriate public education (FAPE), including special education and related services. The EHA set forth procedural protections and mandated the following service components: (a) nondiscriminatory evaluation by an interdisciplinary team that identifies the child's strengths and weaknesses; (b) development of an Individualized Education Program (IEP) that identifies objectives, strategies, and evaluation; (c) assurance that children are served in the least restrictive environment (LRE) (e.g., appropriate participation in general education programs); and (d) recognition of the importance of parents' participation in their children's education program. This law resulted in a dramatic change in the number of children with disabilities served in public education, the quality of services, and the expectations of the parental role. Because most states did not serve all children birth through age 5, there were limited services available for young children with disabilities. As a result, only incentive monies were available to states to encourage services for the 3- to 5-year-old population through the Preschool Incentive Grant (EHA-Part B). These monies were not provided at the same level of funding available for children ages 6 to 18 years. As a result, many states did not provide services for children between the ages of 3 through 5 years as the incentive funds offered to serve this young population were not sufficient to cover total program costs. The Education of the Handicapped Act amendments (Public Law 98-199) extended these preschool incentive grant programs to include children birth through 3 years of age. Although both of these initiatives laid the basis for early intervention at a state level, the EHA endorsements of early childhood special education did not ignite state services for this population; services available for young children with disabilities and their families continued to be limited.

The early intervention movement in special education was most influenced by the Education of the Handicapped Act amendments of 1986 (Public Law 99-457), because it significantly changed the federal government's role in supporting services for young children with disabilities. The primary basis for legislation of this early intervention model was economic (decreased long-term costs associated with early intervention; Woody, LaVoie, & Epps, 1992). This outcome was to be realized by enhancing the development of young children, minimizing the need for special education for this group of children when they reached school-age, and enhancing the capacity of families to meet the needs of their young children with disabilities. This legislation mandated the extension of the right to education to eligible 3- to 5-year-olds (Part B) by 1992 and provided financial incentives to states to provide early intervention services for children birth through 2-year-olds (then called Part H, now referred to as Part C). There was an expectation that programs under Part H would be funded by a variety of sources (e.g., Medicaid, Title V of the Social Security Act, private health insurance), with the goal of coordinated payment from federal, state, local, and private sources. This legislation significantly increased the number of young children receiving services. To date, all 50 states, the District of Columbia, Puerto Rico, and the territories receive these funds.

The Individuals With Disabilities Education Act (IDEA) of 1990 (Public Law 101-476) replaced EHA and its amendments. This broad-based legislation addressed both breadth and quality of services for children, youth, and adults with disabilities (Woody et al., 1992). There were several implications of the IDEA legislation for services for young children birth through 5 years of age. Of particular note is the IDEA's emphasis on inclusion, which promotes enrolling children with disabilities in educational settings with children without disabilities, and its emphasis on the role of the family. Legislation highlighted the responsibility of communities to identify and support settings to serve children with disabilities with their typical peers (Bruder, 1993). As a result, increasing numbers of children with developmental delays began participating in inclusive environments, such as community child care settings, with their peers without delays.

President Clinton signed amendments to the IDEA into law on June 4, 1997. The Individuals With Disabilities Education Act amendments of 1997 (Public Law 105-17) revised provisions and extended the authorization of appropriations for IDEA programs through fiscal year 2002. The amendments allow states to extend the "developmental delay" category of eligibility to children up to age 9 years under a new Part A. Use of the developmental delay category gives states the ability to eliminate the traditional categorical system for eligibility that defines very specific areas of delay (e.g., physical handicap, mental retardation). Use of the developmental delay category is recommended because of concern that young children often are miscategorized during the early years. Its use fosters a broader, whole-child approach to meeting the individual needs of young children (NASDSE, 1997). Part B (Section 619) provides grants to assist states in providing special education and related services to children with disabilities ages 3 through 5 years. Revisions of the program for infants and toddlers with disabilities occurred under a new Part C of IDEA (which replaced Part H). In addition to stating an urgent and substantial need to enhance the development of infants and toddlers with disabilities and to reduce the educational costs to society, Part C (Section 631) recognizes the need to enhance the capacity of families to meet the special needs of their children.

This brief historical review of legislation reflects the culmination of early childhood conceptualizations that occurred over the past 30 years. Four themes suggest themselves from this review:

1. The early years are critical to the developing child, suggesting the need for quality early intervention experiences.
2. Children with disabilities have a right to a free and appropriate public education.
3. Children cannot be served in isolation, suggesting the need for comprehensive programs that provide family support.
4. Integrated service delivery models are essential to provide holistic programs that best support children and families.

Snapshot of Early Intervention Services

In establishing a vision for early intervention services, it is important first to determine the desired outcomes of such programs and then to design specific interventions to best achieve the identified outcomes. The outcomes for early childhood programs continue to emphasize the child in that they "enable the child, with the support of the parents as primary caregivers and other caregivers, to establish a developmental path that will prepare the child for long-term success" (Advisory Committee on Services for Families With Infants and Toddlers, 1994, p. 8). In addition, outcomes are broadened to include the family (e.g., enhancing the capacities of families to meet the needs of their children) and society (e.g., reducing educational costs for later special education and decreased institutionalization). To accomplish these outcomes, early intervention services need to consist of diverse networks of services, providers, and consumers. It is important for psychologists and early childhood providers to be aware of the continuum of service models and to possess skills to address the complex and diverse needs of children and families. In the following section, we describe the diversity in children, families, and services and the challenges that occur in early intervention.

Diversity of Children

It is important to establish who the children targeted for early intervention opportunities are. Although portions of this book are relevant to all young children, our emphasis is on children birth through 5 years with special needs. As reflected in the historical review of early childhood legislation, early intervention first targeted only the preschool-aged child (3 to 5 years). The definition of the early intervention population broadened to include newborns, infants, and toddlers (birth to 3 years) as the importance of the early years became clear.

Early intervention populations are not only defined by age but also are based on a definition of risk. This book addresses a broad spectrum of the early childhood population, those children birth through 5 years who demonstrate a developmental delay, have a diagnosed physical or cognitive disability related to an established condition (see chapter 2) or are at risk for developmental problems. These categories of risk are defined in chapter 2. States vary in their definitions of these categories; however, most consider the developmental domains of cognition, language (receptive and expressive), motor skills (fine and gross), self-help skills, and behavior or social–emotional skills. Factors that place infants at risk for developmental challenges come from many sources, ranging from genetic and chromosomal abnormalities to prenatal complications of birth and teratogens affecting the developing fetus. In addition to these biological factors, social factors such as poverty, inadequate care, and physical deprivation also can have significant negative impact on the developing child (Hanson, 1996). These factors are discussed at length in chapter 3.

The IDEA and its amendments do not require that states identify and report children by disability labels from birth through 8 years, so many states have adopted a noncategorical approach to identification. The intent of the law is to allow for services to children who represent a wide range of ability levels and types of disabilities. The guidelines for children from birth to 3 years of age are even broader (Bailey & Wolery, 1992). States can serve children with a documented delay and also can elect to serve children who are at risk for delays. Many states have opted to define eligibility criteria using the broad category of developmental delay at least through the age of 2 and then either at age 3, or for some states at age 5, choose to use categorical descriptions to define eligibility (e.g., mental retardation, sensory impairment). Georgia proposed extending the category of "significantly delayed" through 9 years (Danaher, 1998). Expanding to age 9 avoids miscategorization of grade-school children who do not clearly fall within one of the traditional eligibility categories. Traditionally, eligibility not only was defined by the category description, but also the degree of delay. Such terminology of mild, moderate, and severe/profound degree of delay was common. Each level implied a set of developmental characteristics and capacities. More recently the American Association on Mental Retardation (1992) promoted a contemporary view of the degree of delay in which the fit between the capabilities of the child and the structure and expectations of the child's environment is taken into account. This functional approach focuses on describing a developmental profile of strengths and less developed areas and on identifying the nature of supports for each functional area.

Diversity of Families

Early intervention service providers will encounter a wide spectrum of families varying in cultural backgrounds, family constellations, and age. The "traditional" two-parent family is no longer the norm. Families in which the father earns an income above the poverty line and the mother stays home to care for the young children represent fewer than 10% of the families in the United States (Arcia, Serling, & Gallagher, 1992). Over the past 26 years, there has been an increasing number of single-parent families. In 1996, 32% of children lived with only one parent (24% mothers and 4% fathers and 4% others), compared with 15% in 1970 (14% mothers and 1% fathers). Between 1960 and 1995 birth rates for unmarried women increased from 5% to 32% (Federal Interagency Forum on Child and Family Statistics, 1997). Although it is inappropriate to make general statements regarding the unique needs of this population of single-parent families, financial concerns often are an identified need. These concerns, coupled with the responsibility of carrying out all family functions without the support of a spouse or other family members, may result in a high degree of stress. An awareness of the impact of these dynamics on the family is important as service providers work with families in developing intervention plans. Early interventionists must be prepared to work with families using individualized approaches that respect family diversity.

The number of families with young children from culturally diverse backgrounds enrolled in early intervention programs is increasing (Sonag & Schacht, 1994). Although programs strive to hire employees from diverse backgrounds, many programs are staffed with providers who have different values, traditions, and languages than the families with whom they work (Lowenthal, 1996). These changing demographics place an urgency on programs to determine strategies that support providers in gaining cultural competencies. Providers need to be aware of the issues they will encounter when working with families of diverse cultures in order to form successful partnerships. Providing opportunities to interact with and to learn from diverse groups should enhance appreciation of diverse families' belief systems and build a repertoire of nonpaternalistic techniques to support families' autonomy. Lowenthal (1996) recommended that such training include topics such as an "awareness of one's own culture, differences in family structures, diverse child-rearing practices, different perspectives about the etiology of disabilities and the value of interventions, the diversity of communication styles, and socioeconomic difficulties" (p. 146). Cultural diversity and its implications on early intervention are discussed further in chapter 4.

Diversity of Services

A range of programs and strategies that support this diverse population of children within the context of their families and communities is clearly needed. Multiple-service delivery options are available for families, ranging from specialized programs designed to serve only infants or young children with disabilities to programs that serve children in natural settings—in other words, places where children typically spend time—including homes or child care settings. Child care centers, preschool groups, Head Start, and kindergarten programs are all settings in which young children with or at risk for developmental challenges participate. It is essential that families understand the broad range of services available and the advantages and disadvantages of each to make appropriate decisions about the services. Those service models that are most typical in early intervention are home-based, hospital-based, or center-based, with an emphasis on prevention or intervention. A summary of this range of service delivery models, settings, and programmatic emphasis is provided in Table 1.2.

Home-Based Services

It is important that families receive the necessary support to meet their goals, and have the resources and guidance to provide a caring and responsive environment for their young children. A *home visitation model* is one approach to help families achieve these goals. As implied, these services occur in the child's home with the primary caregiver. The frequency of the visit is negotiated with the family and may range from weekly to monthly visits. At the core of the home visitation program is the relationship between the caregiver and the home visitor, with both recognizing that the child's development is affected within her or his network of relationships and patterns of interactions (Klass, 1997). These parent-education programs offer support of parent–child interaction (discussed extensively in chapter 6), increase families' knowledge of developmental stages and healthy environments for their children, and build bridges for families to other resources in the community (Advisory Committee on Services for Families With Infants and Toddlers, 1994). The goal of home-based programs is to support families in

- Accepting the parenting role with a sense of confidence, pride, and enjoyment;
- Supporting parents' self-recognition of their strengths and skills;
- Acquiring valuable information about child development and its meaning for interaction with children;
- Understanding and responding to child's behavior in growth-enhancing manner;
- Using available community resources that support families; and
- Supporting fellow parents (Early Childhood Training Center, 1995, p. 7).

In the following scenario, we offer our observations (in italics) of how the home visit failed to achieve family-centered practice.

Jon, the early interventionist, makes his weekly visit to see Anisha. Anisha's mother, Mrs. Jackson, sits on the couch watching Jon play with Anisha. (*Interventionist needs to support Mrs. Jackson's engagement with Anisha.*) Jon comes with a prescribed set of goals and lesson plan that he wants to accomplish with Anisha and describes the purpose of each activity to Mrs. Jackson as he plays with Anisha. (*Intervention is not based on priorities of family.*) Mrs. Jackson had few questions, although she always watched Jon and Anisha play with great interest. As Jon was leaving, Mrs. Jackson commented on how well Jon played with Anisha despite all of Anisha's physical challenges. (*Mrs. Jackson views Jon as the expert.*)

Contrast this example with the following scenario that illustrates building rather than diminishing a parent's confidence in her parenting abilities.

Jon asks Mrs. Jackson to share Anisha's accomplishments for this past week. (*Starts the session by highlighting Anisha's competencies and acknowledging family enjoymont of thcir interactions.*) Together Jon and Mrs. Jackson talk about what they will address during the visit. (*Strategy establishes a partnership and joint ownership of the session.*) Mrs. Jackson expresses concern about Anisha's play with toys because her cerebral palsy and subsequent motor difficulties interfere with her success in manipulating objects. Mrs. Jackson indicates that she has trouble positioning her so she can effectively play with materials at the table. Jon coaches Mrs. Jackson through different ways to sit Anisha on her lap that maximize physical support. Provided with physical stability, Anisha was able to grasp and play with the toys. (*Both joint problem solving and active parent participation in the session are effective parent-education tools.*) When Jon leaves the Jackson's home, he asks Mrs. Jackson how helpful the session was for her. Mrs. Jackson comments how surprised she is that she could make such a difference in Anisha's play. (*Offered a lead, Mrs. Jackson discloses how involved she felt in the session, suggesting that the strategies helped to build her feeling of compotonoo.*)

The home visitation model is used both in prevention and intervention programs. Although each of the following samples of home visitation models target slightly different populations of children and families, each embraces the overall goals of home visitation. Proponents of universal home visitation emphasize that support should be available for all families and

Table 1.2. Typical Service Delivery Models in Early Intervention

Service Delivery Model	Typical Targeted Age Range	Setting	Programmatic Emphasis	Example of National Models
Home-based	Birth through 2 years	Consultation with caregivers in home environment	—Support caregiver–child interaction —Increase parent knowledge of development and health-related issues —Support family access to community resources	—Early Intervention through IDEA Part C —Early Head Start —Parents as Teachers —Prenatal and Infancy Project
Hospital-based	Birth through 5 years	Consultation with careivers and health care providers in hospital setting	—Support caregiver–child interaction —Increase parent knowledge of development and health-related issues —Support family access to community resources —Support child's ability to cope with hospitalization	—Project Continuity
Center-based	3 through 5 years	Direct child-based services in child care, community, and educational programs	—Enhance child development skills through individual and group interactions	—Head Start —Even Start —Early Intervention Preschool Program (IDEA Part B)

not solely for those with children who are at risk as well as those children who have disabilities. This position is grounded in the belief that *all* families benefit from support in their parenting roles. In 1984, Missouri became the sole state to enact legislation for a universal home visitation program, Parents as Teachers (PAT), which mandates that every school district offer parent education and support services to families with children from birth to 3 years of age (Wells, 1997). PAT is widely disseminated and implemented in part by other states.

Home visitation programs for a designated population are more typical. Services provided by programs under IDEA Part C are designed to maximize the child's development and the likelihood of success, to enhance the capacity of families to support their infants and toddlers, and to support the families who often experience unique concerns and stresses. In this model, providers from multiple disciplines are often part of the home visit. In contrast, Early Head Start is a prevention-oriented program that provides comprehensive child development and family support services targeted for families with low incomes who have children under the age of 3 years. In Early Head Start home visitation is one strategy used to develop enriching caregiving environments by supporting parents in their roles as primary caregivers in the educations of their children and to support families in addressing their personal goals (Advisory Committee on Services for Families With Infants and Toddlers, 1994). The Prenatal/ Early Infancy Project, another nationally disseminated home visitation model, targets first-time adolescent mothers for home visits (Olds, 1990). This nurse-based model includes three major activities: (a) parent education regarding influences on fetal and infant development and about women's decisions to return to school, find work, and bear additional children; (b) the involvement of family members and friends in the pregnancy, birth, early care of the child, and in the support of the mother; and (c) the linkage of family members with other health and human services.

Home-based services are a cost-efficient service delivery approach, because they do not require building costs for special facilities or transportation of children and families to facilities. As children remain in their natural setting, it gives opportunities for providers to establish relationships not only with the child but also with caregivers. Disadvantages of this model for the child and family are that it limits opportunities for children to socialize with other children and does not allow for families to meet either formally or informally with members of other families. Clinical supervision is more difficult in this model because observations of the clinician in this environment are not as easily obtained. In addition, home visitors may express feelings of isolation and lack of peer support in their role.

Hospital-Based Services

There are a growing number of young children with special health care needs who are at risk for developmental disabilities and who are hospitalized and will benefit from intervention services (Hochstadt & Yost, 1992). Hospitals are designed for efficient delivery of medical care, with less emphasis on creating environments that facilitate children's cognitive and social development. Multiple caregivers, physical restraint, and painful procedures are potential threats to the emotional and developmental well-being of young children who have been hospitalized (Goldberg, 1990; Goldberger & Wolfer, 1991). The importance of addressing both the developmental needs of children and supporting their families is identified as a key factor in regulations of the Joint Commission on Accreditation of HealthCare Organization's (JCAHO). The JCAHO develops standards of quality in collaboration with health professionals to ensure health care organizations meet or exceed the standards through accreditation and teaching quality improvement concepts (JCAHO, 1992). The challenge is to find effective models of service delivery that hospitals can adopt.

The Project Continuity model has been successful in increasing the consistency of caregiving routines and ameliorating the effects of inevitable changes and transitions on young hospitalized children and their families (Jackson, Finkler, & Robinson, 1992). This model adopts many of the strategies of the home-based model for the hospital setting. Parents are supported in the caregiver–child interaction, in their access to necessary resources during their hospital stay, and in increasing their knowledge of developmental and health-related issues. A unique aspect of the model is the support to the young child and family on the social–emotional effects of the hospital stay and the child's chronic illness on the child and family. A strategy frequently incorporated into the intervention is medical play that provides a venue for the child to express emotions related to his or her experiences through pretend play activities—for example, giving a doll a shot. A challenge in the hospital environment is coordinating care among the numerous adults who interact with the child and implement the care plans. Efforts are typically made to find out how the family approaches daily care routines, so that the nursing personnel may provide some continuity for the child, but often it is difficult to communicate such information to all members of the care team. As a result, the early intervention role is often expanded to that of a consultant who disseminates this information to the health providers (e.g., nurses, physicians). In this role they work with the primary caregivers to make sure all who have contact with the child have a good understanding of the developmental goals to maximize continuity of care for the child. In addition, the developmental goals should become an integral part of the nursing care plans.

Families and providers face the ongoing challenge of the ability of community-based programs to meet the health and educational goals of children with special health care goals once they are discharged from the hospital. Many children end up receiving home-based services, because there are insufficient center-based alternatives that have appropriately trained providers. Communities are beginning to address this gap in services for families by creating new programs that include registered nurses on site to assist in the health care of the children in community-based sites. One such program provides child care to children birth to 12 years of age who have complex medical needs and require skilled nursing care. This program not only provides opportunities for children to socialize with other children (an opportunity that could not be accomplished in a home-based model) but also allows families to strengthen their financial security through renewed employment or school opportunities. This community-based program provides a sharp contrast to the intense atmosphere of the hospital or clinic settings or the isolation of the home-based setting, benefitting both the child and family.

Center-Based Services

Most center-based programs in educational or community settings have targeted the 3- to 5-year-old child with services being provided anywhere from 4 to 15 hours during the week. The typical format includes structured play or care routines (e.g., music, snack), free play time at the child's choice of play centers (e.g., block or dramatic play centers), motor activity, and special activities (e.g., an art activity or field trip outing). The child's individual goals and objectives are addressed within the context of those daily routines. The center-based model of services has the advantage of providing opportunities for peer interaction. More opportunities are available to staff to interact with one another and provide opportunities for team planning and support. Clinical supervision is also simpler with staff being located in one site, as it provides easier access for the supervisor to make observations and provide feedback. However, there are disadvantages to the models as well. These include costliness of transportation, cost of building upkeep, difficulty of establishing relationships with families, and provision of family support services (Bailey & Wolery, 1992).

The center-based model is used both in prevention and intervention programs. Initial efforts in early intervention were directed at children living in poverty because of the increased prevalence of delayed development in this population (Landesman-Dwyer & Butterfield, 1983). These findings, paired with survey results that indicated 25% of the nation's preschool-age children lived in poverty, highlighted the need for action (Martin, Ramey, & Ramey, 1990). The initial rationale for early intervention emphasized benefits for the child, specifically cognitive gains. The underlying premise was that a child's cognitive development would be strengthened through enhanced environmental experiences, such as participation in early intervention programs. This experience was thought to provide the foundation for a greater degree of school readiness, which would increase the likelihood of later school success and, ultimately, economic, social, and cultural benefits as adults (Campbell & Ramey, 1994).

Head Start is one of the most well-known and widely disseminated preschool prevention programs, with its goal to ameliorate the effects of poverty on young children. Head Start is a multifaceted intervention that targets both the child and family by providing a continuum of services including child care, preschool education, and health and social services. Head Start's emphasis on the role of the parents in the planning, administration, and daily activities of the local centers was one of Head Start's unique contributions to early intervention. Even Start programs, another federal education initiative effort, targets family literacy. This comprehensive program has a heavier emphasis on adult competencies and self-sufficiency by supporting parents' attainment of a General Education Development degree (GED) and improving job skills. Center-based services for children are often one component of Even Start. Support of parent–child interaction is reinforced both in center-based services in which the child and parents participate together as well as in home-based services that provide more individualized instruction. Thus Even Start blends service delivery models to best support families.

Some center-based programs are remedial in nature, targeting children with disabilities for intervention (Ramey & Campbell, 1991). Preschool early intervention programs that are now implemented as specified in Part B of the IDEA are examples of such programs. These services, whether implemented in a self-contained classroom or an inclusive setting, are provided to maximize the child's development through a process of individualized educational planning. Descriptions of these programs will be further described in chapter 5. The IDEA and its 1997 amendments emphasize inclusion and have challenged self-contained, center-based programs to examine alternative models. In addition, self-contained classrooms typically only provide part-day services. This is problematic for families who increasingly need to find child care (Voices for Children, 1997). This federal policy, paired with schools' attempts to support families in addressing child care, motivates many schools to partner with local child care providers to allow for more inclusive opportunities for children. Often in these situations, the child attends a child care program that includes typical children, and the educational team provides consultation to the child care staff to assist individualizing the program for the child with disabilities. Some programs incorporate a resource teacher model (funded by the school district), in which the early interventionist works in the child care facility and is responsible for addressing the unique concerns of the children with disabilities. These models provide an opportunity for the integration of best-practices (based on research findings) from both early childhood and early childhood special education, which forms the basis for quality services in inclusive environments. Guidelines are available that support developmentally appropriate practices and individualized programming in inclusive settings (Division for Early Childhood's Task Force on Recommended Practices, 1993; National Association for the Education of Young Children, 1984). Inclusion as a curricular option is discussed in more detail in chapter 5.

Theoretical Perspectives That Guide Early Intervention

A consistent theme throughout this book is the importance of adopting a systems framework that provides a broad context for investigating early childhood development and family–child relationships (Woody et al.,

1992). A systems view focuses on addressing the constellation of interactions rather than a single component of the system and suggests that change in one component ultimately affects the others (Ivey, Ivey, & Simek-Downing, 1987). As early intervention programs begin to embrace a systems approach, the child is considered in relation to the family system, which itself is situated within an assortment of neighborhood, cultural, and political contexts. Each of these units should not be viewed independently but rather seen as a network of interrelated and interdependent components (Bailey & Wolery, 1992). Understanding systems theory is enhanced by contributions of three related theoretical frameworks: ecological (Bronfenbrenner, 1975), social systems (Hobbs, 1975), and family systems (Minuchin, 1974). Each of these perspectives has utility in providing the theoretical foundation for early intervention.

Ecological Theory

Bronfenbrenner (1975) clarified the hierarchical relationships among multiple levels of a system. His social–ecological model highlighted the importance of the dynamic interactions between children and the environments in which they live and the direct and indirect impact in different settings on human behavior (Dunst, Trivette, & Deal, 1988). Bronfenbrenner envisioned the environment as four structural systems, each embedded in the next. At the most molecular structural level is the *microsystem*, which is the level in which children spend most of their time. Typical environments at this level are homes, relatives' homes, and child care centers. The next layer, the *mesosystem*, consists of relationships among individuals in those settings in which the child participates. For young children in early intervention, these could include service coordinator–parent, physical therapist–child, or child care provider–speech pathologist relationships. *Exosystems* consist of the social structures (e.g., local and state agencies, community organizations, churches, or advocacy groups) in which the child does not directly participate but that influence him or her. For example, a family may have a strong informal support system, such as a church or synagogue, that greatly helps the family. The support reduces stress for the family as it allows them to access resources (e.g., respite and transportation) that otherwise would not be available to them. The *macrosystem* includes the cultural and legislative contexts that underlie and influence the organization and practices of the other subsystems.

Analyzing these concentric spheres of influence shows the complexity of the interactions and interrelationships among systems. Impact in one system permeates the other three levels, creating a ripple effect. A prime example is the influence of the IDEA legislation and its amendments at the macrosystem level. This policy can dramatically influence the other three levels. Let us look at one example of how the IDEA affects one child, her family, and their local community providers.

Consuela is a 3-year-old with a diagnosis of spina bifida. She was receiving early intervention services through her local school district four mornings a week. Her parents both work, so after the morning early intervention session, she was bussed to a local child care center. With the passage of the IDEA amendments (*macrosystem level*), the school began to reflect on its practice of providing services for young children in self-contained classrooms (*affecting the exosystem*). Their early intervention team, other community providers, and family members began to meet to examine alternative models. It was decided to pilot an inclusive model with two of their early intervention programs. Consuela's family decided to enroll her in this new program. She received a daily program from 8:00 to 5:00, with a resource teacher on site and consultation by her therapists. The early intervention program would provide a resource teacher who would work in selected child care programs. Five children with disabilities were included in a regular child care setting. The special education resource teacher was responsible for working with the child care staff in addressing Consuela's Individualized Education Program goals in the context of the early childhood curriculum. A close working relationship between the early intervention and child care teacher resulted in new roles and responsibilities emerging (*impact on the mesosystem*). Most important, there was a positive effect on Consuela, whose family agreed to this new placement (*impact on microsystem*). Not only did Consuela benefit from the peer interactions within this new arrangement but also from continuity of providers and consistency in the setting.

This scenario illustrates the need for those individuals who are in the position of influencing change (e.g., administrators, policy makers, and advocacy groups) to think broadly about how proposed new policies or practices might influence all levels of the ecological system. In the design of the IDEA and its amendments, the influences on families and their communities were considered carefully. Less positive outcomes occur when policy decisions are made that focus only on the broad impacts of change and ignore the potential impact on other system levels. For example, state policy makers could recommend a managed care system for families receiving Medicaid services. In designing this policy, it would be important to consider the implication of a policy such as this on children with disabilities, who generally have higher medical costs. This population would need to be excluded from the managed care plan, otherwise primary care physicians may not want to serve this group for economic reasons. To avoid these potential problems, the recommended policy should exclude this population of children from managed care in favor of a system of preferred provider organizations.

As demonstrated by these two examples, not only does the ecological model provide useful insights in understanding the individual child and his or her family, it also offers a useful framework within which to conceptualize intervention policies and practices (Hanson, 1996).

Social Systems Theory

Social systems theory provides an approach to address strategies to strengthen families and community agencies (Hobbs, 1975). The objective of a social systems approach is not merely to ameliorate child difficulties but to make the system work by strengthening typical socializing agencies (e.g., the family, school, church, synagogue, neighborhood) not by replacing them (Hobbs, 1975). Dunst (1985) described a social systems approach to early intervention that highlights a proactive model and empowerment philosophy, which should underlie the design and implementation of early intervention programs. Table 1.3 features how this model contrasts with the more traditional approach to early intervention. The commitment to an enablement–empowerment paradigm (e.g., Dunst et al., 1988) rather than to an expert model challenges traditional notions within many service delivery models (Epps, 1995). In the traditional approach to early intervention, the family seeks the expertise of the provider, who designs services to alleviate provider-determined problems. In this approach the deficits of the family are highlighted and the provider usurps control of the situation by defining the problem and trying to solve it *for* the family. This paternalistic approach is found in numerous early intervention programs (Woody et al., 1992). In contrast, in a proactive approach the role of the provider as expert clearly is diminished and replaced with the concept of family–provider partnerships. Empowerment results from partnerships between families and providers by supporting the family in identifying their concerns and priorities and identifying a plan of action. This proactive approach circumvents the paternalism in the traditional family–provider paradigm, because individuals work together to attain designated objectives by exchanging skills, knowledge, and competencies. Psychologists and others providing services need to reorient themselves toward this global systems view as they address the multidimensional issues of the entire family system (McNulty, 1989).

Empowerment is fundamental to a proactive approach to intervention, which eliminates usurpation of control over family decision making by focusing on family capacities rather than vulnerabilities. This theory maintains that all families have the capacity to become competent. According to this approach an individual's failure to display capabilities is a reflection of a social structure that lacks resources or information to make informed decisions (Dunst et al., 1988). Adopting this assumption engenders high expectations regarding the capacities of families and caregivers, provision of support that matches the family's appraisal of their own priorities, and respect for families' decisions.

Of significance are the implications for practice when embracing a proactive approach, including the role people should play as part of their involvement in the helping process, and the ways in which help givers and help-giving agencies view their roles and responsibilities in interactions with the people they serve (Trivette, Dunst, Hamby, & LaPointe, 1996). For example, enablement results in providers adopting helping behaviors that support rather then "fix" families. A helping approach then results in promoting the family's self-determination and active involvement in decisions related to their child and family rather than a dependency relationship that diminishes the family's capacity. These enabling strategies should be integrated into providers' attitudes, beliefs, and behaviors. Most important, an enablement model entails developing a truly collaborative partnership characterized by mutual respect and acceptance in an effort

Table 1.3. Two Contrasting Models of Early Intervention

	Traditional Model		Social Systems Model
Components	Characteristics	Components	Characteristics
Deficit approach	Differences in behavior are viewed as deficits and weaknesses inherent in the child, family, and their culture. Intervention focuses on the remediation of deficits.	Proactive approach	Differences are viewed as variations in behavior resulting from ecological forces that affect child, parent, and family functioning. Intervention focuses on strengthening families.
Usurpation	Locus of decision making is with the professionals. Interventionists usurp decision making by deciding for families what is wrong, what course of action needs to be taken, when and how often interventions ought to be done, and so on.	Empowerment	Locus of decision making is with the family. Interventions empower families with skills, knowledge, and competencies that allow them access to and control over resources that can be used to meet family needs.
Paternalism	The client (child, parents, family) is seen as someone who has a sickness or pathology and who seeks the expert advice of the professional who prescribes a treatment to alleviate the illness.	Partnerships	Families and professionals work hand-in-hand, on an equal basis, pooling their mutual strengths to devise courses of action that can be taken to meet family-identified needs.

Source: Reprinted with permission of Pergamon Press, Inc., from C. J. Dunst, Rethinking early intervention, *Analysis and Intervention in Developmental Disabilities, 5,* p. 168. Copyright 1985.

to reach commonly recognized goals (Duwa, Wells, & Lalinde, 1993). As providers implement the tenets of an enablement paradigm, it is important to ensure that the intervention supports the family's use of its own resources in a positive way, rather than attempting to "save" the family and in effect squash the family's initiatives. The family should experience the intervention as helping it become more independent rather than more dependent on programs and providers for continued survival (Letourneau, 1988, p. 3).

It is the role of the provider to work with the family to determine the level of support the family desires to successfully complete its goals. For example, in one situation a service coordinator may need to make the referral for a family to a support group, as the family expresses a concern that they could not yet make the call and discuss their child's unique situation. For another family the members may want to initiate the call. It is the role of the provider to negotiate with the family the supports they request, with the goal of increasing the family member's confidence in accessing services. By using this negotiation process, it is less likely that the family's control will be usurped, resulting in a dependent relationship. Often if the provider predetermines the problem and tries to determine the appropriate solution without partnering with the family, the solution will be rejected by the family anyhow, either because the solution is not owned by the family member or the solution does not address the core problem. For example, in one situation the provider assumed a 2-year-old child was not attending the toddler group on a regular basis because of a transportation problem. Based on that assumption, the provider arranged with the school for a van to pick up the child, yet improved attendance still did not occur. In further discussions with the family it was discovered that the family did not feel comfortable sending the young child to school and felt that he belonged home with his mother. Knowing this, the provider with the family would need to investigate other possibilities, such as continued home-based services or perhaps a toddler-based model that also included the mother's participation. These examples illustrate the challenge for programs in shifting from the traditional provider-driven service delivery system to one that is family-driven and builds on family competence.

Family Systems Theory

Family systems theory argues for the importance of interactions between the children and their families, highlighting the importance of the interaction and accommodations between children and their environment (Minuchin, 1974). This perspective recognizes that events in various ecological settings affect children differently, thus emphasizing the need for early childhood programs to address not only the individual child but the multiple sources of influence on the child and family members. Nichols (1984) offered a framework for understanding family structures that influence interaction. Structural family theory offers a clear framework that brings order and meaning to the complex transactions that make up family life. *Family structure* refers to the consistent, repetitive, organized, and predictable modes of family behavior.

Nichols (1984) discussed three constructs that are essential components of structural family theory: structure, subsystems, and boundaries. *"Family structure* is the invisible set of functional demands that organizes the ways in which family members interact" (Minuchin, 1974, p. 51). Repeated family transactions establish enduring patterns of how, when, and with whom to relate. Families are differentiated into *subsystems* of members who join together to carry out its functions. Individuals are subsystems within a family. Dyads are also subsystems (e.g., husband–wife or parent–child). Subsystems can be formed by generation, gender, interest, or function. In different subsystems, a person can enter into various complementary relationships in which she or he has diverse levels of power and differentiated skills (Minuchin, 1974). A woman can be a professional, sister, daughter, mother, wife, and so on. If individuals are mature and flexible, they can vary their behavior to match the different subsystems in which they function. Obvious subsystems such as parents and children can be less significant than covert coalitions, as when a parent and oldest child form such a tightly bonded system that excludes others (Nichols, 1984). Unintentionally, early childhood providers may strengthen a parent–child subsystem to such an extent that other important subsystems are weakened. For instance, the need for a comprehensive program is emphasized for a young child with pervasive developmental disorder. When child and family supports are only offered three hours a week, the parents opt to provide intensive programming themselves. With one parent as the primary wage earner and the other as the "interventionist," little time remains for the parents to nurture their own relationships between themselves, with their other children, and with their informal network of support. Therefore, the impact of a child experiencing developmental struggles can vary across family subsystems by enhancing or encroaching on marriages (Kazak & Marvin, 1984; Murphy, 1982), engendering greater sensitivity in siblings or contributing to adjustment difficulties, and generating closer or more distant ties with the extended family (Vadasy, Fewell, & Meyer, 1986). To prevent this from occurring, a systems approach to early intervention is clearly needed in which the family ecology, rather than just one subsystem of the family, is supported. For instance, a family systems approach to early intervention would attempt to support parents in reserving some time for themselves as individuals and as a couple, siblings in interacting with each other, and the entire family's interactions. A more traditional approach to early intervention focuses on developmental intervention for the child with disabilities (only one subsystem). Even a purportedly contemporary approach emphasizing parent–child interaction often fails to consider other family subsystems. This theory maintains that psychologists and service providers need to continually reevaluate their intervention approaches to ensure they are strengthening families.

The *boundaries* of a subsystem are the rules regulating the amount of contact with others. They serve to protect the differentiation of the system. The interpersonal skills developed in these subsystems is predicated on the subsystem's lack of interference by other subsystems. Developing skills for negotiating and compromising with peers, that is learned among siblings, requires avoidance of interference from parents to settle all disagreements. When young children are permitted to be excessively noncompliant to parent requests and to dictate family routines, the boundary separating parents from children is blurred. The clarity of a family's boundaries is a useful parameter to evaluate family interactional patterns. Rigid interpersonal boundaries are overly restrictive and allow little contact with outside systems, resulting in disengagement. When boundaries among subsystems are blurred, the differentiation of the family system diffuse, resulting in enmeshment (e.g., sharing very personal information with a casual acquaintence; Minuchin 1974; Nichols, 1984). There is no single appropriate pattern, because different cultures have various patterns of family hierarchy (Ivey et al., 1987). Family transactions assume prominence in a systems orientation, in which the young child is not regarded as the "identified target for intervention."

In addition to examining the family structure, family resources, family functions, and family life cycle are important for early interventionists to understand (Turnbull, Summers, & Brotherson, 1984). *Family resources* consist of the descriptive characteristics of the family, including characteristics of the child's developmental and behavioral repertoire. They substantially influence the impact a child with delays has on the family and the family's response to the child's vulnerabilities. Bronicki and Turnbull (1987) addressed three factors in understanding the diversity of a family's resources: (a) characteristics of child's exceptionality, (b) family characteristics (e.g., size, form—foster parents, blended family—cultural background), and (c) personal characteristics of individual family members. For example, a child with severe disabilities including health problems (e.g., an infant on supplemental oxygen) can severely restrict a family's mobility and ability to participate in routine family and community activities. For another family, the personality of the mother is such that she easily becomes overwhelmed when faced with the increasing caregiving demands of her child with special health care needs. The psychologist in this situation would need to take into account her style of responding and determine with her what strategies help to alleviate her stress.

Turnbull and Turnbull (1990) identified seven family functions: (a) economic; (b) daily care; (c) recreation; (d) socialization; (e) self-definition, including self-identity, personal strengths, and weaknesses, and feeling of belonging; (f) affection; and (g) educational/vocational. These functions are not independent, and one function may facilitate or impede progress in another area. For example, economic hardship can substantially interfere with other family functions. Psychologists can be helpful by increasing team members' awareness of these types of family issues and by being available to support families. This is especially critical given the tendency for some educational personnel to concentrate on education development to the exclusion of everything else (Bronicki & Turnbull, 1987).

The family as a system moves through a series of stages across time. Some families, including blended families, may experience several concurrent life-cycle stages—including the child, parent, and grandparent (Terkelson, 1980). The family life cycle is a sequence of developmental stages, spanning from early childhood to adulthood. Each distinctive family unit changes as it progresses through stages and transitions, with each family member facing a unique set of tasks. Families differ in resources and areas of resilience, which influence interaction patterns. All of these factors affect the family's ability to meet its functional needs. It behooves psychologists and other providers to support families struggling with lifespan developmental tasks. Examples of assorted developmental tasks for families with young children appear in Table 1.4. Family systems and developmental perspectives suggest that families have changing priorities and concerns at different stages in the family life cycle. In an ideal situation, agency policies are flexible, because prescribing what programs should provide families is antithetical to the principles of family-centered care and empowerment (Epps, 1995).

From this review of family-related theories, several implications for providers become apparent:

- In planning interventions with the family it is critical to understand the infuences of the family and extended environments.
- Interventions need to target both family and child priorities.
- Team members should build time to reflect on how their interactions are positively or negatively influencing the family structure.
- The goal of intervention is to strengthen and help families maximize their own capacities.

Table 1.4.   Samples of Developmental Tasks for Families With Young Children

- Coming to terms with a diagnosis and violation of expectations for a "perfect" child
- Negotiating the maze of fragmented services
- Becoming an advocate for the child
- Ensuring time for sustained positive interactions with the child
- Nurturing a positive and pleasurable relationship with the child
- Developing synchronous parent–child interaction
- Maintaining relationships with other family members (e.g., siblings, partner, or extended family)
- Managing contextual challenges (e.g., housing, nutrition)
- Clarifying a personal view of early childhood and family services within one's cultural paradigm
- Adopting flexible family roles
- Building informal network of support
- Balancing work and caregiving demands
- Maintaining self-esteem and building sense of competence as parents

Conclusion

This chapter sets the stage for infusing excellence into early intervention by presenting the guiding principles of the service delivery system. Early intervention programs are shaped by the services provided and the children and families for whom they are designed. What specifically delineates current trends in early intervention from the traditional child-centered services is the new emphasis on the family. It is crucial that psychologists and other providers understand the underlying theoretical perspectives of family systems so that they can better recognize the impact of their actions and the service delivery system on the family. Central to services is a systems approach in which the family ecology, rather than the child subsystem alone, is the focal point. It is critical to examine the child within the systems in which they participate, assess the properties of the systems, and design intervention strategies that best support the child and family.

The child cannot be treated in isolation, but rather must be examined within the context of his family and community. The challenge is to (a) develop inclusive environments that provide culturally and developmentally appropriate services that benefit children with diverse educational priorities, (b) address the importance of the interactive accommodations between the child and her or his environment, and (c) acknowledge the family's resilience and uniqueness by addressing the multiplicity of family priorities and concerns through an integrated service delivery system. Community strategic planning is an essential process to achieve positive outcomes for children and families. Through this process of community ownership and community building in partnership with families, community networks are strengthened, thereby establishing accessible, quality services and welcoming neighborhoods that support families in raising their children. Strategies to make this vision a reality are explored in the remaining chapters of this book.

2

Eligibility Pathways to Early Childhood Services: Classification Systems and a Framework of Risk

Jamilla is a 4-year-old whose family just moved from another state. Her uncle, who is her legal guardian, wanted Jamilla to receive similar supports to those in her hometown. The developmental pediatrician diagnosed Jamilla with encephalopathy and suggested early intervention, but the public preschool program, which served young children with identified delays, indicated that first she needed to be reevaluated. The school system, which used a classification system based on its own state administrative regulations, did not find Jamilla eligible for early intervention. What was the uncle to do?

Determining the potential population of children and families who may participate in early childhood services is a formidable task. Programs designed to support children and families are authorized by various child health legislation—for example, Title XIX of the Social Security Act (Medicaid); Title X of the Public Health Service Act (Family Planning and Population Research Act); Title IV (Aid to Families With Dependent Children, Child Welfare, Child Support, Foster Care, Family Preservation and Support Act); and Title V of the Social Security Act (Maternal and Child Health, Children With Special Health Care Needs). The eligibility criteria for participation vary among programs considerably. States must decide whether to include primary prevention strategies for young children at risk for delay or disability or whether to attempt only secondary prevention strategies directed at those already having delays. Eligibility decisions have immense ramifications for states' systems of early childhood service delivery.

Our focus is on young children birth to 5 years of age who participate in a variety of systems of care. These children include those with developmental delay (such as cognitive delay), those with developmental and behavioral challenges (such as social–emotional difficulties), and those with developmental disorders (such as autism). In addition to discussing young children with delays and disorders, this chapter highlights a broader scope of key early childhood populations, including those at biological or social risk. We address eligibility for early intervention services, along with reviewing several classification systems.

Eligibility Conceptualizations

Various nosological systems apply to the classification of early childhood developmental delays and disorders. Several of these are briefly reviewed in this section to illustrate the multiple pathways to classification and hence eligibility for services.

Framework for Diagnostic Classification in Early Childhood

Each taxonomy of the identification or diagnosis of delays and disorders in young children has a different purpose, organizational structure, and implications for early childhood service delivery. Because early childhood providers collaborate with other agencies, they should be familiar with different agencies' criteria for eligibility.

Harmon (1995) suggested that diagnostic classification provides a common system that allows providers and parents to communicate using the same language and builds a common foundation for research. Furthermore, such a classification system may be useful in expanding and improving services for families who build support networks based on their child's classification. As with any classification system, however, there is a potential for negative consequences, such as stigmatization of the child and self-fulfilling prophecies. Harmon highlighted the need for training in what he has labeled "diagnostic thinking" to promote clinical diagnostic skills because knowledge of nosological systems can foster comprehensive assessment of children and their ecological context (discussed further in chapter 3).

Legislative Provisions of Disability Categories

Federal legislation exerts a powerful influence on categories of disability. Legislation has required states to provide services to those children experiencing developmental delay and to those with established conditions that have a high probability of resulting in developmental delay. Established conditions are often medical disorders that are associated with expectancies for developmental challenges. States' inclusion of children at risk for developmental delay (but not an established condition) is voluntary. One of the major challenges state policy makers face under the Individuals With Disabilities Education Act (IDEA) amendments is determining definitions and criteria for eligibility for services. Benn (1993) offered a comprehensive framework for conceptualizing eligibility for early intervention services under Part H (now referred to as Part C) of the IDEA, which also applies to recent IDEA amendments. Benn built on Tjossem's (1976) tripartite classification system of risk conditions (medical, biological, and environmental) in infancy and early childhood. Eligibility for early intervention is based on (a) a diagnosis of developmental delay, (b) a diagnosed physical or mental condition related to an established condition, or (c) the presence of risk factors. (See Table 2.1 for recommended

Table 2.1. Recommended Definitions of Eligibility for Early Intervention Services Under Part C of IDEA

Developmental delay
Eligibility is based on four sources of information:

1. A parent report of a developmental history,
2. Observation of the parent(s) and child together,
3. Health-status appraisal, and
4. Developmentally appropriate formal evaluation measure.

These are used together to arrive at an informed clinical opinion of a delay in one or more areas of developmental functioning.

Established condition
Eligibility is based on a diagnosed or mental condition related to

- Chromosomal anomaly/genetic disorder (e.g., fragile X, trisomy 18, etc.),
- Neurological disorder (e.g., cerebral palsy, neurofibromatosis, etc.),
- Congenital malformation (e.g., patent ductus arteriosis, de Lange syndrome, etc.),
- Inborn error of metabolism (e.g., Hunter syndrome, maple syrup disease, etc.),
- Sensory disorder (e.g., amblyopia ex anopsia, retinopathy of prematurity, etc.),
- Severe attachment and atypical developmental disorder (e.g., autism, reactive attachment disorder, including child abuse, etc.),
- Severe toxic exposure (e.g., fetal alcohol syndrome, maternal phenylketonuria, etc.)
- Chronic illness (e.g., technology dependent, cancer, etc.), and
- Severe infectious disease (e.g., cytomegalovirus, meningitis, HIV-positive, etc.).

At risk
Eligibility is based on the presence of four or more risk factors that may interfere with the caregiving, health, or development of the child. Risk factors include

1. Any serious concern expressed by parent(s) or professionals regarding a child's development, parenting style, or parent–child interaction;
2. Any serious concerns expressed by parents or professionals regarding the prenatal period (i.e., severe prenatal complications, maternal prenatal substance abuse/use, limited prenatal care);
3. The perinatal period (i.e., severe perinatal complications, asphyxia, small for gestational age, very low birth weight);
4. The postnatal period (i.e., atypical infant behavioral characteristics, recurrent accidents, chronic otitis media);
5. Demographics (i.e., poverty, teenage mother, four or more preschool-aged children under age 6, single parent or parent education less than high school or parent unemployed);
6. Ecology (i.e., family has inadequate health care, lack of stable residence, physical or social isolation or lack of adequate social support, parent–child separations); and/or
7. Family's health, caregiving, and interaction (i.e., parent with severe chronic illness, parent with chronic–acute mental illness–developmental disability–mental retardation, parent with drug or alcohol dependence, parent with a developmental history of loss or abuse, family medical genetic history characteristics, acute family crisis, and chronically disturbed family interaction).

Note: This framework for eligibility was originally developed for Michigan under a Part H grant awarded by the State Board of Education. The use of the term *parent* implies the primary caregiver of the child.
Source: Reprinted with permission from R. Benn (1993), Conceptualizing eligibility for early intervention services. In D. M. Bryant & M. A. Graham (Eds.), *Implementing early intervention: From research to effective practice* (p. 27). New York: Guilford Press.

definitions for early intervention services.) How broadly the states have defined their eligibility criteria has been based on several factors, including the numbers and types of children needing or receiving services, the types of services provided, and ultimately the cost of the early intervention system (Shackelford, 1992).

Levels of Prevention

Viewing significant health problems at primary, secondary, and tertiary levels of prevention is a well-established model in public health (Pardes, Silverman, & Wesh, 1989). As depicted in Figure 2.1, primary prevention efforts are aimed at reducing new cases (incidence); secondary prevention is designed to reduce existing cases (prevalence); and tertiary prevention is intended to reduce sequelae or complications of the condition. Primary prevention has a large scope and can range from universal efforts (planned to benefit everyone) to ventures restricted to a particular subgroup with indicated risk status (Gordon, 1989). Efforts at primary prevention attempt to deter manifestation of developmental delays in children at increased or identified risk because of intrinsic (e.g., prematurity) or extrinsic (e.g., poverty) risk indicators.

Primary prevention supports the greatest number of children and families through a diverse assortment of interagency services. Programs for young children with developmental delays or established conditions imply

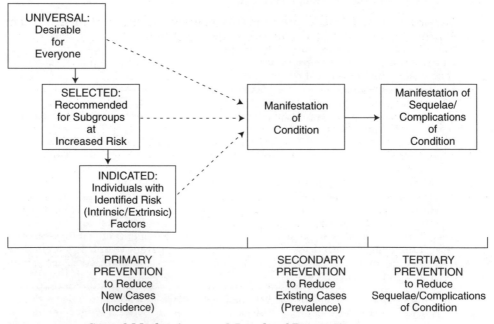

Figure 2.1. Causal Mechanisms and Levels of Prevention
Source: Cited from Simeonsson, R. J. (1991). Early intervention eligibility: A prevention perspective. *Infants and Young Children, 3*(4), p. 49.

a focus on secondary prevention designed to diminish the severity of man-ifestations of delays. The design of tertiary prevention is to diminish child and family sequelae and complications. The numbers of children needing secondary and tertiary services are less, although these services are more complex. Simeonsson (1991) delineated broad services that can be ex-tended to children and their families at each level of prevention (see Table 2.2).

As early childhood programs begin to define eligibility criteria, feasi-bility of implementation raises a host of questions (Benn, 1993). For ex-ample, how many children and families would be included under devel-opmental delay, established condition, or at risk? What are the anticipated expenditures for comprehensive programs that address primary, second-ary, and tertiary prevention? Careful analysis of such questions assists states in incorporating realistic projections into policy decisions. Eligibility criteria may be restricted for states with limited resources. Furthermore, if there are few intervention services available, there may be limited in-centive to identify young children at risk. If criteria for eligibility for ser-vices are narrowly defined, then fewer young children will qualify for ser-vices. Although many states anticipated serving the at-risk population after passage of Public Law 99-457, this expectation was modified because of concerns about costs of services, resulting in definition criteria that were more exclusionary.

Definitions of Developmental Delay

Part C regulations of IDEA amendments specify the areas that are to be included in a state's definition of developmental delay, but leave it up to

Table 2.2. Levels of Prevention

Level and Goal of Prevention	Prevention Goals for Children	Prevention Goals for Families
Primary prevention to reduce incidence	Reduce new cases through promotion of develop-ment and reduction of risk factors	Provide anticipatory guid-ance and promotion of parenting skills
Secondary prevention to reduce prevalence	Reduce duration and se-verity by maintaining, restoring, or developing new skills	Help family deal with re-ality demands of child's disability
Tertiary prevention to reduce sequelae	Reduce direct and indirect effects through correc-tive, augmentative, or compensatory interven-tion	Facilitate adjustment of family in terms of dy-namics, relationships, and values

Source: Reprinted with permission from R. J. Simeonsson (1991). Early intervention eligi-bility: A prevention perspective. *Infants and Young Children, 3*(4), p. 51. © 1991, Aspen Publishers, Inc.

the state's discretion to define the appropriate diagnostic instruments, procedures, and criteria. As a result, there is much variability in the definition of developmental delay across states. Developmental delay has been broadly defined as

> a condition which represents a significant delay in the process of development. It does not refer to a condition in which a child is slightly or momentarily lagging in development. The presence of developmental delay is an indication that the process of development is significantly affected and that without special intervention, it is likely that educational performance at school age will be affected. (Division for Early Childhood, 1991, p. 1)

Shackelford (1992) found a range of criteria for developmental delay in individual states, including (a) the difference between the chronological age and actual performance level expressed as a percentage of chronological age, (b) delay expressed as performance at a certain number of months below chronological age, (c) delay as indicated by standard deviations below the mean on a norm-referenced instrument, or (d) delay indicated by atypical development or observed atypical behaviors. Common measurements of level of delay are 25% delay or 2 standard deviations (SD) below the mean in one or more areas or 20% delay or 1.5 SD below the mean in two or more areas. For example, in Delaware, children may be classified as having developmental delay using one or more of the following criteria:

- Standardized test scores of 1.75 or more standard deviations below the mean;
- A 25% delay in one of the following developmental domains: cognitive, receptive language, expressive language, fine motor, gross motor, social/emotional, and self-help; or
- Clinical judgment to determine a classification of developmental delay provided that written justification is included in the multidisciplinary team meeting minutes (State of Delaware, 1993, pp. 15–16).

The "clinical judgment" stipulation recognizes the trend away from rigid reliance on fixed scores, which cannot capture the full essence of a child's behavioral repertoire or developmental delay in all situations. Part C regulations require this informed clinical opinion to help decision making regarding the need for early intervention services. The necessity for such clinical judgment arose because of concerns related to the lack of reliable and valid instruments for young children and questionable predictive validity of available instruments (Shonkoff & Meisels, 1991).

To determine eligibility for early intervention, estimates of a young child's developmental and behavioral repertoire and family resources are based on systematic, multidimensional clinical assessment and interpretation of both child and context. Eligibility determination should be an ongoing process rather than a fixed occurrence. Young children could move in and out of program eligibility given the fluctuations typical of early childhood development and variations in contextual variables (discussed in chapter 3). For example, assessment of the child may include

- Interviews with significant people in the child's life, such as family members or teachers (or play interviews with the child);
- Observation under a variety of stimulus conditions, such as play with peers, challenging task, or daily routine (e.g., mealtime);
- Family- or provider-completed rating scales;
- Physical examination and appraisal of health status;
- Criterion-referenced, norm-referenced, or curriculum-based assessments; and
- Observation of family–child interaction.

Considering the emphasis on the family within early intervention, observing parent–(or caregiver) child interaction is particularly important. Parent–child interaction is an important component of family-centered early intervention because of its influence on later child development. The early social interactions between parents and children become the foundation for future relationships of the child with parents, siblings, and peers and affect development of child cognitive abilities, language, social skills, and emotional stability (Bailey & Simeonsson, 1988). In fact, early parent–child interaction has been shown to be an even more powerful predictor of cognitive skills at 2 years of age than family socioeconomic status (Cohen & Parmelee, 1983). Such observations yield information about children (such as language and problem-solving skills) that may be more representative of their developmental repertoire because they may feel more secure with their consistent caregivers than with unfamiliar clinicians. Even more significantly, observation of parent–child interaction offers rich data that relate directly to intervention. For instance, is the interaction synchronous (i.e., are the parent and child doing the same "dance")? Does the parent recognize the child's cues (sensitivity), correctly interpret them, and respond appropriately (responsiveness)? The following two brief scenarios illustrate varying degrees of synchrony.

Erykah stands on her tip toes, attempting to reach for the foam blocks. She starts to whine, then crawls away. Her father gets up from his chair, says, "Oh, do you want these?," and gently lifts her up to the shelf. Erykah beams with delight at her father, then sits on the floor and pushes around the blocks. *(Good sensitivity and responsiveness.)*

Garrett moves his left arm to activate a switch toy. The stuffed pig makes an "oink-oink" sound and flips backward. He laughs and looks at his mother. She takes away the pig, asks, "Do you want to read?" then puts a book in front of Garrett. *(Poor sensitivity and responsiveness.)*

Because children with disabilities or delays in development often exhibit greater variability in their interactional cues and responses than typical children, the contingent behavior of their family may be altered, thereby placing both family and child at greater risk for less synchronous interactions.

Massachusetts uses a matrix criteria for delay, which defines different amounts of delay based on the child's chronological age. Specifically, these guidelines suggest developmental delay in one or more areas, including

- 1.5 months delay at 6 months,
- 3 months delay at 12 months,
- 4 months delay at 18 months,
- 6 months delay at 24 months, and
- 6 months delay at 30 months.

Despite the variation in state eligibility definitions, young children must be determined "eligible" by an interdisciplinary team before they can receive early intervention services. Typically, this classification is within the purview of community-based programs designated as a Part C or Part B provider, not an outside agency such as a private diagnostic clinic. Hence diagnoses made using other nosological systems may or may not be accepted by the schools, depending on whether the diagnostic criteria meet the state's eligibility criteria.

Diagnostic and Statistical Manual of Mental Disorders (Fourth Edition)

The *Diagnostic and Statistical Manual of Mental Disorders* (Fourth Edition; *DSM-IV*; American Psychiatric Association, 1994) is widely used by psychiatrists, other physicians, psychologists, social workers, and other health and mental health professionals. As an official nomenclature, clinicians and researchers of diverse theoretical orientations use it. The highest priority in its development was to guide clinical practice, with additional goals of facilitating research and improving communication among clinicians and researchers. The *DSM-IV* also is used as a tool to improve the collection of clinical information and to teach psychopathology.

The *DSM-IV* groups disorders into 16 major diagnostic classes. The first section is devoted to disorders usually first diagnosed in infancy, childhood, or adolescence. Examples of "disorders" include developmental coordination disorder (315.4), expressive language disorder (315.31), autistic disorder (299.00), attention-deficit/hyperactivity disorder, combined type (314.01), and separation anxiety disorder (309.21). A number of disorders placed in other sections also may be diagnosed in children such as major depressive disorder, sleep terror disorder, and adjustment disorders. Therefore, the American Psychiatric Association (1994) recommends that clinicians working with children should be familiar with the entire manual.

The *DSM-IV* uses a multiaxial assessment, with five axes referring to different domains of information that may assist in planning treatment and predicting outcome:

- Axis I: clinical disorders, other conditions that may be a focus of clinical attention;
- Axis II: personality disorders, mental retardation;
- Axis III: general medical conditions;
- Axis IV: psychosocial and environmental problems; and
- Axis V: global assessment of functioning.

The multiaxial assessment is designed to promote the biopsychosocial model, to capture the complexity of clinical situations, and to describe the heterogeneity of individuals with the same diagnostic presentation.

Although diagnostic criteria are listed in the *DSM-IV*, considerable astute clinical interpretation is required to make accurate clinical judgments. For instance, "lack of social or emotional reciprocity" is not operationalized for autistic disorder. Yet the criteria can be helpful in defining the universe of observations that must be made before reaching a diagnosis. Another shortcoming of the *DSM-IV* for early childhood populations is its focus on disorders and problems rather than capacities and resilience.

International Classification of Diseases, 9th Revision, Clinical Modification, 4th Edition *(ICD-9-CM)*

The *International Classification of Diseases, 9th Revision, Clinical Modification (ICD-9-CM*; Practice Management Information Corporation, 1994) was designed to classify morbidity and mortality information for statistical purposes and to index hospital records by disease and operations. This classification system was developed in response to the need of hospitals to have an efficient basis for storage and retrieval of diagnostic data. Over the past 40 years the diagnostic codes have been modified to include more specificity to improve the precision of the system. The *ICD-9-CM* also serves as the basis for diagnostic codes for Medicare/Medicaid, many health insurance companies, and managed care programs reimbursement. Overall, this system generally has limited use for community-based early childhood programs, although many hospitals use the codes. Examples of codes include infantile autism (199.0), mixed development disorder (315.5), and feeding problems in newborn (779.3).

Diagnostic Classification of Mental Health and Developmental Disorders of Infancy and Early Childhood

In 1994 a diagnostic framework was published by the Diagnostic Classification Task Force (1994) of the ZERO TO THREE/National Center for Clinical Infant Programs (currently called ZERO TO THREE/National Center for Infants, Toddlers, and Families). This *Diagnostic Classification of Mental Health and Developmental Disorders of Infancy and Early Childhood* (Diagnostic Classification 0–3) offers a systematic, developmentally based approach to the classification of mental health and developmental difficulties for young children birth through 4 years of age. It can be helpful to psychologists and other providers in conceptualizing young children's emotional, behavioral, and relationship patterns that represent significant difficulties. The manual is designed to complement existing nosology such as the *DSM-IV* (American Psychiatric Association, 1994) and the *ICD-9-CM* (Practice Management Information Corporation, 1994), and therefore does not include categories for all types of developmental and mental health issues.

The framework of the Diagnostic Classification 0–3 is based on a multiaxial system that includes (a) primary diagnosis, (b) relationship disorder classification, (c) medical and developmental disorders and conditions, (d) psychosocial stressors, and (e) functional emotional developmental level. These five axes are described in further detail in Table 2.3. This framework allows the clinician–team to collect and integrate information about the nature of the young child's difficulties and strengths, the level of the child's overall adaptive capacity, the child's developmental levels, the contribution of different areas assessed (e.g., family relationships) to the child's difficulties and competencies, and a comprehensive intervention plan (Harmon, 1995).

The intent of this system is not to find psychopathology or to label a child. Nor is it intended to detract attention from resilience and coping capacities. When used by trained professionals, this diagnostic process should promote greater comprehensiveness in describing a young child's challenges and abilities. Such a thorough diagnosis, then, has the potential for designing more appropriate, effective, and supportive interventions for young children and their families. However, it is clearly heavily influenced by the *DSM-IV* framework and may be more appropriately used by clinical child psychologists and pediatric psychologists with training in differential diagnosis. It is not appropriate for many other early childhood providers, such as teachers and maternal child health nurses, to use the Diagnostic Classification 0–3 to make a diagnosis given their lack of training in its heavily clinical orientation. Even many school psychologists may not have such training.

Framework for Classification of At Risk in Early Childhood

Sources of risk for developmental difficulties in young children include genetic and chromosomal abnormalities, prenatal complications and teratogens affecting fetal development, complications of birth, accidents, and lead toxicity. Sociopolitical factors, such as poverty and social and physical deprivation, also can have a deleterious effect (Hanson, 1996). Although Parts B and C of the IDEA amendments refer to facilitating and improving the early identification of young children who are at risk for developmental delay, most states have not adopted regulations to serve this population.

Univariate Conceptualization of Risk

The "risk" category is probably the most arduous to operationalize. For example, should an infant born preterm be regarded as having a disability or as at risk for developing one? Another consideration relates to the length of time in which problems are manifested before the young child and family are able to access services. As Meisels and Wasik (1990) noted, etiological considerations substantially influence those who are and those who are not viewed as potential recipients of early intervention services. According to these authors, the etiology of risk is of pivotal importance in the first three years of a child's life. For instance, parent–child interactive disorders have been linked to subsequent disabilities in childhood (see chapter 6). They advocate for services for the birth to 3 population that focus on those at risk for developmental difficulties as a preventive measure (i.e., primary prevention). Meisels and Anastasiow (1982) defined two primary categories of risk, biological and environmental.

Biologically at Risk

Children with a history of prenatal, perinatal, or postnatal conditions that could have developmental sequelae are considered biologically vulnerable to developmental delays. Examples of these conditions include genetic deviations; teratogens; maternal metabolic disease, nutritional deficiencies, or infection; obstetrical complications; low birth weight; and anoxia. Prematurity (see Friedman & Sigman, 1992) is a chief biological risk factor, with such related illnesses as intraventricular hemorrhage (a bleed in the brain), retinopathy of prematurity (disorder of the retina), and bronchopulmonary dysplasia (lung disease). Biological insults to the developing central nervous system increase the probability of later developmental delays. Therefore, determining the etiology is often an integral component of the clinical assessment of the young child and may help families have a greater understanding of their child's developmental challenges. However, this goal can be elusive, because approximately 30% of children with disabilities never have a confirmed cause (Crocker, 1989). With the increased survival rates of premature and medically complex infants because of technological advances in neonatal medicine such as high-frequency jet ventilators (Boros et al., 1985), serious questions are raised about the process, context, and developmental outcome of these young children (Crnic & Greenberg, 1987; Epps, 1993).

Because prematurity is not a univariate construct with predictive developmental sequelae (Meisels, Plunkett, Pasick, Stiefel, & Roloff, 1987), it is not known which infants born under which conditions will develop normally and which will not. A further confound is the caregiving environment, which interacts with biologic status to determine outcome. Differential contribution of biology and environment cannot easily be isolated.

Early experiences for infants at biological risk may significantly alter their developmental course. A young child who is more at risk biologically actually may fare better than a less medically involved infant if provided with a more supportive and responsive environment. The following case illustrates an intervention that "modifies the child's vulnerability" (Hanson, 1996, p. 502) by (a) supporting the infant's self-regulation and capac-

Table 2.3. Diagnostic Classification of Mental Health and Developmental Disorders of Infancy and Early Childhood

Axis	Purpose	Descriptions

Axis I: Primary diagnosis	Reflects the prominent features of the disorder	Clinicians conduct differential diagnosis
		• Traumatic stress disorder
		• Disorders of affect
		    Anxiety disorders of infancy and early childhood
		    Mood disorder: prolonged bereavement/grief reaction
		    Mood disorder: depression of infancy and early childhood
		    Mixed disorder of emotional expressiveness
		    Childhood gender identity disorder
		    Reactive attachment deprivation/maltreatment disorder of infancy
		• Adjustment disorder
		• Regulatory disorders
		    Type I: Hypersensitive
		    Type II: Under-reactive
		    Type III: Motorically disorganized, impulsive
		    Type IV: Other
		• Sleep behavior disorder
		• Eating behavior disorder
		• Disorders of relating and communicating
		    Pattern A (aimless and unrelated)
		    Pattern B (intermittently related)
		    Pattern C (more consistent relatedness)

Axis		
Axis II: Relationship disorder classification	Recognizes the quality of the parent–child relationship as a significant component of formulating a diagnostic profile for infants and young children. Considers behavioral quality, affective tone, and psychological involvement.	The Parent–Infant Relationship Global Assessment Scale ranges from "well-adapted" to "grossly impaired." Relationship disorders in Axis II include *overinvolved, underinvolved, anxious/tense, angry/hostile, mixed relationship disorder; abusive (verbally abusive, physically abusive, and sexually abusive)*
Axis III: Medical and developmental disorders and conditions	Used to note any medical, neurological, mental health, and/or developmental diagnoses made using other nosological systems.	Clinicians identify classifications based on other systems, including • *Diagnostic and Statistical Manual (DSM-IV)* • *International Classification of Diseases (ICD-9 or ICD-10)* • Other classifications used by therapists, special educators, or physicians (Note: The American Academy of Pediatrics is developing a diagnostic manual for primary care providers.)
Axis IV: Psychosocial stressors	Considers forms and severity of psychosocial stress that are influencing factors of disorder.	Clinicians examine the psychosocial stress present in the life of the young child. Impact of the stressful event is based on severity of stressor, developmental level of the child, and availability–capacity of adults to serve as a protective buffer.
Axis V: Functional emotional–developmental level	Addresses the manner in which the child organizes her or his experiences. Evaluates age-expected functional developmental level.	Clinicians evaluate processes, including mutual attention, mutual engagement, interactive intentionality and reciprocity, representational/affective communication, representational elaboration, and representational differentiation. The quality of the child's play and interaction with significant others is evaluated.

ity for interaction, (b) building on the family's own competence by providing information about the baby and emotional nurturance, and (c) helping to launch a synchronous family–child relationship.

Kenichi was born at 29 weeks gestation. He currently is 8 weeks old and was transferred from another hospital. His mother was kept alive long enough to deliver him; she then died of cancer. Kenichi's father and his sister live three hours away from the hospital where Kenichi is in intensive care.

Establishing a Relationship With the Family

The psychologist introduces herself to Kenichi's father and paternal aunt, using a soft voice tone. "I see that you have some nice things for Kenichi in his isolette: a stuffed bear, a ball, and a photograph of his mother holding him. I am so sorry about Kenichi's mother. How are you doing?" To set the stage for the family as Kenichi's primary caregivers and to soften her expertness, she then says, "Tell me about Kenichi; what have you noticed that he likes?" *(Rather than, "Let me tell you all about Kenichi's autonomic and behavioral cues.")* In the initial component of intervention, a primary focus is on relationship-based care and determining the family's perception of the baby and themselves as caregivers.

Introducing the Observation

The psychologist explains that together they will have a chance to look at Kenichi in a number of situations to see how he reacts. While he is still asleep, she will point a flashlight briefly to his eyes, shake a rattle, and then ring a bell to see what Kenichi does. She also describes the other parts of her assessment, explaining that babies usually get upset at some point, which will help them learn the kinds of things Kenichi likes and does not like and how he works to calm himself down.

Facilitating the Family's Responsiveness

After several presentations of light, the psychologist supports the family members in sharing their own observations. "Did you see what he did? It looked like Kenichi squirmed around a little. If we look really closely, we can see that he started to breathe a little faster. Now look at him. He has stopped moving around. Yes, you really are good observers; he has gone back to sleep. Good for him; he gets himself back to sleep really well. *(Focusing on Kenichi's strengths rather than deficits.)* Right now Kenichi is in a light sleep state." *(Sharing information with the family.)*

The psychologist slowly turns Kenichi onto his back, saying, "Let's see what he does when we unwrap him." His aunt comments that he is waking up, which provides an opportunity to discuss state changes from light sleep to drowsy. The psychologist describes his color, which is becoming a little red in the face. Kenichi's father then asks why his arms and legs are "sticking out," which provides a segue into a discussion about Kenichi's autonomic and motoric signals.

The psychologist continues, "Kenichi has let us know that he likes to sleep when he is swaddled in a blanket. He is doing a very good job of letting us know what he doesn't like. Remember earlier when he started breathing a little faster? And just then when his face started to turn red? And now he is placing his arms and legs straight out. He is telling us that he is having a tough time keeping himself together when we loosen his blanket. *(Helping the family be sensitive to his cues.)* He likes to have some form of a boundary, or what is sometimes called containment. *(Information sharing.)*

Can you help me wrap this blanket around him to tuck in his legs and arms, with his hands up close to his face?" *(Supporting the family in comforting their baby.)*

"Now if we keep the lights dim, try not to talk, and keep him wrapped or swaddled in his blanket, let's see what he does." As Kenichi begins to open his eyes and focus on his father, his father says, "Kenichi!" When Kenichi startles, squirms, and closes his eyes, the psychologist says, "He looks like he is trying to tell us something." His aunt continues, "He doesn't like something." The psychologist follows up with, "I wonder if we may be talking a little loudly for him. Maybe if we just smile at him when he opens his eyes. We can say, 'Hello, Kenichi' silently to ourselves." *(Beginning of supporting the family's use of cognitive–behavioral strategies to regulate their own behavior.)* When Kenichi again opens his eyes, his father and aunt both grin and move their lips as if talking to him. *(Facilitating the family's responsiveness to Kenichi.)*

This example illustrates how intervention can reduce the impact of biological risk. It also highlights relationship-based care; the building of a trusting, supportive relationship with the family; and the helping of the family to build a nurturing relationship with Kenichi. As his father and aunt become more knowledgable about Kenichi's autonomic and behavioral signals and see him respond positively to their own caregiving, their anxiety and sense of helplessness will likely decrease significantly. As their sensitivity and responsiveness increase, Kenichi's supportive environment will enable him to advance his own self-regulatory repertoire in a continuing transactional manner.

Environmentally at Risk

Children are regarded as environmentally at risk if their life experiences are substantially limited during the early childhood years in realms of caregiver attachment, family organization, poverty, health care, and nutrition and in opportunities for physical and social stimulation. As Meisels and Wasik (1990) indicated, developmental vulnerability can be assumed among children who are environmentally at risk, particularly those living in poverty, although a direct correspondence between a risk factor (e.g., adolescent parenting) and child delay is not supported by the empirical literature. The actual prevalence rate for young children at environmental or biological risk is unknown, considering that children can shift into and out of risk status over the span of their development. Prospective, longitudinal series of investigations of birth cohorts are needed to establish accurate prevalence estimates (Benn, 1993).

Conclusion

Classification systems determine eligibility for early intervention services. Because service providers use diverse nosological systems, there are multiple pathways to eligibility for services. Policy makers face conceptual and methodological concerns related to defining and operationalizing "developmental delay" and "at risk," with considerable variability across states in eligibility requirements. Chapter 3 further discusses the need to consider multiple risk factors in defining eligibility. Substantial variance in eligibility criteria also exists across agencies, with the same child potentially deemed eligible for some services (e.g., state-supported child care) and ineligible for others (e.g., supplemental nutrition). Similarly, families may find themselves receiving only a portion of the supports they have prioritized because of divergence in their eligibility across systems of service delivery. Clearly there is a need for greater consistency in eligibility criteria and semantic clarity in the use of terms. Eligibility criteria for most early childhood special education programs have limited services that are available for those children who are at risk but who have neither an established condition nor developmental delay. Exploration of alternative funding sources therefore becomes necessary.

The emphasis in the IDEA amendments is both intervention and prevention. Therefore, it behooves the early childhood field to explore and to establish primary, secondary, and tertiary levels of prevention. Early prevention and intervention should be viewed as elements of a comprehensive societal effort rather than as independent and singular initiatives. Although numerous multilevel prevention activities are being implemented, they tend to be fragmented across various agencies (Simeonsson, 1991). Framing early intervention services within levels of prevention may help to enhance interagency collaboration.

3

Specific Risk Conditions: Contextual Variables That Influence Risk and Resilience

Madison was born full term, but she was small for her gestational age. She had a hard time nursing because she could not coordinate her sucking and swallowing with her breathing. Her mother was still in the hospital after complications during delivery. Her father was exhausted after spending time at the hospital and work plus trying to keep up with home and school routines of their other four children. He also was concerned about their health insurance. What could Madison's father do? He decided to turn to extended family, his boss, and a woman at their 4-year-old son's Head Start.

This chapter extends the concept of risk in early childhood development introduced in chapter 2. The contextual view of development is discussed at length, with attention devoted to protective factors and the multiplicity of variables influencing risk. The effects to those living in poverty, those young children of adolescent parents, those with growth deficiency, and victims of maltreatment are reviewed to illustrate implications for assessment and intervention when adopting a broad-systems approach. Consistent with one of our guiding principles—that children and families are basically competent—the chapter concludes with strategies for building resilience in young children at risk and their families.

Contextual Approach to Early Identification of Young Children At Risk

The contextual view of development contends that rudimentary categorical models of risk must be discarded, suggesting a multirisk conceptualization of at-risk eligibility. Rather than focusing on single-risk groups of children, numerous authors (e.g., Harbin, Gallagher, & Terry, 1991) advocate a multiple-risk eligibility policy.

Multirisk Conceptualization

Few variables occur in isolation; therefore, exclusively biological or environmental risk is unlikely. Cicchetti and Lynch (1993) discussed the role of potentiating and compensatory risk factors, which influence various levels of the social ecology. (For more on social ecology, see the discussion on Bronfenbrenner in chapter 1.) The *macrosystem* contains the beliefs and values of the culture. The *exosystem* includes aspects of the community in which children and families live, such as schools and neighborhoods. The *microsystem* refers to the immediate environment, typically the family. The ongoing transactions among these risk factors determine the measure of biological and psychological risk that a person faces. Potentiating risk factors increase the probability that developmental difficulties will occur. On the other hand, compensatory factors decrease the likelihood of their occurrence. Both potentiating and compensatory factors may exert enduring or transient influences that transform the likelihood of a particular outcome. As enduring vulnerability factors and transient challenges at various ecological levels increase, developmental problems become more likely.

Without resulting in an inundation of service recipients, a well-conceived model should enable service delivery to those young children and their families in greatest need. Pervasive developmental obstruction most likely occurs when multiple, simultaneous barriers to healthy development are present and when these hindrances exist over time. Perhaps the highest risk situation is a constitutionally vulnerable young child, vulnerable and overwhelmed caregivers, and a nonsupportive social and community context. An exacerbated risk potential also might exist when considering unresponsive or poorly accessible maternal and child health and education programs.

Other than events such as those involving substantive central nervous system dysfunction or significant chromosomal anomalies, most isolated occurrences early in a young child's life do not have predetermined repercussions on the child's development. Indeed, *multifinality* specifies that diverse outcomes are likely to result from any one source of influence (Cicchetti & Toth, 1998). For instance, although children of parents with attention deficits or hyperactivity could be considered at risk (including at genetic risk) for developing attention deficit-hyperactivity disorder (ADHD), clearly not all of these children do develop ADHD, and a broad spectrum of adaptation is seen. In contrast to multifinality, the principle of *equifinality* suggests that the same outcome may emerge from disparate routes.

Because a univariate approach does not offer justification for apportioning risk, an entire group (such as all young children born preterm or born into poverty) should not be presumed to be at risk for suboptimal development. Child delay or medical condition is only one part of a multivariate equation in which family and contextual variables have the capacity to compensate for or exacerbate child risk characteristics in a transactional manner. The interactive effects of biological and environmental risk factors are important in determining both degree of risk and protective influence. Children and their families who experience multiple risks face a more challenging and complex developmental path.

Other contextual factors that must be considered include (a) areas of susceptibility/vulnerability (e.g., racism, sexism, daily hassles); (b) family and community supports (external mediators) and coping strategies (internal mediators); and (c) social, political, cultural, and economic variables. Table 3.1 provides sample questions that help explore various contextual factors that mediate child outcome. The practitioner may use these questions to probe for the vulnerabilities and supports in a child's environment.

With child risk characteristics placed within an ecological context, attention is given to such factors as parent psychological processes (e.g., stress, sense of competence) and sources of support or stress (e.g., restriction of role, relationship with partner). Examples of more refined risk registers include

> enduring characteristics of the family (e.g., number of children, marital and minority status), psychologic characteristics of the parents (e.g., mental health, education, child-rearing attitudes, beliefs and coping skills), and stressful life events that interfere with the family's ability to provide a nurturant context for the child. (Sameroff, 1986, pp. 196–197)

Understanding caregiver reactions can enhance practitioners' ability to provide effective and culturally sensitive intervention supports for families of young children. For example, families have a variety of means of coping in their search for meaning and mastery over challenging life circumstances. Appreciating that some families rely on spirituality can augment early childhood providers' sensitivity to family beliefs and responsiveness to family priorities and concerns (Epps & Nowak, 1998).

Process of Early Identification of Children At Risk

Meisels and Wasik (1990) offered several implications of the contextual view of development for early identification, which regards the environmental context of child development as propelling forward the impact of risk factors and ultimately ameliorating or heightening problems of early childhood (see Sameroff, 1975, 1986). These authors recommended that comprehensive screening models be adopted for early identification that are multifaceted and periodic and that draw from diverse databases. In addition to including information about biological circumstances and developmental competence, screening models should incorporate family variables related to concerns, priorities, resources, support systems, and quality of caregiver–child interaction. Multiple sources of information from family members and providers using various methodologies (e.g., direct observation, interview) are necessary to reduce decision-making error. Because of substantial variation in child and family developmental pathways, screening is recommended on multiple occasions between birth to 5 years of age.

Such comprehensive screening models highlight the integral nature of

Table 3.1.   Contextual Factors That Mediate the Child–Environment Interaction

Familial

- Are there single or multiple caregivers (e.g., single parent, adolescent parent, involved grandparents)?
- Is there extended family (intrafamilial social supports)?
- What is the family type (e.g., blended)?
- What is the family's organization?
- What are the levels of stress, depression, and so on in the family?
- What is the family's sense of competence as a caregiver?
- What is the nature of the relationship between spouse–partner?
- Are there siblings? Do any of them have special needs because of their age or developmental or health status?
- What is the family's cognitive interpretation of their life circumstances?
- What are the family's coping strategies?
- What is the educational level of the primary caregiver?

Sociopolitical

- How supportive is the school–education environment?
- Does the entire family have access to health care?
- Are child and family agencies (e.g., child care, employment) accessible?
- Are public playgrounds, libraries, petting zoos, and so on safe and accessible?
- Are crime and violence issues in the community?
- Do state regulations include early childhood services for those without developmental disabilities but who are at risk?
- Do state regulations include early intervention for established conditions such as prematurity?
- Is there supportive service coordination across agencies that integrates care?

Cultural

- What are the family's culturally based belief systems (e.g., grandparents help raise the children)?
- What are the family's views toward childrearing?
- What are the family's views toward disability?
- What are the family's views toward intervention from persons outside the family?
- What are the extrafamilial social supports available to the family?

Economic

- Is the family experiencing economic hardship?
- Is the community in a depressed, flourishing, or revitalized area?
- Is the housing substandard (e.g., is lead paint chipping)?
- What is the nature of the parents'–caregivers' work environment (e.g., policy toward leaving work to attend meetings for the child)?

interagency collaboration to attenuate gaps and fragmentation in service delivery and family supports. Certain young children and families emerge from screening programs without meeting the eligibility criteria for Part C early intervention services or Part B preschool programs. However, many need some form of intervention and support. Hence comprehensive screening paradigms demand options for broad-based early childhood initiatives (such as therapeutic child care) that are accessible for families (Kochanek & Buka, 1991).

The American Academy of Pediatrics (1988) has endorsed developmental surveillance (a health clinic-based screening process) as a conceptual prototype that embraces the practice of multiple sources of data and ongoing monitoring of development. Developmental surveillance (*The Lancet,* 1986) should be integrated into child health supervision visits. It is not restricted to examining the young child's developmental status. Rather, it is intended to gather information as well concerning family traits, social support, and variables in the home that may unfavorably influence growth and development. Applying this model requires reflective formulation in selecting measures and establishing operational procedures for determining risk. Continued experimentation with screening models for heterogeneous, cross-cultural populations is warranted (Kochanek & Buka, 1991). Dworkin (1989) advised developing large-scale population-based studies to evaluate the reliability and validity of alternative systems of risk classification.

Meisels and Wasik (1990) also emphasized the need to identify the number and weighting of risk factors that increase the probability of delay. Werner (1986), in an 18-year longitudinal study in Kauai, found that the presence of four or more predictors of risk by 2 years of age essentially differentiated children who developed significant learning or behavioral difficulties from those who were able to deal with the developmental tasks of childhood. The predictive factors included biological variables (e.g., perinatal stress, congenital birth defect), caregiving variables (e.g., low standard of living, low rating of family stability in the first two years of life), and other behavioral factors (e.g., maternal ratings of very low or very high infant activity level, delayed development operationalized by psychometric examination). Hence the cumulative nature of risk must be considered in systems of early identification. Sameroff, Seifer, Barocas, Zax, and Greenspan (1987), examining a set of 10 environmental variables in a longitudinal study of 215 children, demonstrated that it was the *number* of risk factors that predicted adverse outcomes. They found that the critical determinant of severity of delay was the cumulative effect of risk. Only by including a fourth risk factor were considerable decrements in performance observed.

Thus states have varying formulations of "at risk," with diverse policies about whether young children who are at risk (as opposed to those who meet identified criteria for developmental delay) are even served. A univariate classification of risk based on etiology is not only too simplistic but insufficiently predictive of adverse outcome. Hence cross-cultural, empirical models of a multifactorial ecological approach to early identification must be designed and refined so that comprehensive preventive interventions can be applied. Future policy development indeed may identify multi-risk definition of eligibility as an established condition (cf. Federal Register, 1992).

Building Resilience in Young Children and Families

Under a variety of risk conditions, both the young child and caregiver are at heightened risk of contributing to relationship difficulties. Yet young children are both uniquely vulnerable and strikingly resilient. Indeed, child and family resilience and social system variables may ameliorate negative sequelae. The presence of enduring protective factors and transient buffers at various ecological levels may help explain why some children deal adaptively and ward off developmental difficulties even in the presence of multiple potentiating risk factors. Table 3.1 offers insight into family resilience as well as vulnerability.

Gest, Neemann, Hubbard, Masten, and Tellegan (1993) emphasized the importance of providers understanding resilience to identify characteristics of children, their environments, and their familial and social relationships that promote adaptive development under challenging conditions. Lessons have been learned from studies of naturally occurring resilience among children at risk and from endeavors to alter the course of competence through early childhood education and preventive interventions. Table 3.2 summarizes characteristics of the child and the environment, derived from empirical investigations, which are associated with (and hence are not necessarily causal) competence or better psychosocial functioning during or following adverse experiences. Among these char-

Table 3.2. Characteristics of Resilient Children

Source	Characteristic
Individual	Good intellectual functioning
	Appealing, sociable, easygoing disposition
	Self-efficacy, self-confidence, high self-esteem
	Talents
	Faith
Family	Close relationship to caring parent figure
	Authoritative parenting: warmth, structure, high expectations
	Socioeconomic advantages
	Connections to extended supportive family networks
Extrafamilial context	Bonds to prosocial adults outside the family
	Connections to prosocial organizations
	Attending effective schools

Source: From A. S. Masten & J. D. Coatsworth (1998). The development of competence in favorable and unfavorable environments: Lessons from research on successful children. *American Psychologist, 53*, p. 212. Copyright 1998 by the American Psychological Association. Reprinted by permission of the author.

acteristics, the two most widely cited predictors of resilience appear to be relationships with caring prosocial adults and good intellectual status (Masten & Coatsworth, 1998). Developmental psychopathology espouses the perspective that to comprehend human development it is essential to appreciate the integration of developmental processes at multiple levels of biological, psychological, and social complexity (Cicchetti & Toth, 1998). The paradigm shift away from a deficit model, with its historical emphasis on weaknesses, dysfunction, and pathology, has led to a contemporary focus on child and family resilience, strengths, coping, and benefits (Epps, 1995). Hence attention needs to be directed to areas of invulnerability and protective factors in children, families, and communities. A contextual approach to early intervention, therefore, must include factors that enhance child and family resilience. Because young children's typical daily environmental experiences strongly predict subsequent well-being and developmental competence (Kagan, Kearsley, & Zelazo, 1978), early intervention can heighten resilience by supporting family–child interaction.

Resilience in young children cannot be predicted independent of the caregiver–child relationship. Both caregivers and young children bring resources to the relationship. Healthy caregivers who are educationally and economically advantaged with available intrafamilial and extrafamilial supports are more likely to protect their young child from a stressful, overwhelming environment and nurture healthy development by providing the cognitive stimulation and emotional support needed to build resilience. The well-equipped young child brings to the caregiver–child relationship an innate capability to initiate and reciprocate interaction. Such a child with an easy temperament even may be able to relax and secure nurturance from an anxious caregiver. Positive developmental outcomes can more likely occur when the vulnerable young child is paired with a caregiver with a reserve of resiliency (Poulsen, 1993). The case illustration of Kenichi from chapter 2 highlights supportive intervention to enhance the protective factor of the family.

As depicted in Figure 3.1, child and family resources and supports build resilience in young children at risk. Table 3.3 lists community supports that enhance resilience in young children, the caregiver–child interaction, and families. The exosystem is the ecological level most directly linked to community supports that can be mobilized when a child or family is experiencing difficulties. In a supportive exosystem, high-quality intervention services are readily available and accessible, which could help reduce the probability and chronicity of problems. What are defining characteristics of quality interventions that support resilience? Epps (1995), Gustavsson and Segal (1994), and Poulsen (1993) have suggested the following:

- Local, community-based, comprehensive, and coordinated systems of care involving interdisciplinary and transdisciplinary teams;
- Enabling supports to ensure linkage of young children and families who are at risk to culturally competent community resources and services;

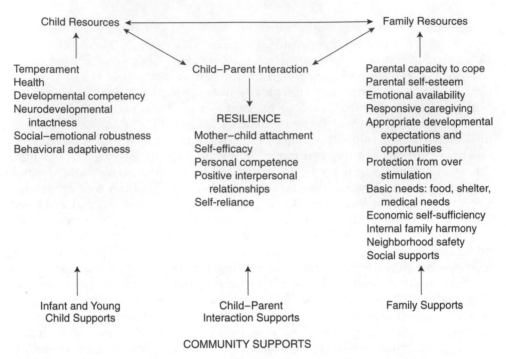

Figure 3.1. Building resilience in infants and young children at risk.
Source: From M. K. Poulsen (1993). Strategies for building resilience in infants and young children at risk. *Infants and Young Children, 6* (2), p. 37. © 1993, Aspen Publishers, Inc.

- Partnerships among service providers across agencies within the public and private sectors;
- Public education regarding the needs of at-risk children and the cost of national neglect;
- Active involvement with local, state, and federal elected officials to advocate for children and families; and
- Evaluation and research.

Specific Risk Conditions: Implications for Child Development

Attempts to intervene before problems arise have led to a focus on risk and protective factors in development. Determining those risk factors that are salient enables the practitioner to identify groups at high risk for adjustment and developmental difficulties. Ascertaining which protective factors are operative helps not only in understanding individual differences in adaptation but also contributes to the design of early intervention and further refinement of characterizations of high-risk groups. Understanding global risk conditions is important, including those at the level of the macrosystem. The role of culture, for example, has contributed to child stigmatization. Levy and Kunitz (1987) found that members of the Hopi

Table 3.3. Community Resources to Support Families and Build Resilience in Children

Infant or Young Child Supports	Child–Parent Interaction Supports	Family Supports
Public health nurse	*Mother–child interaction supports*	Community health clinics
Neonatal intensive care unit follow-up	Developmental services	Family service clinics
Well-baby clinics	Psychologist	Community mental health clinics
Health care	Early interventionist	Welfare and social services
Developmental Screening	Communication specialist	Aid to Families With Dependent Children
Women, Infants, and Children Program	Feeding team specialist	Food stamps
Early identification and referral (Child Find)	Mommy and me classes	Housing
	Conjoint mother–infant therapy	Medicaid
Clinic-based, home-based, and center-based developmental services	*Parental support*	Drug and alcohol recovery programs
	Parent support groups	Job training and job counseling
Public Law 99-457, Part H services	Parent education	Instrumental support for service delivery
High-risk infant program	Parent counseling	—child care
Well-baby clinics	*Social supports*	—transportation
Public health nurse	Church mommy and me activities	—toy loan
Infant and child care	Library mommy and me activities	—translator
Head Start	Parks and recreation Mommy and me activities	Child development warm lines
Public school system		Job availability
Child guidance clinics		Community safety
		Freedom from discrimination

Source: From M. K. Poulsen (1993). Strategies for building resilience in infants and young children at risk. *Infants and Young Children,* 6(2), p. 38.

nation who are at increased risk for suicide included children of parents who had entered into traditionally disapproved marriages, such as marriage across nations or clans of disparate social status. The ensuing labeling of parents as deviant contributed to their children's experience of stigmatization, which thereby contributed to the initiation of a series of stressors.

Although attention to global risk conditions is meaningful, it is insufficient to elucidate risks for a particular child and family. Early childhood providers can misconstrue what appears to be comparable circumstances for families. Similar situations may have vastly different psychological meanings for each child and family depending on their subjective interpretation. For instance, one family experiencing economic hardship may feel ashamed whereas another family may have a sense of pride about how hard everyone works to contribute to the household.

In this section, four specific risk conditions are described: poverty, adolescent parenthood, growth deficiency, and maltreatment. Each has extensive bodies of literature, which are briefly reviewed with regard to their implications for child development and early intervention. It is important to keep in mind that risk factors rarely occur in isolation and the nature of the specific risk variable is less significant than the sheer number of risk factors affecting a child and family.

Poverty

Poverty is a contextual variable evident both in material misfortune and in multifarious social dimensions. Corollaries of poverty include inadequate nutrition, poor prenatal and postnatal care, and substandard housing. Drug use, disorganized family life, and limited resources also may be present. It often denies young children and their families decent health care and places them in tangibly neglected and often geographically and socially isolated communities, sometimes even denying them homes. Poverty is also stigmatizing. It requires people to prove their worthiness for the most basic life supports; then society frequently "defines" them by virtue of their needing such supports. The relentlessness of poverty offers little respite or opportunity for rejuvenation (Halpern, 1993).

There are two different viewpoints on the meaning of poverty. One perspective underscores the shared and genuine burdens and injuries associated with poverty, which evokes public policy implications. The other view emphasizes the uniqueness of experiences of children and families and their interpretation of their adversity, which offers significance to providers in supportive relationships with individual families. Halpern (1993) contended that these two seemingly contradictory perspectives are both necessary to enhancing the well-being of young children.

Young Children Living in Poverty

The 1980s witnessed the juvenilization of poverty (Segal, 1991). In 1990 there were 900,000 infants and 850,000 children 1 to 2 years of age living in poverty in the United States—approximately one fourth of all children 2 and younger (National Center for Children in Poverty, 1990). According to the Children's Defense Fund (Sherman, 1998), in 1996 there were 14.5 million U.S. children who lived below the poverty line, more than one in every five. In 1995, 24% of children under 6 years of age lived in poverty (below $15,569 annual income for a family of four; Federal Interagency Forum on Child and Family Statistics, 1997), and 69% of poor children in 1996 lived in a family in which someone worked (Sherman, 1997). Poverty rates in the United States are two to three times higher than most other industrialized nations (Huston, 1994). Almost two thirds of young children living in poverty live in mother-only families, and slightly more than two thirds live with families supported by welfare. More than half live in households with parents who have not completed high school, and about half live with mothers who began childbearing during adolescence. Of young children living in economic hardship, approximately 40% live in urban areas of concentrated poverty, 30% in rural areas, and the remainder largely in suburban areas or in neighborhoods contiguous to central city high-poverty areas (Halpern, 1993).

In a cohort-sequential design of 534 public school students from 1986–1989, Bolger, Patterson, Thompson, and Kupersmidt (1995) found that second through fourth graders who experienced persistent family economic hardship were behind other children at the start of the study on every measure of school-based competence. Moreover, they generally stayed behind and were less well-adjusted throughout the investigation. Overall, the greatest difficulties in adjustment were exhibited by children whose families experienced persistent economic hardship, followed by those whose families experienced intermittent economic disadvantage. Those children whose families did not experience economic hardship exhibited the fewest difficulties. Negative outcomes occurred even after statistically evaluating the separate and interactive contributions of ethnicity. In addition, boys were more affected than girls by family economic disadvantage in terms of externalizing behaviors. The linkage of economic hardship and children's school-based competence was mediated in part by parental involvement.

The Broad Context of Poverty

There are numerous correlates of poverty, which form the multifaceted context for early childhood development. Poor families residing in high-poverty communities are disadvantaged in multiple ways. They have more stress and conflict; limited learning opportunities at home; fewer transportation options; reduced accessibility to jobs, high quality public and private services (such as child care, schools, parks, and community centers), or informal social supports; greater isolation (e.g., no telephone); lower quality child care; substandard housing (or no housing); poor nutrition; and triple the risk of lead poisoning in their children. They are subject to increased exposure to pernicious environmental stressors, including street violence, homelessness, illegal drugs, and negative role models (Sherman, 1997; Zigler, 1994). This cascade of reasons is why growing up poor indeed matters. They multiply to fill a child's life with heightened obstacles, narrowed horizons, and deepened risks. The scope of problems assailing poor children erode their resilience by compelling them to fight battles on many fronts concurrently.

Poverty and its correlates directly affect infant development from the moment of conception. Women living in poverty are significantly more likely than their more economically advantaged peers to have histories of poor health prior to their pregnancy, to receive inadequate prenatal care, to experience high levels of stress during their pregnancy, and to engage in harmful health behavior during pregnancy. Hence under conditions of poverty, infants are substantially more likely to be born constitutionally vulnerable and to be difficult to care for. Moreover, both the infant and family are at heightened risk of contributing to relationship difficulties (Halpern, 1993). Once a transactional process is set in motion, a negative pattern of interaction becomes increasingly difficult to redirect. For example, an irritable, disorganized, small-for-gestation-age infant is likely to overload the limited psychological and physical resources of an already stressed family facing the risk of homelessness. Similarly, an easygoing, persistent child can contribute to adequate caregiving even in family caregivers with minimal resources to draw on. Infants born into poverty, therefore, are likely to be at both biological and environmental risk, but with pockets of protective factors.

Poverty is too broad a variable for explaining specific processes in the lives of young children and their families. The influence of indigence and its correlates are mediated by such variables as birth order, physical status, and temperament; parents' age, history of nurturance, and intra-familial and extrafamilial social supports; and degree of economic hardship. Family characteristics, infant characteristics, and family circumstances (e.g., neighborhood and housing) interact in complex ways, predicting both positive and negative outcomes. For instance, feelings of powerlessness or power-over-adversity in caregivers can mediate caregivers' responsiveness to their infants. Multiple caregivers and attachments that may ensue also may offer some protection from the unpredictability in the lives of many families. The cognitive interpretation of adversity also must be considered. For some, family economic hardship may represent a challenge to be overcome rather than an agent of suffering and strife. As Halpern (1993) noted, "Even seemingly identical situations and events have a unique psychological meaning for each poor child and family. The only way to understand that meaning is to come to know how that . . . caregiver experiences and interprets those situations and events" (p. 74). Future research needs to investigate mechanisms by which children and families internalize the inveterate stresses associated with poverty.

Family members' own histories of nurturance, as well as how they interpret those experiences to themselves, contribute to what has been termed their "internal representational models." Such models influence their view of what they are like as people, what they expect from others, and what family–child and other relationships are like (Main, Kaplan, & Cassidy, 1985; Stern-Bruschweiler & Stern, 1989). How do families' personal histories affect early childhood providers? A history of adversity, especially experiences of broken or disrupted attachments, can undermine parents' capacity to form supportive adult relationships. Some parents may have adult behavioral patterns (e.g., depressive symptomatology, displaced anger, disinterest) that make it challenging for others, including early intervention providers, to be caring and supportive. It is important for psychologists and other providers to work assiduously toward establishing and nurturing nonjudgmental, relationship-based interactions with the family. Diverse theoretical perspectives offer guidance about how to support families. In addition to family systems theory and cognitive–behavioral approaches, psychodynamic theory suggests helping the family in exploring the pain of their own history of negative or intermittent nurturance (if applicable) and becoming aware of its continuing effects on the pattern in their relationships with their children.

As well as influencing the larger social ecology of young children's lives, poverty affects children's immediate ecology, including daily routines, caregiving roles and responsibilities, and the interpersonal environment of the home. One way to get a better understanding of the real-life experiences of a young child and family is to learn about daily routines. Following are examples of types of information related to sleep and mealtime that can elucidate the developmental appropriateness of the child's behavior, the broad pattern and quality of care, ecological variables, and the family's interpretation of activities (e.g., is the routine pleasant or stressful?).

- *Sleep:* times for going to bed (for naps and at night) and waking up, locations (rooms, households, sleeping in own or other's bed), caregivers (who puts the child to bed?), transition activities (calming down routines to help prepare the child for bed—such as story reading or cuddling while rocking child in a chair), and ways of handling disruptions in sleep (crying in the night, family members coming home from work);
- *Mealtime:* times for snacks and meals, food preparation and selection of food (by whom?), setting (table, floor), presence of others (eats alone, with other children, with various adults), emotional circumstances (stressful, enjoyable), presence of distractions (crying baby, shouting from street), presence of supports (grandmother, older child in family to help set the table).

Rather than questioning families, psychologists and other providers can have a conversation with families. For instance, the provider may begin the relationship-based communication with, "I can appreciate all the demands on your time. It would help me understand some of the difficulties you face if you chatted about what your day is like. Maybe you could start with the morning when Caleb first gets up and go through a typical day." During the conversation, the provider varies her or his pacing and body language to match the family's style, even digressing when the family seems to want to talk about another issue.

Through the course of the dialogue, the emphasis is on nurturing a supportive relationship with the family. In this process, providers gain invaluable information about

- Child behaviors (both positive and challenging),
- Family perception of child temperament,
- Family–child interaction,
- Frustrations and facilitations (i.e., what is helpful),
- Sequence of activities (rather than focus on discrete events) and their cumulative effect (e.g., build up of stressors or calming event somewhere in the day that diffuses tension), and
- Family energy level at beginning and end of day (energized or demoralized).

Protective Processes and Implications for Intervention

Caregiving that is strict and highly directive (such as well-defined house rules, clear and consistent consequences for disregarding rules, close supervision), together with high levels of warmth, helps poor, inner-city children resist forces in their extrafamilial environments that ordinarily would contribute to low levels of achievement. Examples of negative influence include peer pressure against achievement and poor-quality schooling. These parenting behaviors differentiated high-achieving and low-achieving children from poor, inner-city neighborhoods who were exposed to similar stressors (Baldwin, Baldwin, & Cole, 1990; Jarrett, 1995). Parenting behavior is an important mediator of the effects of poverty on children's socioemotional status. It also may be crucial in buffering poor children from the negative sequelae of discrete and chronic stressors that are exogenous to the family (McLoyd, 1998).

Various compensatory factors include nonseparation of child and primary caregiver during infancy; positive parent–child relationships during the preschool and elementary school years; a robust sense of parenting efficacy by the primary caregivers; and parental use of reasoned, developmentally appropriate, consistent discipline (Cowen, Wyman, Work, & Parker, 1990).

There has been ample demonstration of the protective effects of cognitive stimulation provided in preschool education (Barnett, 1995). Poor children who attend large-scale programs such as Head Start and small, model preschool intervention programs demonstrate superior academic-readiness skills or show greater gains than their peers not enrolled in such intervention (Currie & Thomas, 1995). Children enrolled in these programs also demonstrate lower rates of grade retention and special education placement, higher scores on standardized achievement tests, and increased rates of high school graduation (Reynolds, 1994). These positive effects have been replicated in quasi-experimental studies that control for preexisting differences in child cognitive status and background characteristics such as maternal education and presence of father (Lee, Brooks-Gunn, Schnur, & Liaw, 1990). The most enduring effects ensue from interventions that typically are centered on the family because they reduce multiple risk factors. For instance, preschool education could be accompanied by various core services to parents and other family members, parenting education, and assistance with housing and legal problems (McLoyd, 1998).

Unfortunately, cognitive and achievement gains resulting from preschool education programs typically dissipate by the third or fourth grade (Lee et al., 1990). Gains tend to persist longer if children participate in model programs and programs of more than two years duration and significant intensity (Ramey, Ramey, Gaines, & Blair, 1995). Overall, although preschool intervention provides some protection from the deleterious effects of poverty, over the long haul it does not bestow levels of cognitive and academic competence comparable to those seen among children who are not poor in the general population (McLoyd, 1998).

Family members and extrafamilial adults may contribute indirectly to socioemotional resilience in children living in poverty by providing emotional and parenting support to the mother and bolstering parental control (Cowen et al., 1990). Because parental depression is a potentiating risk factor for difficulties in parenting (see chapter 6), variables that protect against parental depression (e.g., companionship, availability of a confidant, assistance in child rearing) are likely to enhance parenting, promote positive parent–child relationships, and in turn cultivate adaptive resilience in children (McLoyd, 1990).

Poverty in the first five years of a child's life attenuates years of schooling completed more so than does poverty experienced during middle childhood and adolescence. One plausible explanation is that poverty during early childhood thwarts the development of preschool readiness skills, launching a pattern of underachievement (McLoyd, 1998). Research on the differential effects of the timing of poverty argues for policies that give highest priority to the elimination of deep and persistent poverty during children's early years of life (Duncan, Yeung, Brooks-Gunn, & Smith, in press). Furthermore, it strengthens the position for implementing Head Start for children living in poverty from birth to age 3 years (Zigler, 1994). Evidence that more intensive preschool intervention produces more enduring effects argues for making Head Start a full-day rather than a half-day program, 5 days per week, year round. Currently, Head Start centers operate on a nine-month school year. Less than 15% provide full-day programs, and 35% are open fewer than five days per week (Hofferth, 1994; Zigler & Styfco, 1994). Such an extension also would respond to child-care needs created by the work requirements of the 1996 federal welfare reform law and help redress the paucity of regulated, high-quality child care (Greenberg, 1996).

The Children's Defense Fund makes a strong case for a prowork, profamily policy to end poverty. Policies must be developed and implemented in which all families can gain the education, wages, health benefits, and other opportunities they require to provide food, housing, and nurturance to their children. Partnerships across business, community, and religious institutions; individuals; foundations; universities; and government can enhance new work- and family-based opportunities (Sherman, 1997). Policies that raise the incomes of families living in poverty may be comparatively more effective in promoting children's development (in addition to being easier to design and to administer) than programs that seek to modify family characteristics, although cost–benefit analyses need to be expanded (McLoyd, 1998). "Two-generation" programs also merit attention. For example, programs to increase levels of education among poor parents can indirectly and positively affect children's cognitive status by providing more stimulating home environments (Smith & Zaslow, 1995).

Adolescent Parenthood

Adolescent parenthood is replete with various developmental risks, yet areas of resilience and protective factors potentially buffer the effects. Risks affect both child and parent and relate to mental health and socio-emotional development. With adolescent pregnancy comes early parenthood, compelling young women and men struggling with their own developmental tasks to assume adult responsibilities. Compared to nonpregnant adolescents, adolescent mothers have been found to exhibit greater identity diffusion, less autonomy, more challenges with trust, greater depression, and lower self-esteem (Osofsky, Hann, & Peebles, 1993). Indeed, there can be a mismatch between adolescent development and infant developmental needs that disrupts adolescents' parenting skills (Osofsky & Eberhart-Wright, 1992).

Conceptual Framework

Adolescent pregnancy is having an immense impact on society. In 1994 there were 195,169 births to females ages 15 to 17, with substantial racial and ethnic disparities in birth rates (16 per 1000 for Asian or Pacific Islanders, 23 for Whites, 51 for American Indian or Alaskan Natives, 77 for Hispanics, and 76 for Blacks; Federal Interagency Forum on Child and Family Statistics, 1997). Accompanying adolescent pregnancy is a family of origin, a network of relationships, a neighborhood, and school or work environments. This ecological context, along with adolescent individual characteristics and experiential base, strongly influence adjustment both to pregnancy and parenthood (Osofsky et al., 1993).

Given that most adolescent parents do not live in isolation, attention to the family system is paramount. In addition, community-based ideologies provide an interpretive model for understanding locally based belief systems (Reiss, 1981), such as mothers staying home with their children, which have implications both for defining stressful situations and designing ecologically appropriate supportive interventions for young children and their young parents.

The realities of economic hardship, addressed in the previous section, offer another contextual factor needing consideration. Poverty augments the challenges facing adolescent parents, increasing their risk for living in areas of high crime and violence, moving frequently, experiencing difficulty coping with daily responsibilities, and receiving less social and emotional support than generally afforded to older mothers (Brooks-Gunn & Furstenberg, 1986).

Mental Health and Biological Risks

Given the data indicating that depressed mothers are less empathic or responsive to their young children (see chapter 6), it is disconcerting that adolescent mothers are more likely to experience depression than older mothers (Osofsky & Eberhart-Wright, 1988). The children of depressed mothers are at higher risk for problems in regulation of affect, including depression and aggression (Field, Healy, Goldstein, & Guthertz, 1990; Zahn-Waxler, Kochanska, Krupnick, & McKnew, 1990).

When variables that contribute to low birthweight and increased mortality risk (e.g., poverty, inadequate nutrition, ethnicity, maternal education, maternal age at the extremes, prior obstetrical history) are controlled for, adolescent motherhood does not contribute to outcome differentially (Hollingsworth, Kotchen, & Felice, 1983). There may be increased biologic risk to infants of very young mothers under the age of 15, although systematic empirical investigations are lacking. With good prenatal care, biological risk can be greatly reduced (McCormick, 1985). However, an amalgamation of gynecologic age, socioeconomic hardships, inferior nutrition, late diagnosis of pregnancy, and fragmented services available to pregnant adolescents mitigates good prenatal care and optimal pregnancy outcome. Although there may be greater physiologic risk for some adolescent mothers and their babies, the overriding concerns influencing outcomes seem to be more in the psychosocial domain (Turner, Grindstaff, & Phillips, 1990).

Protective Factors

The majority of the at-risk literature, for adolescent pregnancy as well as other at-risk areas, concentrates on why those who are at risk flounder. Emerging research questions have focused on how those at risk avoid failure—namely on the protective factors that serve as buffers against the risks. Such areas of resilience may lead to relative invulnerability for adolescent parents and their young children as they recover from or adjust to adversity or chronic life stress (Masten, Best, & Garmezy, 1990). Identifying such protective factors can lead to the design of proactive early childhood supports for some of society's most vulnerable.

There are several protective factors that mediate outcomes for adolescent mothers and their young children. The role of support is extremely important, whether it comes from nuclear or extended family, father of the child, or agencies. At a conceptual level, social support is regarded as a buffer, enhancing a person's ability to manage stress. The availability and use of social support may provide a buffer from potential detrimental effects of negative life events (Brooks-Gunn & Furstenberg, 1986). Osofsky et al. (1993) found that both perception of support and specific support from grandmothers (i.e., mothers of the adolescent mother) positively affected young mothers and their infants and enhanced their interactive relationship. Other studies have found that the presence of a responsive grandmother seems to serve as a buffer and a positive socializing influence on a child's development (Pearson, Hunter, Ensminger, & Kellam, 1990). Further, if a child's father sustains positive involvement with a mother and child over time, he serves as a notable source of support that has a beneficial influence on developmental outcome for both the mother and young child (Osofsky et al., 1993).

An infant's developmental competence has emerged as a protective factor contributing to resilience. Problem-solving skills enhance the number of options available to young children for difficulty-focused coping. Young children with more advanced abilities should have more competent coping skills when responding to demands from their environment (Karraker & Lake, 1991). Temperament also can be a protective factor. Beginning in infancy, friendly, resilient young children tend to have the capacity to procure other people's positive attention (Garmezy, 1983). In their work with adolescent mothers, Osofsky and Eberhart-Wright (1992) found several positive temperamental characteristics in young children that contributed to resilience, including a social nature evident from birth, skill in captivating others, and a verve for living.

Implications for Intervention

For adolescent parents, a comprehensive approach to intervention clearly is indicated, with features of programs tailored to supporting both young children and young parents with their developmental struggles. Interventions must support the caregiver–child dyad and the broader family context. Other important issues deserving attention in comprehensive interventions include social support, education, personality issues, self-esteem, depression, match between young child and mother, and the invulnerability of the person under stress (Osofsky et al., 1993).

A relationship perspective in which trust is developed (cf. Sameroff & Emde, 1989) should be an overarching framework of all early childhood programs and certainly of those with adolescent parents. Intervention programs must address adolescents' basic needs for trust (cf. Erikson, 1972), emphasizing the need to have skilled providers who can sensitively and intentionally use microskills to listen and support young parents. Osofsky et al. (1993) further emphasized the need to support young parents in empathizing with their babies, because adolescence is a developmental stage in which teenagers (although not restricted to this chronological age range) tend to focus primarily on themselves rather than others. For instance, video cameras can be used to help young parents focus playfully on their infants' feelings and to appreciate the impact of their behavior on their babies (Carter, Osofsky, & Hann, 1991).

Growth Deficiency

In general, *failure to thrive* is defined in terms of growth deficiency. The majority of children are diagnosed with failure to thrive when their percentiles for weight or height are low. Others are diagnosed when their growth, plotted on growth charts of the National Center for Health Statistics, crosses percentile lines in a downward trend even though it may not have dropped below the fifth percentile. Failure to thrive is of concern to early childhood providers because malnutrition impairs brain development. Moreover, children with failure to thrive may encounter social and environmental risks as well (Dawson, 1992).

Failure to thrive can be categorized as organic (resulting from illness or other biologic variables) or nonorganic (which intimates pathogenesis as a result of psychosocial factors). Budd et al. (1992) suggested a more detailed classification than the organic–nonorganic dichotomy; they used the terms *only organic, primarily organic, primarily nonorganic,* and *only nonorganic.* Many young children have a fused etiology that blends one or more of these classifications (Frank & Zeisel, 1988). In the spirit of nonpejorative nomenclature, other terms are preferred, such as *growth deficiency, underweight, undernutrition,* or *growth difficulties.* Imagine the anguish of parents of young children diagnosed as failing to thrive when they arrive looking for the "failure" clinic. Failure to thrive is associated with poverty, and almost all studies of failure to thrive have been conducted with low-income populations. Few investigations have been done with the population of children with failure to thrive in affluent populations (Dawson, 1992).

Eligibility and Implications for Assessment and Intervention

If young children with growth deficiency have concurrent developmental delays, they are eligible for services under Part C and Part B. As of 1992, 29 states regarded failure to thrive as an established condition or a biologic risk factor for early intervention. Attachment disorders (which are associated with failure to thrive) also should be deemed a developmental concern. In 1992, 24 states considered attachment disorders established conditions, hence qualifying for early intervention services (Carolina Policy Studies Program, 1992, cited in Dawson, 1992). Insecure attachment has been found in a significantly higher proportion in groups of individuals diagnosed as failing to thrive than in control groups (Dawson, 1992).

Given the potential for cognitive delays or attachment disorders, young children with growth deficiency should be assessed, with provision of services to many. A systems approach makes it necessary to appreciate familial, social, and economic factors that contributed to the development or maintenance of the feeding difficulties. A variety of providers may need to be involved in assessing and intervening, such as a physician (e.g., developmental pediatrician, pediatric gastroenterologist), nurse, nutritionist, speech–language pathologist, occupational therapist, or social worker. A psychologist may be needed to examine behavioral components of feeding–eating difficulties, degree of synchrony of interaction between the child and caregivers both during mealtimes, and other daily routines (refer to the case study in chapter 6), family relationships, and ethical responsibilities toward each family member. In addition to triage to developmental and educational services, child and family supports from the Special Supplemental Food Program for Women, Infants, and Children Program (WIC) may be appropriate.

Maltreatment

Maltreatment of young children is an egregious social problem, with immediate and long-term sequelae. *Child maltreatment* typically refers to caregiving practices regarded as unsuitable by the populace in a given culture in a particular historical period. The term also can be directed to a society as a whole with regard to its attitude toward children. Considering infant mortality, fetal addiction, inadequate health care, economic hardship, substandard housing, violent neighborhoods, homelessness, and deficient preparation for learning, the status of children in the United States has regressed over the past two decades (Fuchs & Reklis, 1992; Mrazek, 1993).

The 1992 report of the Annie E. Casey Foundation and the Center for the Study of Social Policy, the *Kids Count Data Book* (1992) portrays a nation failing to keep abreast of the needs of its children. The United States has made no improvement or lost previous breakthroughs in seven of nine measures of well-being: percentage of low birthweight babies (increased from 6.8% in 1980 to 7.3% in 1995), adolescent (ages 15–19) violent death rate (11% worse), percentage of all births to single adolescents (14% worse), juvenile (ages 10–15) custody rate (10% worse), percentage graduating from high school (no difference), percentage of children living in poverty (22% worse), and percentage of children in families with a single parent (13% more). Infant mortality rate for 1- to 4-year-olds decreased from 12.6 deaths per 1000 births in 1980 to 7.5 in 1994, and child (ages 1–14) death rate decreased from 63.9 deaths per 100,000 children in 1980 to 42.9 in 1994. However, these gains were not shared evenly, with Black children at greatest risk.

Maltreatment should be viewed in manifold contextual tiers. It is a failure of caregiving within individual families, as well as a dereliction of society, to provide built-in safety nets when the child's family languishes in its caregiving role. The mental health needs of many young children and their families often are unrecognized by the health care system. Furthermore, the trend has been of inadequate funding for preventive services such as Aid to Families With Dependent Children, Head Start, food programs, and subsidized child care.

Demographics and Spectrum of Child Maltreatment

Incidence data for 1990 from the National Center on Child Abuse and Neglect indicated more than 160,000 children under the age of 3 years were reported to child protective services or social service agencies as suspected child maltreatment cases. These cases were investigated and corroborated. Of all child abuse victims in the United States, 6% were younger than 1 year, and 19% were younger than 3 years (U.S. Department of Health and Human Services, 1992). In children younger than 12 months of age, the leading cause of death is physical abuse. Homicide accounts for 10% of all deaths in children between 1 and 4 years of age (Waller, Baker, & Szocka, 1989).

The realm of maltreatment includes physical abuse and neglect, sexual abuse, Munchausen syndrome by proxy, fetal abuse, and emotional abuse. Maltreatment typically is an amalgamation. Experiencing one form of maltreatment places the child at risk for other types of maltreatment, concurrently or sequentially occurring throughout childhood. The effects of maltreatment vary depending on the child's developmental stage (Mrazek, 1993) as well as areas of child and family invulnerability and multiple layers of socioecological contextual factors.

Sequelae of Maltreatment of Young Children

Gaensbauer and Mrazek (1981) have depicted four categories of young children who have been abused. According to this system, the developmentally and affectively retarded individuals (40%) have endured substantial stimulus deprivation, with a proclivity for being socially passive and emotionally numb. Depressed individuals (20%) are highly sensitive to rebuffs. Ambivalent, affectively labile (25%) individuals demonstrated ambivalent reactions and emotional lability, shifting from pleasure to withdrawal or anger quickly under stress. They appeared to have received inconsistent caregiving, fluctuating between sensitive and reciprocal interaction and maltreatment. The angry infants (slightly fewer than 20%) displayed high arousal, limited frustration tolerance, considerable anger, high activity levels, and disorganized play. They had been subjected to chaotic, highly charged environments with recurrent, harsh responses from caregivers. George and Main (1979) also found greater anger in abused toddlers compared to nonabused toddlers who were disadvantaged. They directed their anger toward peers and caregivers, hitting, slapping, kicking, exhibiting unprovoked hostility, and avoiding friendly overtures. Carlson, Cicchetti, Barnett, and Braunwald (1989) found that 82% of the maltreated infants they studied could be classified as disorganized–disoriented based on Main and Solomon's (1986) attachment classification. More detail about the influence of maltreatment and its association with insecure patterns of attachment (e.g., Crittendon, 1988) is presented in chapter 6.

Because of variations in type and frequency of child maltreatment, existence of comorbidities, socioemotional status of the caregivers, and developmental tasks facing the caregivers, maltreatment can lead to disparate effects on different children. The various contextual layers (e.g., social isolation, deteriorating neighborhoods) also affect developing young children and their families. The age of the child has twofold relevance. First, distinct sequelae may ensue, depending on the prominent biological–maturational tasks of the age period. The biological status of children younger than 3 years of age is fragile. For the most part, an insult at such a young age will have more impact than at other ages. For example, significant nutritional neglect may lead to irreversible stunting of brain development. Second, child maltreatment can have different effects depending on the relevant psychological issues and developmental tasks of the age group (Mrazek, 1993).

Risk and Protective Factors

Holden, Willis, and Corcoran (1992) categorized several risk factors for maltreatment. Those with strong empirical support are (a) negative maternal attitude toward the pregnancy (Altemeier, O'Conner, Vietze, Sandler, & Sherrod, 1982); (b) high levels of perceived social stress, such as poor health, inadequate finances, and unhappy life events (Altemeier et al., 1982; Friedrich & Wheeler, 1982); and (c) low socioeconomic status, which increases risk for an assortment of detrimental experiences for young children and their families. Those risk factors with less empirical support include lack of financial resources, low intelligence, parent's criminal record, loss of previous child, history of child maltreatment, negative maternal traits, absence of social support and social isolation, and substance abuse of a parent.

The proportion of maltreated infants who have secure attachments in childhood may be in the range of 5% to 10% (Carlson et al., 1989). Although these figures are low, they suggest some potential for invulnerability. Additional investigations are needed about the protective factors (e.g., positive caregiver attributes, child temperament) that facilitate the development of secure attachment in the midst of maltreatment. The effects of maltreatment may be mediated by such factors as number of children, physical status, and intelligence; caregivers' pattern of responsiveness; familial and community social supports; and degree of economic adversity. Indeed, the interaction among risk factors has received insufficient attention. It is possible that a certain variable only becomes predictive when it is associated with another variable or cluster of variables. In this view, one factor may trigger the power of another factor that has remained latent.

Rather than coming from research on child maltreatment, much of the knowledge base about protective factors is derived from related areas of child and family development. In their longitudinal study of a 1955 birth cohort of 505 individuals, Werner and Smith (1992) found that constitutional factors, such as health and temperament, discriminated between resilient young children and their high-risk peers. Furthermore, support from alternate caregivers (e.g., other family members) was a protective factor of increasing importance as children grew older. Protective factors can abide within the child, family, or community. If they are lacking in one of these areas, it is particularly crucial that they exist profusely in another domain (Mrazek, 1993). Hence the benefit of early childhood services is not likely to be realized when services focus exclusively on child-focused intervention. A broader, more comprehensive approach is indicated.

Implications for Primary Prevention and Treatment

Among families with single or adolescent parents or those living in poverty, there is evidence that extended home visitation can prevent physical abuse and neglect (MacMillan, 1994; MacMillan, MacMillan, & Offord, 1992). Other interventions directed at primary prevention of child maltreatment have not conclusively been shown to be effective, such as intensive pediatric contact, short-term home visitation, early and extended postpartum contact, and parent education programs (Hardy & Streett, 1989; Olds, Henderson, Tatelbaum, & Chamberlin, 1988). The first priority of providers is the physical protection of the child, with reporting to the local child protective service agency if maltreatment already has transpired and the etiology is clear. Ethical principles of autonomy, beneficence, and nonmaleficence (discussed in chapter 7) offer a framework for decision making about protecting the child, rights of the parents—legal guardians, and adequacy of caregiving. In many instances, the course of action is not as clear, particularly for such issues as socioemotional neglect. In these situations, efficacy of preventive and supportive interventions is likely to be enhanced significantly by in-home family support providers who develop therapeutic relationships with families and support them over prolonged periods (Olds, 1997).

Early childhood providers in general, and psychologists in particular, should expand their traditional dialogues with families to inquire about caregiving history (in a supportive, nonthreatening manner), contextual factors, and nature of adult—child interaction and attachment to gain a comprehensive view of family resources and vulnerabilities, and ultimately, to enable delivery of the appropriate blend of interagency supports. Such information may reveal caregivers who themselves lacked nurturance and protective parenting, resulting in their own insecure attachment. Helping parents to attain adaptive functioning in current stage-salient issues (e.g., social relations, work achievement) may be beneficial in supporting them in reworking prior developmental incompetencies (cf. Cicchetti & Toth, 1998). Family members with this type of relational history frequently have difficulty developing relationships with their own children. Psychologists can help caregivers in these situations learn different interaction patterns with their child. Strategies that help caregivers develop secure relationships with other adults also positively affect their interactions with their children. See chapter 6 for a detailed discussion of adult relational history on caregiver–child interaction.

Conclusion

Delineating the relationships among risk factors, protective factors, and areas of invulnerability can expand the notions of early childhood programs and embrace the biopsychosocial nature of child and family development. To realize the goals of reducing mortality and morbidity and enhancing developmental outcome, it is important to those in the field to support children and families at risk as well as those young children with identified delays. Rather than using rudimentary categorical frameworks of risk, comprehensive screening models that consider multiple risk factors should be adopted for early identification. These need to be multifaceted and periodic and draw from diverse databases. Screening paradigms should incorporate family variables related to concerns, priorities, resources, support systems, and quality of caregiver–child interaction.

Overall, a contextual view of family resources and vulnerabilities is essential for all early childhood populations to enable the mingling of interagency supports. Young children and their families continue to develop in a transactional matrix of potentiating and compensatory factors at various levels of the social ecology, which influence their adaptation. Primary and secondary interventions (see chapter 2) aimed at altering family and social–contextual sources of risk should incorporate multiple foci and strategies. They are needed to alleviate ongoing contributors to developmental difficulties. More interdisciplinary and rigorous prospective research, incorporating economic analysis, is needed to delineate the array of risk and protective factors; to design, implement, and monitor effective primary prevention and early childhood programs; and to affect public policy. Investigations of competence, psychopathology, resilience, and intervention all highlight the importance of establishing a good start early in development. Children who enter school who are distrustful of adults, have impaired learning capacity, and have significant difficulties in self-regulation of attention, emotion, and behavior are at a marked disadvantage for meeting the developmental tasks of middle childhood. Research has repeatedly pointed to the importance of good parent–child relationships in developing competence. Fostering competence requires the involvement of nurturing, competent adults in a child's life. We believe supporting families at all levels of their social ecology should be a public policy imperative to ensure that all children have this fundamental protective system (Masten & Coatsworth, 1998).

4

Organizing Integrated Service Delivery Systems

Leslie is 19 years old, pregnant, and addicted to cocaine and alcohol. She is very concerned for her baby and has decided she needs help. As she and her mother begin to explore options they find that there is a general shortage of drug treatment openings for women (particularly those who are pregnant) and general unwillingness of many drug treatment programs to accept her in part because of medical uncertainty over optimal medical management during pregnancy and fear of liability. The one program she found for women with addiction problems did not provide adequate prenatal medical services and did not provide care for the infants, which precluded Leslie from participating in treatment.

The Anthony family was devastated when their 3-year-old son was diagnosed with autism. The interdisciplinary team at a medical rehabilitation center recommended a referral for preschool intervention services and thought the family would qualify for Medicaid services through a waiver. Supplemental Security Income was also a potential financial resource. The family called the school, whose intake worker obtained demographic and medical information via a telephone interview. They were surprised when they met with the Medicaid social service worker that they were repeating much of the same information. The family was emotionally drained as they filled out yet another application for SSI. Each worker stressed the importance of this information for determining eligibility. The family was becoming frustrated as they found themselves telling their story over and over again.

"Communities need to embrace and support all families, celebrating the birth of their children and creating an environment where support and resources are mobilized to ensure that a comprehensive, integrated array of services are available and accessible for all very young children and their families" (Advisory Committee on Services for Families With Infants and Toddlers, 1994, p. 4). Dramatic change is needed in the ways agencies work together to realize this vision. The challenge for communities is to examine their service delivery system for families and begin a process that integrates these programs through collaborative family and community partnerships. How do we accomplish such a valuable vision in communities in which traditionally there exists a broad range of social, health, and educational programs that are multifarious, interconnected, and often fragmented? This chapter will begin to address this challenge by providing the foundation for psychologists and others to understand the components and workings of an integrated service delivery system. Key to building such a delivery system is adopting strategies that promote collaborative relationships among providers and between providers and family members. Collaboration with families is built on the principles of family-centered care, adopting practices that are sensitive to cultural diversity, and incorporating quality interpersonal interactions. The contributions of each will be explored. As psychologists and other community providers take a growing role in early intervention services for young children, it is our hope that information from this chapter can build the competence necessary for providers to work effectively in partnership with families to organize an integrated service delivery system that involves joint planning, implementation, and evaluation of services for children and families.

Community Partnerships

The children and families illustrated at the beginning of the chapter all share something in common: Each experienced a complex labyrinth of services that were organized in such a way that divided issues of children and families into distinct categories with separate and often conflicting eligibility requirements and regulations governing distribution of funds. This points to the issues communities face as they struggle to progress toward an integrated system of services. Psychologists and other providers with interests in early childhood will appreciate this complexity of services as they strive to build community partnerships that potentially lead to integrated services for families.

Who, then, are the players needed to make service integration a reality? As described in chapter 1, children and families are receiving services from a wide spectrum of programs. The specific players at the broad systems level are the policy-making agencies at the federal, state, or local level and the public sector through public hearings and advisory groups. Those professionals involved in policy development, including legislators and agency administrators, can work toward a conceptualization of an integrated system with families. Their role in service integration is to review and create policies that promote collaboration and limit gaps in services. Success in this area has been realized in many areas, and most recently occurred as reflected in the new federal Title 21 legislation (1997) that provides funding for underinsured children, who are not eligible for Medicaid. This new policy has significantly affected a large number of children and addresses a gap in services.

At the service-delivery level, potential participants in early childhood programs include a wide variety of interdisciplinary–interagency specialists who provide early childhood services, including early childhood educators, early childhood special educators, psychologists, Head Start providers, therapists, child care providers, service coordinators, social service providers, and health-care specialists. Public administrators (such as agency and department directors in local, state, and federal governments as well as nonprofit organizations) also play a primary contributing role. Their role in building an integrated service delivery system is to design the direct service components.

It is important to recognize the role of each of these participants as part of a successful integrated system of care. An effective liaison among these policy makers, service delivery providers, and family members is critical in designing comprehensive programs. These programs need to be funded flexibly to meet family priorities and concerns and extend beyond the traditionally exclusive domains of any one of these agencies (Epps & Jackson, 1991; Woody et al., 1992). For example, several community agencies may have as one of their goals increased literacy among families they serve. Providers and families from the various programs might believe that a workshop series would be an appropriate strategy to promote literacy in their community. However, there might be limited funds available for a workshop series. Collaborative planning can occur at the community family literacy council meeting, which would include administrators, providers, and family members. Funds can be obtained across agencies to allow for the workshop series to occur. The established collaborative infrastructure of this community family literacy council could contribute to successful outcomes.

Integrated Service Delivery System: A Goal in Progress

It is important, when working toward a goal of integrated service delivery, to understand both the philosophy behind the model and the steps necessary to reach the goal.

Philosophical Framework

For early intervention to embrace and build an integrated service delivery system, it is essential to understand what service integration entails. *Service integration* reflects a major paradigm shift in the way we deliver services to children and families. In traditional service delivery, there are multiple isolated programs, each with its own targeted populations, restricted eligibility criteria, and limited menus of services. In contrast, an integrated system offers seamless boundaries among programs and encompasses a full range of community-based options that are individualized to meet the child's and family's needs. Service integration provides a framework for highlighting important values related to helping children and families. These values are important in shaping interventions, program design and implementation, regulatory and fiscal administrative procedures, and policies that cut across and govern multiple systems. Knitzer (1997) described five value orientations that are the foundation for service integration:

1. Families are the focal point of service integration with services built on family strengths.
2. Collaboration among agencies is crucial to build effective agency connections.
3. Services are delivered within the context of neighborhoods and communities.
4. Services exemplify cultural competence by creating programs that are respectful of the cultural values and traditions of families.
5. An integrated service system is linked to concrete outcomes and positive change in the lives of children and families.

Review how each of the scenarios at the beginning of the chapter clearly violates these underlying values.

What is the meaning of "collaboration?" *Interagency collaboration* refers to providers from diverse areas of expertise working together for the benefit of children and their families. For these interdisciplinary partnerships to occur, providers need to learn to respect one another's history, culture, language, and practices (Davidson, 1998). Collaboration results in a consolidated system of services that is distinctly different from a service-delivery system that uses either cross-agency cooperative or coordinated efforts. As programs strive toward collaboration, it is important to differentiate the term from *cooperative* or *coordinated efforts*. Swan and Morgan (1993) have suggested that these three terms represent a hierarchical progression of interagency efforts, defining each.

- *Cooperation*: Agencies work together informally, with an awareness of each other's activities.
- *Coordination*: This term represents a more sophisticated level of interagency interaction, with each agency defining its responsibilities for service provision to provide a holistic view of the community service delivery system. This coordination results in reduced duplication of services and efforts and identifies resources to fill gaps in services.
- *Collaboration*: This interagency effort emphasizes joint planning, common goal setting, mutual financial contributions, and joint evaluation of outcomes. In collaborative efforts, distinct agency boundaries dissolve. In their place is a collection of services that blend to form a consolidated system of services. This process results in more formal commitment than is found in coordinated or cooperative efforts.

Table 4.1 illustrates these levels of interagency efforts. When communities engage in coordination of services, they can only advocate for cooperative initiatives. These initiatives can result in increased community awareness, building of trusting relationships, and identification of the need for change. The outcomes, however, are insufficient to ensure high-quality comprehensive services. In contrast, collaborative efforts that include interagency agreements can provide leverage to advance common

Table 4.1. Levels of Interagency Efforts

	Cooperation	Coordination	Collaboration
IFSP/IEP meeting	Agencies are invited to the IFSP/IEP meeting that is organized by the school.	IFSP/IEP meetings include members of all agencies and are scheduled at a time that is mutually agreed on with input solicited from all members.	The outcome of the IFSP/IEP meeting is that the school district provides a speech therapist to provide direct services and consultative supports in the Head Start Program.
Service coordination	Each agency has its own designated service coordinator.	A service coordinator is designated in one agency who coordinates services with the family.	Service coordinator is located in one agency but is hired through an interagency interview process and is funded across agencies.
Agency forms	Each agency has its own set of forms (e.g., intake, release of information).	Agencies accept information on other agency forms to avoid duplication and prevent time delays.	Agencies work together to develop common intake and release of information forms.

goals, promote new programmatic directions, and develop fiscal partnerships. The premise underlying these collaborative efforts is valuing the diversity of agency strengths and viewing agencies as equal and mutually beneficial partners.

One community's work to develop an integrated service-delivery system is illustrated in the following case study, including its positive outcomes for families.

The Hamburg Resource Center was established in a small rural community to provide an integrated system of services that families could reach easily. All community early childhood programs were located at this facility, including child care, Even Start (a federally funded literacy program), Head Start, and the early childhood special education programs. (*Illustrates the concept of one-stop services for families.*) In addition, family support programs were located at the center: mental health resources, a food pantry, social services, and health clinics. The Mendez family moved to Hamburg as Mr. Mendez acquired a job at Farmland Industries.

Although both Mr. and Mrs. Mendez spoke some English, Spanish was their primary language. Neither had graduated from high school. Both parents enrolled in the Even Start program at the Hamburg Resource Center. Mr. Mendez worked at nights, but joined the GED classes in the afternoon. Mrs. Mendez participated in the program during the day and their daughter, Lalita, was enrolled in the child care center. Mrs. Mendez felt very comfortable with this situation, as she was able to visit Lalita several times during the day. Mrs. Mendez and Lalita also participated in a parent–child interaction activity as part of the sponsored Even Start program. After a year in the program both parents received their GED. (*Individualized programs result in positive outcomes.*) Even Start staff helped Mrs. Mendez with job interview skills, and she successfully obtained employment both at a community bank and Head Start Center at the Resource Center.

Mr. Mendez decided that he wanted a career as a diesel mechanic rather then just a "job" at Farmland. Multiple agencies needed to mobilize support for the family to help him reach his goal. (*Interagency planning promotes joint problem solving.*) Social services worked with the family to ensure funds to provide for daily living expenses [e.g. , Aid to Dependent Families With Children] during the 18 months that he was in school. Even Start helped Mr. Mendez connect with a diesel mechanic firm who sponsored him by paying for his tools in return for a work commitment of six months following his graduation. Health insurance was obtained via Medicaid. Even Start staff continued to work with Mr. Mendez on his computer skills to facilitate his readiness to enroll in community college courses. Although Mr. Mendez's change in career was a major life transition for this family, the community helped make this goal a reality.

The established collaborative community partnerships at this center, which included an infrastructure at the systems level (regular interagency team meetings and defined mechanisms for problem-solving), allowed for linkages among resources to occur with minimal effort.

Integrating the Service Delivery Maze

The previous discussion focused on the general philosophical framework of the service delivery system and provided an overall definition of terms.

It is now important to examine the mechanisms of how services can be designed and implemented to make this vision a reality. For successful collaborative relationships to develop and be sustained, commitment and involvement of leadership is needed within the context of an interagency administrative team. The importance of the administrative structure is acknowledged in the regulations for Part C, which stipulate the development of a community Interagency Coordinating Council (ICC) to advise and assist each state in designing and implementing early intervention service. The leadership of the ICC can help to articulate the vision, build the necessary consensus from community providers, and sustain the commitment to ensure success over time.

Baldwin, Jeffries, Jones, Thorp, and Walsh (1992) suggest four steps to building collaborative partnerships: (a) forming the group with decisions about membership and roles in mind; (b) conceptualizing a shared vision; (c) developing working groups; and (d) implementing recommended action such as written agreements, professional development to promote changed attitudes, and adaptation of policies. (These steps as they relate to system change will be discussed in more detail in chapter 9.) This planning needs to include not only traditional services for families (e.g., schools, health services, and social services) but also relationships with other community establishments, such as churches, other religious institutions, and civic groups. These less traditional services serve to mobilize community resources on behalf of children and families (Advisory Committee on Services for Families With Infants and Toddlers, 1994).

For successful collaboration to occur, it is essential that there is community ownership of outcomes that reflect local preferences, needs, and circumstances. Two critical variables are essential to develop community ownership: (a) the use of effective communication and problem-solving skills that facilitate decision making and conflict resolution (see chapter 9) and (b) involving family members in this community-building process. Too often when systems begin to redesign their programs, there is little input solicited from the families they serve (Turnbull, Summers, & Brotherson, 1986). Lack of family input often results in frustration, because the end result does not match the priorities of families. The perspective from families enhances supports as services are modified to address what families believe are their most significant issues. Head Start programs exemplify parent participation through their Parent Advisory Council. They also recognize the need to provide training so they can enhance parents' capacity to participate in the advisory council.

Building collaborative relationships takes time and often proceeds along a rough course with varied success. Four dimensions clearly influence the degree and success of interagency efforts (Harbin & McNulty, 1990; Melaville & Blank, 1991). First is the *climate* in which the initiative exists, including such factors as community attitudes and priorities and support of key stakeholders. For example, two agencies may have two different and competing priorities. One agency wants to secure funding for a site for a new program exclusively for children with disabilities. Another agency's belief and priority is that funds should be used to support child care staff development so children with disabilities can be included in those settings. These conflicting priorities most likely will create road blocks to collaboration. In addition, it is crucial that processes are used that build trust and manage conflict. When there is distrust among the service providers, it is less likely that the open communication that is needed for collaboration can occur. Strategies that promote quality interpersonal interactions that are discussed later in the chapter are useful to adopt to overcome problems of distrust and manage conflict.

The policies that support or inhibit partnership efforts and the availability of resources, such as people, money, and facilities to support efforts to continue collaboration, are the other two key dimensions that influence interagency collaboration. This reiterates the importance of working with policy makers to create flexible policies and regulations to address such areas as modifying fiscal incentives to promote community control and multiagency partnerships (Friedman, 1994). In their national survey, Meisels, Harbin, Modigliani, and Olson (1988) found that 50 state directors of Part H (now called Part C) services identified the lack of available funds, inconsistent eligibility criteria, lack of interagency coordination, and inconsistent regulation across agencies as barriers to comprehensive collaborative services for young children and their families. A primary example was the obstacle that resulted from excessive categorization of funding (e.g., funding that is designated for specific uses and for targeted populations). For example, special education funds can support the funding of special education teachers, but they are restricted to providing services only to children eligible for special education. This policy can be counterproductive when attempting to serve children with disabilities in inclusive environments, as it restricts special education professionals from teaching children without disabilities. Friedman (1994) suggested that a solution to this problem of funding categorization is creating sources of flexible funds to support individualized services. For example, Iowa has eliminated fiscal categorized barriers from 32 funding streams (Robison, 1992). This change resulted not only in flexible funding but has generated incentives to provide effective integrated services (Friedman, 1994).

Biro and Daulton (1991) have identified a number of areas for potential coordination across initiatives, including early detection and assessment of children, a central directory of resources and providers, public awareness and prevention programs, family service plans, professional development of personnel, interagency agreements, and data-reporting systems. The following examples illustrate some of the practical collaboration efforts that agencies in early intervention need to address as they redesign early intervention toward an integrated services delivery system.

1. Need for *common intake form*. Families often complain that they frequently repeat core information about themselves and their child with each new referral. A goal of integrated services is to develop a common interagency intake form. The challenge is for each agency to give up ownership of their form and develop a new format based on consensus that works across agencies.

2. Need for a *cross-agency release form*. In establishing community partnerships, it is critical that systems of communication be developed that allow agencies to share information, efficiently and effectively, yet maintain family confidentiality. Many Part C programs have developed a consent form that allows parents to sign one release that allows for cross-agency communication.

3. Access to current *community resource information*. A central directory of community resources is essential to maximize family's access to programs. Maintaining a current listing is a challenge for communities because of the large array of and ongoing change in programs (e.g., eligibility criteria). Website-based referral information systems and community information hotlines are two alternatives to the traditional printed guide to information and referral. Currently in Nebraska a directory of services is available through the Health and Human Services web page. This provides easy access to information for families and providers and is easily updated as programs change.

4. Integrated *data reporting systems*. Another challenge for communities is developing a process for reporting data across agencies. Developing a common database becomes a difficult task because each program has different mandates for the types of data that need to be collected. A further complicating factor is the issue of confidentiality. In addition agencies need to determine a database infrastructure that allows data entry and data access across agencies. In Nebraska, where there are colead agencies, the Department of Health and Human Services (HHS) and Department of Education, designated for implementation of early intervention (Part C), there was success in integrating the data information systems of those two agencies. A database was designed for Medicaid reimbursement of therapy services that are provided in educational settings. The database that is managed by HHS and used broadly by health care professionals in the state was modified to allow for educational therapies to be documented and billed.

A Key Navigator of the Service Delivery System: The Service Coordinator

Service coordination was proposed as one way to promote interagency collaboration and to support families as they come into contact with multiple agencies. The positive outcomes of service coordination for families are twofold: (a) reducing fragmentation and duplication of services and (b) promoting family competence by assisting families in acquiring resources in a way that increases self-sufficiency, self-esteem, and the family's sense of control over life events (Dunst & Trivette, 1989). Service coordination at the community level helps providers in separate service systems become aware of the benefits that parallel agencies may provide and support families in accessing and coordinating services (Brown, Perry, & Kurland,

1994). This awareness can also be an impetus to agencies to begin the process of formulating collaborative efforts.

Service coordination has long been a documented need of children with disabilities and their families (Elder & McGrab, 1985). Overall, it is difficult to capture service coordination in a single clarifying statement. However, the vision of family-centered service coordination is defined as "an active process for implementing intervention services that promotes and supports a family's capacities and competencies to identify, obtain, coordinate, monitor and evaluate resources and services to meet its needs" (McGonigel, Kaufmann, & Johnson, 1991, p. 71). This definition emerged through implementation of Part C and Maternal and Child Health Services Block Grant [Title V] legislation. Rather than managing families as cases, service coordination is intended to facilitate families' active role in planning. With its guiding principle of empowerment, service coordination is intended to advance family independence, self-sufficiency, and resilience as it supports families in mobilizing their resources to address their priorities for themselves and for their children. Most important, service coordinators support children and families to obtain their rights and procedural safeguards as guaranteed in Part C regulations.

Before discussing the process of service coordination, it is important to sort out the many commonly used terms in the human service field. *Case management, care coordination, managed care,* and *service coordination* are all popular terms that reflect some similarities in the coordination roles, yet the terms cannot be used interchangeably among professions. For example, *case management* defined by the nursing profession includes the responsibilities of managing a patient's total care to ensure optimal outcome and to assess and to choose health treatment options (Knollmueller, 1989). By contrast, *case management* defined by insurance companies is designed to restrict access to care and reduce costs (Perrin, Shayne, & Bloom, 1993). In early intervention, *service coordination* replaced the term *case management* with the reauthorization of Part H of the Individuals With Disabilities Education Act (IDEA) in 1990. This change occurred because many families were offended by being referred to as "cases" and did not wish to be "managed." The term *service coordination* more accurately describes the process taking place—that is, services are coordinated, not families.

As states implemented Part H two questions arose: Who should the service coordinators be and what specifically should their responsibilities be? In accordance with the IDEA, service coordination should be provided by "the person most immediately relevant to the infant's and toddler's or family's needs" (34 CFR Pt. 303.6, 1986). This definition suggests that service coordinators can cross disciplines. Implementing service coordination for early intervention has resulted in two basic models. One involves assigning the service coordinator from one of the intervention team members for that child. For example, if a child has cerebral palsy and is receiving intensive physical therapy services in conjunction with early intervention, the physical therapist may be assigned as the service coordinator. This assignment would be made because the physical therapist could best meet the child and family needs—for example, coordination of orthopedics visits, joint visit with an orthodist, and acquiring funding for equipment. The advantage of this model is that one does not have to add yet another team member to work with the family. The problem, however, is that often times there is a shortage of therapists for early intervention services, so that programs want to use the therapists in roles that best take advantage of their unique expertise and assign others the coordination responsibilities.

Some states have implemented a model in which staff are hired to specifically implement a service coordination role with no provision of direct services. The service coordinator is an added member to the interdisciplinary team. These service coordinators come from varied backgrounds, such as social work, education, psychology, or experience as a family member. The advantage of this model is that these service coordinators can build their skills in this very specific role and can exclusively support families around their coordination needs. The disadvantage is the added burden to families in developing yet another relationship with an additional provider.

The exciting prospect in early intervention is the potential roles that parents might assume in service coordination. Initially, many parents may want the support of a service coordinator, but most parents will assume the responsibility of coordination for their own family over time. An important role for the service coordinator is to support families who want to coordinate their own services to develop skills that enable families to advocate for themselves, gain access to necessary services, and attribute positive developments to their own actions and resilience. This emphasis on empowerment is especially critical because parents are the chief participants over the long term from early intervention through various transitions through the service system (e.g., preschool services to school-aged services). These skills will help them navigate through the service delivery system long after their child transitions from early intervention programs.

Although case management has historical roots, there is limited research to guide practice (Bailey, 1987). As states begin to design their service coordination system they need to define the roles, responsibilities, and competencies of the service coordinators. Typically, service coordinators guide the assessment and Individual Family Service Plan (IFSP) process, assist families in securing needed services, and advocate for the needs and rights of the child and family. Because service coordination is a new role in early intervention, there is a need for ongoing professional development opportunities to ensure positive benefits for families. As early intervention programs gain more experience with the service coordination role, further delineation of responsibilities and the competencies needed to implement high-quality services will emerge.

Building Parent–Provider Partnerships

One of the most critical assessments of service integration is how the family experiences the services provided. Early intervention needs to be delivered within the context of a supportive, growth-promoting relationship between the provider and family (Trout & Foley, 1992). For a family–provider partnership to occur, the provider needs to develop skills that build and maintain a relationship including consistency, predictability, warmth, positive regard, and empathy. Communication between parties is essential for successful partnerships to develop. The quality of these interactions affects the extent to which a collaborative partnership that encompasses mutual trust and support is established (Bailey, 1991a). Providers need to maintain attitudes that reflect an understanding of the complex factors that influence family–provider collaboration and convey this sensitivity to parents. A major factor in collaboration is recognizing and respecting the talents and expertise of team members, including the family members, as they strive toward a common goal (Duwa et al., 1993).

As service providers begin to work with families, we suggest that family-centered principles provide the necessary foundation for building those partnerships. Incorporating family-centered care into policies and provider practice is an ongoing process that has no final destination. Family-centered care is based on recognizing that the family is the constant in the child's life and the primary decision maker for both the child and the family. Although many early intervention providers embrace family-centered principles, the challenge is applying these principles to practice. Psychologists and early intervention providers can encourage institutions to examine their approach toward the family and the extent to which the family is integral in all aspects of care. It is urgently necessary that the organization moves away from directive approaches of intervention to a perspective of supporting, facilitating, and enabling. As psychologists and early intervention providers advocate for the reconceptualization of the role families play in decision making, they can support agencies' shift from paternalism to enablement and from judgmental to supportive stances (Epps, 1995). Strategies to help providers develop family-centered practices are found in the following discussions.

Building Partnerships Using a Family-Centered Approach

Family-centered care has evolved in recent years from two parallel movements, including the passage of the IDEA (1990) and Surgeon General C. Everett Koop's initiative in 1987 for family-centered, community-based, coordinated care. These initiatives marked entry into a new era in which program emphasis shifted from a child-oriented, provider-driven service delivery system to one that is both family-centered and family-driven. This shift translates into the need to adopt new agency policies that ultimately influence the roles and practices of providers. A child-oriented focus is evident in the design of their programs, which offered a predetermined package of services (e.g., preschool program, parent support group). In a rather paternalistic fashion, these services were assumed to meet the needs of the children and families they served. The program and service package remain constant, assuming these services met the needs of all children and families. The shift to a family-centered service system has been analogized as a "Copernican revolution" (Turnbull et al., 1986). In this framework, the family is viewed as the constant, with the various service delivery systems moving in and out of the family's life. This model necessitates individualizing services across time to meet the unique priorities and concerns of families and building partnerships that strengthen a family's skills to support their child and to interact with agencies. A multifactorial model views neither the program services nor the family as constant. Rather, it highlights a systems perspective in regarding changing family ecology in which contextual factors affect shifting priorities for families over time. For example, employment of the mother may necessitate the search for appropriate child care and a shift of services that previously was provided to the family at home to a combined service package that includes consultation with the new child care providers and home services.

A program's philosophy and its underlying assumptions regarding families has major implications on how policies are determined and services are delivered. It is important for programs to develop a shared philosophy and to plan as a team so that services are delivered with consistency. Described as a new constellation of philosophies, attitudes, and approaches, family-centered care is reflected in nine principles that form the philosophical underpinnings of the paradigm (Shelton, Jeppson, & Johnson, 1987). Table 4.2 illustrates the roles of psychologists and other service providers in translating these nine principles into practice.

To implement family-centered approaches successfully, providers must respect family beliefs and recognize their own prejudices that may result in judgmental interactions (Duwa et al., 1993). A lack of comprehensive family intervention models and limited personnel trained to work with families can potentially thwart implementation of family-centered programs. Therefore, for this system change to occur, ongoing professional development is essential. To deliver a family-centered approach, providers must learn new behaviors and attitudes toward the family's role in early intervention programs (Bailey, McWilliam, & Winton, 1992). Providers need training in the scientist–practitioner model, in which clinical practice is predicated on systematic training in behavioral science, to gain skills to change and to address these challenges proactively. Winton, McWilliam, Harrison, Owens, and Bailey (1992) have suggested that the most success occurs if training activities are delivered that support a team-based model for change. This model is implemented through a series of workshops and consultations that place decision making into the hands of key players so that family-centered practices are tailored to the unique needs of the community. This decision-based format has team members examine their own practices, determine what techniques work well in their programs, and recommend change. The skill of the team in

Table 4.2. Translating Family-Centered Principles Into Practice: Roles of Psychologists and Others

1. Recognize that the family is the constant in a child's life, whereas service systems and the personnel within those systems fluctuate.

   Because families have the ultimate responsibility for the care of their children, it is essential that providers support them as the primary decision makers, caregivers, and advocates. This support means the providers assist families in gaining knowledge and skills to support their child, to make decisions regarding their child's program, and to feel secure in their relationships with providers. It is important to acknowledge and build on family strengths and resilience and not allow personal judgments to interfere with the support provided to the family.

2. Facilitate parent–provider collaboration at all levels of service provision: services for an individual child, program development, and policy formation.

   The primary goal is to build a collaborative relationship in which providers and the family are equal partners. Families are the ultimate decision makers regarding services. As families need to be respected, so do their decisions, even when they are not congruent with the views of the provider. If the child is physically or emotionally threatened within the family, providers are obligated to take responsible courses of action, but even in extreme situations the providers need to be family-centered, continuing to build on and support the family's resilience.

3. Honor the racial, ethnic, cultural, and socioeconomic diversity of families.

   To develop effective relationships with families, providers must have a sound understanding of their own perspectives and value systems. On a continual basis they need to reevaluate how their own values and judgments affect their perceptions and interactions with families. It is also important to gather information and explore customs central to each individual family.

4. Recognize family strengths, resilience, resources, and individuality and respect different methods of coping.

   An assumption of family-centered care is that all families have strengths. This posture represents a shift from previous practices and focuses on protective factors and vulnerabilities rather than on deficits in family functioning. This change enables families to identify their own strengths and the resources they bring to the situation. Just as families are diverse in their constellation and priorities, they are equally diverse in their ways of coping.

5. Share with parents, on a continuing basis and in a supportive manner, complete and unbiased information.

   In providing information of a technical nature, it is essential to assist the family in gaining clarification (while also avoiding paternalism) until family members reach a comfortable level of understanding. Such support enables the family to assume power and control to make informed decisions and to be self-directed in their child's care.

Table continues

Table 4.2. *Continued*

6. Encourage and facilitate family-to-family support and networking.

   Families determine their own preference for family-to-family support. This support might come from a formalized support group or from an individual family that has had similar experience. Providers can assist the family in identifying contacts. Providers should respect the autonomy of families to determine if and when this type of support is needed.

7. Understand and incorporate the developmental needs of infants, children, and adolescents and their families into service delivery systems.

   The early intervention program is merely one of multiple services that children and families encounter. It is important for early intervention teams to collaborate with other service providers to ensure consistency across each setting.

8. Implement comprehensive policies and programs that provide emotional and financial support to meet the priorities and concerns of families.

   One responsibility of the early intervention team is to assist the family in linking with various service agencies and providers to create a more comprehensive and integrated service delivery system for their child and themselves. One of the many resources families may prioritize is financial support. Creativity is required in finding financial alternatives. Universal to all providers is the emotional support provided to families, which is tailored to each family's circumstance. It is important for providers to be as nonintrusive as possible, recognizing this area of vulnerability.

9. Design accessible service delivery systems that are flexible, culturally competent, and responsive to family-identified priorities and concerns.

   Family-centered services are not implemented overnight. Advocacy at the policy level is important to enhance coordinated supports for families. A key to designing successful service delivery systems is active participation of families.

Source: From Shelton, T. L., Jeppson, E. S., & Johnson, B. H. (1987). *Family-centered care for children with special health care needs.* Washington, DC: U.S. Government Printing Office.

specifying goals and carrying out the action plan is central to a successful outcome.

Striving for Family-Centered Care

Once a program embraces the concept of family-centered care, the important question is what steps do programs take to translate this philosophy into practice. Effective infusion of family-centered care practices across community programs will need to include extensive training and consultation to individual providers and examination of program policies and procedures to ensure that they provide the foundation from which family-centered practices can emerge.

Systems Change Approach

Results of a recent analysis of 75 case studies by the Early Childhood Research Institute at the University of North Carolina at Chapel Hill found that early intervention programs across nine communities were family-centered in their response to the family's priorities but had not yet accomplished family-centered services on the dimension of enabling family members or taking a holistic approach to the family (McWilliam, Tocci, & Harbin, 1995). These results suggest that although there is a recognition that family-centered approaches benefit young children and their families, the totality of these principles generally has not been infused into existing programs. The journey toward a genuine interagency, family-centered approach requires rethinking and reframing the manner in which we relate to families and other providers throughout the assortment of professional activities. Too often it is easier for providers to continue to implement services from outdated practices that are comfortable. The challenge is motivating staff to relinquish these strategies and replace them with innovative approaches that might at first present challenges in implementation. Change at the individual level requires courage, which challenges people to eschew practices antithetical to family sensitivity and partnership building. In many ways, courage drives people beyond comfort zones to realize what is really possible in best-practice early intervention (see Terry, 1993). Chapter 9 provides strategies for programs to facilitate the systems change needed to make these new practices a reality.

Supporting Family Decision-Making Processes

Psychologists and providers play critical roles in supporting the family as the primary decision makers. This new capacity for families does not imply a passive role for the provider, but rather a partnership toward this effort. Families rely on providers to share information and clinical opinions from which they can make informed decisions. Providers are then responsible for creating opportunities for information sharing and dialogue. It is easy to be family-centered when the provider agrees with the family's decisions. Putting family-centered care into practice is much more difficult when the family's decision or underlying values differ from those of providers. It is important in these situations for the practitioner to provide the family with information about their professional opinion, support and respect the family's decision, and negotiate with the family strategies to evaluate the outcome of the plan. Take the following case as an example.

In the Green River Family Center preschool program a family wanted their child, who had a moderate hearing loss, to participate in an exclusively oral rather than a total communication program. The program staff provided the family with information about the advantages and disadvantages of both approaches. When the family opted for an oral approach, the staff supported the family's decision, despite their preference for an expanded total communication approach. In situations such as these, it is essential to set aside judgments and to respect and to support the family's decision. Together with the family, they developed a plan to evaluate the program's success. During the next six months, the team and parents provided each other with ongoing feedback on the child's progress. If at the time of the evaluation the child did not reach expected goals, problem-solving strategies would be initiated at a team meeting to examine possible alternative approaches.

Supporting Infusion of Family-Centered Practices Across Agencies

There likely are differences in family-centeredness among programs for children of different ages. There is evidence that infant–toddler programs are more successful in implementing family-centered principles than programs for either preschool children (Mahoney, O'Sullivan, & Dennebaum, 1990) or public school programs for grade-school children (Hamblin-Wilson & Thurman, 1990). Survey results from 539 parents of infants, toddlers, and preschool children who participated in early intervention programs describe a similar pattern (McWilliam et al., 1995). In this study, parents of children under 3 years rated their early intervention providers more satisfactorily in the area of responsiveness compared to parents of older children. The report on the implementation of the IDEA by the National Council on Disability (1995) found that parents often perceive school officials as failing to respect their opinions and failing to include parents in developing their child's goals or objectives. One parent who was interviewed stated, "I believe parents come to the IEP meeting as an unequal partner. Our signature means only that we were present at the meeting" (p. 57). This perceived lack of respect is often attributed to well-intentioned providers who lack training in how to engage and collaborate with parents. Instead they rely on strategies that are provider-driven.

Urgent attention needs to be given to this lack of continuity of family-centered practices across programs (situations in which the provider takes control and drives the process). Families that experience family-centered practices in one program come to expect these relationships with providers across agencies. This discontinuity of program philosophy can be addressed at two different levels: work with families through parent advocacy groups and work with providers through continuing education efforts that target systems change at the organizational level. (See chapter 9.)

The following scenario illustrates the conflict and stress one family experienced when encountering an educational system that was provider-driven. This illustration could typify any agency for younger or older children and is not intended to be representative of educational programs in general, which often provide exemplary services.

Maria, who is 5 years old, has multiple disabilities, including hearing and vision loss and developmental delays requiring educational and health care resources. She currently participates in an inclusive community-based preschool program. In the spring, the preschool transdisciplinary team, including her parents, began planning with the school for Maria's transition to her community grade school. Two key issues needed to be resolved during the transition: (a) how were Maria's medical cares to be addressed during the school day (as Maria had numerous respiratory problems, including a tracheostomy with supplemental oxygen) and (b) what opportunities would Maria have to interact with peers without disabilities? The school's standard practice was to group children with disabilities in separate classrooms, which resulted in limited interaction with children without disabilities. *(Provider-driven service approach.)* Prior to the final transition meeting, the family had many communications with the school administrator, discussing nursing support and visiting the district's proposed classroom option for Maria. Subsequent conversations between the school administrator and parents were fraught with miscommunications, resulting in mutual mistrust. *(Poor family–provider relationship.)* The parents felt that their concerns were discounted and devalued because the school had already decided on a service plan without their input. The school believed the parents were being unreasonable and controlling. The proposed classroom was unacceptable to the family, but they expressed to the preschool team a fear that they would be labeled as "difficult parents" if they raised concerns, thus jeopardizing the education they believed Maria would receive. *(Fear of judgmental providers.)*

The provider-driven philosophy was of equal concern to the preschool team, which worked diligently in Maria's current program to emulate family-centered services. Before the preschool team could strategize with the family, they needed to reflect on how they felt themselves when they were confronted with this school system's values, which were contrary to their beliefs. *(Need for reflective practices.)* A psychologist serving as a consultant helped the team members contemplate their reactions, which varied based on each person's history of positive and negative interactions with colleagues in varying community agencies and prior experience with conflict. One team member, who previously experienced successful conflict resolution, saw this conflict with the school district as an opportunity for learning and was hopeful that there would be positive outcomes. Others with less experience in working through conflict felt threatened by the situation. Many felt utter frustration with a system they believed was unresponsive to the family and felt anger at the stress the family faced as a result of what they regarded as the school personnel's rigid posture. *(Diverse reactions to conflict.)* The team members needed to address their feelings at a personal level, while at the same time they needed to support the family in identifying strategies that would result in a positive outcome for the child. Consultation played a key role for these team members by helping them integrate the factual information and emotional experiences and develop problem-solving skills that helped them work effectively through the conflict.

The family asked the preschool team to help them prepare for the transition meeting. *(Enhancing family competence.)* Preparation included supporting the family in identifying issues they would like addressed and informal role playing that helped them to use effective problem-solving skills. When the transition meeting occurred, it resulted in positive outcomes for Maria because of the preparation of the family and the establishment of a meeting atmosphere that promoted open communication among all team members. The preschool staff modeled family-centered practices throughout the meeting (e.g., asking the parents to describe their priorities and concerns, asking for their input on program goals for Maria), supporting the family as the primary decision maker of their child's plan.

This scenario illustrates that magically infusing the family-centered philosophy into another agency's practices is unlikely. However, practicing a family-centered approach may effect small changes. Providers must have the courage and commitment to work toward this goal of implementing family-centered practices, recognizing and celebrating small steps as accomplishments. This scenario further demonstrates that family-centered care is characterized not as an overnight revolution but rather as a gradual evolution.

Quality Interpersonal Interactions: A Key to Effective Provider–Family Partnerships

Developing effective communication skills and creating positive interpersonal relationships are the tools of the trade for early childhood providers (Stahlman, 1994). Each person has a unique and individualized communication style influenced by culture, education, environment, and personal temperament (Bryant & Graham, 1993). Developing effective communication strategies is essential to relationship building. The importance of these communication strategies cannot be overstated. Parents describe active listening, with appropriate nonverbal behavior described in the next section, as one of the most helpful strategies. Indeed a frequent complaint by parents is that service providers do not listen to them. Communication that is genuine, clear, jargon-free, respectful, and honest is the foundation of collaborative partnerships between families and providers (Bailey, 1991a). If interpersonal interactions are successful, Bailey (1991a) has suggested the following outcomes result: (a) interactions that are enjoyable for the parties rather than stressful, (b) interactions that build feelings of competence and worth by the parents through being valued and respected, (c) services that are based on family priorities, and (d) service providers with a greater sense of meaning and accomplishment in their work (Bailey, 1991a).

Basic microskills of attending and influencing skills are essential as psychologists and other service providers build relationships with families. Both nonverbal and verbal communication influences the content and process of the interactions. Providers can develop and enhance their communication skills by participating in seminars and workshops and by working with people with different communication styles (Bryant & Graham, 1993). Families learn new communication skills through formal training and from those persons surrounding them, including providers and other role models they encounter.

Nonverbal Communication

Nonverbal behavior plays a significant role in communication and relationships with others. Cormier and Cormier (1979) described three dimensions of nonverbal behavior: kinesics, paralinguistics, and proxemics. Use of any of these behaviors can enhance the family–provider relationship by sending messages of attending–listening to the family. *Kinesics* are body motion, gestures, facial expressions, eye movements, and posture. For example, leaning slightly forward rather than backward with arms crossed is usually more inviting. *Paralinguistics* include vocal cues such as voice quality (level and pitch), fluency in speech (stuttering, hesitations, speech errors), rate of speech, silence, and autonomic responses such as clammy hands and shallow breathing. Some providers may talk quickly and fill in periods of silence with extraneous conversation. Actually, silence can be used strategically and respectfully to enable families to share their own priorities and concerns. *Proxemics* consist of environmental and personal space such as seating arrangement, furniture array, and distance between counselor and family member. In many situations, having a desk between the family and provider may serve as a barrier to communication.

Verbal Communication

Empathic listening, which comprises active and reflective listening skills, allows service providers to learn about families as they develop trust and rapport (Dunst, Trivette, & Deal, 1988). Specific communication skills that enhance dialogue are (a) effective questioning and interviewing, (b) reflecting content or paraphrasing, and (c) reflecting feelings (Winton, 1988; Woody et al., 1992). Sensitive and effective questioning and interviewing are incorporated into a conversational dialogue to gain information from the family about their priorities and concerns. Both open-ended and close-ended questions, paired with nonverbal behavior that conveys interest and a listening stance (e.g., head nodding, eye contact, relatively close physical contact) are effective communication strategies in many cultures, but not all (Winton & Bailey, 1990). Again, it is important to recognize cultural and individual variation in communication strategies. Open-ended questions, which often begin with *what, how, why,* or *could,* promote elaborated responses from the individual. The use of minimal encouragers or restatements to support family members in providing more detail is often beneficial. These may take the form of short comments such as "uh-huh" or a direct repetition of what the family member has just said. In contrast closed-ended questions are used to help clarify, provide focus, or narrow the area of discussion by requiring briefer responses. Excessive use of closed questions can deter conversation and obstruct the development of a relationship, however (Woody et al., 1992).

Paraphrasing or reflecting content occurs when the service provider wants to verify understanding of the content of a family member's communication (Winton & Bailey, 1990). This strategy involves repeating an encapsulated version of the family members' main words or thoughts and clarifying and summarizing the trends of the discussion to present ideas concisely (Woody et al., 1992). Reflecting feelings refers to identifying and reflecting about how family members feel about a specific topic. Reflecting feelings requires skills in perceiving a person's inner feelings accurately and sensitively and in communicating understanding of those feelings in appropriate language, with congruence in nonverbal behavior (Winton & Bailey, 1990). The reflection frequently consists of labeling the emotion such as anger and identifying the context for the emotional experience (e.g., "You feel angry when you are left responsible for all the caregiving responsibilities for Jacob"). Reflection of meaning is an equally important communication skill (e.g., "When you hear Courtney (age 4) say, 'I hate you,' it means she is angry that you asked her to put her toys away, not that she hates you"). This strategy assists the family members in finding a new interpretation or meaning from old information or situations (Woody et al., 1992).

Creating Partnerships That Are Sensitive to Cultural Diversity

Although much attention has been focused on the family, it is only recently that emphasis has been placed on the notion of cultural diversity in early intervention programs (Beckman & Bristol, 1991). Because of the critical impact of culture and families on a child's development, culturally competent intervention needs to be an outcome of early intervention (Bryant & Graham, 1993). The term *family* has permeated our discussion of early childhood. Yet what defines *family* differs from culture to culture. In some cultures, the extended family assumes a variety of forms. Family structures and relationships expected among family members may vary considerably across cultures. In many cultures, children may be cared for not only by their parents but also by siblings, grandparents, other relatives, neighbors, and entire families and communities. *Multicultural* refers not only to ethnically and racially diverse persons but also to nonmajority cultures such as the deaf community. Special consideration also should be devoted to young children and families historically underserved or unsocialized about traditional service delivery systems. They may experience particular difficulties when attempting to negotiate the service delivery system. For example, a family that has just moved into a new community from Mexico is faced with the challenge of navigating the service delivery system. Not only do they have the disadvantage of limited skills in English, but they also are unaccustomed to the large array of service providers that they need to contact to get the support they desire for their family. They have difficulty understanding the providers and interpreters are not available. As a result, the process can be intimidating to them and they soon can became discouraged and do not continue to pursue services. This situation results in what many refer to as "a family that fell through the cracks due to a user-unfriendly system."

Early intervention service providers must demonstrate cultural competence, interacting in a way that matches the behavioral expectations of the members of a specific culture (Hanson, Lynch, & Wayman, 1990). The authors suggest that ethnic competencies come from developing an understanding of the social organization of the community, the prevailing belief system, history of the group, and ways members access services. In addition to examining their own values, early childhood providers must also analyze the ethnographic information relevant to the families they serve (Stahlman, 1994). This ethnographic approach will result in a better understanding of the families participating in their programs and should emphasize the following aspects:

1. Describe the ethnic groups with which the family identifies.
2. Identify the social organization of the ethnic community.
3. Identify the prevailing belief system within the particular ethnic community.
4. Become informed about the history of a particular ethnic group.
5. Determine how members of the community gain access to and use social services.
6. Identify the attitudes of the ethnic community toward help seeking (Hanson et al., 1990, p. 127).

In addition, Anderson and Fenichel (1989) offered an excellent framework for supporting culturally diverse families of young children with developmental challenges. Cultural sensitivity presupposes awareness that cultural differences as well as similarities exist. For example, there is no generic entity of "the Southeast Asian family" or "the Native American family." Rather, each encompasses numerous cultures, with individual members sharing proclivities in some areas but not in others. Individuals and families lie along various points of their cultural continua, from traditional to fully bicultural. Ultimately, this heightened sensitivity will support the relationship-building process that is key for building family–provider partnerships.

Hanson et al. (1990) suggested that communication forms are influenced by culture. For example, high-context cultures frequently rely on situational cues, established hierarchies, and nonconfrontational communication strategies. In contrast, low-context cultures (characteristic of Anglo American culture) generally prefer directiveness, speed, and rely on what is said (Chan, 1990). As providers communicate with families, it is important to recognize the differences in the process of relationship building and the usefulness in understanding and planning learning environments. One's cultural perspective can influence all aspects of the service delivery system, including assessment techniques chosen and the goals that are established (Beckman & Bristol, 1991). Smith and Ryan (1987), in a qualitative study examining the efficacy of services for parents of Chinese American children with disabilities found that language barriers adversely affected every aspect of services, from access to use. For example, a home visitor working with a new family who was Vietnamese commented on how lovely certain pictures in the home were. This was a strategy she frequently used to join with the family. Later she found out that in the Vietnamese culture if someone comments that they like something, the owner feels obligated to give it to them. Later in this same situation, the home visitor was teaching the 18-month-old child how to use the gesture "come here." As she and the mother began to discuss its meaning, the home visitor discovered that Vietnamese only use this gesture to call an animal, never another person. These are just two examples that illustrate that it is incumbent on providers to take time to learn the communication customs of the family they work with and then reflect and evaluate their own verbal and nonverbal behavior to enhance the support they provide to families.

To alleviate rather than exacerbate family stress, early childhood providers need skills in understanding the given culture's manner of seeking and using assistance. Anderson and Fenichel (1989) advised providers to appreciate the challenge of describing early intervention because specialized teachers do not exist in most cultures. Members of the extended family may function as service coordinators or home visitors. Moreover, basic definitions of disabilities are cultural constructs influencing beliefs and practices. Pachter (1994) extended this formulation by examining the culturally constructed meaning of illness and culturally mediated health beliefs and behaviors. Different disabilities and illnesses may engender sundry concerns in assorted cultures. For instance, congenital hip dislocation may cause little concern in traditional Navajos, whereas epilepsy may be regarded with apprehension. Family members in some cultures tend to judge providers slowly and may take some time before voicing their priorities and concerns. Hence if service providers change relatively frequently, there may be no one in a position to build sufficient trust to establish effective partnerships with families. Rather than unintentionally compelling families to choose between traditional helping practices and early childhood services, providers must be competent in effecting an integration of the two approaches when a family so desires (Anderson & Fenichel, 1989).

Agencies have an obligation to promote cultural competence of its staff. Becoming culturally aware and responsive does not ensue from a single incident or workshop; rather, it is a lifelong journey. Providing culturally competent services entails adapting and responding to the cultural patterns of families rather than expecting families to adapt to agency practices. Programs on cultural and ethnic issues are strengthened when persons from the communities served by the agency are involved. When educational staff and health care providers learn about such issues directly from families, their learning is enhanced. Families can speak for themselves and do not need early childhood experts to offer the sole interpretation of the family. For instance, parents may communicate their discomfort when inundated by questions from providers. Family members also can communicate their own cultural pattern of making decisions. For example, school or hospital staff who expect immediate decisions may not be respecting the family's need first to talk with extended family members (Johnson, Jeppson, & Redburn, 1992). Examining the cultural background of providers and families helps to provide the framework through which their actions are filtered (Lynch & Hanson, 1992). Provider respect for diversity among families implies recognizing and providing for the need of family members to participate in different ways in their child's programs (Stahlman, 1994). Not all families will have the same experiences with programs. Use the checklist in Table 4.3 to determine how sensitive you and your program are to diversity issues.

Providers often fail to recognize their own ignorance or prejudices, which may result in inappropriate judgmental interactions with families. Divesting provider relationships with families of personal opinions and values can be a difficult task (Bryant & Graham, 1993). Self-insight

Table 4.3.   A Checklist for Honoring Family Diversity and Values

---

Do we
- Learn who is included in the family and who needs or wants to be involved?
- Learn what support the family wants?
- Find out each family's customs or preferences regarding language, food, religion, holidays, health practices, and kinship?
- Honor family values, customs, and preferences?
- Support families in identifying and using their preferred support networks?
- Enable families to use their preferred spiritual resources?
- Recruit staff who share the languages and ethnicity of communities served by the hospital?
- Make translators available, in addition to providing information in the family's own language?

Source: Reproduced with permission of the Association for the Care of Children's Health, 7910 Woodmont Ave., Suite 300, Bethesda, MD 20814, from *Caring for children and families: Guidelines for hospitals* (1992) (p. 196) by B. H. Johnson, E. S. Jeppson, & L. Redburn.

and reflection by providers become increasingly important as providers gain sensitivity regarding their feelings and responses about both their own culture and that of others. Reflective process is crucial given the relationship-based, systems-oriented nature of early childhood supports; the complexity of the early childhood context; and the necessity for organizational support for change and growth in early childhood practice. Reflective process significantly enhances the likelihood of individual and organizational change to become more responsive to families (see chapter 9). This reflective process can be facilitated both through formal training experiences for providers and during provider clinical supervision sessions. Identifying the providers' own beliefs allows them to be sensitive and to cope with the nuances of another culture. With interaction with other cultures, understanding of one's own culture is refined and appreciation of others is enhanced (Nugent, 1994). Given their appreciation for cultural diversity, psychologists and other providers can advance nonjudgmental postures for families of diverse cultures, values, and lifestyles (Epps, 1995).

The following scenario illustrates potential problems when providers do not consider the influence of culture on family values.

Dr. Lawrence was asked to present a workshop on discipline. This workshop was part of a family education series for a community neighborhood resource center. She talked briefly to the program director to determine the content of the workshop. She used a previously designed workshop for early childhood staff that reviewed the overall principles of time-in and time-out and key "do's and don'ts" of behavior management. Dr. Lawrence was quite surprised that her typically well-received workshop was met with disdain. The family participants were particularly angered with her firm discounting of spanking as an effective discipline strategy. This suggested the need to adopt an approach that would not alienate the audience, but still disseminate the principles of discipline. *(Need to individualize content, being sensitive to cultural beliefs of the audience.)*

Dr. Lawrence decided to talk with her colleagues to identify what she could have done differently. *(Reflection to increase provider sensitivity.)* As they began to problem solve together, it became clear that Dr. Lawrence was viewed as an expert who did not understand the community. Her colleagues recommended that she needed to adopt an interactive inservice approach rather than a didactic approach that "proclaimed what was right." *(Interactive strategies enable the presenter to have a better understanding of the values of the group.)* Dr. Lawrence decided that she should have allowed time to listen to their issues regarding discipline and identify the strategies with which they felt most comfortable. A series of open-ended questions would easily serve this purpose:

"I understand tonight's topic is how to handle your child's difficult behavior."

"What are some questions you would like to have addressed during this session?"

"What are the three biggest challenges you have regarding your child's behavior?"

"What kinds of discipline is ok with you?" or "What kinds are not ok?"

This type of dialogue may open up a willingness to examine alternative ways of disciplining children that were not threatening to the value system of the audience members. By prefacing the workshop with the assumption that there are multiple ways to do things and that families and practitioners are working toward a common goal is a major step to joint problem solving.

Conclusion

The outcome of strengthening community networks through community–family partnerships will be accessible and welcoming neighborhoods that support families in raising their children by providing a diverse array of services. The challenge for early childhood providers is how to create an integrated service delivery system to address the needs of a highly heterogenous population of young children and their families. Such integration of services requires thinking differently about community services and includes planning with significant input from families so that *systems* of care are emphasized rather than individual programs. An integrated service delivery system can best be described as a comprehensive and accessible network of services that addresses the priority concerns of the family in such a way that the family perceives the services as an organized whole. This service system that is built on collaborative partnerships reflects joint planning, shared procedures, and commitment to build a continuum of complementary services.

The variables that influence collaboration between providers and families are extensive and complex. Positive relationships are enhanced when providers reflect an understanding of and sensitivity to the unique concerns of each family. Parents respond to this sensitive treatment and are likely to be eager to assist staff in meeting the needs of their child when strong collaborative relationships are established, resulting in greater satisfaction and better services for children and families. Service providers can encourage examination of their institution's approach toward family-centered care and the extent to which the family is integral in all aspects of services. Psychologists and other service providers can play a significant role in assisting team members in enhancing their skills in working together with families to shift services to support these dimensions of family-centered care.

Part II

Building Blocks of Early Intervention

5

Creating a System That Works: Components of a Collaborative Program Design

A family's agenda—its priorities for how early intervention will be involved in family life—shapes the entire family-centered planning process for early intervention (Kaufmann, McGonigel, & Hurth, 1991, p. 17).

Implementing meaningful services for young children with disabilities and their families is an ongoing challenge for providers. Uncovering the strategies to successful planning for such services is a key to a system that works to support children and their families. Issues regarding appropriate assessment processes and curriculum approaches are factors to consider as practioners begin to develop, implement, and refine their programs. Expanding services from child-related to holistic family-support programs and from self-contained classrooms to inclusive programs are ongoing challenges faced by early intervention programs as they strive to provide quality services for children and families. This chapter discusses these elements and provides a step-by-step guide to the planning process, highlighting not only the individual aspects of early intervention but also its complexity and interwoven nature.

A Foundation in Theory

It is critical that assessment and intervention practices are theory driven to address the complex needs of the child with disabilities. The key question becomes, "Which theoretical approach or approaches should be adopted?" Our position is that in working with young children and their caregivers, developmental, ecological, and behavioral paradigms offer substantive utility, particularly in combination. Each of these paradigms is discussed extensively in the literature, so for the purpose of this chapter, only key aspects of each perspective is reviewed.

The developmental approach has gained widespread recognition as a viable theoretical perspective, with strong support from the National Association of the Education of Young Children (NAEYC) and National Association of Early Childhood Specialists in State Departments of Education (NAECSSDE; 1991). This framework conceptualizes development as an ongoing process that becomes reorganized at each stage of development. Developmental theory suggests that children are born intrinsically motivated to explore and interact in the environment. Young children develop as a result of physical maturation and through exploration and interactions with their environment. Typically, addressing the child's interests and providing materials and activities that match the child's developmental level is paramount to a developmental approach. Intervention is designed to meet the developmental needs of young children and takes into account the integration of curricular activities across developmental domains (i.e., cognitive, behavioral, social–emotional, communication, motor, and self-help).

The behavioral perspective focuses on learning as central to children's growth and development, which is based on the belief that children develop as a result of experiences with their environment. Typically this philosophy embraces the principles of behavior modification. Skills are sequenced and target behaviors are specified and taught using strategies including modeling, prompting, fading, and reinforcement approaches (Stayton & Karnes, 1994).

Ecological theory was addressed in chapter 1. Comprehensive clinical approaches to early intervention need to integrate the multiple domains of development (e.g., cognitive, social–emotional, behavioral, physical, and communication) while concurrently considering the child within the context of interactive family and social patterns (Greenspan, 1990). This ecological approach has broadened both the developmental and behavioral approaches to include a naturalistic perspective that considers the child, parent, family, and family–child behaviors with the goal of increasing the child's interaction in natural social and physical environments (Noonan & McCormick, 1993). This broad-based strategy involves incorporating goals to support the family, individualizing the curriculum so that it is responsive to the priorities for the child, and assimilating intervention strategies within the natural routines of the child's and family's daily activities.

Because each of these theoretical perspectives contributes to understanding children, it is important that providers use a blended theoretical framework. Such a perspective is consistent with a general theory orientation (Ivey et al., 1987) for early intervention in which components of multiple theories are organized into a coherent and systematic framework to enhance the number of responses providers have in their therapeutic repertoire. Rather than arbitrarily drawing from a particular theory, the general theorist strategically draws from multiple theories based on the particular circumstance. For example, a combined behavioral and developmental approach supports children in learning new adaptive and prosocial behaviors; extending variations in appropriate behavior; and reducing potentially dangerous or challenging behaviors of an externalizing (e.g., hitting) or internalizing (e.g., nervousness) nature that interfere with family routines. Greenberg and Speltz (1988) proposed the integration of behavioral and attachment constructs to address difficulties in the pre-school years. For example, chronic uncertainty of the toddler regarding the responsiveness of his or her caregiver may relate to feelings of anger and frustration and become manifested as a tantrum or aggressiveness toward the caregiver. The case study at the end of the chapter illustrates such a blended approach.

A Team Approach

A team approach is critical because of the complexity of the challenges for young children and their families. The terms multidisciplinary, interdisciplinary, and transdisciplinary are used to describe interactions among team members in assessment and intervention practices. Although early intervention providers appreciate the need for holistic approaches to intervention, most typical intervention reverts to targeting individual developmental components (e.g., intervention session focuses on motor development exclusively) through a multidisciplinary service delivery approach. A *multidisciplinary team* comprises members from multiple disciplines, but each remains relatively independent and is affected little by the actions of other team members. For example, the psychologist and physical therapist would both assess the child and make recommendations independent of each other. Given the importance of collaboration, this model is often counterproductive. Because there is no formal structure for communication in this team model, the potential exists for duplication of effort or contradictions in intervention approaches (Gallagher, Garland, & Kniest, 1995). Practitioners proposed alternative approaches, interdisciplinary or transdisciplinary team processes, to ameliorate these problems.

An *interdisciplinary team* involves greater interaction among team members, with each member relying on the others for important information and suggestions. Typically, interdisciplinary teams conduct separate assessments, but the final product is an integrated plan of services that involves significant cooperation among disciplines. Within this model, there is a call for a particular discipline to perform certain activities. In an interdisciplinary developmental group, all team members are likely to be involved, each performing unique roles (e.g., physical therapist facilitates gross-motor activities, speech–language pathologist focuses on oral–motor stimulation and speech and language development). The major difference between a multidisciplinary and interdisciplinary team is the increased communication and coordination among team members.

A *transdisciplinary team* is one in which multiple disciplines work together in the initial assessment (or in periodic reassessments), but one point of contact typically provides the services. Providers from each of the disciplines relinquish their roles to the direct service provider. The other disciplines consult with the direct provider and support the provider in delivering the intervention. The point is that each provider facilitates child development in all domains rather than exclusively in her or his central domain. All providers support synchronous parent–child interaction and everyone genuinely listens to families (not solely social workers and psychologists). Proponents of the transdisciplinary approach suggest that it reduces the intrusiveness of having many providers working with the family, while maintaining comprehensive services through both direct services and consultation. Adopting this approach also raises issues of staff development and support so that all providers are skilled and feel comfortable providing a variety of activities. Overall, there is no empirical support for using a transdisciplinary approach over an interdisciplinary approach.

Following is a scenario of a transdisciplinary home-based intervention:

Jasper, a home-based teacher, has been working with Anthony, a 2-year-old and his family during the past year. *(One provider is designated as the primary interventionist.)* Anthony has multiple developmental issues because of his medical diagnosis of cerebral palsy. When Jasper arrived, Anthony was seated in his adaptive chair. The first part of the session involved play with a wind-up musical toy. The purpose of this activity was to see if Anthony would systematically signal for more music by vocalizing and reaching for the toy when the music stopped. This activity addressed both the cognitive skill of cause and effect but also expressive communication. Following this activity Ms. Jacobs, Anthony's mother, requested that Jasper support her with strategies to help Anthony roll over. As they both worked with Anthony in this activity, Jasper observed that Anthony's leg and ankle appeared tighter and resisted manual attempts to flex it at the joints. Ms. Jacobs had a similar concern. Jasper recommended having the physical therapist join them at the next home visit to reevaluate Anthony's muscle tone and provide them with additional strategies to promote flexion. *(Transdisciplinary approach provides consultative support.)* At the conclusion of the visit, Ms. Jacobs asked Jasper to discuss community child care options for Anthony at their next visit, because she was interested in returning to work.

This scenario illustrates the teacher's ability to incorporate multiple child and family goals within the intervention session. When the mother's concerns about the child's motor skills arose, the teacher understood the need to gather information to share with the therapist and the need to arrange to have the appropriate team member back for a reevaluation and consultation.

Planning Processes

Planning and documenting a child's education is an important process for successful intervention and provides important safeguards for the family. For early childhood providers there are two planning processes, the Individualized Family Service Plan (IFSP) for young children birth to 3 years and the Individualized Education Program (IEP) for children 3 through 5 years. Although there are similarities in these planning processes, there are some unique differences.

The Individualized Education Program

The IEP was a key educational provision of the Education for All Handicapped Children Act (EHA; Public Law 94-142; discussed in chapter 1). The primary participants of the IEP planning process are the school personnel and the child's parents–guardian. The law mandated a written document that included the following:

1. Statement of the present levels of the child's educational performance;
2. Goals, including short-term instructional objectives;
3. A statement of the specific education and related services to be provided and the extent to which the child participates in a general education program;
4. The projected date for the initiation and anticipated duration of the services with appropriate objective criteria and evaluation procedures; and
5. Transition services.

The EHA represented the first attempt to promote parent–provider relationships (Turnbull, Strickland, & Goldstein, 1984). Although the law promoted active parent participation in the IEP process, actual implementation fell short of the original expectations, with families reporting that they believed that they were not frequently viewed as meaningful contributors to the process (Turnbull & Turnbull, 1990). Parent involvement was solicited in the context of a service delivery system that was child focused and professionally driven. As a result, "Highly individualized programs for children were reflected in the children's Individualized Education Programs (IEPs), but there tended to be only a single package for involving parents" (Bristol & Gallagher, 1982, p. 149). Although Part B of the EHA amendments (Public Law 99-457) does not mandate a family-driven provision explicitly, this legislation and the IDEA of 1991 promoted a family-driven IEP process.

The Individualized Family Service Plan

The cornerstone of Part H (now Part C) of the IDEA is the IFSP (McGonigel et al., 1991). The IFSP serves as a blueprint for families and includes the development or enhancement of family support systems and the mobilization of community resources to address family priorities and concerns (Deal, Dunst, & Trivette, 1989). This model represents a departure from the earlier parental-involvement intervention models in that the family plays an integral role in the IFSP process and the parent is viewed as the primary decision maker. The IFSP process marks a shift in the service provider's role from strictly providing direct services to the child to the addition of a consultant role to the family. In this new role, the provider supplies information and makes recommendations but does not determine the final decision (Leviton, Mueller, & Kaufman, 1991). Bailey (1991a) suggested that the consultant model "offers a balance between the discipline's expertise and the family's decision-making authority and responsibility for the child and itself" (p. 33). It is important for the provider to support the family, enabling members to make informed decisions. The approach to developing and implementing IFSPs described in this chapter operates on the assumption that an effective early intervention service delivery system must be dynamic, with continuous identification of the child and family priorities and the services provided. This assumption suggests a fluid rather than a static system of services. A key to the success of such a service delivery system is a responsive and proactive approach that strengthens families and their natural support networks by enabling families to enhance their competencies (Hobbs et al., 1984). Therefore, both the process and the format of the IFSP need to be flexible and functional to build on the family's social network and maximize the mobilization of resources to address the family's concerns (Deal et al., 1989). This process is illustrated in the case at the conclusion of this chapter.

The notion of individualized family-centered intervention has received widespread attention (Bailey, 1987; McGonigel et al., 1991; Winton, 1990) and is influencing the design of early intervention services and the IFSP process. In 1989 this shared philosophy of family-centered intervention was articulated by the IFSP Expert Team and Task Force appointed by the National Early Childhood Training Assistance System (NEC*TAS) and the Office of Special Education Programs, U.S. Department of Education, as they developed the principles underlying the IFSP process (McGonigel et al., 1991). These principles, described in Table 5.1, form the framework of the required IFSP components. The key activities of this IFSP process described in this chapter and outlined in Figure 5.1 are the following: (a) identifying family priorities, concerns, and resources; (b) assessing the child; (c) developing child and family outcomes; and (d) implementing and monitoring the progress toward accomplishments of IFSP goals.

As these descriptions of the IEP and IFSP processes unfold, several differences become apparent. The primary difference between the IEP and IFSP process are the beneficiary of the intervention and the team-member constellation. The IFSP identifies both the child and family as targets for intervention, with planning accomplished through an interagency team, service coordinator, and family members. In contrast, the IEP process, which primarily benefits the child, limits the planning team to members of the education system (e.g., teachers, therapists, and school administrator) and parents. Whereas both processes require a statement of the child's present level of development, the IFSP also includes a system for families to identify their own resources, priorities, and concerns. Developing an educational plan also differs in emphasis. The IEP describes the level of resources, goals, and short-term child instructional objectives, whereas the IFSP identifies family and child outcomes and states the early intervention services needed to achieve the identified outcomes. The IFSP process highlights the importance of service coordination to support the families

Table 5.1.   Principles Underlying the IFSP Process

- Infants and toddlers are uniquely dependent on their families for their survival and nurturance. This dependence necessitates a family-centered approach to early intervention.
- States and programs should define *family* in a way that reflects the diversity of family patterns and structures.
- Each family has its own structure, roles, values, beliefs, and coping styles. Respect for and acceptance of this diversity is a cornerstone of family-centered early intervention.
- Early intervention systems and strategies must honor the racial, ethnic, cultural and socioeconomic diversity of families.
- Respect for family autonomy, independence, and decision making means that families must be able to choose the level and nature of early intervention's involvement in their lives.
- Family–professional collaboration and partnerships are the keys to family-centered early intervention and to successful implementation of the IFSP process.
- An enabling approach to working with families requires that professionals re-examine their traditional roles and practices and develop new practices when necessary—practices that promote mutual respect and partnerships.
- Early intervention services should be flexible, accessible, and responsive to family-identified needs.
- Early intervention services should be provided according to the normalization principle—that is, families should have access to services provided in as normal a fashion and environment as possible and that promote the integration of the child and family within the community.
- No one agency or discipline can meet the diverse and complex needs of infants and toddlers with special needs and their families. Therefore, a team approach to planning and implementing the IFSP is necessary.

Source: Reprinted by permission of the Association for the Care of Children's Health from the *Guidelines and recommended practices for the individual family service plan* (2nd ed.) by M. McGonigel. Copyright © 1991.

in accessing and coordinating services. There is no provision for coordination in the IEP process. Transition is a key component of both.

In summary, the IFSP includes the following:

1. Establishing a state Interagency Coordinating Council to create a structure for agency collaboration in meeting the needs of children with disabilities;
2. Expanding the eligibility determination to include children who are at risk for future developmental challenges;
3. Assigning a service coordinator to support families in coordinating services;
4. Developing an IFSP that identifies both child and family outcomes; and
5. Emphasizing transition planning to preschool or other community services.

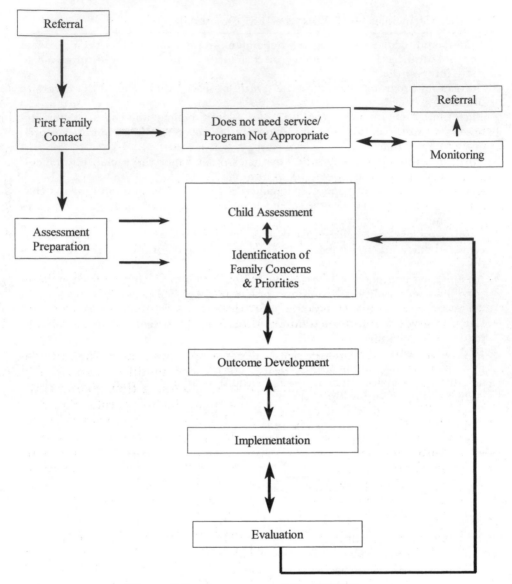

Figure 5.1.   A sequence of the IFSP Process.

Overall, the IFSP provides a holistic approach to early intervention services and embraces a family-centered approach. Many practioners implementing the IEP process are beginning to adopt many of the family-centered components central to the IFSP. Support for a family-centered IEP process is seen at the federal level in that the authorization of the IDEA of 1991 allowed for the use of the IFSP process through age 5 (with state, school district, and family agreement) as long as the IEP requirements are met (Rosenkoetter, Hains, & Fowler, 1994). Children and families benefit from the continuity of services that occurs if there is a commitment of all early childhood services to include IFSP processes across ages birth through 5.

Step 1: Identifying Family Concerns, Priorities, and Resources

Ecological theory provides the basis for assessment strategies for examining the relationships among child, family, and social context variables. Part C of the IDEA expands previous child-based data collection by requiring an assessment of family concerns, priorities, and resources to assist in program planning. When first conceptualized, the legislation referred to meeting family needs. This language was replaced by "family concerns, priorities, and resources" to avoid approaching families from a deficit model (hence we do not consider them "needy families"). Family concerns are defined as issues or problems that influence the family's capacity to support their child directly (e.g., transportation, child care) as well as indirectly (e.g., employment, GED classes for the parent; Kaufmann, Hurth, & McGonigel, 1991). This approach is based on the premise that identifying family concerns, priorities, and resources enhances the development of the infant or toddler (Mahoney, O'Sullivan, & Dennebaum, 1990; Sheehan, 1989).

The IDEA and its amendments reflect a philosophical change in the family's role in the assessment process. Although families have always been considered an important data source in assessing their young children, federal legislation suggests a much more inclusive role. Squires, Nickel, and Bricker (1990) found that although parents were reliable sources of information, they were often untapped resources. At the core of a family-centered process is the recognition that families can identify their own concerns, priorities, and resources (Kaufmann et al., 1991). Currently there is no consensus within early intervention programming for best practice procedures with regard to using parents as resources (Kraus & Jacobs, 1993). As part of a qualitative study using focus group interviews, parents reported that their concerns need to be shared at their pace and level of understanding (Slentz & Bricker, 1992). The implication of this finding is that the family assessment process needs to be completed over time to allow for the provider to develop a relationship with the family. The authors caution that the process of the family assessment can carry a hidden message to families—namely that because their child has a disability their family has "problems." Slentz, Walker, and Bricker (1989) reported that families who participated in early intervention indicated that family assessment was one of the most threatening and uncomfortable facets of the IFSP process.

A variety of formal and informal methods and measures are currently used to elicit family concerns, priorities, and resources. Initially, a large number of these family assessment instruments were developed or adapted from family therapy and clinical research tools for use in early intervention programs not for administration by early interventionists without clinical training. Slentz and Bricker (1992) expressed concern about using many of these tools because they are incongruent with the tenets of early intervention and inappropriate or even detrimental to the goals of the IFSP. Families recommended that other types of family assessment (e.g., Parental Stress Index; Abidin, 1986) should be excluded from the process (Summers et al., 1991). Measures of family stress, coping strategies, and family environment, integral to family assessment in clinical approaches, were not intended for use in developing the IFSP. Slentz and Bricker contended that if the family does not identify any of these areas as a priority or concern, collecting such data can be confusing or disturbing. As a result, the term "family assessment" is avoided in the IFSP process to help differentiate the process of identifying family priorities, concerns, and resources from traditional clinical family assessment. Should families identify concerns related to clinical issues (e.g., stress or resource management difficulties), the IFSP would include referrals to resources where in-depth family assessments and intervention can be provided by trained family specialists (e.g., psychologists or family therapists).

Most commonly used formats of evaluating families' concerns include interviews and written surveys. In selecting appropriate measures and methods, family-centered criteria should be considered, including the degree to which it is respectful of families, nonintrusive, nonjudgmental, and jargon-free. As programs begin to select assessment tools, the checklist for evaluating family-centeredness of assessments in Table 5.2, developed by Duwa et al. (1993), may serve as a helpful guide. Summers and her colleagues (1991) found that families preferred tools that measured self-assessed family priorities and concerns (e.g., Survey of Family Needs, Bailey, 1988). In addition, parents reported that the assessment was most

Table 5.2. Checklist for Evaluating the Family-Centeredness of Assessments

1. Will the completion of the assessment result in a family-generated identification of concerns, priorities, and resources, not a label or diagnosis of family functioning?
2. Does the family have a choice about participating in the assessment?
3. Is the assessment tool free of acronyms and program jargon?
4. Is the answer to every question going to play a role in planning and serving the family according to its own identified needs?
5. Are the answers based on the family's perception of itself and its needs?
6. Can the family answer the questions in privacy if they wish?
7. Will/could the process involve the entire family unit?
8. Do family members have the opportunity to discuss the questions with the interviewer or each other?
9. Is the tool culturally sensitive and available in another language, if necessary?
10. Can the resulting information be used by other agencies and programs with family permission?
11. Were families involved in the creation and development of the tool to be used?

Source: Reprinted by permission of The Guilford Press from Creating family-centered programs and policies in *Implementing early intervention: From research to effective practice* by S. M. Duwa, C. Wells, & P. Lalinde. Copyright © 1993.

meaningful when information was gathered in a conversational style characterized by nonintrusive questions (Summers et al., 1991). This technique was preferred to structured interviews or written surveys. Other evidence indicates that written surveys can be helpful and user friendly (Bailey & Simeonsson, 1988; Sexton, Snyder, Rheams, Garron-Sharp, & Perez, 1991). Sexton et al. (1991) found that 51% of the families interviewed preferred written surveys and 49% preferred personal interviews. These data suggest that a multimethod approach may be beneficial, where families identify their preferred method of assessment. Compare the following two interview formats:

Beth, the early intervention service coordinator, was making her second visit with the Finora/Sanchez family. On arriving she notified the family that she needed to do a family assessment. *(Family should have prior notice regarding purpose of visit.)* During her previous home visit, Beth observed much arguing between the parents on appropriate child rearing. She also noticed conflict among the siblings. Shortly after she arrived, she began her interview. Some of the questions she asked included, "Do you see the marital conflict you are describing affecting your relationship with your child?" or "Describe typical tensions that arise among your children." *(Such clinical questions, particularly of this stilted nature, are not appropriate in the IFSP process.)* Mr. Finora and his wife, Ms. Sanchez, were quite reserved in their responses and provided only minimal information. Once Beth had left, they were baffled with the line of questioning and did not see how this information would help their child. They were beginning to have misgivings that they had agreed to this new program.

Although the line of inquiry used by the service coordinator may be appropriate for other purposes, this type of questioning was not the intent of the family assessment process outlined in the IDEA. Instead of assessing family dynamics, the focus of the interview needed to help identify the priorities—concerns of the family. A family dialogue would more likely resemble the following:

At Beth's last visit with the Finora–Sanchez family, she discussed with them the need to identify any concerns they would like addressed and what they saw as priorities, both for their child and family. Once she had an opportunity to greet the family she began to ask some questions, including, "Are there areas that you think Lucas needs help?" Throughout this discussion, the family felt comfortable with Beth and her genuine listening. They then began to express concerns they had with the constant conflicts between Lucas and his brothers. Beth asked if they would like support in helping the boys to get along. The family indicated addressing this conflict would be a priority for them. Beth proposed that this priority could be addressed in the upcoming IFSP meeting, where suggested resources could be identified. After Beth left, the parents expressed how eager they were to join the team at the IFSP meeting to develop a family plan that they hoped would help address their concerns.

A key goal of the initial family assessment process is to acquaint the provider with the child and family and to gather information from the family that identifies mechanisms for best supporting them. The outcome of a successful family–guided assessment process is attaining adequate information to effectively plan services. Most important is recognizing the dynamic nature of the process. Family circumstances, concerns, priorities, and resources change over time. Therefore, it is crucial that early intervention programs develop a responsive system that offers opportunities for families to share information and to identify outcomes on an ongoing basis. The challenge to the field is to continue to design studies that provide useful data to guide and refine practice.

Step 2: Assessing the Child

The purpose of child assessment in early intervention is to determine eligibility for services, to identify the child's unique needs, and to describe the child's current status in a variety of developmental areas to decide the nature and extent of needed services (Kaufmann et al., 1991). During the planning process, the family can express any concerns about their child and assist in determining the place and time of the assessment, in addition to whom should attend (Turnbull, 1991). The goal of this type of interview process is parent input; however, the degree to which a family identifies and articulates its agenda varies (McGonigel et al., 1991). The manner information is obtained from family members regarding their child determines the success or failure of family participation. Kjerland (1986) found that interviews with families using the questions depicted in Table 5.3 elicited information potentially useful to team members. Throughout the assessment process, the family can adopt the role they find most comfortable. Table 5.4 summarizes different ways that family members can contribute to the assessment process.

This discussion on child assessment is applicable to either the IFSP or IEP process. The intention of the assessment process is to gather, share, and exchange information among team and family members that enables families to make informed choices about services and the intervention plan (Kaufmann et al., 1991). To accomplish the assessment process as outlined in the IDEA and its amendments it is important to develop a procedure that determines the child's level of developmental abilities across domains. This procedure allows for the provider, with the support of the family, to identify strengths that enhance the child's development and those weaknesses that may limit the child's learning and performance (McCune, Kalmanson, Fleck, Blazewski, & Sillari, 1993). Successful assessment is based on the assumptions that development (i.e., motor, social, communication,

Table 5.3.   The Family's Assessment Focus

- I would describe my child in this way: _____
- A typical day with my child includes _____
- What my child is really good at or likes to do is _____
- What my child needs help with or avoids is _____
- My child is really interested in _____

Source: Reprinted by permission of Project Dakota from *Early Intervention Tailor Made* by L. Kjerland. Copyright © 1986.

Table 5.4. Options for Family Participation in Assessment

To assist in the assessment of their child, family members may

- Determine to what extent and how they would like to prepare for the assessment.
- Make choices regarding assessment procedures.
- Provide familiar toys or activities for assessment.
- Observe their child's behaviors in a variety of situations and with a variety of people in preparation for sharing information about their child with the team.
- Share information with the rest of the team related to their child's behaviors and reactions to people and things that may affect the assessment.
- Identify child strengths or abilities as well as their family's concerns related to child development.
- Identify the outcomes they desire for their child and themselves related to the development of their child.
- Answer questions about their child and family in the assessment setting.
- Ask questions about the assessment process.
- Observe their child's behaviors and level of skill during assessment.
- Demonstrate for the team typical interactions with their child.
- Use specific intervention strategies they have learned from other team members to elicit child behaviors the team would like to see.
- Identify discrepancies between their child's performance in assessment and in their daily environment.
- Provide the team with feedback about the assessment process.

Source: Reprinted by permission of Child Development Resources from *Caring for infants and toddlers with disabilities: A manual for physicians* by F. G. Gallagher, C. W. Garland, & B. A. Kniest. © 1995.

cognitive, behavioral, and affective) is interrelated and that each area should not be assessed in isolation (Trout & Foley, 1992). For example, the child's ability to acquire sitting balance allows the child freedom to manipulate materials and to discover more complex actions with toys. Based on this assumption, there needs to be a shift from traditional intellectual assessment to practices that target a number of interrelated systems in young children (McGonigel et al., 1991). Such a technique requires expanding the traditional measures that typically quantify a child's abilities (e.g., norm-referenced, ordinal, and curriculum-based assessments) to those that tap the equally important qualitative aspects of development, including such areas as social competence and attentional skills (Hauser-Cram & Shonkoff, 1988), representational development (Cicchetti & Wagner, 1993), and self-regulation. These approaches are of particular utility for populations of young children with sensory, physical, or severe disabilities for whom traditional measures are not valid. Recognizing the societal and social influences on the child's development has broadened assessment practice from the narrow perspective of child behaviors to interactions between the child and significant others or events in the environment (Katz, 1989). (Chapter 6 provides a detailed discussion of conceptualizations of parent–child interaction and its implications for development.)

The assessment component ought to emphasize functional skills within a developmental context rather than test scores; describe child strengths; and report any functional challenges the child faces that would likely affect intervention (Bailey, 1988). Assessing functional abilities in this population of young children increases content validity, because it samples behaviors that are fundamental to their daily routines (Haley, Hallenborg, & Gans, 1989). For example, functional assessment evaluates achievement of independent locomotion, no matter what the mode (e.g., with assistance of a walker or partial participation) because walking may never be a realistic goal for a child with a severe physical challenge. Assessment needs to be an ongoing process, because it only provides a momentary picture of the child's repertoire of skills. Part C regulations also require that assessment be in the native language of the child and include multiple measures that are not racially or culturally discriminatory. Each program must reexamine the types of assessment tools used and the appropriateness of the assessment process as a whole in light of the cultural background of the children and families in the program (Nugent, 1994).

Neisworth and Bagnato (1988) have suggested that a multidimensional assessment process should include multidomain assessment as well as data from multiple sources and contexts. Multicontextual assessments incorporating input from a variety of settings (e.g., home, school, and child care) and diverse sources (e.g., parents, teachers, child care staff) can further clarify areas of difficulty and result in well-informed decisions (Cicchetti & Toth, 1987). The overall challenge to this broad-based, multidomain approach is integrating socially valid, diverse assessment outcomes into a comprehensive assessment process (McCune et al., 1993). A play arena assessment is one possible model that meets these criteria (Linder, 1990). Implementing this assessment format is illustrated in the following:

Josie is a 4-year-old who was referred for intervention because of suspected developmental difficulties. She was brought to the preschool center for assessment by her mother. The assessment starts in a playroom that has a pretend-play and block area. The psychologist begins by introducing Josie and Mrs. James to the play area. The speech pathologist and teacher are observing behind a one-way mirror. Josie's play is observed initially during free play. Gradually the psychologist introduces new materials to probe Josie's understanding of additional early preschool concepts. Josie continues to check back with her mother and bring her toys, requesting that her mother join her in play. Mrs. James accepts Josie's offer. This parent–child interaction provides the psychologist an opportunity to observe their dyadic interaction (e.g., how Mrs. James responds to Josie's requests and the strategies she uses to sustain an interaction with Josie). In addition, Josie's interactions with familiar versus unfamiliar adults are noted. After about 45 minutes, two children from the preschool join Josie. The psychologist observes Josie's interactions with other children. First the children begin to join in pretend activities using a picnic set. Later in the session, the psychologist leads the children in a music activity, which is a typical routine in the preschool. They then move into the gym. Josie and the psychologist play in a motor maze and join in a game of ball. They then return to the play room for a snack.

This play assessment presents many advantages for both the child, family, and intervention team. According to Linder (1990),

1. Assessment is completed in an environment that is inviting with many familiar materials.
2. The child only needs to develop a relationship with one unfamiliar clinician.
3. Families are part of the assessment process.
4. There is flexibility in materials used, settings, alterations of sequence, and content based on the child.
5. The method gives the family and team an opportunity to view the child at the same time, allowing everyone the same frame of reference for discussion.
6. The method provides useful information for planning intervention.

Play assessment offers one approach to gathering child development information using an ecological approach. Procedures such as these are recommended to optimize the validity of the information obtained during the assessment.

Step 3: Collaborative Goal Setting

The goal of the IFSP process is to develop a service and outcome plan, based on data from both the child and family assessment. The challenge to early intervention providers is to engage in collaborative goal setting (Able-Boone, 1993; Bailey, 1987). Bailey and Bricker (1986) recommended that in developing IFSP outcomes, optimal success occurs when there is a good match between the unique characteristics of the child and family with the demands, expectations, and outcomes as designed in the IFSP. One of the most important characteristics for providers to consider is the cultural background of the family. Nugent (1994) suggested that findings of cross-cultural research point to the importance of providers, administrators, and policy makers questioning the appropriateness of each program outcome used in light of the cultural background of the child. Further discussion of the influence of culture on intervention can be found in chapter 4.

Beckman and Bristol (1991) provided a useful framework for describing both the child and family outcomes that make up the IFSP. This framework accounts for the varying emphases on the child and family and their important reciprocal impact on each other. This framework, as it relates to child-related outcomes, is also applicable to the IEP process for the preschool child. Beckman and Bristol identified two categories of child outcomes: child-related outcomes and family-related outcomes. Both target the child for intervention. The child-related outcomes emphasize changes in child behavior across stimulus conditions (e.g., settings), and monitor child progress rather than family support. For example, the plan may identify specific language goals for the child to increase the words the child uses to communicate. In contrast, family-related outcomes target child changes that affect the family. For example, the family may want support in how to address their child's behavior in public places or suggestions about bedtime routines. It is important for these child outcomes to be operationalized in behavioral terms to allow for observation and monitoring (Bagnato & Hofkosh, 1990; Bailey & Wolery, 1989).

Equally important in the IFSP process are outcomes, including child-related family outcomes and general family outcomes (Beckman & Bristol, 1991). Child-related family outcomes identify areas in which families can be supported based on their self-identified priorities that are clearly related to having a child with a disability. Respite care, family support groups, or financial support are all examples of child-related family outcomes. In contrast, general family outcomes address family needs that may be unrelated to having a child with a delay (e.g., identifying housing, relationship difficulties). Unlike the behaviorally written child outcomes, Summers et al. (1991) recommended that family outcomes be defined more broadly. In addition, these outcomes need to be written in terms of the family's expectations for the providers, rather than the providers' expectations of the family (Beckman & Bristol, 1991). Too often plans are written with the family being assigned responsibility for each outcome. Not only can parent assignments potentially place an undue burden on the family, it is contrary to a family-driven paradigm.

To determine how the IFSP process is implemented, it is important to turn to families for guidance. Results of interviews from nine consumer-focus groups found that families preferred the IFSP to be informal, responsive to their identified priorities, and supportive of their family as a whole (Bailey & Blasco, 1990). In an ideal situation the skills and expertise of each participant are used to develop a collaborative plan that maximally benefits the child and family. Essential to the success of the IFSP or IEP process is collaboration among team and family members to obtain mutually agreed on outcomes. To achieve this outcome, negotiation is necessary. Collaboration is an interactive process that enables teams of people with diverse expertise to generate creative solutions to mutually defined problems. The benefit of this approach is that outcomes are enhanced and altered from solutions that no one team member would produce independently. Negotiation includes considering multiple alternatives to find one that has common agreement. The benefits of this approach are twofold: (a) all team members are more likely to be invested in the outcome or activity, and (b) collaboration will foster parent independence as they continue to learn to advocate effectively, to make decisions, and to solve problems (Bailey, 1987). Consider how collaboration worked for this IFSP team:

Michael was 6 months old and had multiple medical problems and developmental delays. His parents lived together and both had a mild mental disability. At the time he was referred for early intervention, Michael was living in a foster home placement. Social services was working with the family in attempts to have Michael live at home. The key community service providers that were part of the IFSP team included social services, the home health care agency, and early intervention providers. There were many challenges that faced Michael's parents (the Hahns) as they worked with the agencies. The parents expressed that they were overwhelmed with the number of health cares Michael needed, including gastrointestinal feedings and supplemental oxygen. Daily caregiving activities, such as diapering and bathing, were initially difficult for them to learn as well. Supporting the family around health care was a priority; yet the developmental needs of Michael also needed to be addressed.

The family and providers met to develop a plan that would ensure success. Small steps needed to be defined and accomplished to help the family gain sufficient skills to effectively care for Michael. Initially the family visited Michael at the foster home with the support of the home health provider. These visits provided them opportunities to learn how to administer g-tube feedings. On the request of the Hahns, the early intervention team worked with the foster family addressing child-related outcomes. After working for several months, the parents learned the basic skills needed to care for Michael. The community team supported the family's decision to bring Michael home. The home health agency provided 18-hour nursing care during the first month home to provide the necessary support to the family. The early intervention teacher began to play a dual role of liaison to both the family and the home health provider. This provided the home health provider with information that she could use to directly support Michael's development and allowed her to continue to support his parents integrate this developmental information with his other caregiving routines. *(Collaborative intervention benefits the child.)* The team had ongoing meetings with the family to assess how the intervention was working for them and modified strategies as needed.

Several factors entered into the success of this transition, including a motivated family who was open to learning; agencies who were willing to provide the supports needed, which promoted family competence; and providers who were willing to work together to create an individualized plan.

Sometimes in the planning process potential conflict can occur when there are differences between provider and family priorities, values, identified outcomes, or methods of intervention (Bailey, 1987). Look at the following example:

Taquille is a 4-year-old with significant communication difficulties. Those involved in her early intervention believe that she would benefit from a preschool classroom where she would have opportunities to interact with peers who would serve as good language models. The parents want to keep Taquille at home, because they want her to have home schooling as her older brother and sister had. *(Value conflict.)*

DeGangi, Royeen, and Wietlishbach (1992) found that parents and providers differ in the solutions that are generated, suggesting that each brings to the IFSP a differing but equally important perspective. For example, Winton and Turnbull (1981) found that parents prefer not to be teachers of their child, leaving that role for providers. In contrast, the philosophy of many providers is that their role should be a consultant to the parents who then can integrate the strategies into their interactions with their child. It is important to recognize these differences and to discuss them openly, either modifying expectations of the key players or integrating both the family and provider viewpoints into the planning process. This conflict also can occur when families accustomed to a family-centered process encounter a child-centered orientation. For example, although the family as the decision maker is a recommended guiding principle, Duwa et al. (1993) found therapists often were resistant to this premise because their authority to make decisions was threatened. This finding suggests the need for further staff development to help providers make the individual change to incorporate this principle into practice. Potential negative outcomes can occur for the family when conflict is not effectively resolved (discussed further in chapter 4).

For parents and guardians to become equal members of a collaborative team process, they need to have opportunities to develop balanced partnerships with providers. If not, often well-intended assistance and support are offered that are not valued by the family, because the intervention does not address the family priorities. Although family–provider partnerships are the goal of most early intervention programs, achieving these relationships is difficult (Bailey, 1987; Winton, 1990). Family participation in the IFSP or IEP process is limited by providers placing too little value on input from family members (Nash, 1990). Family members' expertise and their role in the program decision-making process needs respect from the outset of the planning process. Developing collaborative family partnerships can best be achieved when providers demonstrate good communication and listening skills, flexibility, and open-mindedness and provide a nonjudgmental atmosphere (DeGangi et al., 1992). Family access to understandable information about their children and community resources enhances their role in the planning process and allows them to make well-informed decisions.

Step 4: Choosing an Approach

Early intervention programs need to consider strategies to address both child and family outcomes. Turning to the research literature can help program planners in designing the intervention components. The following provides information regarding alternative child-based approaches, intervention variables needing consideration, strategies to promote inclusion, and family support networks.

Alternative Child-Based Intervention Strategies

Intervention for young children with disabilities is based on the assumption that specialized strategies will affect positively the child's rate of learning (Ramey & Ramey, 1998). However, there is no simple answer about what is the best intervention approach or curriculum to use with young children. Most evaluation efforts provide limited insights into the functional relationship between independent (e.g., instructional strategies) and dependent (e.g., child change) variables (Dunst & Snyder, 1986). Just as providers need to draw on multiple theoretical practices, a blended approach is also called for in planning interventions. Different curricular and intervention approaches used in early intervention programs frequently are based on one or more theoretical perspectives. This section describes the multiple intervention approaches used in early childhood programs and the expected child outcomes.

A social contingent responsive interactional approach emphasizes the importance of the interventionist's differential and contingent responding to child behavior. Contingent responding functions as a reinforcer to maintain or promote further child behavior. Research with young children with disabilities suggests that this responsive interactional approach is associated with a number of areas, including facilitating vocabulary and early semantic relations (Warren & Kaiser, 1986), improving sensorimotor skills (Mahoney & Powell, 1988), accelerating developmental growth (Shonkoff, 1992), and increasing social engagement with adults and peers (Dunst et al., 1990). This and other research suggest that a responsive interactional approach is an effective determinant of competency across areas, which underscores the need for early interventionists to focus on supporting the caregiver–child relationship (Dunst et al., 1990). Specific strategies to support the caregiver–child relationship are described in chapter 6. In situations in which a responsive approach is deemed appropriate, these strategies promote and enhance child development. Interventionists who use a social contingent responsive interactional approach often pair it with a cognitive-based curriculum. This curriculum, which is derived from developmental theory, stresses broad thinking, planning, and self-directing skills that enable young children to "learn how to learn." This curriculum emphasizes the development and generalization of cognitive processes, such as comparison, classification, perspective change, and sequencing, which are assumed to underlie learning (Dale & Cole, 1988).

Incidental teaching, the use of responsive approaches in natural contexts and within daily routines, is another strategy interventionists use. In Warren and Kaiser's (1986) review, the importance of incidental teaching as an intervention strategy became evident. They found that this approach was related to children's increased communication skills and the generalization of those skills across situations as compared to groups in which structured learning strategies were used. Furthermore, Wetherby (1986) found that young children with autism acquired increased communication skills when intervention targeted increasing verbal and nonverbal acts within natural learning environments. Incidental teaching with children with autism also resulted in significant child progress in cognitive, communication, and socioemotional development (Rogers, Herbison, Lewis, Patone, & Reis, 1986).

Incidental teaching is compatible with a functional curriculum, which evolved to address the needs of children with severe physical or mental disabilities for whom cognitive or academically based curricula have less content validity. For example, instructional objectives address functional motor independence (or increasing partial participation in daily routines) rather than normal motor function. Functional curricula proponents propose that this ecological approach supports children's learning, especially those children with more severe disabilities. It proposes that skills are generalized if they are learned within the context of daily routines. For example, a young child may learn spatial skills by taking cheerios out of a container during snack time or throwing away her napkin.

Direct skill instruction is an intervention approach that uses strategies to teach targeted skills directly. Its foundation is in behavioral theory. Key to this behaviorally oriented approach is generalization of skills to new contexts through adult- versus child-directed strategies (Yoder, 1990). Compared to a responsive interaction approach, direct-skill instruction is at the opposite end of the spectrum. Advocates of direct-skill instruction claim that specific objectives and task-analyzed activities are necessary for children with disabilities to learn skills efficiently (Bailey & Wolery, 1984). Direct-skill instruction is compatible with those providers using an academic-based curriculum, which is also based extensively on task analysis of academic skills (Gersten, Woodward, & Darch, 1986). The emphasis of the academic-based curriculum, which is drawn from learning and behavioral theory, is the use of approaches that teach specific skills needed to succeed in school.

Research findings with direct skill instruction indicate that short-term benefits include increased cognitive skills (Bailey & Bricker, 1986), improved developmental rates (Wolery & Dyk, 1985), and increased number of objectives mastered (Wolery & Dyk, 1985). Advocates of direct-skill instruction suggest that specific objectives and task-analyzed activities are important for skills to be learned efficiently (Bailey & Wolery, 1984). However, as discussed earlier, directive styles were also correlated with slower rates of development (Mahoney & Powell, 1988). Unfortunately, there are few studies that evaluate the differential effectiveness of the two approaches. In one comparative study, Yoder, Kaiser, and Alpert (1989) found that the relative success of an intervention approach was dependent on the child's initial skill level. Infants and young preschoolers benefited most from a responsive approach, whereas older preschool children learned better in direct-skill instruction. These findings suggest that different aspects of development at different ages may influence the effectiveness of the approach adopted.

Dale and Cole (1988) conducted an efficacy study contrasting the differential effects of cognitive and academic-based curricula with children ranging from 3 through 6 years of age. They found that each curriculum differed in its focus and philosophy. Results found differential effects on language development. The results indicated that the academic curriculum facilitated development of specific language skills that were convergent in nature (i.e., responses to items that were more specific and focused as measured on the Basic Language Concepts Test; Gersten et al., 1986). The cognitive curriculum facilitated language skills that were more generalized or divergent in nature (i.e., responses to items that were more open ended as measured on the McCarthy Verbal and Memory Scales; McCarthy, 1972). These results were supported by Cole, Mills, and Dale (1989), who found similar patterns of differences. This empirical support suggests that each approach has value in promoting specific skills. The differences in content emphasis of each of these curricula and intervention approaches may differentially benefit children with varying disabilities and should be a consideration in their use. Therefore, these two studies suggest that individualization of interactional approaches based on child characteristics is very important. In future program planning, interventionists might consider taking an informed eclectic approach (i.e., general theory), with flexibility to take advantage of the strengths of each curriculum and approach. Continued investigations need to be conducted to ascertain the relative effectiveness of such a blended approach.

Intervention Variables

Evidence gathered over the past 25 years suggests that early intervention programs can produce positive effects on children's cognitive and social development (see review by Ramey & Ramey, 1998). Information obtained from these studies can guide programs in planning and designing early intervention programs. Ramey et al. (1992) have derived several principles regarding the efficacy of early intervention that also have direct relevance to policy development and resource allocation.

In general, early initiation of intervention maximizes benefits to children (Campbell & Ramey, 1994; Casto & Lewis, 1986; Shonkoff, 1992). These studies suggest that programs that enroll infants resulted in greater benefits that were longer lasting. However, these data do not suggest that there is a "critical period" for intervention such that intervention is not beneficial after a designated age (Ramey & Ramey, 1998). Although Shonkoff and Hauser-Cram (1987) found similar results with infants with mild delays, these same effects were not true of young children with severe disabilities. Time of enrollment did not predict outcomes of young children with severe disabilities, suggesting an interaction of level of disability with initiation of services. Nevertheless, these findings highlight the importance of child-find efforts in early intervention programs. Child-find can be hindered if physicians, who are in a primary position to influence the diagnostic and referral process for young children, adopt a "wait-and-see" approach. Epps and Kroeker (1995), in a survey of 155 family practice physicians, found that the younger child (20 month old vs. 40 month old) was twice as likely to be identified as having no disorder despite the fact that mild delay was present. Further dissemination of information about the importance of intervention and effective mechanisms for referral by physicians is crucial.

The service delivery mode (e.g., direct education versus intermediary route to change child competencies such as parent training only) and intensity of program, including the duration and frequency of services, were also found to be factors in child outcomes (Ramey & Ramey, 1998). Results of the Early Intervention study (Shonkhoff, Hauser, Cram, & Upshur, 1992) suggested that greater increases of children's growth in cognitive skills were found when services provided one-on-one contact between the service providers and the child. Therefore, the benefits of individualized programming for children and families are indicated. Wasik, Ramey, Bryant, and Sparling (1990) also found similar effects with environmentally at-risk populations of young children. Their randomized trial study indicated that combining daily center-based intervention with weekly home visits resulted in significant cognitive gains for children, whereas weekly home-visit programs had no measurable benefits on the child's development. These results "challenge the basis for the popularity of intervention that rely on infrequent home visits only" for the economically disadvantaged, high-risk children (Ramey & Ramey, 1998, p. 5).

Meisels (1992) disputed that intensity, as defined by the number or length of program contacts or the exposure of children and families to activities, alone contributes to child outcomes. He proposed that active experience, the child's and family's interest and active participation in the program, is the key program variable to success. Hence it may be necessary for program designers to move away from a days-per-week framework and to redirect their focus to operationalizing active involvement. Meisels's proposal suggests there is a motivational component to program involvement. Liaw (1991), cited in Meisels (1992), tested these hypotheses empirically and found research support for Meisels's Active Experience Model. Liaw reanalyzed data from the Infant Health and Development Program (Ramey et al., 1992) a multisite randomized study that examined the efficacy of an early intervention study. Results indicated that the family's level of active experience accounted for 12% more variance than the number of contacts or level of exposure. The implication is that programs need to incorporate validated strategies that support children and families. Furthermore, programs should promote the active role and involvement of the child's and family's participation.

This sampling of research findings reinforces the contention that human development is complex and as a result the interaction of multiple variables affect the ultimate benefit of early intervention on the developing child (Bricker & Veltman, 1990). Characteristics of the population of children and families should be considered carefully because programs are designed with emphasis on individualized programming. Adequate resources need to be obtained to allow for the intensity of programming that will be sufficient to make a difference. Further research is needed to continue to clarify the relative importance of particular program variables' contributions to effective interventions.

Implementing Services in Natural Environments

It is important to determine why there is a growing movement toward inclusive settings. In the forefront are legislative requirements. The amendments in the IDEA (1997) make it clear that young children with disabilities are best served in their natural environments. In their position paper, the Division for Early Childhood (1993) defined a natural environment as "one in which the child would spend time if he or she did not have special needs" (p. 3). As early intervention began to implement services within inclusive environments, their goal was to find settings in which children with disabilities could actively interact with typically developing peers. Stainback and Stainback (1992) recommended that the percentage of children with disabilities enrolled in these settings should be similar to the proportion of persons with disabilities in the general population. Full inclusion should not be restricted to educational and child care settings but expanded to include other family–child community activities (e.g., parenting classes or playgroups). The IDEA amendments (1997) added, "The provision of early intervention services for any infant and toddler occurs in a setting other than a natural environment only when early intervention cannot be achieved satisfactorily for the infant or toddler in a natural environment" (p. 9). Part C strengthens this provision by requiring a statement of the natural environments in which early intervention services shall appropriately be provided and including a justification of the extent, if any, to which the services will not be provided in a natural environment.

Much of the call for inclusion comes from parents of children with disabilities who advocate for their children to have opportunities in the mainstream community (Bruder, 1998; Guralnick, 1994). Their position is that inclusive environments offer more opportunities for their children to learn and socialize in a less stigmatizing setting (Siegel, 1996). The increasing demand for child care services for families with young children is another incentive for services being provided in inclusive settings. Half of all women in the United States with infants under the age of 1 year are in the labor force (Bruder & Staff, 1998). Within this group are large numbers of mothers who have children with disabilities that need child care (Fink, 1991). For these families, a collaborative partnership between early childhood special education and child care programs can serve dual purposes of providing both high-quality educational services to young children and needed child care. To meet this growing need, providing early childhood intervention services are becoming more prevalent in child care settings (Craig & Haggart, 1994). Although there is a trend to use community-based services, it is important to recognize the potential administrative problems (e.g., blending funding streams, monitoring programs that the early intervention does not administer, and ensuring quality services; Smith & Rose, 1993). Community leaders need to take a proactive stance to begin to address these issues to eliminate potential roadblocks to inclusion. (See chapter 9 for specific systems-change strategies.)

Although philosophically inclusion of children with disabilities into child care is being promoted, it is not without caution. Critics have voiced concern regarding the quality of existing child care programs and suggest that providers in community early childhood programs may not be able to meet the developmental tasks of the children with special concerns (Howes & Hamilton, 1993). Also of concern is the lack of specialized providers in the child care environment (Wolery et al., 1993). It is essential that efforts be made to increase the quality of child care for all children. One step toward improved quality is support of child care providers in gaining their child development associate's (CDA) degree or their participation in ongoing inservice programs. Ideally follow-up consultation in the classroom or home settings is recommended to help the child care providers generalize these skills learned in the formal training activities to everyday practice. For example, after participating in a workshop on creating a learning environment, the consultant collaborates with the child care staff in evaluating their environment and suggests adaptations based on the information they learned at the inservice programs. Efforts such as these, paired with partnerships with early intervention programs will increase the quality of child care for all young children.

In a recent study, Bruder (1998) examined the effects of classroom setting type, inclusive (classroom experience of 6 hours per week) or self-contained (4 hours per week of intensive services) for toddlers with moderate to severe disabilities. She found that there were no differences in effectiveness as measured by developmental outcomes in a one-year follow-up. She concluded that this preliminary evidence suggests that settings, such as child care classrooms, can meet the needs of children with disabilities as well as self-contained classrooms and need not have a detrimental effect on toddler development. Buysse and Bailey (1993) also found in a review of 22 studies that developmental outcomes did not vary as a result of segregated versus integrated educational settings.

It was not the intent of IDEA to simply place children with and without disabilities together. There is both an art and science to inclusion that encompasses careful planning and adequate supports. The challenge is to set up the supports needed for community programs to provide the quality services needed for children with special concerns. For successful inclusion to occur, the characteristics of the child's environments need to be assessed to identify the skills the child needs to participate in the settings and to determine any necessary environmental adaptations (Epps, Thompson, & Lane, 1985; Noonan & McCormick, 1993). Early childhood staff need guidance in identifying the strengths and less well-developed areas for children with disabilities to include them in meaningful activities. For example, a child with autism may excel and attend well to spatial activities, building, and putting shapes into the formboard. In contrast the same child may have great difficulty sitting during a music activity that requires attending to the teacher and interacting with the other children. In the music activity, the early childhood special education teacher or psychologist can collaborate with the early childhood teacher and mutually develop strategies to facilitate the child's participation in music. Environmental adaptations may be another area of concern for some children.

Joey, who is receiving home-based services, was going to be enrolled in the neighborhood preschool program in the fall. Joey is 4 years old and has spina bifida. He is quite independent in maneuvering with his wheelchair. The preschool meets the requirements of the Americans With Disabilities Act, so he could easily access the building and the restrooms. Prior to beginning preschool, his parents asked if his physical therapist would evaluate the classroom layout with the classroom teacher to make sure he could navigate easily in the environment. During the visit, the teacher and physical therapist found they only had to make slight modifications such as making wider aisles between the table and chairs and moving some cabinets to make larger openings into the special-interest play areas. This preplanning with the team and family contributed to his successful transition.

One of the goals of inclusion is increased interactions with peers. Odom and McEvoy (1996) found that peer interaction is most successful when actively facilitated by adults. In fact, decreases in interaction occurred when adult support was stopped (Anita, Kreimeyer, & Eldridge, 1994). Types of adult-facilitated activities include structured integrated play activities (Odom & McEvoy, 1996), group friendship activities (Cooper & McEvoy, 1996), and direct support of children during classroom routines (Rule et al., 1987). The following scenario provides one example of adult facilitated interaction.

Ms. Bhavano, the preschool teacher, gathered six children to participate in a special activity, pretending to be firefighters. Jasmine, a 5 year old with a speech and language disorder, was part of this group activity. During the planning phase of this activity Ms. Bhavano asked the children what they would need to play firefighters. She used a picture as an extra cue for the children and made sure Jasmine had an opportunity to respond. Jasmine told the group they needed hoses. *(Provides opportunity to demonstrate skills.)* Ms. Bhavano asked Jasmine and Jose to find the hoses and provided the other children additional props to find. The children began to give each other roles. Jasmine chose to be a firefighter. Ms. Bhavano suggested that firefighters always have partners. She asked Jasmine and Maddie to choose whom their partners would be. *(Pairing up children helps to build interactions and friendships.)* The play sequence evolved, starting with calling the firefighters to put out the fire. After Ms. Bhavano helped the children set the stage for the play activity, she stepped back and took on an active observer role. She only entered the children's play to encourage new interactions or to help expand their problem solving skills.

This play activity offered all the children a rich learning experience that targeted social, representational, and language skills. Ms. Bhavano actively facilitated the interactions with minimal intrusion to ensure that Jasmine was integrated throughout the play experience.

One of the concerns of inclusion is the potential for children to be stigmatized. One way to ameliorate this problem is to arrange situations in which the strengths of children with disabilities are highlighted. This strengths-based strategy provides a foundation for building mutual respect among the children. Early childhood programs that offer multiage grouping have been found to favorably influence the performance of children with and without disabilities (McWilliam & Bailey, 1995). In these multiage settings the staff is already accustomed to adapting the curriculum to different age levels, so it is often easier to provide instruction that accommodates the diverse characteristics of children in the program. When a classroom teacher is accustomed to instructing children who are all 4-year-olds, it is sometimes more difficult to make the modifications in curriculum instruction for the child with disabilities who may have skills below the 4-year level. Mutual respect among peers can also occur by eliminating any fears or questions that the child with disabilities might present. Answering questions that the other children have openly and honestly helps to allay these fears or uncertainties. In the situation described with Joey, for example, the teachers might choose to let the children try out his wheel chair when first enrolled so it is seen as something familiar.

Addressing Family Outcomes

It is appropriate for early intervention programs to embrace parental so-cial support as a primary program goal, given the positive effects of ade-quate social networks on both children and families (Shonkoff et al., 1992). The results suggest that psychologists, through developing a relationship with the family and open dialogue, can help families identify ways to ac-cess both informal and formal supports that the family regards as helpful. Research suggests that families participating in a mixed-service delivery mode (i.e., a combination of home-based and center-based services) in-creased the support networks they used and reported a decreased level of stress and perceived family difficulties (Shonkoff & Hauser-Cram, 1987). These benefits were attributed to parents' access to multiple-service pro-viders and interactions with other parents.

Providing social support networks in early intervention programs is based on the assumption that support buffers individuals from potential negative effects of stress (Dunst, Trivette, & Cross, 1986). Social support networks are defined as a "set of interconnected relationships among a group of people that provides enduring patterns of nurturance and pro-vides contingent reinforcement for efforts to cope with life on a day-to-day basis" (Garbarino, 1983, p. 5). Levitt, Weber, and Clark (1986) found that social support was related to mothers' well-being. Specifically, when moth-ers of young children reported adequate support, defined as maternal sat-isfaction with spousal and friendship support, there were resultant de-creases in parental stress and increases in life satisfaction and satisfaction with parenting (Crnic, Greenberg, Ragozin, Robinson, & Basham, 1983; Levitt et al., 1986). Although the relationship between spousal support and maternal well-being was found, further clarification of "what is adequate support" is necessary to better guide clinical practice. Overall, these find-ings point to the interdependencies between family system variables and child outcomes (Dunst, Trivette, Hamby, & Pollock, 1990).

The important question related to early intervention efficacy is the degree to which parental well-being influences child outcomes. Social net-work theory proposes that family functioning affects parenting behavior, which in turn influences the child. This proposed relationship has been supported by a number of studies. Research has investigated the impact of social support on families with children with disabilities. A study of 47 mothers and their preschool children with disabilities examined the re-lationship between social support, personal and family well-being (Dunst et al., 1990), and two dimensions of child behavior (measured by the Bayley Scales of Infant Development; Bayley, 1969; and Carolina Record of Individual Behavior; Simeonsson, 1981). The results indicated that enhanced personal and family well-being were significantly related to greater social responsiveness of children, suggesting a close relationship between the social–affective behavior of both parties. In addition, the greater the amount of family support (i.e., contact with social network members), the less aversive behavior the child displayed. Shonkoff, Hauser-Cram, Kraus, and Upshur (1992) found increased parental stress (measured on the Parenting Stress Index; Abidin, 1986) was related to less effective maternal interaction strategies (rated on the Nursing Child Assessment Teaching Scale; Barnard & Kelly, 1990). Dunst, Lowe, and Bartholomew (1990) reported a positive relationship among parental role satisfaction, social support, and changes in children's developmental rate. Trickett, Apfel, Rosenbaum, and Zigler (1982) also found that providing support services to families who had infants at risk was related to increased child receptive language skills. This evidence suggested that family context may influence the magnitude or presence of a wide range of intervention effects.

Conclusion

The 1990s marked a time of changing roles for both family members and providers. The ability of both of these parties to develop collaborative partnership is a key factor in successful early intervention. It is important to recognize that differences in values, expectations, and priorities of families are likely to influence each aspect of the service delivery system. Creating a system that works relies on effective planning, implementation, and monitoring of services. Based on this assumption, the IFSP–IEP processes were developed and provide the plans and directions for service implementation. Although the IFSP process is only mandated for services from birth through 2 years, many of its underlying assumptions and processes have utility in services for young preschool children with disabilities and indeed for older children as well. Incorporating these principles into practice for the preschool population needs consideration to provide a seamless family support service delivery system for all young children and their families. It is critical that providers continually individualize the intervention strategies to meet the unique needs of children and examine ways to provide services in inclusive settings. Expanding services to include family support programs that provide adequate social networks to children and families is essential. This program change can only be accomplished through service delivery systems that provide multiple service options for families. As service delivery systems begin implementing these revolutionary services for young children and their families, there needs to be an emphasis on accountability to ensure that families and providers work together to implement an integrated service delivery system that embraces the principles of family-centeredness. Without this accountability and commitment to quality services, the system will do nothing more than change the name of the process (Duwa et al., 1993).

Family Story: Tiara

Tiara was born at approximately 34 weeks gestation age when her mother's pregnancy was complicated by placental abruption. Tiara was delivered by emergency C-section and transferred to the closest tertiary care center. In addition to prematurity, diagnoses were made of birth asphyxia and seizures, with episodes of apnea and bradycardia. Tiara required temporary ventilatory support and placement of a gastrostomy-button for feedings. For the first several weeks of Tiara's hospitalization, her parents seemed to be struggling with balancing their own work and home demands with being at the hospital with Tiara. Furthermore, they were grappling with the initial diagnoses, uncertainty about long-term prognosis, reactions of extended family members and friends, and violation of their expectations of having a "perfect" baby. They also seemed hesitant to touch her when she was on the ventilator. Therefore, genuine efforts were made to embrace her parents early on, encouraging their participation in decision making regarding their child's care. *(Supporting families as decision makers.)* Ongoing nurturance of their relationship with their baby *(supporting the attachment relationship and parent–child interaction)* was provided. Actively fostering their sense of some degree of control and influence on their child's care was encouraged across staff to support her parents in reducing their stress and enhancing their problem solving in uncertain situations. *(Building family self-confidence.)*

When Tiara's acute care needs were largely met, the health care team introduced the availability of community-based early intervention services. Her parents indicated that they were not able to focus on such services at that time, and the team tried to convey respect for the family's priorities. *(Respecting family decisions.)* Several weeks later, Tiara's primary nurse reintroduced the possibility for early intervention. At that point, the parents indicated an interest in learning more about early intervention.

Identification of Family Concerns and Priorities

The psychologist met with Tiara's parents to provide general information about the range of early intervention supports and to describe assessments and the IFSP process. To identify their most pressing priorities and concerns, a combination of brief surveys and an informal, sensitive dialogue with the family was used. After the psychologist indicated that the family could have others join them at the IFSP meeting, the parents chose to have one of the grandfathers present, a close family friend, and one other member of the hospital team. When Tiara's mother and father inquired about a service coordinator from their area, the psychologist provided the telephone number of the Part C program, pausing to try to sense whether the family preferred to call themselves. When they indicated that they could call, the psychologist reviewed the type of questions the agency would probably ask them. *(Family questions guide child assessment process.)*

Child Assessment

Tiara was assessed by a transdisciplinary team of early childhood providers, including a speech–language pathologist, occupational therapist, and psychologist. Tiara's parents were integral in the assessment process. With some guidance, they were encouraged to express their priorities for assessment. They indicated that they wanted to know how to "hold" her (i.e., postural supports) and "do things" with her (i.e., synchronous interaction). They also were concerned about whether she would be able to "talk" and "eat" and whether Tiara would be able to play with the same toys her older sister had used when she was a baby.

IFSP Meeting

The parents indicated a convenient meeting time. Tiara's mother and father had contacted the early intervention program in their community, and a service coordinator was able to participate in the meeting as well. After introductions were made, Tiara's mother and father did not talk readily, so the staff used a variety of communication strategies to support their autonomy and to counteract the potential for provider-generated goals. For instance, when the father continued to avoid eye contact by looking down as others were talking, the psychologist interjected (while one of the health care providers was speaking), "You look like you wanted to say something." A genuine, flexible, nonrigid approach was used to support Tiara's parents in expressing their priorities and concerns and in jointly (with providers) formulating a plan. Listed below are Tiara's parents' prioritized concerns and the plan generated by the group.

1. Tiara's future development. Her parents were most concerned about how Tiara's diagnosis would affect her future development and what kind of support she might need. The team problem solved with her parents about developmental activities that would support Tiara's learning. The family asked if there would be any support in their home once Tiara was discharged, which led to discussion of home-based options and times that would enable participation from both parents.
2. Sibling's adjustment to her new sister. Tiara's parents expressed concern about their 4-year-old daughter, Sonia, and how she would adjust to a new baby. They were worried about how she might feel in the future, having a sister with special needs. The psychologist offered to arrange times when Sonia could visit Tiara in the hospital (with the support of either the psychologist or child life specialist if the parents so desired). In addition, Tiara's parents were told about resource books for families and siblings that were available for them to borrow. *(Need to consider whole family.)*
3. Medical finances. Although Tiara's parents would be eligible for state funds for children with special health care needs, they still had concerns regarding future medical costs and special equipment needs their daughter might have. They had heard that "everything would have to be reviewed" (i.e., Medicaid had contracted with health maintenance organizations [HMOs] in their state). The team indicated that a social worker could meet with them privately regarding these issues. *(Team respects confidentiality of sensitive issues.)*
4. Family support. Tiara's family was worried about finding respite care for her because they had few extended family members available for support. A group discussion led to a plan to provide the family with information about their state's respite program and a Family Friends program to provide in-home support. This information would be given to the family to use at their discretion. Tiara's father indicated that he would like to follow-up on this plan. *(Need to address family outcome.)*

Implementation of the Plan

Developmental Intervention

With Tiara's parents in agreement, the plan was put into effect at the end of the meeting. Continued developmental supports were provided to Tiara and her family during the remainder of her hospitalization, including collaboration with Tiara's primary nurse and joining Tiara's parents for some of the times when they were with her. A daily schedule was developed and bedside developmental suggestions were posted to promote continuity of care. A communication notebook also was placed at Tiara's bedside to assist the family in feeling informed about Tiara's activities during days and nights.

Referral to Services

Tiara's family had already contacted their community early intervention program, and the service coordinator was facilitating Tiara's transition. The social worker supported the family in making an application for Supplemental Security Income.

Transition

By the time of discharge, Tiara's parents had made necessary connections with several community resources. They felt comfortable with Tiara's physical cares and indicated they were prepared to take her home. Within the first month after Tiara was discharged, she experienced an unexpected respiratory arrest. Emergency measures were taken, but she was not able to be revived. Tiara died in the emergency room of their neighborhood hospital. The tertiary hospital was notified, which in turn notified the community service coordinator. The hospital's bereavement program was initiated, providing ongoing support to family members. *(Integrated service delivery system.)*

Reflective Process

Considering the providers' empathy with the family, strong emotions over Tiara's death, and questions about whether they had "done everything," managing their emotional distress was crucial. The psychologist assumed a role in supporting other providers in self-reflection and reframing their distress through ongoing interaction individually and in teams. *(Support in ethical deliberation and reflective process.)*

6

Interventions to Support
Caregiver–Child Interaction and
Developing Relationships

The 8-week-old gazes at her father's face. Her father smiles and says, "How's my little girl?" Her face lights up with a bright smile. The synchronous dance begins.

Interactions between children and their caregivers are the building blocks of a relationship, one that provides the context for infant learning. Not only are interactions important to developing relationships, recent advances in neuroscience suggest that these relationships influence how the intricate circuitry of the human brain is "wired" (Shore, 1997). This interplay between nature and nurture is a much debated topic. Early assumptions placed a heavy emphasis on the role of genes on the development of the child. However, recent evidence suggests that brain development hinges on the complex interplay of the genes and experiences, with both factors being critical (Shore, 1997). Gains in medical technology (e.g., Positron Emission Topography [PET] and Magnetic Resonance Imagery [MRI]) provide neuroscientists with new tools that allow a closer look at the functioning of the brain. Research shows us that although the infant is born with a 100,000 billion brain cells, there is limited density of the synapses. These synapses form the primary circuitry or connections of the brain and are the basic equipment of the brain that humans need for a lifetime of thinking. By the time the child is 3 years old, the child's brain has 1,000 trillion connections, yet by adolescence one half of the synapses have been discarded (Huttenlocher, 1984).

We are interested in brain development in relation to caregiver–child interactions because the process of selectively producing and pruning excess synapses has substantial implications for early intervention. There is growing evidence that the infant's early experiences shape the development of these connections (Chugani, 1997). Researchers are finding that relationships can make a difference in the development of the efficient neural pathways and the processing of information. Although there are new advances in neuroscience, much needs to be learned to better understand what kinds of experiences wire the brain in certain ways. Researchers propose that there are critical periods that are optimal for learning, with most occurring during the first years of life. For example, if a baby is born with cataracts and does not have them removed until 2 years of age, visual problems will remain despite the corrective surgery. Of interest to early interventionists is whether the social–emotional environment of the young child can have similar dramatic effects. Although less is known in this realm of research, preliminary findings suggest that responsive interactions (those in which the child's signals are interpreted and responded to appropriately) can influence developing patterns of neuronal connectivity (Dawson, Hessl, & Frey, 1994). These new research developments suggest the importance of the developing caregiver–child relationship. As a result, providers are turning to the literature on the caregiver–child relationship for guidance. The term *caregivers* is chosen for this chapter to represent not only the child's parents or guardians but to be inclusive of other primary adults (e.g., grandparents, child care providers) who may interact with the child. This chapter explores the literature that provides clinicians with an understanding of the complexity of dyadic relationships and application to clinical practices.

Attachment: The Theoretical Backdrop for Caregiver–Child Interaction

Attachment theory based on the joint work of Bowlby and Ainsworth (e.g., Ainsworth & Bowlby, 1991) is instrumental in guiding our practice of supporting caregiver–child interaction. It has contributed greatly to the field of psychology by providing a conceptual foundation and useful framework to understand the complexities of the development of attachment behaviors, related socioemotional abilities, and the significance of the parent–child relationship. Bowlby (1969) proposed an ethological theory of attachment formation in which the survival of infants depended on their ability to maintain proximity to adults to gain nourishment, comfort, and protection. He conceptualized attachment as a goal-directed control system in which goal states or functions of behavior, rather than the infant's discrete behaviors, are important. Attachment behavior develops as part of the attachment control system and is the outgrowth of an innate need (genetic based) for social interaction in human infants. The survival goal of the attachment system is seeking and maintaining proximity to this individual. It is accomplished when the caregiver responds to the infant's signal, which may include smiling, reaching, or crawling toward the caregiver. The efficiency of the infant's signals is dependent on both the promptness and appropriateness of the adult responses, illustrating the transactional nature of these interactions. This theory underlies the emphasis in early intervention on why responsive and sensitive caregiving is an important strategy. The infant's early relationships interact within a social context to influence later socioemotional behavior. Attachment lays the groundwork for later socioemotional development through what Bowlby (1969) described as internal working models. Internal working models emerge as the infant begins to have generalized expectations concerning self and others.

Attachment can best be defined as "specific, enduring emotional bonds whose existence is of major importance in the process of sociopersonality development" (Bornstein & Lamb, 1992, p. 417). Ainsworth (1969) examined individual differences in the development of attachment relationships, classifying behaviors as either secure or insecure (avoidant or ambivalent). These patterns of attachment evolve as a result of the infant's experiences with the caregiving environment. Those infants who form insecure attachment patterns inhibit expression of feelings of fear, desire, and anger toward an insensitive caregiver (Type A, avoidant attachment pattern) or become increasingly angry with or fearful of an inconsistent caregiver (Type C, ambivalent attachment pattern). Recently, a fourth type of attachment pattern (Type D, disoriented or disorganized) has been described (Main & Solomon, 1986). Infants who are disoriented appear confused or apprehensive and display contradictory behavior patterns that include incomplete movements. In a community-based childcare or preschool program, one might see manifestations of these patterns of attachment. For example, children rated as disoriented often have more difficulty physically moving and negotiating their environment, exhibiting reckless and accident-prone behavior (e.g., inability to move safely through space or lack of anticipating consequences of their physical actions). Lieberman and Pawl (1990) suggested that this pattern is developed as young children attempt to manage their uncertainty of the caregiver's availability, so they court danger, rather than seek protection. Crittenden (1995) suggested these insecure behavioral patterns serve as an adaptive and protective response to their unique family circumstances. However, these same behaviors may be problematic if used in a context outside of the family.

Attachment theory provides a useful paradigm for exploring the developmental sequelae of this early relationship (Silber, 1989). A recurring theme is the positive influence of an attentive and responsive caregiver on cognitive and social development (Beckwith & Cohen, 1984). Researchers have shown that responsive interaction is associated with increased infant interest in exploring the environment (Yarrow, Rubenstein, & Pederson, 1975). Sensitive and responsive caregiving during infancy is also related to improved cognitive competence (Mahoney & Powell, 1988). In a review of the literature, Lamb (1997) found that father–child attachment influenced child development, regardless of maternal attachment. Sroufe, Egeland, and Kreutzer (1993) found that elementary schoolchildren with histories of secure attachment are less likely to demonstrate difficult behavior problems (e.g., aggressive behavior) when encountering stress. DeKlyen, Speltz, and Greenberg (1998) found that the quality of father–child relationship was associated with the likelihood of referral for early onset of conduct problems. This is consistent with evidence that mother–child insecure attachment is linked with challenging child behavior. These studies show the significance of either parent's relationship with subsequent child behavior.

Findings of neuroscience research are beginning to answer the question of why there is an association between difficult behavior and attachment. Gunnar (1996) investigated young children's reactions to stress by measuring levels of cortisol (a steroid hormone) in saliva samples. Results indicated that increased cortisol levels are produced when individuals are faced with adverse physical or psychological events. Cortisol is known to alter the brain by making it vulnerable to processes that alter neurons and reduce synapses. Specifically, the damage occurs in the hippocampus, which results in memory lapse, anxiety, and the inability to control emotional outbursts. Of interest to Gunner was the differential effect of stress on the young child. She found that young children who experienced nurturing and sensitive care in the first year of life produced less cortisol than other children when encountering stress. She concluded that these early experiences served as a protective buffer. Perry (1996) found that when young children were emotionally neglected, brain-related functions, such as empathy, attachment, and affective regulation, were impaired. These studies suggest that early social environments affect the child's emotional regulatory capacities.

The Dynamic Interplay Between the Characteristics of the Caregiver and the Child

Through the process of social interaction and bidirectional influences, the caregiver and young child begin to adapt, adjust, and change their behaviors in response to each other (Barnard, 1997). This statement captures the essence of the transactional model by describing the mutual effects of the child on the environment and the environmental context on the child (Sameroff, 1987). These tenets of the transactional model greatly influenced the direction of early intervention and the current emphasis on the family, and more specifically caregiver–child interaction. The conceptualization that the adult and child mutually influence each other throughout their relationship guided researchers to examine the contributions of both the parent and the child. The mother's and father's relationship with their child may be parallel in many ways, whereas in other respects they are distinct (Lewis, 1997). For example, mothers typically provide more caregiving than fathers, whereas fathers spend higher proportions of their time in playful, roughhousing interactions. How these quite different functions and styles of interaction affect the developing caregiver–child relationship and subsequent child skills needs investigating. Unfortunately, although transactional theory stresses the importance of all caregivers' relationships on the developing child, the majority of research in this area focuses on the maternal–child relationship. Although we also focus on this relationship, we make great efforts to share research findings related to father–child relationships in this chapter. More research is needed regarding the influence of other caregivers (grandparents and child care workers, for example) to better understand the familial, social, and cultural factors that impede or enhance the child's development.

The Young Child's Contributions to Interaction

In recent years there has been an emphasis on the importance of the characteristics of infants in their transactions with the world (Goldsmith & Campos, 1982). The infant is no longer seen as a passive receptor of stimulation but rather a unique entity affecting the way the social world interacts with him or her. Stern (1977) suggested that "the infant arrives with an array of innately determined predilections, motor patterns, cognitive and thinking tendencies and abilities for emotional expressiveness" (p. 10) that contribute to interactions with others. Multiple characteristics potentially influence how others interact with the infant and vice versa. Goldberg (1990) suggested three qualities of infant behavior that influence the interaction: (a) predictability of the infant's behavior, (b) social responsiveness, and (c) readability of cues.

Mrs. Henry describes her granddaughter, Daniecia (a 2-month-old), to her pediatrician as being a "very intense baby." Daniecia is difficult to soothe (*poor self-regulation— unpredictable behavior*) and transitions very quickly from a quiet-alert to agitated-fussy state (*poor state control*). When her grandmother tries to cuddle her, she increases her fussing and stiffens her body. When Daniecia looks at Mrs. Henry she interprets this as an invitation to play and begins to talk to her. Daniecia, begins to fuss and turn away (*difficulty reading her cues*). Mrs. Henry is frustrated and feels badly that she is not a better caregiver.

This interaction pattern illustrates the early influence of temperament on the parent–child interaction. Daniecia presents as an infant who classically portrays characteristics of a "difficult" temperament. Researchers have hypothesized that infant irritability results in altered relationships by changing the parental response to the infant. Some studies report more responsive parenting with irritable babies, and others report parents demonstrating less contact with babies with these characteristics. Van den Boom (1994) hypothesized that the issue could be further clarified by examining the influence of social context. This contention is supported by research showing the interactive effects of infant irritability with other parent risk factors (e.g., low social support) on the quality of the caregiver–child relationship (Crockenberg & McCluskey, 1986). (For extensive discussion on risk, see chapters 2 and 3.) Van den Boom found that mothers of irritable infants who faced the stressors related to poverty demonstrated less responsive interactions with their infants as compared to mothers with irritable infants who had adequate financial resources. However, she further found that mothers facing stressors related to poverty could be provided support to be sensitive, and the increased sensitivity resulted in increased numbers of infants rated as securely attached.

To support Mrs. Henry's capacity to adapt to Daniecia's mode of interacting, it is important for the pediatrician to adopt an ecological approach that takes into account both the child and family circumstances. First, the pediatrician could provide practical suggestions that would help the infant to calm herself—for example, swaddling Daniecia by wrapping her snuggly with her blankets to limit extraneous movements, yet keeping her hands up by her face to give her opportunities to suck her fingers. Second, the pediatrician would want to determine if other familial issues, such as ongoing verbal disputes with adult members in the household, were present that could be exacerbating the difficulties in the interaction. If so, the family could be referred to other community resources for support (e.g., counseling).

Woody et al. (1992) suggested that "interaction difficultness" does not strictly reside within the child but is evident in the interactions between the temperament characteristics and environmental demands or the "fit" between child and caregiver characteristics. Any child can appear difficult if he or she violates the expectations of the caregiver's definition of appropriate behavior. Turecki and Wernick (1995) suggested that compatibility is crucial. They propose that often when young children have difficulties, there is a mismatch between the child's innate nature and the environment. Because this variable of "fit" plays an essential role in the quality of the interaction, the role of temperament in establishing the attachment relationship is difficult to investigate and may account for variability in findings (Bornstein & Lamb, 1992). The following example illustrates the "goodness of fit" concept:

Juan, a 3-year-old, is quite gregarious and rowdy. He fits in very well in his family where there are several siblings in a home environment that provides him with sufficient space to play without bothering family members. His family views his "outgoing behavior" as one of his strengths. In contrast, Julian, a 3-year-old, who has the same characteristics, is viewed as difficult by his family. He is the only child who lives with his parents in a small apartment in a large metropolitan city. His parents are fairly stressed because of their obligations to their extended family. They find his behavior quite disruptive, in part because it is a contrast to their quiet, reserved styles. The concern of the psychologist working with the family is not only the external conflict the family expressed but the potential long-term effect on Julian's self-esteem. The psychologist can support the family in articulating their expectation for Julian, the stress they experience, and feelings about him by reflecting on their feelings (e.g., it sounds like you are feeling overwhelmed when Julian gets wound up). In addition, the psychologist can set up activities the parents like to do with Julian and focus on his enjoyment with them. This type of strategy builds their confidence as parents and ultimately encourages positive interactions.

The cultural influence on characteristics, such as temperament, is also important to consider. Cross-cultural studies using Brazelton's Neonatal Behavioral Assessment Scale (1984) found that both Chinese American and Japanese American infants are more easily self-soothed, habituate quicker to light and sound, and experience fewer state changes than European American infants (Freedman, 1984). Chinese American infants were found to be more active and labile than European American infants (Birtchnell, 1988). Birtchnell (1988) also found similar results when European American neonates were compared to Kenyan neonates, with Kenyan infants demonstrating more activity and lability. These results suggest that providers need to take into account cultural differences as they assess and intervene with young children and their families. Cultural awareness and sensitivity are discussed further in chapter 4.

Interactions With Young Children With Special Health Care Needs/Disabilities

Most research on caregiver–child interaction has been based on observations of "normal" infant–mother dyads (Field, 1987; Goldberg & Simmons, 1988), yet little is known about the child with special health care needs or the child with disabilities (Cerreto, 1986). Such young children may have characteristics (e.g., irritability, passivity, reduced expressiveness and opportunities for interaction, and less mobility) that may negatively influence interaction and subsequently affect the child's development by altering parents' behavior (Goldberg & Simmons, 1988). Infants born premature were found to demonstrate less positive affect and game playing during interaction than infants who were full-term (Field, 1987). Plunkett, Meisels, Stieffel, Pasick, and Roloff (1986) also found that mothers of preterm infants appeared to work harder to engage their babies, played fewer games, and received less positive feedback from their infants. This interaction pattern suggests that although parents strive for optimal interactions with their babies, infants who are preterm may be less responsive to typical patterns of parent stimulation. Barnard, Bee, and Hammond (1984) investigated the impact of these early patterns of interaction on later interaction. Their longitudinal study of preterm infants found interactions of mothers and their 4-month-old infants to be characterized by intense maternal involvement and limited infant responsiveness. By 8 months and then at 2 years of age, these interactions were characterized by a less attentive mother. These results clearly illustrate the transactional and dynamic nature of caregiver–child interaction. The relationship changes over time based on the interaction pattern, and that relationship may be adversely affected if mutuality is not established (Barnard & Kelly, 1990).

Some consistent patterns in how children's disabilities affect interaction with their parents have been reported. Young children with disabilities are typically less active and less responsive and provide fewer communicative and affective cues (see Rosenberg & Robinson, 1988, for a review). These behavioral characteristics ultimately make interaction more difficult and less rewarding for the child's interactive partners (Rosenberg & Robinson, 1988) and result in increased levels of directiveness for mothers with children with cognitive delays and with children who display both cerebral palsy and a cognitive delay (Hanzlik & Stevenson, 1986). This difficulty in sending clear signals may affect the attachment process and points to the need to focus intervention with caregivers on being sensitive and responsive to these subtle child cues (Hadadian, 1996).

Brooks-Gunn and Lewis (1982) found that mothers of both infants with disabilities and their typical peers tailored their play to the child's ability and behavior. Mothers of children with disabilities initiated more of the play and controlled the interaction longer than mothers of typical children, suggesting a more directive style. Interactions may be less reciprocal and more mother-dominated with infants with disabilities because of the differences in infant characteristics (Barnard & Kelly, 1990). Gen-

Table 6.1. Types of Regulatory Disorders

Neurobehavioral Level of Development	Type of Regulatory Disorder
Basic organization of physiological and sensory systems	Severe sensory or developmental disorders—e.g., blindness or severe disability
Dynamic coordination of physiological and sensory systems; basic homeostatic functions	Persistent and severe regulatory disorder with sensory hypersensitivities, mood and state dysregulation; difficulties accepting regulation from others
Organization of overt behaviors in non-contingent situations	Mild to moderate regulatory disorders; ability to accept regulation from others; may be able to use one sensory regulatory mechanism
Organization of contingent responses in social situations	Affective and mood dysregulation with or without sensory component

Source: G. A. DeGangi, Assessment of sensory, emotional, and attentional problems in regulatory disordered infants: Part 1, *Infants and Young Children, 3* (p. 6). Reprinted with permission. Copyright © 1991 Aspen Publishers, Inc.

erally, as the infant does less, the parent does more to keep the interaction going. This finding is concerning, because data suggest that a responsive approach that is less directive has better developmental outcomes for children (Mahoney & Powell, 1988). Interaction strategies that promote a responsive nondirective approach are discussed later in the chapter. A more detailed description of the impact of disabilities on the attachment process can be found in Hadadian's (1996) review.

A Young Child's Self-Regulation Difficulties and Interaction

It has been recognized that neurobehavioral markers signaling atypical self-regulation or constitutional difficulties may offer early predictors of neurodevelopmental disabilities (Neisworth, Bagnato, & Salvia, 1995). These difficulties in self-regulation may include poor state control, poor autonomic control (e.g., breathing), hyperirritability, or difficulties in other regulatory capacities (e.g., sensory, attentional, socioemotional, or neuromotor). DeGangi (1991) proposed a neurobehavioral model that identifies four levels of regulatory disorders, outlined in Table 6.1. Infants with regulatory disorders frequently demonstrate typical developmental skills but have difficulties in behavior organization and adaptive functioning (DeGangi, 1991). Neisworth et al. (1995) suggested that extreme problems in self-regulation may lead to serious maladaptive interaction patterns.

Infants with patterns of atypical self-regulation present families with unique challenges. DeGangi, Craft, and Castellan (1991) proposed a family-centered intervention approach that recognizes the stress that coping with a child with these difficulties places on the family. Psychologists can play a critical role on the intervention team by addressing family concerns, family stresses in coping with their child's specific behaviors, adaptive and maladaptive family–child interaction, and depression or marital relationship conflicts that may be secondary to the child's constitutional difficulties. Multiple intervention strategies can support families. For example, psychologists can help families to strengthen protective factors such as facilitating intra- and extrafamilial support. (See chapter 3 for further discussion of protective factors.) DeGangi et al. (1991) also pointed to the importance of addressing the emotional aspects of interaction, such as identifying play activities that are mutually enjoyable. The efficacy of the integrated model of intervention for children with regulatory difficulties that blends caregiver guidance techniques, counseling approaches, and child-centered activities needs further study.

Contributions of the Caregiver to the Dyadic Interaction

Both attachment theory and the transactional model stress that parent characteristics play an important role in developing a relationship with the child. Bornstein and Lamb (1992) suggested that parents' personalities and perceptions of their roles are influenced by the social situations they encounter, which further influence their behaviors toward their child. These findings emphasize the importance for providers to recognize and examine factors outside of the dyadic interaction that may influence caregiver behavior (Bailey & Wolery, 1992). Financial and social stress, the availability of resources, and the social support in parents' lives are all variables affecting the general well-being and quality of interactions with their child (Levitt et al., 1986). Overall, it appears that mothers who encounter difficult life situations (e.g., lower education level, limited social support, or high life stress) have interactions with their infants that are less optimal than mothers with fewer difficulties (Crnic et al., 1993; Egeland & Sroufe, 1981). Barnard and Kelly (1990) found that maternal education, family income and occupation, and total amount of social support for the mother were related to child scores on cognitive assessment. In addition, well-supported mothers are less restrictive and punitive with their infants than less supported mothers. What is critical is that intervention that focuses on caregiver–child interaction not result in additional stress to the family that is already overwhelmed. When working with families who face these types of broad life issues, the intervention needs to support the family in seeking social support, reducing stress, or reducing caregiver demands (Dunst, 1985). Only when these issues are addressed can the family focus their efforts on the quality of their interactions with their child.

Challenging Caregiver Characteristics and Their Effect on the Dyadic Interaction

Child or caregiver behavior can often be a signal of problems in the caregiver–child relationship, including persistent caregiver complaints of severe behavior challenges, indications that the child is rejecting the caregiver, caregiver use of excessive punishment, or caregiver detachment from the child. Any of these behaviors may indicate the need for referral to a mental health provider. Three categories of adult characteristics place the dyadic relationship at significant risk: caregiver relational histories, caregiver depression, and caregivers who maltreat their children.

"Ghosts in the Nursery": Influences of Adult Relational History

It is important to examine the context in which parental behavior is rooted. Fraiberg (1980) suggested that relational patterns during childhood help to construct a parent's contemporary working model of attachment that may be related to the attachment status of their children and also influence their parenting. In a retrospective study, Main et al. (1985) found that mothers' reports of their early nurturance (or lack thereof) was strongly associated with secure or anxious patterns of attachment at adulthood. These maternal histories were associated with independent assessment of their attachment with their children. The results indicated that secure–autonomous adults tended to have infants classified as secure. Dismissing adults had infants classified as insecure–avoidant, and preoccupied adults had infants classified as disorganized. The findings of this and other research studies suggest that relationships are internalized and carried forward to new relationships (Morris, 1982).

The quality of these future relationships is related to caregivers history of relationships and current social support (Sroufe & Fleeson, 1986). The authors suggest that these findings may reflect issues the adults encountered with their own childhood attachment figure. Chinitz (1995) proposed that parents who themselves lacked nurturing and protective parenting or experienced physical or sexual abuse develop representations of themselves as unlovable or incompetent in the context of relationships. This representation of attachment contributes to problematic relationship development with their own children. Fraiberg (1980) described these as "ghosts in the nursery," which influence subsequent caregiving for their child. Bowlby (1969) suggested these parental attachment experiences provide for the caregiver's internal working model that affect relationships and subsequent interactions across the life span. These relational histories of the caregivers then influence their interactions with their children, which in turn accounts for the intergenerational transmission of attachment patterns.

These research findings highlight the need for providers to help adults who themselves had poor relationships learn different interaction patterns with their children. These new interaction patterns potentially provide a positive context for a new caregiver–child relationship. However, research has shown that altering these basic relationship patterns is not an easy task (Sroufe & Fleeson, 1986). In situations in which the caregiver has many personal issues that need addressing, it is important for providers to establish a network of services for both the child and the family, including referral to community resources and to providers with expertise in adult clinical issues. It is crucial to provide a safety net for the child, who cannot merely be put on hold until the caregiver addresses her or his own needs. This research suggests that other alternatives to support the child must be built in simultaneously to the family's treatment plan. The following case study deals with parental attachment experiences.

Rhanda is a single mother who currently uses illicit drugs and alcohol. She lives with her boyfriend and is pregnant. She has a 15-month-old son, Tony, whose father has no contact with him. Child protective services are involved as Rhanda was reported for child neglect. A psychologist's conversation with Rhanda reveals that her former step-father was physically abusive and that her mother was rejecting, shaming, and nonprotective. (*Problematic relationship history.*) Observations of Rhanda and Tony revealed similar relational patterns of rejection and put downs. (*Parent internal working model affects current relationship.*) She most often ignores Tony and has difficulty engaging him in an appropriate rewarding play interaction. Whenever Tony initiates an interaction, she typically responds by rebuffing him.

The dilemma for this family preservation team was to determine an intervention plan with the family that addressed the mother's difficulties, but at the same time protected the child. As a result, Tony was enrolled in a high-quality child care program as one means to address his developmental and caregiving challenges. (*Essential to provide safety net for child.*) Several steps were taken to address Rhanda's situation. The psychologist began by building a relationship with Rhanda. Rhanda's consent was obtained, so the psychologist could speak with Rhanda's obstetrician to explore support options and to enhance the intrauterine environment for her unborn child. The family preservation team talked to the drug–alcohol treatment center staff to discuss possible modifications in their program, which included family counseling with her mother and opportunities for supported interactions with Tony and her boyfriend. The family preservation team also wanted to ensure that there was adequate discharge planning from the drug and alcohol treatment center, with communication across providers and real community-based support.

Influences of Caregiver Depression

Maternal depression, which depletes the caregiver's energy and engagement, contributes to attachment and behavioral difficulties in infants and young children (Chinitz, 1995). Green (1993) suggested that often caregivers do not recognize their symptomatology of depression; therefore, it is important for clinically trained practitioners to explore the state of the caregivers' well-being or assist their access to clinical services. Birtchnell (1988) found that depression in adults occurred frequently within the context of marital conflict and divorce and was associated with the selection of spouses who also had disturbances (Birtchnell, 1988). These findings suggest that it is the accumulation of these multiple adverse circumstances that contribute to risks for their children, which is consistent with the multirisk model discussed in chapter 3. The findings of Goodman, Brogan, Lynch, and Fielding (1993) also support this multiple-risk factor model. In their study of 96 families, they found that fathers' psychiatric status and mothers' marital status were related to children's (ages 5 through 10 years) decreased social and emotional competence. For these same group of children, maternal depression in itself was only related to their children's decreased popularity (e.g., social networks with peers) as rated by their teachers. These results suggest that the interaction of multiple familial factors—maternal depression, paternal psychopathology, and divorce—contribute to less effective social competence in older children. Of great concern is the link of maternal depression with generalized negative effects on children (Goodman et al., 1993). Field (1987), in her study of mothers experiencing postpartum depression, found that their infants responded less positively during face-to-face interaction than did infants of nondepressed mothers. Field has argued that the infants mirrored the behavior and affect of their mothers. Giannino and Tronick (1988) also found that mothers who were depressed were less responsive to infant signals, which resulted in inadequately coordinated interactions. Cohn, Matias, Tronick, Connell, and Lyons-Ruth (1986) found similar results with a group of older infants whose mothers were of low socioeconomic status and displayed high levels of chronic depression. These mothers demonstrated lower levels of positive affect and less contingent responsiveness than mothers without depression. In addition, when their infants were 12 months of age, the mothers with chronic depression were more hostile and interfered more with their infants' goal-directed behavior than the typical control mothers. Another pattern of maternal behavior suggested that mothers who were depressed showed labile behavior alternating between disengagement and intrusive overstimulation with their infants (Lyons-Ruth, Zoll, Connell, & Grunebaum, 1986). These findings are not surprising, given that caregiver emotional unavailability and insensitivity are highly associated with caregiver depression. At the same time there is evidence that these are the primary predictors of insecure caregiver–child attachment (Ainsworth, Blehar, Waters, & Wall, 1978).

Interventionists have been concerned with these caregiver behaviors because research demonstrates that infants and toddlers are at risk for developmental problems of affect disturbance, insecure attachment, and lowered cognitive performance when at least one caregiver has a history of depression (Giannino & Tronick, 1988; Tronick & Field, 1986). Field (1987) found that infants whose mothers were depressed were withdrawn and demonstrated limited positive affect when compared to their peers. A number of studies found that depression had increasingly greater impact on many aspects of child development, suggesting the cumulative nature of adverse effects (Egeland & Sroufe, 1981; Gaensbauer, Harmon, Cytryn, & McKnew, 1984; Spieker & Booth, 1988).

In their review of the literature, Cummings and Davies (1994) found that a wide range of challenging child behaviors was associated with caregiver depression. Zahn-Waxler, Iannoti, Cummings, and Denham

(1990) found that behavioral difficulties of 2-year-olds predicted more externalizing problems at 5 years of age in children whose mothers were depressed than in children whose mothers were not. Data from a longitudinal study implied that maternal depressive symptoms and maternal hostility were present from early on in the lives of children with conduct problems and that these children were more likely to be rated with an insecure pattern characterized as disorganized during infancy (Lyons-Ruth, Alpern, & Rapacholi, 1993). Forehand, Lautenschlager, Faust, and Graziano (1986) found support for the mediating role of poor child management techniques in the development of challenging behaviors in children of caregivers who were depressed.

Brain research is giving providers a better insight into the role of caregiver depression on the developing child. Based on the premise that caregiver behavior influences young children's ability to express and modulate emotions, Dawson et al. (1994) examined the impact of maternal depression on the biological systems, specifically the frontal cortex. The results of the research based on infants 13 to 14 months of age found that maternal depression impedes the babies brain activity, specifically the part of the brain associated with expression and regulation of emotions. Results of EEG indicate reduced brain activity on the left frontal region, which was associated with outwardly directed emotions such as joy, interest, or anger. Dawson et al. (1994) found that when mothers' depression was treated or went into remission, their infant's brain activity returned to normal. In light of this data, the need for early detection and intervention to support parents experiencing depression becomes crucial. This can be accomplished through appropriate referrals for counseling for parents, while simultaneously supporting parents' interaction with their children, requiring both a developmental and behavioral approach. The role of other family members is also important. Early intervention providers can support the other family members to take an active role with the child, as research has found participation of the nondepressed father and a strong relationship between the infant's parents moderate the impact of maternal depression on young children (Shore, 1997).

Influence of Maltreatment

Protection is one of the primary functions of caregiving. When there is a breakdown in this role, negative impacts on the child are seen. Risks to relationships are especially evident in situations of abuse and neglect. Overall, maltreatment was found to be associated with insecure patterns of attachment behavior (Crittenden, 1988), decreased social competence (Trickett, 1993), and impaired cognition for some children (Graziano, 1992). Although there are different categories of maltreatment (i.e., physical, sexual, and emotional abuse and physical and psychological neglect), it is often difficult to delineate types and sequelae because different forms of maltreatment so often occur simultaneously (Schneider-Rosen, Braunwald, Carlson, & Cicchetti, 1985). Although some caregivers, but certainly not all, report maltreatment during their own childhood, there is no clear explanation of why some families show an intergenerational pattern of abuse and others do not (Beckwith, 1990). Strauss (1980) suggested that it is a multitude of factors that predicts abuse, including a history of violence in one's own childhood, concurrent interspousal violence, and few satisfying social supports (e.g., lack of a supportive relationship or marriage, rare attendance at religious services, and no organization affiliations) that are predictive of abusive situations.

To identify caregivers who potentially are abusive prior to their violent behavior, there has been extensive research to determine patterns of interaction that lead to child maltreatment. Research proposes that mothers who are abusive are less sensitive to their infants by interfering with their infants' goal-directed behavior more frequently and displaying more hostile behavior (Lyons-Ruth et al., 1986). There are also differences in the behavior-management techniques used with their preschool children. Oldershaw, Walters, and Hall (1986) found that caregivers who are abusive used more commands and more power-assertive and less positively oriented strategies than nonabusive caregivers. Different patterns were found with mothers who were characterized as neglecting. They typically show decreased interaction, greater physical distance from their child, absence of affective expression, and decreased eye contact when compared with normative groups (Crittenden & Bonvillian, 1984).

Recent research showed that abuse and neglect influenced brain development, specifically the left hemisphere, where language and logical thought are processed (Perry, 1996). Results indicated that there were differences in brain electrical activity, with fewer nerve-cell connections between areas of the brain in children who were abused than children in nonabusive relationships. Those with the most abnormal recordings were most likely to be aggressive. In addition, Perry (1996) found that the cortex in groups of neglected children was 20% smaller on average than the control group. These results suggest that a preventive model of maltreatment is critical. MacMillan (1994) found that high quality home visitation programs that were initiated at birth were effective at preventing abuse and neglect. This type of program is successful when it can help parents reduce stress of parenting before unhealthy interactional patterns develop.

A multiple intervention approach that includes educational, vocational, and financial emphasis and draws from interagency supports can best support families who are abusive. Often provision of in-home family preservation services is key to successful intervention. Some children may need individual child therapy, but this treatment should not be offered in lieu of family–child therapy. Children can also be supported in high-quality child care. The family and family preservation team need to carefully select and monitor the child care program, where staff ensure safety, set behavioral limits, provide opportunities for positive peer interactions, and nurture and express affection. All of these efforts help to connect the child and family with community supports and need to be combined with long-term support and follow-up.

Assessing Caregiver–Child Interaction

This chapter has presented three strong arguments that propose that early relationships and caregiver–child interaction are critical for healthy child development:

1. Early caregiver–child interactions and relationships influence child development;
2. Secure attachments between caregivers and infants are related to positive cognitive, behavioral, social–emotional outcomes; and
3. Early dyadic relationships can influence brain development.

Knowing that dyadic interactions play a critical role in development, the important question is how can providers assess and support caregivers in their interactions with their children? There is now substantial data to guide intervention in supporting parents' interactions with their children (Rosenberg & Robinson, 1988). Conclusions drawn from these data have been used to formulate early intervention models that "promote interaction styles presumed to foster optimal development and to discourage those associated with negative outcomes" (Lussier, Crimmins, & Alberti, 1994, p. 13).

MacDonald and Carroll (1994) identified five adult interactive styles that support positive caregiver–child interaction. These include (a) balanced interactions, (b) interaction matched to the child's developmental ability, (c) sensitivity and responsiveness to the child's signals, (d) emotional engagement through mutually reinforcing interactions, and (e) interactions that are nondirective. The potential benefits for children when their interaction partner uses these interaction styles are outlined in Table 6.2. Similar frameworks have been proposed by Bromwich (1981), Mahoney and Powell (1988), Barnard (1976), and Rosenberg and Robinson (1988). Each of these researchers also developed a scale that providers use to assess adult–child interaction. Assessment of dyadic interaction determines the strengths of the interaction and the behavior patterns that promote high-quality interaction that are mutually satisfying. Assessing interactions that are less satisfying can provide useful information that can guide intervention practices. Bailey and Wolery (1992) caution providers that assessment and intervention should be implemented with care so that families do not perceive this as a judgment of their adequacy as a caregiver. The rationale and supporting empirical evidence for the selection of these variables is discussed in the following section.

Interactions That Are Balanced and Nondirective

Balanced interactions indicate that both the child and the adult take turns in assuming the lead in the interaction. It is a synchronous dance with a fluid change of leads. Frustration will likely occur when one partner dominates (Trad, 1990). Bruner (1975) found that when the interaction is bal-

Table 6.2. Potential Consequences for Children When Their Interactive Partner Uses Facilitative Adult Styles

Adult Style	Consequences for Child
Balance: Interact frequently and as much as the child	Child learns to take turns, to give and take Child moves from passive to active role Child develops an expectation to interact Child learns to respond reciprocally Child acts more socially competent Child is more motivated to communicate when he or she has frequent control and success Child is allowed to interact at his or her pace
Match: Act and communicate in ways the child is able	Child is motivated to attend when adult matches Child more easily learns matched actions, sounds, and words Child has more opportunities to construct meanings at his or her own developmental pace Child learns more from models he or she can do Child is more motivated to communicate when adult's ideas are matched to his or her interests
Be responsive: Respond sensitively to the child's world	Child learns that adult response is reinforcing Child is rewarded for small developmental steps Child's self-esteem increases; thus child is more motivated to continue learning Child learns to know the differences between developmentally acceptable and unacceptable behavior Child learns his or her little developmental steps are valuable Child learns to stay in social interactions Child learns that his or her nonverbal behavior can have communicative effects
Be nondirective: Allow the child guidance with the freedom to be expressive	Child becomes more active and less passive Child stays in interactions longer Child experiences more successes that support increased competence Child receives models of what he or she can do when adults use comments rather than questions that test more than guide Child learns to communicate from his or her own ideas rather than from the adult's ideas
Emotionally attached: Be mutually reinforcing with the child	Child learns to enjoy being with people and returns for frequent learning opportunities Child becomes more interested in being with people than in being alone Child is likely to take communicative risks Child is motivated to communicate Child feels competent and successful

Source: From *Infant-Toddler Intervention: The Transdisciplinary Journal*, Vol. 4(3), by J. D. MacDonald and J. Y. Carroll. © 1994. Reprinted with permission of Delmar Publishers, a division of Thompson Learning.

anced, the child is more likely to learn to be social and communicative. Mahoney and Powell (1988) found that infants with disabilities whose mothers allowed them to take the lead and supported child-initiated activities had the highest developmental abilities as measured by the Bayley Scales of Infant Development (Bayley, 1969). These data suggest that it is vital to have a balance between adult-directed and child-directed interactions to obtain the desirable outcome of reciprocal exchanges.

Specific strategies to facilitate a balance of child- and adult-directed interactions are described in the following illustration:

Tanya, a 15-month-old, was referred for early intervention services because of her physician's concerns about her overall developmental delays. No medical diagnosis was determined, yet the developmental assessment completed by the early intervention team suggested overall delayed development. During an initial home visit, the early intervention provider observed Mr. Johnson, Tanya's grandfather, and Tanya playing. It was clear that her grandfather wanted Tanya to succeed as he was very directive, picking the toys for Tanya to play with, and demonstrating to her how to play with the toys (*adult directed interaction limits active learning*). He frequently guided Tanya through the motions when she did not respond correctly (*need to allow for the least amount of prompts that will ensure success*). Tanya responded to this approach by becoming more passive, which led to the transactional effect of Mr. Johnson becoming more directive. This pattern of interaction was counterproductive and was frustrating for both Tanya and her grandfather.

The provider demonstrated two strategies that helped Tanya take the lead: (a) giving Tanya choices and (b) imitating Tanya's behavior. The provider served as a supportive coach in this situation, gently guiding Mr. Johnson through the interaction. Together Mr. Johnson and the provider identified two of Tanya's favorite toys. When Mr. Johnson presented the toys, Tanya looked at them. Mr. Johnson began to reach toward Tanya's hand to guide her to touch the toy. The provider coached him to wait a little longer and to shake each toy slightly to help attract Tanya's attention to the toy. (*Coaching enables the caregiver to remain active*). Much to Mr. Johnson's surprise and delight, Tanya reached toward the slinky and began to shake it. Her grandfather was encouraged to imitate Tanya's shaking movement and then to pause. Tanya watched and then repeated the motion (*mutually enjoyable interaction is likely to be repeated*). The result of this interaction was that Mr. Johnson began to view Tanya as competent, and Tanya began to become an active play partner. Most critical was that both enjoyed the interaction.

Matched Interaction to the Child's Developmental Abilities and Interests

Developmental match occurs when interactions with the child are developmentally meaningful and match the child's interests (MacDonald & Carroll, 1994). Presenting activities at the appropriate level increases the likelihood of the child maintaining interest in the activity and learning new concepts (MacDonald & Carroll, 1994; Mahoney & Powell, 1988). When a mismatch occurs, the child is more likely to leave the interaction and miss a learning opportunity. In her work with infants born preterm, Field (1987) highlighted the importance of sustaining an optimal level of "stimulation." Mothers who were overstimulating had an increase in disengagement cues by their infants. These findings suggest the need for developmental assessment to identify and evaluate interactions to optimally match the interaction with the child's abilities. Vygotsky's (1978) concept of proximal zone relates to this discussion and has implications for intervention. The *zone of proximal development* refers to those abilities that the child can display during an interaction with the adult but cannot show independently. Vygotsky recommends that activities be presented that are slightly discrepant from the child's current repertoire. The parent then facilitates the child's independence by providing graduated cues (the process of *scaffolding*) to support him or her in solving the problem (Silber, 1989). Effective use of scaffolding is associated both with increased levels of cognitive competence in young children (Wood, 1980) and communication with peers (Martinez, 1987). See the following example:

A 2-year-old is presented with a narrow container and a strand of beads and then observed to determine if he could manipulate the beads into the container. He may first use a trial and error approach, by trying to place one bead in at a time. When they keep falling out, he then hands them to the adult for help. The adult models an approach, such as dangling the strand into the container, then hands the materials to the child to see if he imitates the response. If this strategy is not helpful, the adult may help him by placing part of the strand into the container and verbally or manually prompting him through the steps. The outcome of this "least to most" scaffolding process is to allow the child success with the least amount of help, yet providing him the necessary support for his success. His pride in doing it himself helps support both cognitive development and self-esteem.

Sensitivity and Responsiveness to the Child's Signals

The interaction style that receives the most attention includes sensitivity and responsiveness, the adult's capacity to "perceive and interpret the child's signals and interventions and to respond quickly and appropriately" (Beckwith, 1990, p. 56). Early attachment research primarily focused on the maternal contributions to the development of attachment behavior, with sensitivity being a key ingredient. Ainsworth, Bell, and Stayton (1972) found that mothers who behave sensitively, responsively, and positively to their infants promote secure attachment behavior. Other research demonstrates similar relationships (Goldberg, 1990; Plunkett et al., 1986). Goldberg reported that increased sensitivity, responsiveness, and accessibility positively related to the development of secure relationships. Conversely, insecure attachments were characterized by interactions in which the mother was minimally involved, unresponsive to infant signals, or intrusive, resulting in less synchronous interactions.

Thompson and Lamb (1983) suggested that mothers' sensitivity in responding appropriately to their infant's signals also influences their infant's skill in regulating states of emotional arousal and their use of emotional signals. Girolametto, Verbey, and Tannock (1994) found that increased maternal responsiveness resulted in increased joint engagement (i.e., the ability to initiate and sustain interaction). Lussier et al. (1994) used a within-subjects design to investigate the effects of adult interaction styles on infant engagement. They found that infants whose parents responded to their cues appropriately spent more of their time in interactive forms of engagement. In contrast, infants with an unresponsive adult spent a large percentage of their time either disengaged or focused on object play. These results lend empirical support to the belief that infants respond rapidly and differentially to differences in interaction styles.

Thompson and Lamb (1983) discussed two alternative interactive patterns to well-synchronized interaction between parent and child: those that are predictably unresponsive or those that are markedly inconsistent. Take the following example:

Kyle's grandmother, who is his primary caregiver, provides for his basic needs (e.g., food, and shelter). She typically feeds Kyle, who is 9 months old, by giving him his bottle as he lays in his crib. She has limited time to provide him with social interaction, as she has many other caregiving demands from her other children and grandchildren. Kyle's cries are often unattended. When he cries, he eventually falls asleep or self-quiets. When the early interventionist made his first home visit to get acquainted with the family, he was struck with how solemn Kyle was. When he tried to engage him, Kyle engaged visually, but was aloof and did not respond socially.

Thomson and Lamb (1983) suggested that infants who encounter unresponsive social environments, such as described with Kyle, potentially result in a flattened range of affect. In this situation, the provider would want to problem solve with the grandmother about how to reduce some of the caregiving demands that she encounters. If these strategies worked and resulted in the grandmother being more socially accessible to Kyle, then the provider could begin to support her in being more socially responsive to Kyle.

The second alternative to synchronous interactions is inconsistent responding (Thompson & Lamb, 1983). Experiencing inconsistent responses to regulatory signals may lead the infant to persistent demands.

Latisha crawls to her mother, raises her hands, signaling that she wants up. Her mother immediately picks her up and gives her a big hug. Later that day her mother is preoccupied as Latisha begins to vocalize that she wants to play. Latisha persists with several bids for her mother's attention, tugging at her pant leg, and vocalizing, and when she is unsuccessful she begins to cry. Her mother picks her up roughly and scolds her for always needing attention.

Latisha learns from this situation that persistence and crying result in being picked up. The provider will want to coach Latisha's mother to read Latisha's cues earlier, so that she does not reinforce Latisha's negative signals. Both the cases of Kyle and Latisha illustrate interaction patterns that are likely to result in lessened coping capacity for the infant. Giannino and Tronick (1988) labeled these as abnormally stressful interactions and also suggested that infants will learn abnormal patterns of self-regulation and coping from these experiences. It is critical for providers to recognize these stressful caregiver–child interactions and support the family in developing with their children consistent positive patterns of interaction.

Emotional Engagement–Attunement

Emotional engagement, often described as parental warmth, plays an important role in caregiver–child relationships. Research suggests that parental warmth, measured by expression of positive affect and emotional signaling systems such as facial, postural, and vocal cues, is associated with improved short-term cognitive performance (Clarke-Stewart, 1973) as well as long-term effects of positive academic performance (Estrada, Arsenio, Hess, & Holloway, 1987). Such cues serve to regulate caregiver and infant interaction (Beckwith, 1990). Warm interactions of the mother also provide the foundation for compliance and internalized controls (Maccoby & Martin, 1983). Fathers' positive engagement was also associated with low externalizing scores and fewer school behavior problems (Mosley & Thompson, 1995), whereas lack of paternal involvement and unaffectionate father–son interactions were associated with serious antisocial problems (Baker & Heller, 1996). These studies suggest fathers' relationships with their sons influence subsequent social behavior. Furthermore, DeKlyen et al. (1998) suggested that limit-setting and discipline may be less effective in the absence of positive, warm relationships.

Emotional availability of the caregiver is related to the degree to which infants explore their environments (Sorce & Emde, 1981). In a naturalistic study, emotional availability was shown to affect the level of children's pretend play and the duration of the play episodes positively (Slade, 1987). Stern (1984) discussed the importance of attunement—in other words, whether the adult plays back the child's inner feelings. For example, if the mother soothes her crying infant or laughs and smiles in delight in response to her infant initiating a pat-a-cake game, the mother is attuned to the infant's emotional state. In contrast, if the mother shouts at the toddler to stop crying when he falls down or ignores his joy of building a tower and knocking it down, she is emotionally out of sync. In these circumstances, providers can assist the caregiver in being a better observer and interpreter of the infant's emotional state and support him or her in "playing back" these feelings to the infant.

Interactions That Are Nondirective

Children learn by doing. This is based on the assumptions of developmental theorists who emphasize the importance of the child's active, social–constructive role in learning. Research suggests that children learn more readily when they share control and directions (Goldberg, 1990; Mahoney & Powell, 1988). These results do not mean that all directions and controls are eliminated but imply that social and communication development is enhanced when children are self-motivated rather than having their behavior constantly regulated by adults (MacDonald & Carroll, 1994). Mahoney and Powell (1988) found that adults using nondirective interactive styles have children who have higher levels of communication skills and are more actively engaged in play activities. In contrast, directive mothers' children demonstrated increased avoidance, ignoring, and passive watching styles of interacting.

Lussier et al. (1994) found a somewhat different pattern of outcomes. Their data indicated that children exposed to highly stimulating directive styles engaged in the activity, but were passive, exhibiting primarily watching behavior. Therefore, it is important for providers to support parents in self-monitoring their own behavior when interacting with their child and to facilitate opportunities for the parent to build on the child's interest in play.

Supporting Caregiver–Child Interaction

Of utmost importance is for early intervention to provide individualized services to support caregivers in interaction with their young children. Psychologists play a vital role as both direct providers in supporting the family–child relationship and as consultants in facilitating other providers' journeys toward family-centered intervention that targets dyadic interaction. The goal of early intervention in relationship to caregiver–child interaction is twofold: (a) supporting the caregivers' interaction with their children to support the child's development and (b) changing the maladaptive patterns of interaction and insecure models of attachment to support both the child and parent to achieve a satisfactory relationship (Chinitz, 1995). A theme of this book is that intervention with families and their young children requires a multitude of approaches based on the family's priorities, concerns, and resources. Typically the intervention team provides guidance on developmentally appropriate intervention, explores adaptations based on the child's unique repertoire, and supports the family in accommodating their parenting style to their child's particular capacities (e.g., decreased affect, restricted schemes, or limited communicative intent). Psychologists and other providers can be instrumental in addressing clinical issues with the family. Intervention may include dialoguing with families to explore relevant issues in their own histories that affect their child-rearing tendencies or relationship with their child, supporting the family in altering less supporting interactive patterns, or managing difficult behaviors (Chinitz, 1995). The challenge for early intervention programs is to ensure that one component of their intervention focuses on interaction strategies. Typically, early intervention providers' training focuses on promoting children's development, with less attention to strategies that support caregiver–child relationships. Both preservice and inservice programs need to be implemented to enhance provider skills to gain competencies in this area. (See chapter 8 for further discussion.) A caregiver-mediated model is often implemented to address difficulties in parent–child interaction. The outcome of such a model of intervention is the creation of a working partnership with caregivers on behalf of the child (Seitz & Provence, 1990). McCollum and Yates (1994) have identified six strategies, described in Table 6.3, to promote family-centered interaction. Caregiver support includes providing information about the appropriate developmental content as well as the adult interactional strategies that promote reciprocal and mutually satisfying interactions. The provider does not assume an "expert" role with the family but may model interactions with the child and quickly focus the child's enjoyment with the provider to strengthen that relationship. The provider can assist parents in enhancing their interactional styles by occasional but infrequent modeling, sharing information in a nondidactic fashion, and fostering problem solving. Take the following example:

A provider may observe a 4-year-old child begin to protest and move away from a play activity that his father has presented. The provider can encourage the father to share his ideas about why his son lost interest. Possible alternatives may be that the child is tired, the toy is too easy or too difficult, or a preceding setting event (e.g., tantrum by a sibling) adversely affected the young boy's play. Each of these alternatives may suggest a different interactional strategy. The provider then can support the father in reengaging his son based on the proposed solution.

In this case they identified that the multipiece puzzle activity was too difficult. By choosing a simpler puzzle, the father enabled his son to be successful. Not only did the child become reengaged in the activity, but his father experienced positive feelings about the interaction and his caregiving.

This scenario demonstrates the importance of providing sufficient support to enhance the father's parenting efficacy, while enabling him (rather than the provider) to foster the interaction (cf. McCollum & Yates, 1994). In

Table 6.3.   Overview of Caregiver–Child Intervention Strategies

1. *Establish a supportive context.* Elements of the environment are arranged or rearranged by the interventionist to increase the probability of playful interaction.
2. *Acknowledge caregiver competence.* Developmentally facilitative behaviors of the caregiver are warmly recognized and expanded, as are characteristics of child competence.
3. *Focus attention.* Aspects of the interaction are commented on, questioned, or expanded to draw the caregiver's attention to particular competencies or actions.
4. *Provide information.* Information about the child's developmental agenda is given within the context of play.
5. *Model.* Dyadic interaction roles are momentarily taken on by the interventionist.
6. *Suggest.* The caregiver is given a specific suggestion as to what to do with the child.

Source: J. A. McCollum & T. J. Yates, Dyad as focus, triad as means: A family-centered approach to supporting caregiver-child interaction, *Infants and Young Children* (p. 56). Reprinted with permission. Copyright © 1991 Aspen Publishers, Inc.

Table 6.4. Guidelines for Promoting Caregiver–Child Relationships

Help families understand the importance of early caregiver relationships on later child development.

Provide young children with consistent environments to avoid child distress and promote healthy interactions.

Identify with families the stresses associated with coping with their child with poor self-regulation patterns and provide supports to reduce stress.

Help children become self-motivated by providing them choices and letting them take the lead in play interactions.

Present children with play activities that are at an appropriate developmental level.

Support caregivers to become contingently responsive to their children.

Help caregivers to be emotionally available to their children by demonstrating positive affect and warmth.

Help caregivers to develop reasonable limit setting for their young child within a developmentally supportive context.

addition, the intervention promotes building family alliance and gains treatment acceptability from the family.

Intervention can potentially have long-term benefits by assisting caregivers to gain skills in observing their children, understanding the importance of play, and adjusting the complexity of the play activities as their children continue to grow and develop (Seitz & Provence, 1990). Providers need to support families in using play activities as a vehicle both for promoting the child's learning and for supporting the child in expressing emotions. (See Table 6.4 for guidelines that promote parent–child relationships.) Within this play context, the child learns to process and to react to environmental information. Caregiving routines serve as a context for interaction (Carmen, 1994). Helping the parents to incorporate the child's goals within these naturally occurring routines can facilitate generalization and simultaneously provide a framework for mutually enjoyable interactions. (For further discussion, see chapter 5.) The case study at the end of the chapter demonstrates strategies to facilitate caregiver–child interaction within the context of naturally occurring routines.

Supporting Caregivers in Managing Challenging Behaviors

Other textbooks present greater detail about specific behavioral interventions with young children. Watkins and Durant (1992) offer a useful reference, which considers developmental issues and environmental factors in addition to behavioral techniques. This section of the chapter contributes a more clinical focus, such as recommendations for cognitive–behavioral reframing in caregivers. It also presents guidelines for supporting other providers who extend interventions to families with young children experiencing difficult behavioral patterns.

Promoting Interactions Through Use of Developmentally Appropriate Time-In

Paternal as well as maternal negative discipline is associated with externalizing child behavior (DeKlyen et al., 1998). Specifically, fathers' negativity is related to increased negative peer interaction and increased aggressiveness and uncooperativeness (Katz & Gottman, 1995). These two studies suggest that there is a need to help parents learn positive approaches with their children. One of the first priorities in addressing behavioral challenges of early childhood is ensuring an adequate "time-in" environment in which the child's primary interactions with the adult are positive. Sensitivity and responsiveness to child cues by supporting yet not over prompting can be difficult, particularly for young children with poor self-regulation, limited sustained attention; or high activity levels; significant aggression; or social reciprocity difficulties. Young children who have restricted repertoires of a stereotypic nature and who also may withdraw when an adult or other child approaches may need providers with expertise in multisystem developmental delays (e.g., self-regulation, social, motor, and cognitive difficulties).

The critical issue is ensuring an interaction environment that is sufficiently engaging for the particular child and family. Some children have a lengthy history of grossly inadequate family or community environments, which may further complicate ensuring adequacy of the activity or interaction. In supporting parents and guardians, the goal is reasonable limit-setting for young children within a developmentally supportive context. The parameters around the limits usually can vary somewhat in terms of leniency to accommodate families with diverse parenting styles. Caregivers with a more permissive style may need support as they attempt to impose some limits on their young child who exhibits a significant degree of opposition to adult direction.

Caregiver Self-Monitoring and Self-Reinforcement

Attention to time-in should not be restricted to a child focus. Caregiver time-in is crucial as well, both in interactions with young children and in adult-focused activities with a partner, friends, or alone. Family members need to rejuvenate themselves to have the physical and mental energy to manage young children's difficult behaviors. Therefore, it is important for providers to be sensitive and responsive to caregivers' cues (e.g., uncertainty, displeasure, emotional disengagement, inconsistency, and harshness) that they are overwhelmed. Because all providers do not have such training, psychologists should support others in recognizing areas of family difficulty and in promoting synchronous caregiver–child relationships.

For example, if a family member's nonverbal behavior suggests discomfort (e.g., facial expressions, blushing, moving away from child), the sensitive provider might offer a reflection of feeling (e.g., you seem a little uncomfortable) or occasionally even use self-disclosure (e.g., I felt uncomfortable, too, the first few times I used this strategy with young children). Sometimes it also can be helpful to normalize the family member's reaction (e.g., many parents of children who are aggressive wonder how they can stay calm enough to play with their child). Other strategies include labeling the family member's behavior in a nonjudgmental fashion (e.g., you closed your eyes and shook your head when your child talked back to you), commenting on the child's behavior (e.g., she talked very loudly at first, but now she is quieting down because you have ignored her behavior), and backtracking using a supportive statement along with a gentle reminder of the next step in the interaction with the child (e.g., you're doing a great job of praising your child; now you can ask him to put away the toys). In their attempt to be supportive and responsive, providers need to be aware of the timing of their input. Sometimes remaining silent and waiting for a later time to comment is the most appropriate form of support.

The potential for misusing behavioral strategies, such as contingent ignoring the child's tantruming when denied a cookie before dinner or brief chair time-out if the child hits a peer, is great. However, these strategies may not be used with sufficient fidelity to protocol to effect behavioral improvement. Even minor deviations for some children can preclude the positive gains caregivers are expecting. For example, for some young children, caregiver failure to set limits for even fairly minor noncompliance can lead to rapid escalation of very difficult tantruming. At this level of intensity, caregivers may avoid implementing a behavioral strategy altogether. They also may attempt a consequence only to experience such an aversive situation that they avoid attempting the strategy again. Cognitive–behavioral strategies, such as verbal mediation, can supplement developmental and behavioral techniques for family members experiencing high degrees of stress, particularly if combined with strategies that enhance family members' internal coping mechanisms or support their access to external family and community resources. Caregivers can be guided to use self-talk (self-mediation) in key features of the protocol (e.g., remain calm, do not yell, do not restrain, do not use force to implement a brief chair time-out) as well as self-reinforcement (e.g., good for me, I'm ignoring the burst in my child's whining; great, I noticed my child was becoming panicked at the loud sounds and helped him self-calm). In addition, supporting their partner relationship and social contacts so that they are energized may be indicated. Helping families adopt these types of strategies is another key component in intervention that targets supporting caregiver–child interaction and relationship building.

Conclusion

As family policy is translated into early intervention practice, it is critical to understand the dynamics of the caregiver–child relationship, which is at the heart of intervention (McCollum & Yates, 1994). The goal of this approach is to enable families to interact with their children with pleasure and success and to achieve satisfying relationships and positive outcomes for their children (Tronick & Field, 1986). This chapter provides a backdrop for providing early intervention by illustrating the usefulness of attachment theory and the transactional model in understanding the caregiver–child relationship and the ecological contexts that affect the relationship. This review suggests the need for a blend of theoretical paradigms in providing interaction-focused intervention within the context of naturalistic family routines and settings. This approach promotes incorporating the cultural and personal values of families by accommodating to the social customs of the family and community life. Therefore, generalization and maintenance of synchronous interactions are far more likely.

For a variety of reasons, caregivers may be facing challenging life circumstances. Although a child-focused approach, whether developmental or behavioral, certainly can facilitate child development, we strongly advocate a broader family-systems orientation in which the effect of child intervention on the family is considered. Some young children exhibit extremely challenging behaviors. Furthermore, caregivers may be exhausted from providing medical cares for their child, managing siblings, and attempting to balance the demands of caregiving and work. Some families also may be encountering people who are "experts" in what they should or should not be doing for their child, thus potentially undermining caregivers' and guardians' sense of competence. Infusion of an interaction-based intervention approach into early childhood programs underscores the need to have skilled providers who can assess social–interactive behavior and strategically use microskills to support families in nurturing a "goodness of fit" with their young child (cf. Aydlett, 1993). For effective early intervention, it is essential that programs recognize the importance of supporting the caregiver–child relationship and build staff competency to implement this family-centered approach.

Adelaide: A Family Story

Adelaide is a 15-month-old girl who was referred by a state department of social services to a developmental pediatrician for "nonorganic failure to thrive." Height and weight measurements from the WIC office (where her 31-year-old mother, Ms. Edel, obtained vouchers for Similac with iron) at 12 months was significantly below the 5th percentile. The developmental pediatrician was concerned that Adelaide's feeding history provided by her mother was not "reliable" given Adelaide's limited weight gain. Because concerns that adequate feeding could not be ensured in the home environment, given Adelaide's pattern of poor weight gain over the previous year and the ruling out of an organic basis, the pediatrician recommended temporary foster placement to document Adelaide's ability to gain weight. Concurrently, referral was made to pediatric psychology to gain a better understanding of Ms. Edel's basic caregiving repertoire.

History

Adelaide was born full-term and delivered by C-section for breech presentation, with birth weight of 4 pounds, 9 ounces. Adelaide has had several episodes of otitis media, but no chronic or recurring upper or lower respiratory infections. Her mother reports that Adelaide has no problem with emesis and that she has regular stool patterns without diarrhea. Living with Adelaide's mother are a 7-year-old son (who manifests substantive externalizing behaviors both at home and at school) and an 8-year-old daughter (who has academic difficulties). Ms. Edel is uncertain about whom Adelaide's father is. Social services referred Ms. Edel for a psychological assessment (elsewhere) "to determine cognitive ability and current mental health status." This assessment, combined with the discharge summary from a psychiatric hospitalization three years earlier, indicated dysthymia, borderline cognitive capacity, remarkably low self-esteem, suicidal ideation, insecure attachment, and dependent personality traits (*relational history and current mental health concerns may affect her ability to interact successfully with Adelaide*). Ms. Edel sustained physical and mental abuse from her ex-husband, who is an alcoholic.

Initial Assessment

Initial activities with Adelaide largely consisted of parallel movement as Ms. Edel forcefully depressed or rotated knobs that activated sounds on a toy, averting eye contact with her daughter (*lack of emotional engagement*). On the occasions when she helped Adelaide activate a musical toy, she did not allow her time to experiment with it (*need to promote active exploration by the child*). During feeding, Ms. Edel gave Adelaide a bottle and laid her on the floor in the midst of toys (*indication of a lack of emotional engagement*). Ms. Edel herself played with the toys, intermittently glancing at Adelaide and occasionally smiling at her. Adelaide accepted a few bites of toast when her mother offered it, but refused when her mother continued to place the toast in her mouth. Throughout the session, Adelaide typically wandered about the room. Adelaide played with a variety of toys (musical shape box, pegs, piano, telephone) from approximately 3 seconds to 1 minute per toy. There were several safety concerns as Ms. Edel infrequently responded to Adelaide's climbing on furniture and putting small toys in her mouth.

Intervention

Intervention clearly needs to be systemic and collaborative across agencies to safeguard all three children, particularly the vulnerable status of Adelaide, and to enhance Ms. Edel's strategies for managing her own challenging issues. The ultimate goal is an accelerated rate of weight gain for Adelaide, which Ms. Edel identified as her aim. To begin with, then, empathy is expressed for the mother as her concerns and priorities are acknowledged, thus helping to establish a therapeutic relationship. Given Ms. Edel's own fragile state and prolonged history of feeling devalued and incompetent, a directive therapeutic approach is strongly contraindicated. Both a developmental and behavioral approach can be clinician directed. It is not the paradigm that determines the degree of directiveness but rather the pattern of influencing and microskills the clinician uses.

For example, for the goals of reducing Adelaide's level of wandering and building her repertoire of developmentally appropriate play, the following scenario illustrates a blended developmental and behavioral approach, but from a perspective that falls to consider the low sense of caregiving self-efficacy in the mother. Such an approach is ill-advised for this particular family.

The clinician models play with Adelaide, building on "putting in and dumping out" schemes by placing a geometric shape into a container and then appropriately waiting until she dumps it out on her own. When Adelaide looks at the clinician, signaling "do it again," she begins laughing as the clinician merely holds the shape towards her, enabling Adelaide to place it on her own. When Adelaide smiles at putting the shape into the container, the clinician also vocalizes delight.

The same play theme is incorporated into a mealtime where Adelaide is provided opportunities to take out pieces of dried cereal from a zip-lock baggie and to drop them back in while the clinician talks to her and feeds her several spoonfuls of baby food thickened with cereal (*intervention should provide a context for naturally occurring home routines*). When Adelaide, sitting at the table, refuses to open her mouth and swats at the spoon, the caregiver is requested to look away to reduce the reinforcement of the interfering behavior.

This strategy can help determine techniques that actually are effective with Adelaide. Moreover, it can be an efficient means of modeling a developmentally appropriate and nonaversive, behaviorally supportive approach for caregivers. However, such a tactic would likely serve to enhance Ms. Edel's sense of inadequacy (*my child laughs and eats for the clinician, but not for me*), and therefore, would serve an iatrogenic function. Moreover, implementing an extinction procedure (e.g., ignoring the child to eliminate negative behaviors) is not generally appropriate when caregivers engage in so few positive interactions with their child.

As an alternative, some degree of modeling initially is necessary if the caregiver has a minimal repertoire in developmentally appropriate play, sensitive and responsive interactions, and child care routines. This tactic, though, is quickly diminished, with a deliberate reframing of the "directive" from the clinician's perspective to that of the child. For instance, rather than saying, "You can smile at Adelaide when she takes a spoonful of cereal," the clinician can use the following approach, "Adelaide really likes it when you smile at her. She really smiles when you're smiling at her." This subtle distinction can offer a profound means of building caregiver self-confidence as well as skill.

Because the feeding routine is a complex social activity and not merely a mechanical procedure, a primary goal of intervention with this family is social interaction between Adelaide and her mother, which in turn can facilitate Adelaide's weight gain and overall development. Ms. Edel's own developmental history and experiential base make responsive caregiver–child interaction extremely difficult. Developmental sequelae of very poor quality interaction, limited sustained focus on play materials, and a disturbed eating pattern have resulted. This child repertoire has a transactional effect on this mother, who becomes increasingly unresponsive to her child's needs. To strengthen basic caregiving skills, the family support provider attends sessions and serves as the key link in supporting Ms. Edel in sustaining some degree of responsive social interaction and caregiving in the home.

7

Emerging Ethical Perspectives in Early Childhood

A family is finding it increasingly difficult to care for their 5-year-old son Aidan, who has severe disabilities and health problems, especially with the demands of their 2-year-old twins. What is in the best interests of Aidan? What is in the best interests of his family? The parents seek out others to support them as they deliberate this ethical dilemma.

Early intervention programs are finding families seeking support in many ethical situations, but it is unclear if caregivers are up to the task. Ethical principles and deliberation have received substantially less attention in the early childhood literature than any other content area we address in this book. Such a minimal emphasis on ethics is apparent both in undergraduate and graduate school and employed practice.

Interagency collaboration of community-based programs supporting young children and their families can present numerous ethical challenges as diverse providers attempt to balance their own ethical framework with support of the family's autonomy. Similarly, with rapid technologic advancement, there are new confrontations in values in the care for neonates who are medically fragile. Attention to ethical problem solving can assist psychologists and other providers in dealing with the challenges encountered in early childhood service delivery. Too often discussion of ethics related to early childhood populations is restricted to medically related situations, where providers support families who are faced with life-and-death decisions. Indeed, the literature is replete with examples related to infants who are medically fragile, with a striking inattention to ethical pondering in community-based programs.

This chapter illustrates the importance of gaining a broader perspective of ethical decision making by addressing how ethics is applied in early intervention and in the public policy arena. Theories and principles provide a conceptual basis for ethical deliberation and a solid foundation for considering ethical issues across the full range of early childhood populations and contexts. For a review of ethical theory and principles, see Beauchamp and Childress (1989); Fowler (1989); and Sandling, Carter, Moore, and Sparks (1993). These theories and principles are complex, requiring diligent study. Without an understanding of them, however, providers are not likely to be capable of the sophistication and sometimes tenacity necessary for ethical decision making in early childhood contexts. Examples are provided to illustrate ethical principles, which underpin family-centered care. This chapter addresses the need for reflection in ethical problem solving and professional codes of ethics. Most important, guidelines are proposed to enhance better-informed and broadly acceptable ethical decision making.

Ethics: Application to Early Intervention Practices

Ethics is a complex concept with a multiplicity of dimensions. The study of ethics examines the factual description of moral beliefs, "what is" (descriptive ethics) or "what ought to be" (normative ethics). As a branch of philosophy, ethics considers competing values to arrive at the best possible outcome in a particular situation. It involves the study of rational processes for determining the most morally desirable course of action in the context of disharmonious value choices. An ethical dilemma exists when values conflict and each value is morally defensible (Sandling et al., 1993).

Normative ethics serves three functions for the early intervention practitioner: (a) clarification, (b) illumination, and (c) comfort. Ethical reasoning helps to abate moral uncertainty by elucidating the questions and ethical components of the circumstance, thereby providing a degree of comfort. Ethical arguments help to clarify moral dilemmas by revealing general and specific obligations and values. Furthermore, they assist in diminishing moral distress when they are used in framing institutional policies that promote moral action (Fowler, 1989).

Principles of Ethics

Autonomy (considering the client's wishes), beneficence and nonmaleficence (considering the client's best interests), and justice (considering the client's best interests based on social factors) are the three predominant principles that guide ethical judgments in early childhood intervention. Because principles may conflict, they must be prioritized to determine which principle takes precedence (Sandling et al., 1993). Ethical principles form the core of ethical deliberation because they assist people in ascertaining their moral obligations and duties. Each principle assumes diverse interpretations and applications in clinical practice and interrelates with the other principles. Decision makers bring their own values, experiential base, and a personal ethical theory to clinical situations, all of which influence the dynamics of the ethical decision-making process.

Autonomy: Supporting Families in Ethical Decision Making

Autonomy is the respect for the rights of individuals to self-government or self-determination. The principle of autonomy asserts that individuals should decide for themselves what is in their own best interests. This respect for the moral agency of individuals is operationalized through the doctrine of informed consent. To appreciate the autonomous decisions and actions of families, they must be provided with adequate information to make a decision (full informedness). Furthermore, families must be sufficiently free of internal or external influences such that their decisions can be viewed as free participation (free consent or voluntariness). Rather than requiring that all information be provided, *the reasonable person standard* applies in situations in which the family of a young child must have all the information that a hypothetical reasonable person in a comparable situation would require to make a similar decision. It has gained acceptance in about 60% of the states in the United States. The reasonable person standard requires disclosure of all information applicable to a meaningful decision process for the family regarding both the proposed intervention and its inherent risks. The fundamental motivation for this standard is the "underlying belief that informed consent in law is a doctrine fashioned to permit [families] to be the agents of decision making and authorization" (Beauchamp & Childress, 1989, p. 88). The majority of supporters of the reasonable person standard assert that considerations of autonomy (client wishes) typically outweigh those of beneficence (best interests).

A fundamental premise applying to many ethical issues is that family-centered care and intervention should foremost be supportive of the family. It is important for providers in early childhood contexts to act in a manner that supports families' autonomy. Therefore, addressing all potential risks or limitations of early childhood services should be addressed openly. For instance, potential disadvantages of providing pull-out services (such as problems with generalization) in which students are removed from a general-education classroom and served in a separate special-education room or offering home-based services only during the day (possible unintentional reinforcement of disengagement or exclusion of working parent) should be presented to satisfy the reasonable-person standard. Clearly, early childhood providers must not coerce a family in making a particular decision about their young child. However, Fowler (1989) contended that providers can "attempt to persuade" (p. 960), although extending their point of view into undue influence must be avoided. Indeed, autonomy must be respected when families disagree as well as when their decision is one practitioners would have them make. In such circumstances, reflection on the ethical principles can help to manage emotional distress that may ensue. Autonomy is not absolute; families cannot oblige providers to act against their professional judgment in providing care.

Paternalism is a roadblock to autonomous decision making. In the best-interests standard from the paternalistic perspective, one individual "knows" the best course of action. Interventions that are paternalistic limit the individual's autonomy and freedom. For example, providers who believe they know what intervention context is best for a child might impose their recommendations on the family, which then limits the family's autonomy in determining treatment parameters for their child. Beauchamp and McCulloch (1984) regarded the essence of paternalism as an outweighing of the principle of autonomy on grounds of the principle of beneficence (doing good). They define paternalism as the intended restriction of the autonomy of one person by another, where the person of beneficence for the person whose autonomy is confined. Some degree of paternalism may be needed. For instance, a teacher may decide to describe to parents the benefits of using hand splints with their child and the potential risks that are presented if treatment is denied, even though the teacher believes the family will object. There still remains an intrinsic and enduring problem with deciding whose paternalistic judgment generates the best outcome for the young child (Engelhardt, 1986). The issue becomes whose substituted judgment would lead to the best outcome. In the *substituted judgment standard* of proxy action, the responsibility of the proxy moral agent is to make the decision the child would have made if competent. This standard grants the "incompetent" young child regard as a moral agent deserving autonomy.

Beneficence and Nonmaleficence: A Balance of Benefits and Harms

According to Beauchamp and Childress (1989), beneficence broadly asserts "an obligation to help others further their important and legitimate interests" (p. 194). Equally important to the obligation to confer benefits and actively to prevent and remove harms is the obligation to weigh and balance the possible goods against the possible harms of an action. Providing benefits is the principle of positive beneficence.

In addition to positive benefit to another, beneficence includes removal of harmful conditions and prevention of harm (Fowler, 1989). The demands of beneficence take us into the empirical literature to determine "harmful conditions" for young children and families. As an example with high-risk, premature infants, ambient noise, particularly associated with staff activities, has been found to effect a decrease in transcutaneous oxygen tension, followed by a rise in intracranial pressure, in turn followed by increases in heart rate and respiratory rate (Long, Lucey, & Philip, 1980). Nonsupportive handling (Long, Philip, & Lucey, 1980), poorly timed social and caregiving interactions (Gorski, 1983), and lack of opportunity for nonnutritive sucking (Anderson, Burroughs, & Measel, 1983) also have been associated with decreased transcutaneous oxygen saturation. In addition, preterm infants exposed to diurnally cycled lighting have demonstrated greater rate of weight gain, were able to be fed orally sooner, spent fewer days on the ventilator and on phototherapy, and exhibited augmented motor coordination compared to infants in noncycled lighting (Miller, White, Whitman, O'Callaghan, & Maxwell, 1995). Hence the principle of beneficence compels a method that removes deleterious conditions.

A principle of nonmaleficence indicates that the main goal is to do no harm. Beneficence and nonmaleficence are two distinct principles that on occasion may come into conflict. In such situations, nonmaleficence often outweighs the principle of beneficence. Duties of nonmaleficence include not imposing risks of harm as well as avoiding inflicting actual harm. It is possible to breach the obligation of nonmaleficence without acting maliciously and without being cognizant of or intending the harm or risk of harm. The following example illustrates an unintentional risk of harm to a family.

An early intervention team appreciated the extensive intervention needs of 20-month-old Jordan, who has a complex developmental presentation. The transdisciplinary team, with the home-based teacher as the primary provider, tries to compensate for the few hours they are able to provide direct services. They work with the father to help him learn the intensive treatment protocols. Although Jordan is making progress, his father is becoming exhausted and beginning to feel guilty about not spending more time with his 5-year-old daughter and wife. Fortunately, the psychologist on the team raised the issue of their duty of nonmaleficence and described a systems approach with regard to the family. The team gradually became more aware of the need to balance both beneficence and nonmaleficence. They then opened up a dialogue with Jordan's parents to revisit and revise their approach.

From a traditional medical viewpoint, the noninfliction of harm concentrates on avoiding physical harm through the use of medical intervention. From an expanded perspective, inflicting harm assumes a much broader scope to include psychosocial, spiritual, moral harm, or harm to the child's dignity (Fowler, 1989). Some authors assert that the principle of nonmaleficence should be applied to the effect of treatment decisions on the family as well as the infant (Silverman, 1992; Strong, 1984). There may be unintentional infliction of harm as a result of an intervention by a well-meaning provider, if there is not a thorough analysis of the child's developmental repertoire and experiential base and the family's acceptance of treatment approaches. For example, a psychologist may be working with a family who is concerned about their child's extreme noncompliance with most family routines. Time-out is one component of the intervention. The child cries inconsolably throughout the time-out procedure, and the family becomes quite distressed. It is incumbent on the psychologist to monitor if the distress is beyond what the family can handle emotionally (limiting risk of harm) and to modify the intervention as needed. In this light, nonmaleficence requires broad-based considerations and reflection.

The criteria for demarcating obligatory, optional, and wrong treatments derive from the client's wishes (a consideration of autonomy) and the client's best interests (considerations of beneficence and nonmaleficence). These criteria include whether the treatment would afford a reasonable likelihood of benefit and whether benefits would outweigh the burdens to the client (Beauchamp & Childress, 1989).

Following is an illustration of ethical principles applied to the decision-making process of a team of early childhood providers.

A school-based early childhood special education team may design a comprehensive intervention plan for a 3-year-old with pervasive developmental disorder, including participation in a five-day per week program with staff having expertise in language disorders, relationship difficulties, and rigid-play repertoires. Members of the team believe the program contains numerous best practices, such as transdisciplinary programming, inclusion of typical peer models, formative evaluation to provide frequent monitoring, and integrated services rather than pull-out treatment sessions. Hence the team recommends the program to the child's grandparents, who have custody.

When the grandparents object to such a program for their grandchild, the team reiterates its recommendation more strongly, emphasizing the benefits of a comprehensive program for their grandchild. When the grandparents intensify their objections, the team begins to process the grandparents' reactions and gradually confronts its own *paternalism*. In an effort to support the *family's autonomy*, the team listens more closely to their priorities and then provides information about several other programs. The grandparents express being comfortable with a twice a week, two-hour program. The team is satisfied that they have supported the family's autonomy while still upholding the principle of beneficence for the child (i.e., an early childhood program) and reducing the potential for nonmaleficence (i.e., withholding of intervention).

Justice

Distributive justice refers to just distribution in society, the implicit and explicit moral, legal, and cultural rules and principles under which individuals are obligated to cooperate. The weighing of risks, costs, and benefits is typical in circumstances of distributive justice (Beauchamp & Childress, 1989). As we examine issues of justice in early intervention, several questions emerge. Following are examples of justice-related ethical dilemmas.

- *Is there justice in early childhood programs?* Perhaps there is greater justice for families who are facile in negotiating the fragmented maze of maternal and child health programs; intergovernmental activities; and public and private interagency connections.
- *Is there equal justice given inconsistent or incomplete operationalizations of "need" (e.g., diversity in eligibility criteria, exclusion of behavioral and social–emotional needs)?* There are issues of justice when a family discovers that their child no longer qualifies for early intervention as they move to another state, although both states implement Part C services. It may also be viewed as "injustice" if a child has a social–emotional relationship disorder but cannot receive services because the state did not conceptualize this difficulty as part of its Part C eligibility criteria.
- *Who should reap the benefits, and who should bear the risks or costs?* Does a state decide to provide services for children at risk? If so, who funds this broad initiative?

A number of material principles of distributive justice have been proposed: to each person an equal share, to each person according to need, to each person according to effort, to each person according to contribution, to each person according to merit, to each person according to free-market exchanges (Rescher, 1966). Conflicts among these still can beget a serious quandary about priorities, including public policy debates. Even beginning with the a priori belief that everyone is of equal worth, disparities in allocation remain. Family constitution may create additional considerations because family resources are not infinite. Providers judge how to support families in making the best decisions for their children considering their own personal resources. Just allocation of resources to satisfy an adequate standard of educational and developmental supports, health care, and mental health care is especially troublesome as resources become increasingly sparse. Distributive justice relates to societal or macroeconomic issues. Macroallocation decisions relate to how much should be expended and what types of goods are to be made available in society. Such decisions are made by Congress, state legislatures, health insurance agencies, administrative agencies, and school boards, among others. At an individual or microeconomic level, microallocation decisions address the competing claims for resources among involved persons.

Sandling et al. (1993) addressed the tension in balancing macroallocation and microallocation policies, which are not mutually exclusive. At a micro level, according to Sandling and colleagues, it is morally wrong to consider finances in the equation of allocating health care. Such reasoning also would apply to Part C and Part B eligibility for early intervention and preschool services for young children with developmental delays. Similarly, if remaining open depends on a high collection rate from the majority of a hospital's patients, then the consequences of providing care at no charge must be weighed.

Such ethical decisions are very real for providers practicing in a variety of settings where "billable hours" are reality. The dilemma arises when sufficient revenue must be generated to cover costs associated with one's salary and benefits plus additional costs for interns and fellows, and at some facilities, expenses related to clerical and other support staff as well as facility overhead. When faced with the potential to work with a family with Medicaid coverage but from another state where reimbursement is very low, macroeconomic forces are likely to influence the microeconomic effort to support the particular family. Similarly, service coordinators may be able to find developmental services for young children only if the delay is significant (as measured by the state's criteria), thereby enabling funding.

Revenue issues aside, according to the American Psychological Association's (APA) 1990 "Ethical Principles of Psychologists," Principle 6, section d:

> Psychologists make advance financial arrangements that safeguard the best interests of and are clearly understood by their clients. They contribute a portion of their services to work for which they receive little or no financial return. (p. 393)

There is a two-fold quandary in providing young children and their families with developmental and family supports: (a) in setting limits so that sufficient resources are available for everyone and (b) in delineating standards so that all receive equal services. The moral questions underlying the principle of distributive justice relate to the issue of regulation —namely, what institution should set the standards? For instance, should it be laypersons; federal, state, or local government; consortium of hospitals; interagency council; school districts; or ethics committees? As technology extends treatment options, setting priorities becomes crucial. Such advances in either technologies or training of providers will engender new debates over allocation of resources (Sandling et al., 1993).

Need for Reflection in Clinical Practice

In the decision-making process, individuals enter in midstream, influenced by their past experiences, emotional responses, and moral sentiments (Callahan, 1988). When an ethical "workup" is initiated, substantive issues are identified and processed, continually checking and adjusting new debates and emotions. Actually effecting a decision necessitates determining who shall decide, the criteria by which these individuals are allowed to do so, and subsequently, the means by which the decisions or actions are to be set in motion in an acceptable manner that does not prevail over others' values (Thomasma, 1978). Table 7.1 offers guidelines to ethical deliberation in early childhood practice.

A crucial issue is the family–provider relationship, which should encourage the illumination of values, beliefs, and emotions of all concerned. Actively supporting parents–guardians early on can encourage their participation in decision making regarding their child's care. Not only should developmental and educational information be discussed thoroughly and with sensitivity, but ongoing support of the attachment relationship and parent–child interaction is critical. Parenting self-efficacy and sense of some degree of control and influence in their child's care can help to reduce their stress and to encourage problem solving in uncertain situations.

A mechanism for examining one's own values, expectations, and paternalism should be in place to facilitate ethical problem solving and support of the family's autonomy. Because the "possibility of self-serving rationalization" remains (Haas & Malouf, 1989, p. 14), self-reflection and a thoroughly personal engagement, dialogue with colleagues, imagining moral scenarios, and processing of factual data and emotional experiences are important. Indeed, "Sound ethical reflection is an essential component of professional development and practice" (Jordan & Meara, 1990, p. 107). However, examining one's personal history (e.g., contertransference) and feelings about a particular family and context may not have been emphasized in professional training or current practice. Following are sample questions that require personal reflection:

- How do I feel about relating such a diagnosis to a family?
- How do I feel when a parent challenges my judgment?
- How do I manage my frustration when there are no comprehensive, community-based early intervention programs for a given child?
- What about my own life experiences influence my perception of this child and family?

Table 7.1. Guidelines to Ethical Deliberation in Early Childhood Practice

For each child and family, identify the particular developmental and medical (if relevant) history and family and agency circumstances.

Delineate participants in the decision-making process and determine if an ethics committee should be consulted.

Convey the ethical dilemma.

Consider ethical theories to explore multiple morally acceptable actions and outcomes.

Delineate ethical principles and prioritize them if they conflict.

Examine and reflect on one's own life experiences and personal ethical theory.

Articulate and respect divergence in values.

Explore all notable consequences of ethical decisions to the child and family.

Process and integrate emotional distress to reach an equilibrium of emotion and reason.

Adopt an inclusionary model of ethical discussion, ensuring meaningful participation by all.

Promote institutional openness to divergent opinions.

Assume the role of devil's advocate to check and recheck rational and emotional defensibility.

Support other providers in reframing their moral distress and suffering.

Nurture the family–provider relationship.

Be empathic, flexible, and culturally sensitive when speaking with families.

Support family members' emotional regrouping to enhance their ethical deliberation.

Champion family autonomy and informed decision making, with attention to potential risks.

Refer to professional codes of ethics to elucidate ethical obligations.

Be knowledgeable about relevant legal principles and adhere to federal, state, and local laws and ordinances governing one's practice.

Individually or when appropriate as a team, reach an ethical decision.

Seek ongoing professional development in ethical deliberation (e.g., mentor and peer supervision).

The large majority of respondents in a sample of members of the National Association of School Psychologists (NASP) had completed formal coursework in ethics and acquired other training in ethics. However, their limited recognition of ethical dilemmas raises concerns about whether their training, indeed, prepared them to engage in adequate ethical problem solving (Basel & Woody, 1991, cited in Woody et al., 1992). The respondents' lack of familiarity with the APA and NASP ethics codes poses the possibility that they over rely on their own internal belief systems. Furthermore, their general denial of having experienced many ethical dilemmas in the previous two years (as Basel and Woody's survey discussed) suggests that they may have underdeveloped skills in recognizing ethical dilemmas. In addition to university-based training in ethics, providers should seek ongoing professional development (see chapter 8).

Professional Codes of Ethics: A Foundation for Ethical Decision Making

Professional ethics is not pure ethics. Rather, it is a combination of ethics, law, and etiquette (Haas & Malouf, 1989). Early childhood providers should be well-versed in the ethics and standards relevant to the practice of psychology in general and early childhood in particular. In addition to the APA (1990) Ethical Principles of Psychologists and the NASP (1984) Principles for Professional Ethics, the Code of Ethics of the Division for Early Childhood (DEC) of the Council for Exceptional Children (adopted in September 1996) is applicable. Several standards of the DEC Code of Ethics are compatible with the ethical principles of beneficence and justice. Qualified and prepared providers are more likely to ensure quality indicators across the range of early childhood supports than unprepared ones. As a result, more good and less harm will ensue for children and families. Qualified leadership personnel are better prepared to manage fiscal matters, better ensuring fair allocation of available resources.

Professional ethics are not of the same authority as law. All psychologists are governed by the laws of the jurisdiction in which they practice, but only members of the professional association are subject to the relevant code of ethics. Somewhere in the chain of influences on the practice of psychology, between the human (e.g., children, families, educators, health-care providers, administrators) and governmental (e.g., federal and state laws, board of education and department of health policies) sources, is the professional association.

Conclusion

Ethical theories and principles combine with emotion to guide ethical analysis and judgment in practice. Ethics require that psychologists and other early childhood providers respect children and families, fully communicate with parents and guardians and obtain their informed consent, do good, avoid inflicting harm, and prevent harm and remove harmful conditions. These tenets establish high ideals and substantive demands on providers to recognize ethical dilemmas and to make ethical analysis explicit on a continuing basis. Hence ethics should be among the primary priorities in early childhood practice, including institutional policies and ongoing professional development. In grappling with ethical problem solving, the goal is a rationally and emotionally reflective integration of reason and emotion. Achieving this goal requires providers to develop sensitivity to the presence of ethical concerns and the capacity to think in ethical terms. It is incumbent on professionals in leadership positions to articulate ethical principles in a clear and explicit fashion in their rationale for the decisions they make. Such role modeling should emphasize ethical deliberation as an inherent part of professional psychology in general and in early childhood practice in particular. Hence students and providers alike will be prepared to develop in their ability to respond appropriately to ethical demands in their areas of practice and in new situations.

Part III

Structural Supports for Early Intervention

8

Professional Development in Early Childhood: Quality Indicators in Training

Given the vast universe of relevant content, it is the duty of professors and practitioners alike to provide those in training with an expanded array of expertise to provide excellent services to young children and to establish effective alliances with families and other providers. The major tenets of early childhood practice, such as collaboration and family involvement, should be reflected in the processes of training as well as the content.

Establishing a cadre of highly trained early childhood professionals presents an immense obligation. Indeed, as noted in Ethical Principle 7, Section C of the American Psychological Association:

> Psychologists who employ or supervise other professionals or professionals in training accept the obligation to facilitate the further professional development of these individuals. They provide appropriate working conditions, timely evaluations, constructive consultation, and experience opportunities. (APA, 1990, p. 393)

We need to examine the practice of preparing psychologists and other service providers to be early interventionists for several reasons. First, under federal legislation, states opting to participate in Part C programs are required to develop and implement policy related to personnel. Each state must implement a Comprehensive System for Personnel Development (CSPD) to ensure that professionals have opportunities to become qualified. Such opportunities may vary considerably from preservice (predegree) to inservice (postdegree) and from one didactic session to on-site supervision. Special issues of journals (such as the 1991 miniseries on initiatives in professional preparation in *School Psychology Review*) or sections of journals (such as the section on innovations in professional training in psychology in *Professional Psychology. Research and Practice*) have examined current efforts and future directions in professional development. These offer testimony to the diversity of training models. Second, the capacity to meet the goals of early childhood services depends on the caliber of the professional personnel. Each state must develop and implement policy in two areas: (a) setting standards for entry-level personnel and (b) providing training alternatives to ensure that these standards are met for current personnel as well as for future personnel (McCollum & Maude, 1994).

This chapter offers direction for the preparation of the next generation of early childhood psychologists and other providers who must function in complex roles. Rather than focusing exclusively on training activities for the direct service provider, this chapter addresses preservice and inservice programs as well as supervision and mentoring. Various sections of the chapter discuss the rationale for early childhood specialization, the balance in competencies as a generalist and specialist, content and processes of training, and issues related to licensure and certification. Skills needed in relating to families and skills necessary for cultural competence are delineated in chapter 4.

Logic for Early Childhood Specialization in Psychology

Federal legislation has led to a substantial increase in early intervention programs for young children with developmental disabilities. Hence the number of needed specialists with transdisciplinary and interagency experience has expanded significantly. The roles of early interventionists, which are highly complex and multifaceted, diverge from the roles of providers working with older populations (McCollum & Maude, 1994). As early as 1985, the Division of Personnel Preparation in the U.S. Office of Special Education Programs offered the first year of funding for a special grant competition for programs preparing personnel for work with children birth to age 3 years of age.

Insufficient Preparation and Current Shortages of Qualified Psychologists

Problems confronting trainers of psychologists pertain to preparing a sufficient number of psychologists who can deliver best-practice supports to the participants in early childhood programs. Many psychologists have received little academic training in the area. Furthermore, many personnel already working with young children may need retooling to provide services more reflective of the theoretical and systemic changes stemming from legislation, policy, and the expanding database about effective early intervention. Therefore, many existing early intervention personnel need retraining as roles and responsibilities are redefined.

Although many universities have established early childhood education and early childhood special education programs, the emphasis historically has been on 3- to 5-year-olds, with minimal training provided with children in the first two years of life (Bailey, Farel, O'Donnell, Simeonsson,

& Miller, 1986). Specialized knowledge and skills with the 0- to 2-year age group require specialized training different from that for preschoolers (Bricker & Slentz, 1987). Very few clinical child and school psychology programs offer early childhood training other than at an exposure level. Moreover, university training in early intervention is often dependent on extramural funding (Klein & Campbell, 1990). The authors' provision of graduate-level early childhood training has been fully funded by federal grants. Another factor weighing against early childhood program development in higher education is the lack of state certification specifically for early childhood psychologists (discussed later in this chapter). States are hesitant to develop specialized certification when there are an insufficient number of personnel to fill early childhood positions (McCollum & Maude, 1994).

A survey by the Carolina Institute for Research on Infant Personnel Preparation at the University of North Carolina (Bailey, Palsha, & Huntington, 1990) indicated that even in early childhood programs, the average student receives only a small amount of information relevant to infant intervention and family support, working with families, team process, and service coordination. The survey found little indication of major changes in curriculum in the near future to meet the learning needs of students wanting early childhood specialization because of extensive preexisting course requirements and limited number of faculty with expertise in the area.

Additional challenges facing those who want early childhood preparation include inadequate numbers of seminars and coursework, limited access to early childhood special populations, insufficient opportunities to reach criterion (e.g., work with very few infants), and use of an easy-to-hard teaching sequence in which students are exposed largely to typical children and hence develop insufficient professional repertoires to provide effective services in complex cases (Epps, 1991; Epps & Jackson, 1991).

In a national survey of 248 clinical child and school psychologists' training and expertise in early intervention, Epps and Nelson (1991a, 1991b) found substantial deficits in their exposure to early intervention with populations with developmental delays. The authors found that only 9.4% had taken coursework on medically complex young children, and 69.5% had minimal or no supervised experience with this population. Although 64.6% reported that they had formal training in assessing preschoolers, only 30.5% had training in assessing infants and toddlers, and only half (51.2%) had coursework in family assessment. Extremely low percentages had received any formal training in curriculum planning for infants and toddlers (2.8%) or preschoolers (10.6%). Less than half had formal training in counseling parents of exceptional children (43.1%), and very few (9.8%) had coursework in grief counseling with parents. Percentages of respondents with supervised clinical experiences were similarly low. There was a striking deficit in the school psychologists' supervised experience with infants and toddlers; 57.7% had minimal experience or none at all.

Uniqueness of Population and Diverse Roles of Early Childhood Providers

Professional development opportunities are critically needed because of unique role requirements necessary for working with young children, their families, and the diverse array of providers and other participants in early childhood programs. Innovative models of professional preparation are essential because of the considerable heterogeneity in the population of young children; the complexity of contextual familial, social, cultural, political, and economic factors; and the multifarious intermingling of interagency and intergovernmental supports. There is a need for early childhood psychologists to work with children in neonatal and pediatric intensive care units, medical specialty clinics, the child's home, child care facilities, toddler and preschool programs, and rehabilitation centers rather than solely in typical classroom settings. This expanded professional preparation can significantly enhance transdisciplinary and interagency collaboration to avoid parallel yet uncoordinated and fragmented services and to address the comprehensive needs of young children and their families (e.g., Peterson, 1991).

The roles of early childhood providers are diverse. Indeed, applying any particular role may be quite varied, depending on the provider's employment. Early intervention programs differ on multiple dimensions, with implications for roles and thus for personnel preparation. These diverse settings are significant contexts in which competence must be viewed (McCollum & Maude, 1994). For example, if providers work with a developmental intervention group for 2-year-olds, they must be well-versed in curricular issues and transdisciplinary teaming. If they work in a program whose mission is to support families at risk, they must be knowledgeable about diverse interagency supports, cultural sensitivity, and relationship building. Providers working with children with medically complex conditions, in either community programs or hospitals, need an understanding of medical nomenclature. University programs are faced with substantive administrative obstacles to requiring additional interdisciplinary coursework given already crowded curricula and different policies across colleges (e.g., College of Education and College of Arts and Sciences). Because no university program or internship can prepare graduate students to be competent to function in all early childhood roles, some flexibility in required coursework and creativity in opportunities for applied experiences are appropriate. Training programs guided by flexible policies can enhance the integrity of educational experiences.

Focusing exclusively on the content of early childhood personnel preparation is misguided. What about the *processes* to be used for training? The major tenets of early childhood practice (e.g., collaboration, family involvement, relationship building) should be reflected in the processes of training as well as the content. Following this logic, a collaborative, interdisciplinary approach would be a critical component of predegree and postdegree professional development programs. Developing and implementing this training process requires faculty from different disciplines both within and across colleges to interact. Bailey (1989) suggested that programs could be combined into courses of study that lead to dual certification or new interdisciplinary courses could be created and used across departments. Other process considerations include family participation in training and new approaches to supervision as students are supported in achieving self-awareness and competence in their diverse roles. Families as training partners as well as supervision are discussed at length later in the chapter.

Although a medical model is not advocated, an understanding of a biopsychosocial model and its implications for developmental intervention, a basic awareness of health care treatment procedures, and skill in facilitating continuity of care and health care education liaison are highly recommended (Epps & Jackson, 1991). Such training increasingly becomes necessary for psychologists working with early childhood populations and will not be the exclusive domain of hospital-based pediatric psychologists as greater numbers of these children with medically complex conditions are served in community-based programs. Moreover, the IDEA amendments specifically address the need to facilitate the transition of infants with or at risk for developmental delay from medical care to early intervention services.

Key Elements of Professional Development Opportunities

There are a number of key features of professional development in early childhood specialization. These include (a) training across disciplines as well as within disciplines, (b) core competencies, (c) family involvment in teaching, (d) interaction with a variety of young children and families, (e) quality supervision and mentorship, (f) personal reflection, and (g) support from colleagues.

Cross-Disciplinary and Within-Disciplinary Training

Given the need for an integrated approach to serving at-risk young children and their families, transdisciplinary perspectives are needed to delineate the content necessary for early childhood specialization (McCollum & Thorp, 1988). Because disciplines and agencies overlap in their service delivery, professional development is best fostered by a cross-disciplinary and cross-agency model that supplements within-disciplinary training. Continuous opportunities to interact and to collaborate with students and professionals from various allied health and education disciplines are needed. Such transdisciplinary training can build on skills typically not addressed in preservice programs, including family-centered supports, service coordination, transdisciplinary teaming, and interagency collaboration (Bailey, Simeonsson, Yoder, & Huntington, 1990). Furthermore, there has been speculation that cross-disciplinary training may heighten the "market value" of psychologists who have the necessary skills to conduct a variety of billable services that provide reimbursement (Johnstone et al., 1995).

How can cross-disciplinary training be coordinated? Suggestions from numerous authors advocate for partnerships with interagency coordinating councils, institutions of higher education, state-level personnel across agencies (e.g., Department of Health and Social Services and Department of Public Instruction), the foundation and philanthropic community, and professionals from multiple disciplines (e.g., Bruder, Klosowski, & Daguio, 1991; Epps & Jackson, 1991; Johnson, Jeppson, & Redburn, 1992; U.S. Department of Health and Human Services, 1994). Such collaboration can significantly enhance state resources for training and reduce duplication of effort. It is critical to have opportunities to teach and to learn across disciplines and agencies. Interns and other providers-in-training can participate together in a variety of forums, such as direct services; team care conferences; psychosocial rounds; discharge and transition-planning meetings; and seminars. Such cross-disciplinary activities build collaborative professional partnerships by enriching perspectives, enhancing exposure to unique expertise, and breaking down barriers associated with unfamiliarity.

Davis, Thurman, and Mauro (1995) address barriers to cross-disciplinary training at the university level, highlighting the need for administrative support to foster cooperation among faculty from different departments. Early childhood expertise is also required. Unfortunately, survey research conducted on a nationwide basis indicated that higher education faculty in early intervention disciplines cannot be assumed to have skills in early childhood (particularly infancy), family, and interdisciplinary issues (Bailey, Simeonsson, Yoder, & Huntington, 1990). Although higher education faculty need renewal and support, historically universities have not demonstrated an administrative commitment to faculty retooling (Eash & Lane, 1985). Winton (1996) summarized the challenge: (a) knowledgeable and skilled trainers are needed; (b) university faculty are a potential resource for offering such training, but they themselves need professional development in early intervention; and (c) institutions of higher education are not likely to offer faculty opportunities to upgrade and expand their skills.

To address the challenge of insufficient numbers of trainers, the Early Education Program for Children With Disabilities, in the U.S. Department of Education Office of Special Education Programs, funded four regional faculty training institutes from 1992 to 1995. The Southeastern Institute for Faculty Training (Winton, 1996) provided 30 to 35 instructional sessions across four days. Content areas addressed key components of early intervention using various innovative instructional strategies (e.g., role play, case-study method, and interactive activities). This federal initiative represents an innovative approach that addressed both training content and processes. Follow-up support and technical assistance also were offered for a period of six months. The potential increase in knowledge about key domains (e.g., family-centered practices) would appear to be significant, particularly if collaboration occurs among institute participants when they return to their home sites. Are all professional development needs addressed by this model? Not all skills could be developed by such an approach. Those related to actual direct service delivery, such as reflective listening or strategies to engage a young child in communicative exchange, need to be fostered by quality applied experiences and supervision.

Despite the emphasis on cross-disciplinary training, professional development—unique to psychology—remains important. For example, psychologists have unique training in psychometric theory and cognitive and social–emotional assessment. Strong identity and competence within one's profession are as critical to successful service integration as is the collaboration across disciplines to address complex problems (Short, 1997). The following scenario illustrates both common and unique areas of expertise across disciplines. The repertoire depicted of these particular providers is not intended to suggest that all professionals within these disciplines necessarily have or do not have these skills.

Anwar was born at 32 weeks gestation 3 weeks ago. He was in respiratory distress at birth and required ventilation for two days. His cardiac and respiratory function were monitored, as well as the oxygen saturation in his blood. Anwar has difficulty sucking (breast or bottle) and keeping himself alert and calm. His mother and father both are 14 years old. His father seems to like to hold him, but his mother often looks away from Anwar when she is near him. She frequently becomes teary and does not seem to enjoy changing his diapers or clothes. His care team consists of a neonatologist, neonatal nurse practitioner, nursing staff, speech pathologist, occupational therapist, social worker, and psychologist. The team wants to support the family without overwhelming them with so many different providers. The challenge is in balancing the need for unique expertise *(each provider's within-disciplinary training)* and continuity of care.

The occupational therapist provides range-of-motion activities, and the speech pathologist examines oral–motor capacity. The social worker has a basic understanding of depression and has contacts with the public high school where Anwar's parents attend. The psychologist has been cross-trained by a nurse who was a certified lactation consultant as well as by a speech pathologist who is an expert in feeding disorders and dysphagia (swallowing difficulties). Therefore, she has specialized skills related to breastfeeding and examining suck bursts. The psychologist has generalist skills in professional psychology (e.g., systems theory, clinical microskills), school psychology (e.g., models of school programs), clinical psychology (e.g., mood disorders), and developmental psychology (e.g., attachment, adolescence). She also has highly specialized skills in infant neurobehavioral assessment. With this combination of cross-disciplinary skills, within-disciplinary skills, general skills across subspecialties of psychology, and specialized skills, the psychologist serves a unique role on the team. By understanding depression and its implications for parent responsiveness, feeding disorders, breastfeeding, infant state organization, and attachment, she is in a prime position to support parent–infant interaction and parenting self-efficacy.

This example illustrates the need for cross-disciplinary training and interprofessional competence, within-disciplinary training, and balanced competencies as a generalist and a specialist. All four are necessary for competence in early childhood service delivery.

The National Center for Infants, Toddlers, and Families (previously called the National Center for Clinical Infant Programs) recognizes four elements of training that seem particularly likely to foster competence in early childhood practitioners: (a) a common framework of cross-disciplinary concepts, (b) opportunities for direct participation with diverse children and families, (c) quality supervision, and (d) within- and cross-disciplinary collegial support (Fenichel & Eggbeer, 1991). Each involves a blend of content and process.

A Common Framework of Cross-Disciplinary Concepts

The need for qualified early childhood providers relates both to entry-level personnel and to those professionals already in the field who lack the relevant knowledge and skills to support young children and their families. This book offers testimony to the extraordinary range and depth of knowledge, skills, and experiences that are necessary to implement quality early childhood services. Because each chapter highlights the conceptual understanding and skills necessary for competence, this chapter does not attempt to provide a summary list of competencies. Of course no provider ever becomes fully "competent." The ongoing evolution toward increasing concordance with best-practice tenets (e.g., continuous quality improvement) should be the goal.

Core Competencies

Thorp and McCollum (1994) outlined four general domains of training programs for early childhood services: (a) infant-related competencies, (b) family-related competencies, (c) teaching competencies, and (d) interagency and advocacy competencies. Fenichel and Eggbeer (1991) recognized that delineation of a restricted number of core constructs is arbitrary. Nevertheless, they offered seven areas as substantive integrators of information across fields of inquiry and as generic guides for practice: (a) endowment, maturation, and individual differences in the first three years of life; (b) the power of human relationships; (c) transactions between the infant and the environment; (d) developmental processes and their interrelationship; (e) risk, coping, adaptation, and mastery; (f) parenthood as a developmental process; and (g) the helping relationship.

Both sets of authors contend that training programs need to establish a unique set of core competencies for students wanting to specialize in early intervention. The core areas identified are related to the major themes of this book, including relationship-based care, the transactional nature of child and family development, a contextual view of resources and vulnerabilities, and an integrated service delivery system.

Families as Training Partners

As Schwab (1991) noted, "Families are the community faculty from whom students can learn about aspects of the health care system that no one else can teach them" (p. 5). They also are in a prime position to teach about the degree of family-centeredness in child care centers, preschool groups, Head Start, and kindergarten programs. Involving families at all levels of design, implementation, evaluation, and revision clearly is crucial. To absorb principles of family-centered care, students and providers-in-training must interact with families along a variety of dimensions. They need the opportunity to hear the family perspective in courses and seminars, the time to establish long-term relationships with families, the occasion to work alongside family members, and the chance to receive feedback from families regarding their professional development (Whitehead, Jesien, & Ulanski, 1998).

Johnson et al. (1992) described several initiatives in which parents participate in planning and conducting training sessions. For example, the American Occupational Therapy Association, with funding from the U.S. Department of Education, developed continuing education programs to help occupational therapists build their collaborative skills with families and work in an interagency system of health, education, and social services. Of the 18 faculty in the model project, 6 were parents of children with special needs (Hanft, 1989). For ongoing revision of their training program, Epps and Jackson (1991) used evaluative data from parents regarding graduate students' professional etiquette, organization and flexibility, clarity and utility of information provided, and degree of enablement and confidence building. Such feedback was particularly helpful because these parents and their children were direct participants in early childhood programs.

Davis et al. (1995) also developed several mechanisms for including parents of diverse cultural, ethnic, and socioeconomic backgrounds in an interdisciplinary seminar for graduate students and faculty from nine different disciplines. They participated in role playing and shared their experiences as members of panels and via lectures and discussions. These parents were paid for their time through extramural funding or university funds. It is especially noteworthy that a parent advocate was added to the faculty who was compensated at the same level as other faculty and was given equal status.

What are other ways to infuse family involvement in personnel preparation? In addition to serving as guest lecturers and coteaching with faculty, family members may participate on advisory boards, in focus groups to determine training needs, in developing and reviewing training curricula, and in various mentoring programs. Capone and Divenere (1996) developed one such program, which represents at least two levels of collaboration: (a) joint funding from the University of Vermont and the U.S. Office of Special Education Programs and (b) the Early Childhood Special Education graduate program of the University of Vermont and Parent to Parent of Vermont. Although no psychology students participated in the program, it serves as a model for providing students with opportunities to reflect on family-centered principles in practice by spending five to seven hours per week with families who have a child with a disability. Within this model, the families become the educators and their homes become the field placement. Students gain a greater appreciation of the challenges and joys of raising a child with special needs; professional development programs that invest the time and energy in developing and maintaining such a family mentoring program are providing a valuable service that deserves to be emulated.

Jeppson and Thomas (1995) recommended the following framework of guidelines when involving families in personnel preparation, to which we have added.

- *Involve families who represent diverse experiences.* For instance, include family members who have children of different ages and developmental repertoires. Families with children currently receiving early childhood services as well as graduates can be invited. Strive to include families with experiences with various agencies as well as families of diverse ethnic and cultural backgrounds. Providers with good intentions sometimes invite families who are the most articulate and happiest with services as well as those who are able to provide their own transportation and child care. The challenge is in finding creative ways to invite and welcome participation from the full array of families.
- *Make the process accessible.* It is important to consider the time and location for training, particularly when families may need to rely on public transportation. Support with transportation and child care should be considered.
- *Compensate families for their time and reimburse them for their expenses.* Families deserve reasonable payment for developing, conducting, and evaluating training programs. Furthermore, costs related to travel and child care should be reimbursed.
- *Support families in acquiring knowledge and skills that are needed for personnel preparation.* For example, some may want practice in using overhead transparencies or slides, and others may want a review of the components and process of the IFSP. When training sessions are offered for staff, families might be invited to attend. When providers and families spend time together in learning activities, they can better appreciate each other's roles and perspectives. Other helpful facilitation might include clerical support and work space.

Opportunities for Direct Participation With Diverse Children and Families

Another key element of training is observing and interacting with a variety of children and families. Fenichel and Eggbeer (1991) illustrated by describing a neophyte who gains an initial awareness of risk factors (see chapters 2 and 3 for an extensive coverage of risk) and then reaches precipitous deductions about child and family vulnerabilities and causes for "delay." For example, the inexperienced provider labels a child as having a cognitive delay as a result of her single mother's smoking during pregnancy and the baby's low birthweight. In this case, the provider fails to understand that the prematurity resulted from the mother's incompetent cervix and that the mother has a very supportive extended family. Observations, interactions, and facilitative supervision build competence in early childhood practice by providing

- Enlightenment in real-world complexity;
- Opportunities to become familiar with typical and optimal development, and in turn, to become discerning about those children and families in need of additional supports;
- Involvement with a child and family over time and in natural home and community surroundings to generate appreciation of the effect of typical developmental change, as well as distinctive challenges;
- Appreciation of tremendous individual differences in vulnerabilities and resilience of children, families, and communities;
- Exposure to cultural differences and diversity within a cultural paradigm; and
- Edification of the breadth of cultural, adaptive, growth-enhancing reactions that caregivers have to developmental tasks along with the less accommodating responses.

Those in training can learn a great deal by observing a skilled provider's interactions with children and families and by having sensitive clinical supervisors observe and support their interactions. Ongoing opportunities for interacting with children and learning directly from families are particularly important for those in administrative, policy making, or research roles. Periodic direct contact can enhance these professionals' understanding of families' experiences with service delivery contexts and factors that obstruct their accessing supports. Hence such professionals can better appreciate the actual impact of policies and programs on children and their families and design socially valid empirical studies.

It also may be helpful for university programs to identify program tasks that outline expectations for trainees. These program tasks represent professional activities that reflect the role responsibilities of psychologists who serve young children and their families. They can be used formatively as an ongoing tool to provide direction throughout the training period or as part of performance evaluation. Table 8.1 provides sample program tasks. It is the responsibility of the sending university to consider quality indicators of training sites and to build cooperative arrangements with field sites that adopt contemporary best-practices. For instance, programs that support young children with delays as they interact with typically developing children should be priorities. Too often practica occur in nearby school districts, mental health facilities, or health care centers regardless of whether quality indicators are present. Another obstacle to quality field-based training includes the press for billable hours in some facilities, which may create a disincentive for psychologists to provide in-depth supervision.

Table 8.1. Sample Program Tasks for Early Childhood Trainees

Descriptor	Program Tasks	Evaluation Criteria
Assessment/intervention	*Educational Assessment* 1. The student will administer a sensorimotor assessment based on Uzgiris-Hunt scales to three typical children, to four children with developmental delays, and to two children with chronic illness. These children should be of different ages.	The student will be videotaped and will meet criterion at the mastery level. All protocols must be scored accurately upon review by the supervisor.
	Clinical Assessment 2. Students use the Diagnostic Classification 0–3 to formulate a systematic, multiaxial framework of mental health and developmental issues for three young children over three sessions.	After reviewing data sources and observing the child, the supervisor will discuss the accuracy and comprehensiveness of the diagnostic formulation.
	Intervention 3. The student will plan and conduct an intervention session for at least four young children of different ages who are hospitalized, at home, or in a school. The student will be responsible for the following: (a) Review assessment and intervention history (b) Identify child and family goals and strategies for implementing (c) Plan for intervention session (d) Summarize session (e) Plan for next session	The supervisor will review the plan, monitor the intervention, and review the summary notes.
Parent education in child behavior management	1. For three children with challenging behaviors, the student will, with supervision, develop a program designed to increase the frequency of one or more desirable alternative behaviors while decreasing the frequency of difficult behaviors. The intervention must include the following elements:	Programs must be judged acceptable to the supervisor and families and receive any necessary human subjects' approval prior to implementation. Students must maintain performance data across all relevant stimulus conditions, and programs must reflect any data-based modifications

The supervisor will observe a session to check for accuracy in description and implementation of the intervention and family opportunities to accept or reject treatment components.

(a) Description of the context
(b) Behavioral statement of the challenges
(c) Review of intervention history
(d) Documentation of collaboration with family and providers
(e) Functional analysis
(f) Specific program objectives
(g) Measurement system
(h) Baseline performance data
(i) Description of intervention plan
(j) Plans for enhancing generalization and maintenance
(k) Plan for supporting family and providers in implementation
(l) Child behavioral data
(m) Social validity data

2. During the development of the behavior change program and throughout intervention, the student will assess treatment integrity and acceptability.

Family-based experience

1. The student will participate in routine family activities for one young child with developmental challenges several hours per week for one month. She or he will maintain a weekly journal of activities and reflection on experiences, including both thoughts and feelings. In coordination with the family, she or he will participate in such activities as:

(a) Mealtime
(b) Bedtime routines
(c) Appointments with medical or allied health specialists
(d) Family errands
(e) Family support or informational group
(f) Community-based recreation activity
(g) Child direct services
(h) IFSP/IEP meeting or other meeting with providers
(i) Respite

A parent-to-parent supervisor will monitor all student activities and provide resources and support. The university or field-site supervisor will review students' journals weekly and offer comments to extend students' interpretation of their experiences. The university or field-site supervisor also will facilitate discussion in the seminar.

Quality Supervision

Another essential element of training that Fenichel and Eggbeer (1991) offered is individualized supervision, which provides an opportunity for reflection. Effective supervision is very much a process of supporting others in uncovering and examining personal values and thoughts and feelings evoked from professional practice and then framing ethical, professional, and sensitive responses that are rationally and emotionally integrated. It provides a safe haven where resilience is facilitated and vulnerabilities are reframed; these are then partnered with supports. Given the potential for self-serving rationalization and personal filtering of professional judgments, mentors must support honest self-reflection and an utterly personal engagement (in themselves as well as in their protégés), dialogue with colleagues, and integration of factual information and emotional experiences. As discussed in chapter 7, reflection on ethical principles can help to manage the emotional distress that may ensue from challenge situations in practice. Quality supervision from a mentor or peers can be key in reframing professional or moral distress. Clinical supervisors also provide ongoing support as students and providers-in-training struggle with the demanding and diverse array of needed skills. Supervisors model high standards of ethical and professional practice, self-exploration of their feelings, and strategies for coping with the emotional realities of working within and across agencies.

A developmental model reflects the changing nature of supervision over time as trainees gain knowledge and experience (e.g., Worthington, 1987). Epps and Jackson (1991) adopted a four-stage model of supervision that enables graduate students to join activities early, with supervision faded as they develop greater autonomy: (a) observation, (b) partial participation, (c) cotherapy, and (d) independent practice with supervision. Because of the potential complexity of situations as a result of contextual factors, substantive supervisor time typically is necessary to ensure a fusion of theoretical and practical issues, rationally and emotionally reflective integration of cognition and affect, and cultural awareness.

Quality supervision, which should include reflection, collaboration, and regularity (Gilkerson, 1992), is not intended to be a monitoring event or vehicle for crisis management. It is based on trust within a relationship, which requires nurturance over time. Supervision sessions should not be postponed or missed, which potentially sends the message that this activity is less important than other more pressing demands. It is important for organizations to provide sufficient time and support to supervisors to enhance the quality and depth of supervision (Fenichel & Eggbeer, 1991).

Self-Reflection

Self-reflection should be a significant element of a graduate program in psychology and postdegree employment. The following are examples of questions that might arise when reflecting on one's experience as a provider:

- How do I avoid defensiveness when I start to feel incompetent?
- How do I feel when a colleague challenges my judgment?
- How do I manage my sense of futility when a vulnerable family remains poorly supported by fragmented services?
- What about my personal history influences my formulation of a treatment approach?
- Do I dare propose another theoretical paradigm with this supervisor if necessary?

Contemplating one's life experiences (cf. countertransference), values, history of interactions with colleagues and supervisors, and perceptions of a given family and ecological context may have been poorly developed in some providers' training or current practice. Hence professional development at a dual level is crucial—namely learning how to (a) self-reflect about one's own reactions in early childhood practice and (b) support other providers in self-exploration and integration through ongoing interaction individually or in groups as well as via periodic focus groups. Therefore, one key component of supervision is the support of students and providers-in-training in developing reflection skills.

Mentoring Relationships

A mentor is an experienced individual who relates well to a junior employee and facilitates her or his personal development for both the individual's and organization's benefit (Noe, 1988). There is diversity in types of mentorships. Even same gender-mentoring relationships are heterogeneous, with variation in such variables as age or area of specialization. The advantage of a mentoring process is that it provides a venue for active learning and helps apply information to the individual's context. Results of a program evaluation of a staff mentoring project found that mentoring led to significant changes in practice (e.g., development of skills to implement play-based assessment) and had an impact on alterations in the assessment process at the respondents' places of employment (Wischnowski, Yates, & McCollum, 1996). Within early childhood, there is a huge range of possibilities for mutually beneficial mentor–protégé relationships. Agencies need to be creative in nurturing innovative models of mentorship. For example, more experienced teachers could mentor inexperienced psychologists.

Another issue is the simultaneous role of being a mentor and a protégé. Because having a mentor can be useful throughout a professional career, the protégé role is not automatically discarded as one advances through the life cycle. Indeed, early childhood providers can be concurrently both mentors for junior colleagues as well as protégés of policy analysts or clinicians. Rather than assuming that all parties have the requisite skills, professional development regarding the mentoring relationship may be appropriate. Protégés are likely to need to learn how to initiate a mentoring relationship and how to use mentors effectively.

Agencies can encourage supportive developmental relationships in two ways. First, educational intervention allows individuals to learn concepts, skills, and attitudes that make up supportive work relationships (e.g., managing conflict and intimacy, providing and receiving feedback). Second, structural intervention creates systems and practices that support mentoring functions. For example, facilities can examine their reward systems to ensure that senior staff are encouraged to provide mentoring functions to junior colleagues (Ragins, 1989). Certainly, educational and organizational interventions designed to nurture effective developmental relationships should be systematically evaluated, particularly in the early childhood field where the efficacy database is minimal.

The Limitations of Mentorships

It is important to place mentorships in perspective. Mentoring has been aggrandized and presented as a panacea to a number of professional development problems and oversimplified as a relationship easily created and maintained. What is in order is a more realistic and sufficiently complex view of this type of developmental relationship, thus making it a more viable resource for professional development in early childhood. If the potential benefits and limitations are understood, individuals and agencies can create conditions so that mentorships can benefit mentor, protégé, early childhood programs, and ultimately children and families.

Within- and Cross-Disciplinary Collegial Support

Another essential element of training is collegial support throughout one's professional career (Fenichel & Eggbeer, 1991). Interdependence is a guiding principle, acknowledging the boundaries of one's expertise; learning from families, those in training, and colleagues; trusting the collaborative approach; and sharing a sense of connectedness with others. As noted in APA Ethical Principle 7:

> Psychologists act with due regard for the needs, special competencies, and obligations of their colleagues in psychology and other professions. They respect the prerogatives and obligations of the institutions or organizations with which these other colleagues are associated. (1990, p. 393)

One alternative to the mentor relationship is the peer relationship, which not only provides some critical mentoring functions but is relatively available to individuals. The absence of a hierarchical dimension in a peer relationship also facilitates mutual support and collaboration. According to Kram (1985), peer relationships provide both professional development functions (e.g., information sharing, job-related feedback) and psychosocial functions (e.g., emotional support, friendship). We have found peer relationships to be crucial in internship programs. Prospective research efforts can clarify the role of peer relationships in professional development, thus contributing a data-based perspective into the range of possible developmental relationships. Future collaborative efforts among researchers, human resources personnel, policy makers, directors, and clinicians could make up a potentially fruitful agenda.

Fenichel and Eggbeer (1991) encouraged students to observe group process and their own contributions to group accomplishments or difficulties, with guidance from more experienced staff. For instance, mentor and protégé attend the same parent conference. Occasionally during the activity, the mentor can point out certain events. Afterward, the mentor can facilitate a discussion about what the protégé or group of protégés observed (e.g., sequence of individuals talking, degree of inference in statements, clarity of communication—complex vernacular versus phrasing understandable to laypersons—and manner of talking at families versus dialoguing with families).

After clinical activities, we generally ask interns about their observations. Invariably, they focus on the dependent variables—namely, on what the child and family did. Rarely, at least early in the internship, do they also indicate their observations about the independent variables— that is, what the provider is doing to facilitate the session. We recommend providing support in interpreting observations. Indeed, one former intern remarked on the limitations of processing with other interns alone that interns could comment on certain events but sometimes "got stuck" in making sense out of the confusing data and dynamics or misinterpreted the theoretical, clinical, and organizational implications of the event.

Professional activities with young children, their families, and other providers are extraordinarily rewarding yet complex and at times draining. All participants, including direct service providers and administrators, need to work together to create an ambiance of collaboration and openness in expressing and subsequently integrating ambivalent feelings. Psychologists and other early childhood providers need skills in reframing as an enabling process. For instance, rather than thinking that one's team or agency has antiquated policies about early childhood services, providers can reframe their views, considering instead how much more family-centered and developmentally supportive they are becoming.

Provider morale may plummet without opportunities to acknowledge and examine the range of feelings that sometimes ensue when working with young children and families or unhealthy organizations (e.g., anger, helplessness, sadness). Fenichel and Eggbeer (1991) recommended mechanisms for ensuring opportunities for sharing satisfactions and frustrations and then rechanneling such emotions into sensitive, productive, and collaborative professional responses. If providers are isolated from each other or feel overburdened by daily demands, they may neglect their own need for dialogue with colleagues.

An important skill is actively combating the potential for isolation from supportive colleagues. Involvement in early childhood organizations (e.g., National Center for Infants, Toddlers, and Families; International Society for Infant Studies; Division of Early Childhood of the Council for

Exceptional Children) can provide a feeling of connection and reinvigorate the commitment to best-practices. As Gilkerson (1992) noted, "We must build around ourselves supportive processes as dependable as gravity, processes which hold and contain us, and which renew and launch us back again" (p. 21).

Personnel Preparation and Standards

Rather than listing specific competencies required for early childhood specialization (i.e., the content of training), it is critical to determine how training occurs (i.e., the *processes* of training). Flexible systems of professional development blend coursework, inservice workshops, supervised applied experiences, and mentoring relationships. Furthermore, such early childhood best-practices as collaboration and family involvement should permeate training activities.

Fundamental Features of Professional Development

Several features basic to the structure of professional development include competency-oriented training that is individualized and closely supervised. Best-practices need to be emphasized through integrating both research and exemplary service efforts. Rather than simply attending seminars and amassing information, those in training must demonstrate competence in complex tasks that actually reflect the diverse role requirements of the job. Training that is heavily field-based with close, supportive supervision is essential. Professional development activities should emphasize the performance of desired skills in the environments in which they naturally should occur. Applied experiences need to provide exposure to the range of young children with developmental concerns as well as to typical young children who provide a foundation for understanding normal development and who serve as peer models in center-based programs. Furthermore, applied experiences should occur in settings that promulgate best practices. In addition to benefiting students, field-based training programs can contribute to the enhancement of early intervention and staff development. Thus a quality training program is indirectly a tool for systems change (see chapter 9).

Although there are generic competencies to be mastered by all psychologists and universal proficiencies to be acquired by all early childhood providers, students and providers-in-training should be supported in self-determining their own particular area of interest and specialization. For instance, some may wish to build special expertise in providing developmental care in intensive care nurseries (e.g., VandenBerg, 1993). Whitehead et al. (1998) used an individualized learning plan (ILP) in their federally funded Family-Centered Interdisciplinary Training Program in Early Intervention. The ILP parallels the IFSP process, providing students an opportunity to reflect on their own learning priorities. Students identify outcomes and strategies to meet the outcomes, resources they believe they will need, and a time line. The ILP, which can be revised at any time, guides the student's learning activities.

Recommended Practices

Dialogue related to competence extends to discussions about how these competencies are to be acquired and at what level of expertise. We do not propose rigid guidelines about which skills should be acquired in graduate school and internships and which should be gained by continuing education. Rather, we advocate a model of professional development that blends preservice, inservice, supervised applied experiences, and mentoring relationships.

Preparation at the Preservice Level

For graduate programs in psychology, early childhood issues might be incorporated into degree programs at some level. Adding didactic content may be less difficult than offering quality applied experiences and close supervision, with appropriate university and administrative sanction for time commitments required of faculty. One challenging issue relates to breadth versus depth of training.

Rather than rigid recommendations for one level or another for beginning early childhood training, we suggest flexible systems of professional development. Early childhood practice is heavily centered on the family, which includes various subsystems. Those with training with older children and adolescents can support families with older siblings and be particularly effective with adolescent parents with young children. Those with experience in adult development may be especially supportive of families facing crises related to employment, relationships, or mood disorders. Professionals with expertise in organization development may be expressly suited to support early childhood staff in the reflective process. There is little or no empirical investigation to elucidate the extent to which more narrowly focused early childhood training early on versus more broadly based experiences across the life span engender higher levels of competence. The authors themselves took somewhat different journeys.

Abundant preexisting requirements in degree programs are necessary, and we do not advocate that all professional psychology programs offer comprehensive opportunities for early childhood specialization. Institutions of higher education clearly should be able to define their own missions, there is a plethora of worthy specializations removed from early childhood. However, general knowledge of the vulnerabilities and resilience of young children and their families is necessary given the likelihood of contact with this heterogeneous population and the obligation, at a minimum, to triage appropriately. Furthermore, familiarity with medical complications and developmental sequelae can no longer be the sole purview of pediatric psychologists as increasing numbers of young children with chronic illness or history of biological insult are being served by the schools. Hence some measure of early childhood exposure is appropriate for many professional psychology graduate programs, particularly given its guiding principles (e.g., cultural awareness and family-centeredness). These best-practice tenets, then, could infuse excellence into all areas of applied psychological practice.

Preparation at the Inservice Level

Adult learners are depicted as self-directed, entering educational activities with a developed personal and professional experiential base that serves as a reservoir for learning, and motivated to learn when they perceive a need for knowledge or skill for more effective practice. Adults prefer to pursue self-growth activities when granted the opportunity to be self-directing. Their orientation toward learning shifts to problem centeredness to enhance immediacy of application to address a problem or to contend with change (Knowles, 1980; Sakata, 1984). Such adult-learner characteristics are significant in designing effective models that enable providers to build competence. Contemporary, best-practice models of professional development are steering away from large workshops and conferences and moving toward designs that promote greater individual control over the training experience. Participants' active involvement in planning and participating in experientially based learning opportunities is crucial (Bennett, Watson, & Raab, 1991).

Inservice activities should reflect a collaborative effort among the participants, including recipients and facilitators. Rush, Sheldon, and Stanfill (1995) described an Individualized Team Training Plan, which outlines the interdisciplinary and interagency team's self-determined goals and plans for professional development, prioritized by team consensus. True interagency collaboration offers a concerted, coordinated effort to support training with such in-kind contributions as clerical support, audiovisual materials, space for sessions, and photocopying. Family members are integral participants as well. Benefits of ongoing interagency staff development include a diminished sense of territoriality and expanded perspective, which should effect greater sensitivity and responsiveness to families.

Needs assessments of participants, focusing on competencies needed in the work setting, recognize the background of participants, enriching those experiences that are relevant to each person's circumstance and highlighting the participant's own goals (Stayton & Miller, 1993). Direct responsiveness to issues identified by those in the field is important. Rush et al. (1995) recommended an annual needs survey and subcommittees of teams, including parents, that help develop topic areas for training and identify possible trainers. Winton (1993) further recommended that inservice training be coordinated with the state's Comprehensive System of Personnel Development plan, that training is actively endorsed or attended by administrators, and that continuing education units (CEUs) are available to disciplines needed to renew their certification or licensure.

Opportunities to Express Resistance

The journey toward a genuine interagency, family-centered approach requires us to relinquish outdated, comfortable strategies and to forge innovative approaches. Change at the individual level requires courage, which challenges persons to eschew practices antithetical to family sensitivity and partnership building. In many ways, courage drives people beyond comfort zones (see Terry, 1993), to realize what is possible in best-practices in early intervention. In designing professional development activities, the nature of resistance to change must be considered. Johns and Harvey (1993) recommended creating opportunities for participants to express their resistance and then using such feedback to adjust training. They point out the important relationship between interactions with families and personal beliefs, with many providers unenlightened about their own values about caregiving styles and childrearing practices. There are a variety of ways in which providers exhibit resistance to refining their manner of interacting with families. They may make statements that they have no difficulty with families or that they can perform their role without involving families. If the facilitator is from another discipline, some providers may resort to their unidiscipline position to support their current interaction style with families. Some providers may insist that the facilitator's ideas may apply to their setting but not to the participants' context. An indirect form of resistance may occur when participants openly agree with the content of training yet continue with their traditional methods when returning to their agency. Resistance may be apparent with late arrivals and limited participation.

What is the basis of resistance? It may occur across several tiers. At the organizational level, obstacles to genuine participation may occur when the agency has policies that do not reflect family-centered principles. There may be minimal support for taking time for professional development for building partnerships with families and other agencies. Crucial organizational supports such as mentoring and peer relationships or collaborative teams also may be lacking. At the professional level, the tenets of best practices in early intervention may seem inconsistent with the image some providers have of themselves. Some providers view family support either as supplemental or tangential to their primary professional role within their discipline. Providers trained in a narrow, within-disciplinary approach may have particular difficulty integrating notions of role release and shared responsibility into their practice. Our contention is that professional development endeavors should provide experiences for providers across disciplines to facilitate a child's development in all domains (e.g., cognitive, behavioral, social–emotional, language, motor) rather than exclusively in their sole discipline. The goal is for everyone to support synchronous parent–child interaction and to listen genuinely to families. It should not be the unique purview of social work, psychology, or psychiatry to be supportive of families.

At a personal level, resistance may occur in some providers because of unresolved issues about their relationships with their own families or about their role as parents. Sometimes personal values and expectations promote judgmental postures and thwart genuine relationship building with families. Cultural, language, or age differences between providers and families may engender misunderstanding and discomfort as well as poor interpersonal skills (Johns & Harvey, 1993).

To support providers in their professional development toward family-centered care, the nature of resistance should be identified. Johns and Harvey (1993) recommended observation over time in diverse contexts as providers interact with families in casual encounters and under more formal circumstances. Providers' self-assessment in defining their own learning needs can be helpful, although they may identify technical skills rather than relationship-enhancing techniques. Our experience is that interns initially focus on specific tools (e.g., behavioral observation, Bayley Scales of Infant Development-II, Bayley, 1993) in expressing their goals for early childhood rotations rather than the metaskills of reflective processing. In addition to supportive mentoring of interns and junior protégés, self-assessment surveys may be useful, particularly when they enhance framing of needs around an interpersonal perspective. For instance, it might be important to determine one's less well-developed skills related to handling differences of opinion at staffings; or determining what makes one most uncomfortable when interacting with families might be important. Feedback from families, such as via focus groups, is a priority in assessing how they perceive providers' interaction styles and manner of support.

A good deal of resistance is a normal part of change in practice. In professional development activities designed to reconfigure ways of relating to families and other providers, frustration and disequilibrium may be stressful, yet often serve as a catalyst for pivotal change in perspective (Weider, Drachman, & DeLeo, 1989). Hence, a safe training environment, with techniques that promote a high degree of trust within the group and a spirit of fun, combined with activities that build on providers' personal and professional experiences, can help to overcome resistance (Johns & Harvey, 1993). More detail about strategies for managing organizational and consultee resistance is presented in Woody et al. (1992).

Administrative Innovations

There are a number of logistical and enabling factors at the inservice level. Financial and geographic accessibility and scheduling to minimize interfering with participants' job demands are important. Furthermore, explicit administrative sanction is needed such as release time, salary increases, and perhaps most significant, enablement of change in service delivery (Stayton & Miller, 1993). Winton (1996) described an important component of a professional development model for higher education faculty. Faculty were supported by a letter sent to deans and department heads, which helped legitimize faculty participation in training activities and assisted them in obtaining travel support. Challenges remained, however, including competing priorities for faculty members' time. Linking higher education and state agency efforts might assist in "buying out" faculty time.

On-Site Professional Development

Workshops may be appropriate for some purposes. However, there is often a mismatch between early childhood content (e.g., collaboration) and the pedagogic format chosen to teach it. There tends to be an overreliance on workshops at the expense of experiential approaches that require time, commitment, and patronage from faculty. On-site training offers advantages related to costs, requiring less time away from work and lower travel expenses. Furthermore, administrators are more likely to be able to participate in activities and to support application to practice. On-site endeavors also facilitate networking with providers clustered within a geographic region. An advantage for trainers includes enhanced appreciation of the individualized learning needs of staff (Bennett et al., 1991).

Administrative supervisors or directors with little expertise with early childhood populations are unlikely to offer best-practice guidance to providers. In all cases, support in reflective processing is critical as those in training expand their more traditional boundaries to the diverse early childhood arena. Johns and Harvey (1993) emphasized the importance of sponsoring a series of professional development activities over a period of 12 to 18 months, preferably with participation from administrators, to provide consistent training and support over time.

Epps and Nelson (1991b) found that a national sample of 246 clinical child and school psychologists significantly preferred inservice workshops over supervised employment, part-time graduate school, full-time graduate school, or post-doctoral training. Although inservices can be useful in providing information, they are insufficient for skill development without substantial supervised activities with culturally diverse young children and their families in a variety of contexts. Various administrative innovations to supplement inservices include release time, opportunities for ongoing quality supervision in actual employment settings by experienced early childhood providers, part-time clinical experiences, and consultative follow-up. Support provided in actual employment settings facilitates transfer of training and appropriate application of principles. Generalization-enhancing techniques must be incorporated into all professional development activities, such as teaming of dyads and work groups who then collaborate and support organizational change in their employment settings.

Evaluation

Formative and summative evaluation are critical throughout both proservice and postdegree development activities to improve training and to facilitate self-feedback. Bennett et al. (1991) indicated that evaluation strategies should be practical learning exercises in which participants extend their professional repertoire by applying new knowledge and skills to problem solving or exploring a new approach. For instance, for the goal of developing skills in role release to contribute fully on a transdisciplinary team, the evaluation strategies of role play, interaction, and feedback from team members can be used to enhance participants' skills and self-appraisal.

Critical incident or work sampling is a useful means of evaluating the performance of interns and providers-in-training. It is an objective technique that records representative examples of appropriate or inappropriate performance (Klingner & Nalbandian, 1993). This technique can be used to highlight successes such as sensitivity to family needs (accurate and responsive use of microskills) or decreased latency in dictating clinical reports (completing dictation within 24 hours). We also recommend a longitudinal perspective whereby interns and staff are followed in their future employment to determine their self-evaluation of their skills as well as their supervisor's evaluation of their skill level (contingent on the individual's permission). Analysis of work and training conditions can help the early childhood agency consider means of improving its human resource development. A facilitative environment of formative evaluation and frequent behavior-specific praise and nurturance can significantly enhance adoption of best-practice precepts.

Distance Education

Ludlow (1994) described an innovative model of personnel preparation that uses interactive telecommunications technology and distance education formats, supplemented with frequent contact, comprehensive print materials, and participant support strategies to build early childhood competencies. Such an approach can be particularly beneficial in rural regions. A key component of the model is building in techniques for participants to relate to each other as real people (e.g., sharing of personal information such as hobbies) and to cultivate the foundations for a personal and professional support network. Hence the program includes an assortment of components to facilitate participant interaction. Sample cooperative activities include sharing ideas about a case study and role playing. Advantages of the model include technical assistance from highly trained professionals as well as enhanced accessibility to training. Disadvantages relate to technology costs and time and effort required to develop packet materials, write broadcast scripts and obtain broadcast releases, acquire the skills to use telecommunications technology effectively for interactions, and travel vast distances to supervise on-the-job practicum components. Satellite transmissions, microwave broadcasts, fiber optic telephone lines, and computer networking offer an expanding array of options.

Balancing Training Needs With Quality Care

One challenge facing professional development programs is balancing the needs of students and providers-in-training to experience and practice the full gamut of care with the rights of children and families to receive the highest quality of family-centered care. The potential is high for over-whelmed students or novices (and more experienced providers as well) to compromise the principles of psychosocially sound care when trying to meet the demands of the training program. Supporting those in training (and in practice) when they make family-centered, developmentally appropriate decisions may necessitate pivotal rethinking in some programs (Johnson et al., 1992). As Schwab (1991) stated, "We need to make an environment in which the student could confidently say on rounds, 'I didn't examine the child because he had just fallen asleep and his father said it wasn't the right time.' We need to have role models around who will say, 'Good choice, you did well'" (p. 5). Balance in both the art and science of care is needed.

Clearly there are criteria for competence in technical skills when considering the readiness of a student or provider-in-training for early childhood practice. No child or family should have to endure unnecessarily prolonged distress to afford practice for the inexperienced. Johnson et al. (1992) advised training programs to establish criteria that include competence in communication and caring skills based on knowledge of child development and family support. Consistency, continuity, and coordination are fundamental features of quality care. Although a diversity of training experiences is necessary, such variety often unsettles rather than champions continuity of care. To build their appreciation of the changing priorities of the young child and family, professional development opportunities should enable students and providers-in-training to interact with children and families over time. Training programs need to ensure that policies are in place that advance continuity and minimize disruption for families. Given the commitment to training, supervision, and mentorship of individuals with varying levels of expertise, a primary goal is professional development over the long term to enhance individuals' knowledge, skills, and abilities needed for early childhood best practices in future employment. The ultimate goal is contributing to young children, their families, and the early intervention community.

Certification in Early Childhood

The Division for Early Childhood (DEC, 1993) has assumed a leadership role in delineating standards for the preparation of early childhood special educators. The National Association for the Education of Young Children (NAEYC) also has issued guidelines to describe the common core of knowledge and performances that are desired outcomes of preparation programs for early childhood professionals. Recently, DEC, NAEYC, and the Association of Teacher Educators (NAEYC, 1995) generated a blending of personnel standards given their shared vision, acknowledging the appropriateness of flexibility across states regarding decisions about the length of preservice training and the level at which training must occur. These have implications for a core set of standards for psychologists who work with young children and their families.

Table 8.2. Log of Professional Development in Early Childhood

Relevant Coursework, Seminars, Inservice Workshops, and Training Institutes

Title	Date	Contact Hours	Trainer (Name, degree, & discipline)	Audience (disciplines attended)	Family Participation	Objectives	Home-Site Work

Applied Experiences

Dates	Supervisor (Name, degree, & discipline)	Format and Process of Supervision	Agency/Site (quality indicators)	Population Served	Description of Activities

Mentoring Relationships

Dates	Mentor (Name, degree, discipline, & agency)	Format and Process of Mentorship	Description of Activities

What certification or licensure is appropriate for early interventionists? This question is complex, requiring consideration of required competencies and policy and pragmatic issues. Psychologists are obligated by their professional and ethical principles to limit their practice to areas of competency. As discussed in APA Ethical Principle 2:

> The maintenance of high standards of competence is a responsibility shared by all psychologists in the interest of the public and the profession as a whole. Psychologists recognize the boundaries of their competence and the limitations of their techniques. They only provide services and only use techniques for which they are qualified by training and experience. (APA, 1990, p. 390)

It could be argued that no special certification is required for early childhood practice because clinicians are ethically bound to avoid working with young children unless they have sufficient training. On the other hand, an early childhood endorsement of some sort could assist the public in making informed judgments about professionals' qualifications. We neither anticipate nor recommend special licensure in early childhood practice for psychologists whose credentials and CEUs are evaluated by state examining boards (e.g., Bureau of Professional and Occupational Affairs). For school psychologists, however, an early childhood endorsement may be on the horizon. Certification in school psychology typically is managed by State Boards of Education, which also certify early childhood teachers. At a policy level, if states are hesitant to promulgate early childhood certification (particularly for infant specialization and for psychologists) because of a lack of personnel to assume positions, this reluctance poses a barrier to requiring the certification in the first place. In the event of early childhood certification or licensure, or even for documentation of CEUs, we suggest keeping a log of professional development activities. Such a log also could be included in one's individualized learning plan (ILP) in graduate school or used to expand a professional portfolio (e.g., attached to or incorporated into a curriculum vita). A sample log is depicted in Table 8.2.

Conclusion

Shortages of highly competent personnel for early childhood service delivery evoke a compelling consideration of the nature of professional development. A key ingredient of professional development activities is continuous formal and informal communication among all participants, including planning personnel, providers, and families. Applied early childhood experiences in quality sites, with supportive mentoring and reflective processing, can extend learning so that family-centered thinking, beliefs, and practice become firmly established in one's professional repertoire. Given the rapidly changing service delivery environment for young children and their families, training in the scholarly scientist–practitioner model is critical so that providers have the skills to be flexible to change and to address challenges proactively. Psychologists and other providers are faced with challenges about funding mechanisms for professional development endeavors. Hence needs assessment, pooling of resources, and coordination of cross-disciplinary training via partnering across agencies (e.g., a consortium) are necessary to infuse relevance and cost-effectiveness into strategic, long-range planning.

As states strive to develop cohesive and effective strategies of staff development, a system that provides a range of training options is essential. The mentoring process provides one such training option. It offers an individualized, collaborative approach that reflects features of sound training practice while also influencing current practice. Models of mentorship and peer supervision and other creative alternatives to traditional workshops are crucial. They should provide experientially based, supervised activities across transdisciplinary and interagency contexts; opportunities to learn from culturally diverse families with different areas of vulnerability and resilience; and organizational support throughout all phases of training, including design, implementation, follow up, evaluation, and refinement.

Professional development activities will be pressed to demonstrate ethnic and cultural diversity in faculty and those in training. Loosening of particular program structures in the accreditation process can engender greater creativity and innovation so that psychologists can expand their more traditional roles to the broader areas of early childhood practice. Indeed, a framework of ever-expanding competencies applies to early childhood. Early childhood providers, ranging from volunteers to attending staff and directors, need both technical knowledge as well as humanistic, relationship-building skills. Just as we advocate a shift of family approaches away from teaching, allowing, and evaluating to a perspective of sharing and facilitating, we also champion such an enablement paradigm in professional development endeavors in which students and providers are respected as self-directing their learning.

The evaluation of training should not be based on face validity. Rather, an infusion of innovative and rigorously investigated models of professional development is fundamental to enhancing quality in cohesive systems of care that have strong partnerships with diverse families and agencies. Although effecting substantive paradigm shifts in models of professional development may not be imminent, seeds of best-practice training can be planted over time in a cycle of continuous quality improvement.

9

Effecting Change: Challenges to Building Integrated and Collaborative Systems

Change in early intervention services cannot be realized through wishful visions. . . . it requires building blocks of principles and behaviors that form a coherent set of steps for action. (Dalziel & Schoonover, 1992, p. 13)

Early childhood education services have been thrust into an era of profound change as programs begin to reevaluate their practices and strive toward an integrated service delivery system that is based on collaborative relationships. Pressure for change in early intervention originated from two primary sources: advocacy groups and federal initiatives (see chapter 1), which promoted a new social value of family-centered care and interagency collaboration. The challenge is to translate that vision into action at the local level. As early intervention program efforts begin to reconfigure patterns of relating to families, the culture of early intervention is being redefined. Ultimately, development of this new system of services means restructuring programs through a process of change. Developing an understanding of change-agent principles and identifying effective strategies to manage change are crucial for those responsible for supporting personnel and programs. The success of agencies in managing this transformation of services depends on multiple factors. This chapter describes essential considerations of the change process that can be instrumental to early intervention programs as they continuously strive to improve services for young children and their families. It also provides a theoretical backdrop to guide practice, which is particularly useful in addressing these complex, novel situations.

Components of Successful Change

"Change is not a discrete event that occurs by linear progression; rather it unfolds on many different levels simultaneously" (Conner, 1993, p. 10). As early childhood intervention programs strive to implement an integrated service delivery system, multiple layers of change are inevitable.

These include a need for all agencies working with families to make changes (macro-level change) and individual providers changing the ways they support children and families (micro-level change). Change in one aspect of an early childhood program easily affects other aspects of practice, which denotes the idea of *systems change*. Therefore, in trying to understand the role of change in one's agency, it is crucial to regard the entire pattern of change rather then focusing on snapshots of isolated aspects of the innovation (Senge, 1990).

Cummings and Worley (1993) provided a helpful framework for analyzing systems change, suggesting that change can be organized into five major activities (as illustrated in Figure 9.1): (a) motivating change, (b) creating a vision, (c) developing political support, (d) managing transition, and (e) sustaining momentum. These activities become part of a circular process, which results in ongoing monitoring and evaluating clinical practices and program services that potentially can provide data to improve the quality of services for children and families (Appel, 1991; Senge, Kleiner, Roberts, Ross, & Smith, 1994). Some describe this process of system change as Continuous Quality Improvement (CQI; Cumming & Wolery, 1993). It is one tool that assists organizations as they seek to improve services and implement change initiatives that will meet or exceed the expectations of families and collaborating service providers (Shortell, Buehler, Levin, O'Brien, & Hughes, 1995). As applied to early intervention programs, improvement efforts result in teams that are working toward high-quality clinical, research, and support services that are family-centered and coordinated. Cohen and Bradford (1990) found that organizations implementing a quality improvement process had employees that were significantly more satisfied with their services, had greater perceived impact on productivity and profitability, and reported more statistically significant cost savings than those who did not. The following section provides a practical guide to implementing each of the activities of this circular process and is further illustrated in the case study at the end of the chapter.

Motivating Change

The impetus for change comes from dissatisfaction with current services and practices, which creates the tension that motivates change. The source of dissatisfaction is not easy to pinpoint. Administrators and providers need introduction to new ideas to begin to identify "what could be" in a service delivery system. Ongoing exposure to new ideas and practices through external networks of information by visiting other organizations, participating in conferences, and reading professional journals can increase an organization's awareness of alternative service delivery practices and provide a basis for comparing its current practice to providers' and consumers' views of best-practice methods. Proponents of the change initiative can help other staff begin to identify the discrepancies between current and desired outcomes. Once convinced that change is necessary,

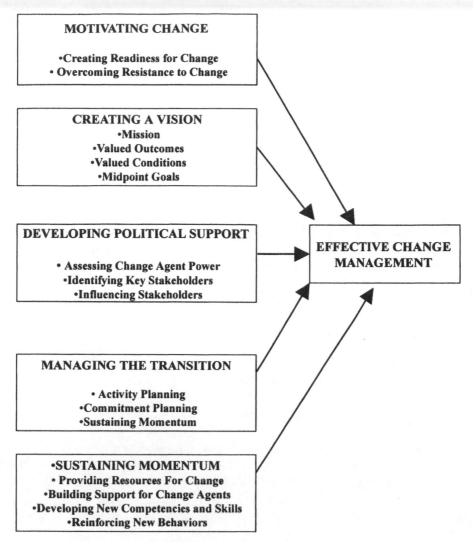

Figure 9.1.   Activities Contributing to Effective Change Management
Source: Reprinted by permission from p. 145 of *Organization development and change* by T. G. Cummings & C. G. Worley; Copyright © 1993 by West Publishing Company. All rights reserved.

the key to successful implementation of change is creating an environment that expects success. This expectation can serve as a self-fulfilling prophecy as staff are more likely to be committed to the change process and direct more energy toward change if positive outcomes are expected (Cummings & Worley, 1993).

Programs also gain awareness of new ideas by developing a system of ongoing contact with families and consumers (e.g., parent participation on advisory councils, parent focus groups or satisfaction surveys). Although the utility of parent satisfaction measures has been questioned because often high satisfaction ratings are reported, Upshor (1991) suggested that the data provide valuable feedback for program planners. Information gathered from families through focus groups or satisfaction surveys heightens a program's awareness of its strengths and weaknesses and provides an impetus to change. Families also are valuable resources in planning and implementing innovations.

A study by McWilliam and Bailey (1995) illustrated how one program effectively used family data to identify programmatic issues, which resulted in program planning to address dissatisfaction in their services. Through an interview process with families participating in center-based early intervention services, McWilliam et al. (1995) found that families prioritized direct therapy for their children and were dissatisfied with the current level of therapy services available in light of the shortage of specialists. Because of this shortage the program created two alternative approaches, including a consultative or transdisciplinary model. Many families interviewed were not satisfied with either of these models and were advocating for more frequent child-directed therapy. To address this issue, a family-centered approach was implemented that demonstrated the successful outcomes of parent–provider partnerships in addressing therapy shortages. Parents were offered information and given opportunities to experience different approaches to make well-informed decisions. This investigation found that initially 80% of the children were pulled out for therapy sessions. Once families were provided choices of six possible intervention models ranging from pull-out sessions to consultation (see chapter 5 for descriptions of these models), two years later 90% of the therapy was occurring in the classrooms. These findings demonstrate the efficacy of a family-centered approach in which partnerships between families and providers address difficult program issues and underscore the value of an open exchange of information on which to base decisions.

Creating a Vision

Critical to implementing innovation is the capacity to build a shared vision among program providers. In developing an integrated service delivery system, this vision must be expanded across agencies. This shared vision provides the overall framework for change, which is a reflection of the values and preferences of the individuals within the organization or across agencies. Following is a sample mission statement formulated by an early intervention team:

> The mission of the Early Childhood Team is to enhance the development of young children with developmental challenges. Our mission is also to support social interaction and the attachment relationship. We use family-centered care, empowerment, and interdisiplinary models to provide high quality, inclusive services that preserve dignity and strengthen collaborative partnerships with other agencies.

Leaders need to establish a climate that promotes creativity in the vision development process to facilitate positive outcomes throughout this visioning process. It is critical for leaders to confront superficial unity (e.g., Terry, 1993) in developing the shared vision to prevent resistance during the implementation phase. Conflict may occur often throughout this process, and resolution of that conflict can actually mobilize the visioning process (Cummings & Worley, 1993). The outcome of a shared vision is creation of a common identity, with a common sense of purpose and operating values (Senge, 1990). As states begin to implement early childhood services, adopting a shared community vision can energize communities to build an integrated service delivery system. The IDEA amendments provide communities with guidelines, yet local communities need to make this vision their own. Central to this process is an agency-wide commitment to the vision, recognition of the benefits, and sense of responsibility for the outcome, rather than mere compliance to meet the minimal expectations of the law. The shared vision provides the foundation from which program policies and practices emerge.

The following scenario demonstrates a community's attempt to build a vision for an integrated service delivery system for universal home visitation:

A capacity-building committee was formed in one urban community to address concerns about the fragmentation and accessibility of services for families. (*Leverage due to dissatisfaction.*) This concern was based on data from family and provider focus groups that were conducted by the United Way. The outcome of several meetings was a vision statement: "We believe that all infants and their families should be welcomed into their neighborhood by providing the necessary supports for parents through a universal home visitation program that is part of an integrated community service delivery system." The committee recognized that to realize success, this vision needed to be embraced by the community. A series of meetings were conducted to provide an opportunity to discuss those issues as well as the proposed vision statement. During these meetings, the meeting facilitator encouraged divergent thinking that resulted in lively debate. Many agencies were territorial, believing their model of service delivery was the best. They were concerned about joining a network in which they might lose resources to support this broader initiative. The vision was clarified and modified to address these concerns and gradually through this process was "owned" by a broad array of providers. (*need for community ownership of the vision*) and the committee began to address specific strategies that could ameliorate the fragmentation and accessibility issues identified.

Developing Political Support

The influence of politics in implementing change is best understood through the social–interactional theoretical framework (Bennis, Benne, Chin, & Corey, 1976). This theory suggests that each person belongs to a network of social relationships that influences his or her behavior. The individual's place in the network (centrality, peripheral, isolation) is a good predicator of his or her rate of acceptance of new ideas. For example, the clinician who is part of the planning committee (*a position of centrality*) is more likely to accept the recommended change in the child assessment process than the therapist who was not part of that planning process (*a peripheral position*). Therefore, in relating theoretical principles to change, it is critical to comprehend the impact that the change will have on the balance of power among individuals and groups within the organization (Nadler, 1987). As community agencies begin to establish collaborative relationships to promote an integrated service delivery system, key stakeholders need to be identified to develop political support. Successful implementation of change depends on key stakeholders being active partners in the decision-making and change process (Counte, Glandon, Oleske, & Hill, 1992). In this context, stakeholders can be defined as internal customers (e.g., providers, administrators) or external customers (e.g., families, other agency service providers). The next step is assessing and identifying strategies to influence stakeholders (Cummings & Worley, 1993). Failure to do so may hinder successful adoption of new strategies or programs.

Examining research findings in the area of inclusive education provides further insights to the role that existing attitudes and values have in influencing the successful change in practice. Results of a survey of 220 preschool teachers and administrators, which examined both the teachers' attitudes regarding inclusion as well as their skills to serve this population of young children, indicated that they had limited experience serving children with developmental difficulties and little exposure to the concept of inclusion at the preschool level. Furthermore, although they agreed with the idea of inclusion only moderately, they perceived themselves as having the skills to serve children with diverse special needs if there were major changes to present practices (Eiserman, Shisler, & Healey, 1995). In addition, there was a significant difference between what providers reported as ideal placement for children with diverse concerns and how they perceived their capabilities to serve this population of children (i.e., they were more likely to accept children with various challenges if they believed they were capable of serving them). The authors suggest that if providers are introduced to philosophies about inclusion that are significantly discrepant from what they can provide, they may reject the inclusive philosophies as untenable. These findings have implications for communities as they are planning outreach efforts to expand inclusive environments, suggesting that infusing new philosophies and skills may occur most successfully when the unique attitudes and needs of community providers are understood and planning and staff development efforts are initiated at the level that matches these expectations. Although full inclusion may be the community's goal, this goal may best be accomplished slowly over time, with small and gradual steps.

A second important political consideration for program planners is the need to analyze ways in which the innovation may threaten or challenge existing roles. Simultaneously, program planners need to build administrators' and providers' sense of ownership of the innovation by emphasizing their value in the change process (Woody et al., 1992). Ensuring that team members are involved in setting goals for their work and are given a balance of autonomy and supervision to successfully complete tasks supports a collaborative climate. A collaborative climate built on trust and supportive relationships leads to team effectiveness (Larson & LaFasto, 1989). (See chapter 4 for further discussion of collaboration.) Consider the following scenario as an illustration.

An Interagency Coordinating Council (ICC) was convened to plan the implementation of Part C services. The team consisted of service providers and administrators from multiple agencies (e.g., education, health, and social services) and families. The group recommended a single agency for the delivery of service coordination across agencies. This recommendation was then forwarded to the special education directors for their review because the early intervention services were administered by education. They rejected the recommendation, believing that service coordination needed to be housed in each of the school districts to have closer proximity to the educational teams. In the discussion with the teachers, the administrators also found that the creation of this new role was threatening to early childhood teachers who believed that this activity should be part of their role. Unfortunately, the ICC had not assessed the political–power structure of the education agencies. By excluding this influential stakeholder (the early childhood teachers) in their planning process, their change initiative failed. In hindsight, a partnership with the directors needed to be formed at the start of these discussions to build support for the change process. This team needed to (a) recognize the influence of the special education directors and teachers, (b) include these stakeholders as representatives on the team, (c) identify the benefits of the change for this stakeholder group, and (d) clarify the advantages of service coordination and how this role would affect the teachers' activities.

Transitioning and Maintaining Change

When the vision is established and the political support gained, the next challenge organizations face is translating this vision into practice through careful planning and implementation of the innovation. Quality improvement process serves as a facilitative tool for program planners. This process includes gathering data, careful planning, piloting, and maintaining momentum to implement the recommended practices. Often assigning a team leader and facilitator supports the team process. The team leader is responsible for scheduling the meetings, leading the team in applying problem-solving processes, leading the meeting according to an agenda, and trying to help the team accomplish its objectives within a specified time frame. The facilitator encourages participation from all team members, brings closure to discussion, assists the team leader in planning and evaluating the meetings, and serves as a support resource person to the team. Together the team leader, facilitator, and team members help identify strategies to maintain the innovative practice so that the organization does not fall back to "familiar patterns." The following section discusses each of these steps.

Step 1: Data Gathering and Analysis

The first step to a proactive planning process is *data gathering* and *analysis*. Taking the time to gather information about the changing patterns and needs of the communities provides useful data to guide program planners in articulating how services need to be changed to improve quality (Johnson et al., 1992). For example, as a community embraces the vision of family-centered services, information gathered from families suggests an increasing number of both parents working out of the home. This information results in offering programs during evenings and weekends to accommodate the preferences of some families. This illustration and the one that follows suggest that although quality improvement process does not currently have widespread use in early intervention networks, it has considerable utility in improving programs.

The following example illustrates the importance of collecting data regarding the extent to which family-centered practices were implemented in a program's early intervention services.

Data collection was accomplished by two parent observers who were randomly selected from a list of recommended parents. Both observers had a child with a disability between 3 and 5 years of age and previously experienced home intervention from multiple disciplines. A consultant met with the parent observers to review the guidelines for their observation visits. The orientation focused on how to make objective observations and to take notes. The parent observers were paid for training, observations, and meeting time. Observations of home visits and IFSP meetings were completed. The parent observers were requested to identify strengths and weaknesses in the delivery of services by addressing the following areas: (a) are the services flexible and responsive to family concerns/priorities; and (b) is there effective communication between families and providers?

The positive feedback from the parent observations indicated that the team promoted a working partnership with families, including (a) respect for family lifestyle and rhythms; (b) flexibility with family schedules; (c) options for service delivery; (d) acceptance and encouragement of relationships between provider and family; and (e) use of natural environment and routines for learning. Recommendations for improvement targeted helping the team explore with families the priorities and concerns that go beyond child-related outcomes. The team identified strategies to address these recommendations and planned on follow-up satisfaction surveys as a method of ongoing review and improvement of the program.

Step 2: Planning

Implementing and sustaining new practices in early childhood programs requires the development of a *clear, succinct road map* that has realistic and well-defined measurable goals (Cumming & Worley, 1993). These new practices are most likely to be adopted if they fit with the organization's overall vision and goals. As the planning process proceeds, continual reflection to determine if the steps of the master plan match the organizational goals is needed. If significant discrepancy exists, resistance is likely to ensue. Once made, these plans are not static but continue to be modified and changed as team members gain further insight as specific tasks have been completed. Many well-intentioned early intervention programs fail to do this iterative process, so advocates must continue to support programs to keep cycling through the improvement process.

A pediatric unit at a children's hospital was committed to supporting young children's development during their hospitalization. A team leader and facilitator were identified to help the unit with their planning. The staff met to determine their vision for developmental supportive care. (*Identifying a vision.*) Many staff members believed that they needed to do a better job of screening the children's development and planning interventions during their hospitalization. The unit decided to adopt a formal screening assessment. They trained all of the staff and instituted the screening process. During the first month, the nurses reviewed how the screening process was going. (*Build in reflection of practice.*) Overall, staff had many concerns. The assessment they chose took too much time to complete in their already busy schedules. They were also discouraged, because the screening did not help them to plan interventions that they could incorporate into their care plans. (*Plan did not meet defined goal.*)

The nurses were committed to this project's goal, but it was clear that modifications were needed in their plans. (*Modify plans as needed.*) The unit director and team leader continued to praise the staff for their efforts and reflected with staff how frustrating it is to go back to the "drawing board." (*Use of cognitive–behavioral strategies are important to support perseverance, not merely for results.*) The staff worked with the unit psychologist and found another developmental assessment that provided them with useful information for their care plans. This process helped build excellence into the pediatric unit practices.

Step 3: Piloting the Innovation

Dalziel and Schoonover (1992) suggested that change needs to be absorbed slowly into the organization. Sometimes it is advisable to select only one segment of the organization to *pilot the change* before full implementation. When Public Law 99-457 was first enacted, it built in five years of planning to ensure the slow adoption of a significant change initiative. Some states embraced Part H early (Nebraska), whereas others adopted practices much later (Delaware). During this five-year time frame, Nebraska, for example, piloted two early intervention projects. Program evaluation was built into the process to allow ongoing feedback to improve the projects. Information from these two projects was used to refine protocols that later were disseminated when implementation of Part H began across the state (Jackson, 1992). Staff in these programs were also available to provide training and consultation as statewide implementation began. These pilot projects provided the opportunity for staff to experience the results of a new way of service provision and allowed visibility to other program staff who were affected once the pilot was fully implemented throughout the state.

Step 4: Maintaining Momentum for Implementation

A significant challenge to implementing change is *maintaining momentum* to carry out the innovation. Among the most difficult aspects of implementing innovative practices is motivating people at all levels of the organization and maintaining the momentum of the effort to implement the change (Dalziel & Schoonover, 1992). Strong tendencies exist for individuals to return to familiar practices unless there is ongoing support and reinforcement to continue movement toward proposed change. Parish and Gemmill (1993) found that both the commitment of a program's adminis-tration and use of a team effort to solve problems by reframing vulnera-bilities into opportunities are likely to enhance the successful adoption of the innovation. Providers must recognize that change requires both hu-man and financial resources to support activities such as training staff to behave differently (including technical and social skills), data collection, and ongoing meetings.

Making Change a Reality: Contributing Factors

Individuals within the organization are key ingredients to the successful adoption of new practices. Effective leadership and cohesive team partic-ipation by individuals within the organization are contributing factors to successful change process. The role of each are explored in the following section.

What Is Needed for Effective Leadership

For most programs the goal is to create and support an environment in which providers and families collaborate on teams, set goals, and pool skills to accomplish these goals (Salisbury, 1992). Effective leadership and management that supports building cohesive and goal-oriented teams are key factors in successful early intervention programs (Hogan, Curphy, & Hogan, 1994). Leaders must have the skills to guide the course of program development. The following have been identified for effective early inter-vention leadership (Johnson et al., 1992):

1. Knowledge of the availability of community services;
2. Skills in team interaction, conflict resolution, and interpersonal communication;
3. Ability to evaluate programs;
4. Effective communication skills in cross-agency interactions;
5. Clear sense of goals or mission;
6. Ability to inspire and maintain the trust of others; and
7. Clear understanding and effective use of one's own skills.

Garland and Linder (1994) suggested that these skills should be the min-imum performance expectations for leaders. With the new challenges pre-sented by the IDEA and its amendments, they suggest that administrators need to embrace a commitment toward new goals for early intervention services.

Leaders used to be viewed as special people who set directions and make key decisions. This view of leadership is counterproductive to an organizational structure that enables the individuals to participate in vi-sion building and promotion of innovation, however (Senge, 1990). Leadership needs to embrace quality-improvement approaches (Barsness et al., 1993) and promote manger–staff partnership models rather than those based on control models (Cohen & Bradford, 1990). In this new culture, effective leaders help reframe the thinking of those they guide and enable them to view change as an achievable outcome (Conner, 1993). Leaders need to expand the capabilities of staff to understand and to clarify the vision, to implement the innovation, and to reflect on ways to improve the system. Typical areas affecting team performance include the skills of leaders in communicating a clear vision, developing talent, planning and organizing work activities, and acquiring needed resources (Hallam & Campbell, 1992, in Hogan et al., 1994). In this climate, leaders need to help others see how things might be different in the future.

"Early intervention programs require teamwork; family-centered decision making; interagency collaboration, external financial and political support; and public accountability" (Garland & Linder, 1994, p. 134). Implementing these components requires innovative approaches to leadership. Terry (1993) proposed a model of authentic (an integrated approach) leadership that draws on six diverse perspectives of leadership (e.g., inclusive personal, structure and unstructured team, positional and functional, power with, visionary leadership, and ethical leadership theories). The primary points of each of these theories follow.

- *Personal theory* attributes both certain inherent traits and acquired skill to leaders.
- The *team situational leadership model* suggests that leaders need to modify their styles to match the needs of those they lead.
- *Functional theory* is attentive to the leadership demanded by cultural change.
- *Political leadership* initiates change either by focusing on accomplishing the will of the leader (power-over) or the will of the followers (power-with).
- A *visionary leader* teaches, providing insight so that persons understand not only the future's possible content but also the process by which that content is predicted or created.
- In *intrinsic ethical theory*, values are intertwined in each phase of the administrative process.

In his comprehensive theory, Terry depicted leadership as authentic action that acknowledges, accesses, and embraces all six diverse perspectives of leadership. In arguing against simple acceptance of a single theory, he elucidated the limitations and perils each paradigm possesses when applied in isolation. In many ways, Terry's approach relates to a general theory orientation (Woody et al., 1992), which involves knowledgeable and systematic movement among theories using transtheoretical skills and concepts. This approach relates to what Terry referred to as "convergent thinking," in which diversity is synthesized into new structures and novel unified directions are proposed. In transcending general theory, he proposed leadership with "divergent thinking," in which old thought forms are challenged by extending boundaries and devising new connections. The following discussion integrates several of the leadership theories to early intervention practices.

In the situational leadership model, leaders can rely on a continuum of supportive and directive behaviors that are manifested in a variety of strategies, such as delegating, supporting, coaching, and directing. Therefore, just as counselors can act with intentionality, leaders can generate alternative behaviors in a particular situation, approach an issue from different vantage points, and avoid being bound to one course of action. Hersey and Blanchard (1988) suggested that leaders need to adjust their direction and support as needed to be dynamic. The specific traits needed for success depend on the context, including the task, the leader, and the group members. Therefore, it is important to identify the task behaviors of the situation (e.g., when, where, and how the tasks are to be accomplished) and the relationship behaviors needed (e.g., establishing trust among members, openness to ideas). Support of the contextual nature of leadership was found in a study of 33 coordinators of local Interagency Coordinating Councils (ICCs; Morgan, Guetzloe, & Swan, 1991). These results suggest that a high task–high relationship style was the most successful in leading the ICC, because of the task-oriented nature of the ICCs paired with the critical need for coordination among agency representatives.

As communities begin planning to create an array of services that are available and accessible for all young children and their families, problems can occur if community leaders assume a visionary stance (*visionary leadership skills*) that results in action without thorough consideration of the implications of implementing the plan. Equally detrimental to effective implementation is the leader who devotes too much time to how people feel, when providers actually need action-oriented leadership and guidance (Dalziel & Schoonover, 1992). Some leaders become so focused on the outcomes of change and the details of implementing the proposed plan that they fail to consider the staff concerns. Successful leaders foster broad-based ownership to sustain staff motivation and commitment, which becomes even more challenging when community agencies are trying to reach a goal through collaboration, as suggested in the implementation of Part C of the IDEA. A leader in these situations needs to be attentive to the cultural change in early intervention that promotes collaboration (*functional theory*). Successful collaboration can occur when a concerted effort among community agency leaders tries to diffuse ownership by soliciting feedback and having community stakeholders participate in planning key dimensions of implementing the change. Ownership of the plan is crucial if implementing new practices is to be inculcated into their agency procedures (Fullan, 1982). The value of team process in promoting innovation is exemplified in the ICC structure. These ICCs provide a collaborative effort to implement an integrated community-based service system for young children and their families.

Supporting Staff in Building Collaborative Teams

"Planned change relies on getting the right people with the right attributes into the right role at the right time" (Dalziel & Schoonover, 1992, p. 67). One of the major challenges of implementing change is identifying the members of the team and ensuring maximum participation (Winton et al., 1992). A primary consideration of group membership is identifying those individuals who are affected by and who will affect the proposed change.

A team approach is not unique to early intervention but is based on many of the concepts derived from a human relationships model (Garland & Linder, 1994). These concepts emphasize the importance of using group methods to build effective working relationships. Well-functioning teams do not just happen. Positive experiences on teams, which result in team members assessing the need for change and identifying strategies for enhancing change, is another powerful learning experience that enhances individual skills in implementing change (Bailey et al., 1992). For teams that have a long-term, ongoing relationship, providing activities that allow for a better understanding of the members' interactive style in team setting is advantageous. Olson and Murphy (1997) recommended that team members complete exercises that help individuals identify their personality style when they participate on teams. Samples of items of their scale, Personality Types and Team Interactions, include ratings such as (a) takes a strong stand/seldom takes a strong stand or (b) quick to act/takes time before acting. This self-evaluation process assists the team in creating an appreciation for the strengths of each of their team members and a better awareness of how these contribute to the team interaction. These individual characteristics affect team dynamics and contribute to the team's functioning, including the decision-making process.

In an effort to maximize the effects of team group dynamics, it is important to have a variety of people serve different functions. This diversity of team member roles results in generating different points of view that are necessary for creativity in the problem-solving process. Optimal results of this group processing occur if the meeting culture promotes deferment of negative judgments and values diversity. Dalziel and Schoonover (1992) identified the following roles needed for an effective team:

- *Inventor*: Integrates trends and data into concepts, models, and plan; envisions the "big picture" first; adapts plans.
- *Entrepreneur*: Instinctively focuses on efficiency and effectiveness; identifies critical issues and new possibilities; actively seeks advantages and opportunities.
- *Integrator*: Forges alliances; gains acceptance of the team and its program; relates practical plans to strategic plans and organizational issues.
- *Expert*: Takes responsibility for the technical knowledge and skills required for the change; uses information skillfully and explains it in a logical way.

- *Manager*: Simplifies, delegates, assigns priorities; develops others; gets the job done.
- *Sponsor*: Ensures support and resources from the highest levels of the organization; communicates where the change fits in the over-all organizational vision. (p. 67)

The following scenario demonstrates that these complementary, yet individual styles that are important to the team process during planning for implementation of the innovation.

Two policy makers, a state senator and director of Health and Human Services, wanted to address the quality of child care throughout the state through an innovative training program that would maximize the use of technology. (*The inventors.*) They challenged a small group of community stakeholders, including child care providers, trainers, public television staff, and faculty to develop a proposal to make this vision a reality. After several meetings, it became clear that each of the participants had unique skills to contribute to the planning process. Two of the committee members emerged as *experts* in their respective areas and began to take responsibility for planning the details of the project. The faculty and trainers took the lead in developing the training curriculum. Simultaneously, the public television staff arranged for technical presentations on the delivery mode options (e.g., public television programs, Internet courses, CD-ROM productions). The director of the training center proceeded to explore options to obtain funding from national sources or to develop partnerships with other states that are addressing similar issues. (*Entrepreneur.*) The faculty from continuing education challenged the group to examine practical issues such as making sure the inservice hours can be used for continuing education credit and helped blend the curriculum ideas with the appropriate delivery mode. She was valued for her ability to weave the parts into a holistic perspective. (*Integrator.*) After a six-month planning process, the proposal was completed and shared with the policy makers for distribution to potential funders.

Successful community agencies are those that grow and adapt by promoting change and continual improvement as a value of their culture, which results in change being integrated into the day-to-day practices of team members (Dalziel & Schoonover, 1992). *Training* is one strategy to achieve the outcome. Gaucher and Coffey (1993) recommended that training needs to be team-based and problem-focused and emphasize knowledge as well as skill-building. There is limited research in early intervention regarding the impact of training on successful adoption of innovative practices. Turning to the health organizations, several studies demonstrate the need for training. A recent national survey of 3,303 community hospital directors of quality improvement found that inadequate training was cited as one of the primary barriers to implementing improvement strategies. These findings suggest that ongoing communication and training is necessary to clarify with staff the direction of the organization and to provide the tools necessary to implement the innovation (Barsness et al., 1993).

Parish and Gemmill (1993) evaluated the results of change initiatives in 48 hospitals. Results of a Quality Success Rating survey found that positive satisfaction ratings of the quality improvement training for hospital staff had a statistically significant, positive correlation to the quality of services provided by the hospitals. These results were supported by Fabi (1992), who also found that the amount of training provided to leaders and members of teams was significantly related to the success of the implementation of the team recommendations. Advanced skills related to leadership and organizational development are delineated in chapter 8. In addition, *emotional support* is essential for staff and change agents to support their ability to cope with challenges that occur during the change process. The need for these resources (training and emotional support) is frequently underestimated (Cummings & Worley, 1993).

The following example illustrates the careful planning and supports necessary for implementation of an innovative service coordination program:

As one early intervention program planned to add service coordination to its existing early intervention services, administration recognized the need to support the service coordination staff in their new roles, as well as integrate them into the existing early intervention team. This support was accomplished by providing training and extensive clinical supervision. (*Need for ongoing training.*) Much attention and recognition was provided to the service coordinators and early intervention team members (e.g., praise of individual coordinators, public recognition of their accomplishments at the ICC meeting, and newspaper publicity) as they gained competence in their roles and implemented services. (*Recognition promotes change.*) It is important to note that these strategies were used with both the service coordinators and the existing team members to build a team ownership to the process and a sense of pride in all team members as they incorporated this new program component into their service delivery system. (*Building team ownership.*)

This example highlights the importance of supporting staff through training and a system of recognition and reinforcement, including the intrinsic reward of experiencing success in the change effort. Strong tendencies exist for individuals to return to familiar practices unless there is ongoing support and reinforcement to continue movement toward proposed change. Therefore, it is imperative to provide a supportive environment that helps to maintain momentum to carry out the innovative practices in early intervention.

Challenges to Collaboration and Service Integration

As community programs begin to plan and implement new ways to deliver services, it is important to anticipate what factors may create potential barriers. Change initiatives can cause reverberations throughout the interdependent components of the organizational system. Such initiatives require adaptation of procedures and professional roles that threaten system homeostasis and frequently result in anxiety as individuals leave the familiar and tread into the unknown (Woody et al., 1992). Such anxiety is felt by many early childhood special education and child care teachers as self-contained classrooms are being dissolved and replaced by inclusive child care settings. Although many staff embrace the challenges and stimulation of this new approach for serving children with disabilities, there will be others who resist changes to current practices. They view change as a threat both to themselves and the system. Change is most likely adopted if the process discussed earlier (including creating a vision and gaining political support paired with careful planning) in the chapter are followed; however, even with the adoption of these strategies, there will always be those who resist change. Resistance is a natural response to the desire for system maintenance and is often an attempt to preserve one's existing role. It is crucial that resistance be managed effectively or the change initiative can fail altogether. It is the responsibility of leaders within early childhood programs to identify the potential sources of resistance proactively. Resistance stems from multiple sources and for many reasons. For example, the child care teachers may feel inadequate in caring for the child with disabilities or the early childhood special education staff may fear losing control of the day-to-day curriculum. Based on the source of the resistance, administrators can work with the providers to identify strategies to ameliorate such resistance. In the case of the child care worker, training may alleviate fears with the proposed inclusive program. For the early childhood special education staff, the program planners need to build in collaborative planning of the curriculum.

Conner (1993) suggested that resistance is accentuated in situations in which staff view the change as causing negative consequences, doubt that the change will result in positive outcomes, or fear the unknown. Resistance can be overt or covert. Overt resistance is much easier to deal with as the concerns are articulated, which provides opportunities to address them. Overt resistance should be encouraged from the start of change efforts, because covert resistance is often not visible until it has undermined the change project. Harkness, Hermansen, and Mentzel (1993), in their implementation of three pilot quality improvement projects, encountered resistance that interfered with their success. They found that providers may resist change even when there are documented benefits, highlighting the need to understand these systemic cultural patterns when planning the change process.

Rodd (1994) identified several sources of resistance to change that can be applied to change initiatives in early childhood programs:

- Fear for staff's future, including fear of unknown and anxiety about losing job;
- Changes in organization beliefs and values that are different from individual staff;
- Misunderstandings about the need for, purpose of, and scope of change;
- Lack of trust in the leader;
- Lack of ownership by individual staff; and
- Agency history of frequent change without careful decision making.

When resistance emerges, it can be addressed if its source is recognized and strategies are used to ameliorate the potential negative impact. Communication, empathy, and support are important to approaching staff resistance to change. Understanding individuals' concerns regarding the change initiative can occur only through a process of active listening, which demonstrates the genuine interest of the listener (addressed in chapter 4). This communication strategy provides a climate that promotes a dialogue between resistors and change agents that can help clarify the basis of the resistance and provide input—modifications of the implementation plan. For example, if the staff primarily is worried about their job security, team meetings clarifying the need for the change will not help lessen resistance. Rather, the leader needs to meet with those staff regarding their jobs and how the position or role will be affected by the change. Staff need opportunities to voice their concerns so the root causes of the resistance can be identified and to prevent staff attempts to sabotage program efforts (Rodd, 1994). Participation in joint problem solving to overcome identified barriers and a system of ongoing communication are crucial to clarify the consequences of the change.

Conner (1993) suggested that Kubler-Ross's five-stage model (Kubler-Ross, 1996) of grief is relevant to understanding individuals' responses to change when the change is viewed as negative. This negative response to change is illustrated in Figure 9.2. Immobilization is often the response to the news of upcoming change when it is regarded as negative. Conner suggested that the recommended change is so different from the individual's frame of reference that she or he is unable to relate to what is happening. This initial response is often followed by denial, resulting in people ignoring and rejecting the innovation, assuming that the change will not take place. As it becomes evident that implementation is moving forward, the individual responds with anger. Anger is followed by the individual negotiating to avoid the negative impact of the change. Conner (1993) suggested that bargaining behavior marks the beginning of acceptance. For example, the early intervention provider may be willing to provide therapy within the classroom setting if they can be in charge of leading the music session. Depression is not an uncommon response and is manifested through recognition of failure, lack of emotional and physical energy, and disengagement from one's work. It is essential for individuals to regain a sense of control in their work environment to move beyond the feelings of depression. When the individual begins to reframe and gain this sense of control, she or he begins to redefine goals and find ways to succeed within the new culture. As we begin to examine resistance to change, let us examine one community's experience.

An early intervention program decided to change its team model from a multidisciplinary to a transdisciplinary approach. Two therapists particularly were threatened by the transdisciplinary approach. They thought the teacher would be assigned the primary intervention role and they would be left only to consult. Not only did they not like to consult, they were worried that they did not have the requisite skill and that their time would be reduced. (*Fear about personal future.*) They believed the decision to implement transdisciplinary teams was a cost-savings strategy and was not being

NEGATIVE RESPONSE TO CHANGE

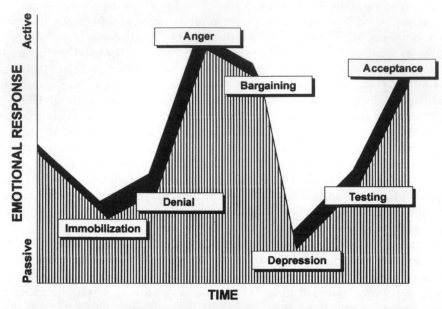

Figure 9.2.   Negative Response to Change. From *Managing at the speed of change* by Daryl R. Conner. Copyright © 1993 by Daryl R. Connor. Reprinted with permission of Villard Books, a division of Random House, Inc.

adopted to benefit families. (*Misunderstanding about the purpose and lack of trust of program administrators.*) They began to voice their concerns to some of their colleagues and felt families should know about the "real" reasons for their change. (*Potential for sabotage.*)

This scenario presented many red flags that needed to be addressed for this new intervention initiative to see positive outcomes. Clearly a dialogue needed to occur that allowed opportunities to understand the motivation for the transdisciplinary approach. This dialogue would result in clarifying misunderstandings regarding the need, purpose, and ramifications of the change. For some staff members, better understanding of the rationale for change allows them to shift their position and gradually accept the proposed change. The following is just one strategy to facilitate team communication:

The team leader was told that some team members were upset with plans to adopt a transdisciplinary model. She was surprised that at previous meetings these feelings were not expressed. The team leader decided to try a new strategy. Once the group met, she passed out note pads and asked everyone to brainstorm by writing ideas on the notes about the advantages of the transdisciplinary approach. After five minutes, the group was asked to work together to arrange the notes on the wall into thematic clusters. The same strategies were used regarding disadvantages and concerns. This process generated many new ideas for and against the proposed team process. The remainder of the meeting was spent clarifying the issues.

This process began the first step to consensus building toward a collaborative model. The team needed to believe and feel they were part of identifying the concerns and strategies for enhancing this new process. Strategies began to be modified, so the team as a whole seemed more comfortable with the recommended approach. The leadership skills of the team leader facilitated this consensus-building activity.

Agencies need to consider the unique blend of environmental influences (e.g., social, cultural, political, and economic factors), the culture of the organization and community, and the skills of individuals and teams in planning for change. Incorporated in this planning is determining whether the agency has the capacities (e.g., trained facilitators) and the motivation to change (Conner, 1993). Often change fails because there are unrealistic expectations, with administrators and staff failing to recognize the costs (e.g., financial, emotional) of the proposed change. Careful analysis at the beginning of the planning is necessary to determine if the potential benefits outweigh the costs associated with the innovation. If there are too many competing factions at the time of proposing new approaches, it can be overwhelming and create an atmosphere of chaos. These factors need to be considered when implementing and sustaining the momentum of change initiatives. For example:

The consultants began the planning process to implement developmental supports in one of the pediatric hospital units. Several factors accelerated this unit's readiness to change their current practice: (a) recent participation of nurses in a national conference, which increased their awareness of the importance of developmentally supportive care for young hospitalized children; (b) emphasis on supporting the psychosocial needs of children in national accreditation standards; and (c) availability of technical assistance through a state training project.

A team of stakeholders, including family members, met to develop an action plan for change. (*Importance of planning for change.*) The first step was to design a developmental assessment and intervention process. The components of the process included identifying standard assessment tools and defining roles and responsibilities. Parallel to this process was implementing inservice workshops to provide the team with skills to carry out the procedures.

Shortly after this process was initiated, hospital administration announced a hospital-wide initiative for redesign. These competing initiatives exacerbated rather than synergized the change process. (*Costs for implementing change need to be determined.*) There was much uncertainty about how the unit innovation would work together with the larger hospital design. In addition, staff did not believe they had adequate resources (i.e., emotional, time, and human resources) to assimilate both change processes simultaneously. As a result, the unit innovation was placed on hold until further clarification of how the hospital redesign would affect the unit.

This example illustrates that the key to optimal organizational success is adopting change initiatives that do not exceed the organization's capacity to assimilate the change. Failure to implement the unit innovation occurred because individuals could not absorb the change without potentially displaying dysfunctional behavior (e.g., immobilization and decreased productivity).

Each individual's unique characteristics influence the pace at which she or he accommodates to change. Therefore, the perceptions of those responsible for carrying out the change affect their rate of adoption and need careful consideration to determine the degree of resistance and the potential success of overcoming this resistance. Rogers (1983) proposed that adoption of innovation follows a normal, bell-shaped curve when tracking the time it takes individuals to implement the recommended change. Individuals are rated on a continuum of adopter categories, ranging from innovators who readily engage in new activities to slow adopters who resist change and only accept the innovation when all the uncertainty is gone and the majority of individuals are safely implementing the change. Slow adopters adapt more slowly than the pace of change is occurring because they have low tolerance for ambiguity (Conner, 1993). There are many important differences between those who are early or late in adopting innovations. Scientific data support the credibility of the innovation and provide important information to sway an innovator, but later adopters place greater credibility in the subjective experiences of their peers (Rogers, 1983). Early adopters tend to be resilient and can be characterized as positive, focused, flexible, organized, and proactive (Conner, 1993). These distinctions are important to make, suggesting that change agents should use different approaches with each adopter category to facilitate the change process.

Conclusion

The field of early intervention is faced with many challenges as it moves toward an integrated service delivery system. There is an urgent need for more empirical investigations in early childhood community-based programs to determine the obstacles they face and the successes they experience in implementing systems-change efforts. As health care, education, and social service organizations and community early intervention programs engage in proactive strategic planning and organizational change endeavors, psychologists can contribute to the stakeholder analysis by supporting the fundamental building blocks for change that have been discussed throughout this chapter. Psychologists can assist in effecting substantive paradigm shifts by planting seeds of developmental and family-centered care over time in a cycle of continuous quality improvement. Considering their particular specialization in behavioral, developmental, and psychosocial issues, psychologists can contribute to a vision of success in early intervention organizations as they enhance their developmentally appropriate and family-supportive care. Even encouraging providers of the need to obtain family input on redesigning the health care or early intervention settings can seem like a novel idea to many providers. At the heart of reform at a broader level is the development of community-based systems of care involving interagency teams. Such reform efforts are consistent with the conceptual underpinnings of much of psychology.

There is no simple recipe for change procedures that can be adopted by programs, as each program is unique. Therefore, the process must be individualized to match specific characteristics of the program context and be guided by theory. As agencies attempt to institute change, individuals need to be reminded that both building a commitment and implementing change are slow processes, requiring an initial investment of time and energy and systematic approach. The complex and critical nature of policy development effort in the areas of interagency collaboration and family-centered care needs to be addressed with caution. Given that unresponsive, uncoordinated, or poorly accessible systems of care significantly compromise benefits to young children and their families, fostering organization change and development in a journey toward excellence is crucial.

Case Study

This illustration represents a summary of organization development activities with an early intervention team, the members of which wanted to examine their assessment process. The director of this agency promoted the use of the CQI process, providing strong leadership support for the effort. This early intervention program, which is part of a private organization that provides services for individuals with disabilities, is located in an urban setting. The mission of the agency is to provide a full range of exemplary services, necessary research pertinent to these activities, and technical assistance to state programs in developing new and innovative ways to provide full inclusion in the community. This interdisciplinary agency has more than 50 specialists across eight disciplines.

Description of the Work Group and Focus of Change

The agency director charged the team with the task of examining its assessment and staffing process. The team will look for inconsistencies in the current process and make recommendations for improvement to allow the process to fully satisfy the needs of the customers. (*Identification of common vision.*) Volunteers were solicited for membership of the team, including representatives from multiple disciplines and family members.

The purview of the team's activities is extremely broad, greatly complicating the CQI process. The entire range of activities (referral, intake, scheduling, assessment, services coordination, staffing, follow-up, and evaluation) needed to be addressed. Both internal and external factors created a set of conditions causing a need for change. The broad environment was turbulent with the uncertainty of managed care, capitation, and contracts with school districts. Moreover, there was growing emphasis within the organization on generating revenue from direct services. Hence there is an increasing focus on quantity rather than quality of services, potentially jeopardizing interdisciplinary collaboration, which is increasingly difficult to justify as cost-efficient. With the expanding recognition that to satisfy external customers, a more family-centered system (e.g., evening and weekend hours) is on the horizon, generating anxiety among providers having their own families. Internally, the agency has faced problems with its service coordination of assessments in terms of which departments should assume primary responsibility and which model is the most family-centered. A second issue is the devaluing of interdisciplinary teamwork by one department. These factors collectively were key to motivating change within the agency.

Gathering Data

Multimethod assessment was conducted, including extensive interviews, question-naires, and process observation. Interview data appeared to be a valid reflection of the thoughts and sentiments of those interviewed because of the comprehensiveness of the questions; the considerable time devoted to each interview; and the use of microskills to probe, clarify, and encourage candid responses.

Diagnosis of Group's Strengths and Weaknesses

Terry's (1993) Action Wheel was used to enable multiple framing, which facilitated an analysis of historical context, competing cultures, and organizational and team struc-ture. As data were gathered and preliminary diagnoses made, feedback was provided to key stakeholders.

History

There is an atmosphere of uncertainty about the role of the interdisciplinary team given the move toward capitation in managed care and restricted funds from the schools (which refer children to the agency). Several members of the team remarked that administration's commitment to interdisciplinary team evaluations is shrinking because of the focus "on numbers"—namely, the number of children seen to generate revenue for the agency. Many comments also suggested a significant level of frustration and learned helplessness, with some feelings that administration will not listen to the team's recommendations. In addition, there was the perception that the administration did not place as high a value on implementing a family-centered service delivery assessment process as did the team. All of these problems directly affect interdisci-plinary evaluations in general and this CQI team in particular.

Culture

There is a perception of some schism in the culture at the agency. Members of the team were unanimous in their commitment to CQI and to interdisciplinary collabora-tion. They believe that CQI is beginning to change the culture where department di-rectors alone make decisions for their own departments, yet they also tend to be skeptical about the incomplete commitment to CQI. A striking theme throughout the interviews was the strong dissatisfaction with one department for its values that were regarded as incongruent with interdisciplinary teaming.

Mission and Meaning

The overall vision is rather diffuse, which is part of the reason for the CQI team to reassess who its customers are and what their needs have become given the evolving environmental context. For instance, does the team want to be family-centered, and if so, how is this concept operationalized? Who are the clients that will be served, and are they different from those served in the past? Most members of the team highlighted quality clinical services, which in their view necessitates interdisciplinary collaboration. This cross-discipline contact and support are significant factors in the meaning they ascribe to their professional work. Some members questioned how they would feel about their work if activities of the interdisciplinary teams were curtailed. Many of those interviewed doubted the values of some department directors who only nominally sup-port the interdisciplinary process.

The team's mission statement indicates that it will "study the Interdisciplinary Team Evaluation process." Yet there may be other "missions" that the team has not fully explored. For example, will this CQI team lead to greater political clout at the agency? Will the team assist the agency in transitioning to a new health care environment that supports fewer full interdisciplinary team assessments? The agency's strategic plan, which calls for the agency to "be the premier interdisciplinary program focused on developmental disabilities and special health care needs," suggests sponsorship of a potentially broader mission after the team's initial charge is addressed. This evolution illustrates the unfolding process of a CQI process that is crucial in examining the entire pattern of change rather than limiting the focus to one isolated part of the innovation. Developing a vision that has shared meaning for the team and ultimately for the agency will affect the eventual outcome of the success or failure of the change initiative.

Organizational and Team Structure

This agency has "flattened administrative structure," with considerable authority in the hands of the department directors. The clinical service system is "heavily structured," with most of the clinics, charting, and billing centrally administrated. From the perspective of many group members, most issues have to go to top administration prior to implementation. Although all group members interviewed voiced strong convictions about the worth of egalitarian participation, interview data, survey responses, and process observation suggest that some members of the team do not feel as comfortable speaking up as do others. This reticence may occur because of what they regard as their positions within the organizational hierarchy, their own insecurities, or their learning histories (e.g., family upbringing).

Several questions arose about how group membership was determined. Some members, although very positive about the team, felt compelled to serve on the team when asked by their director. The original solicitation for volunteers went out on e-mail, but not to all potential internal customers, only to department directors. The team, with its hierarchical organizational context, seems to be in the early stages of reaching out to a broader base of customers, denying the opportunity for nondirectors to have the voice advanced by CQI principles. Although apparently not an issue for this particular group, unequal representation across departments (e.g., two physical therapists and one social worker) could be problematic, particularly from a political perspective. In addition, having random selection by the department directors limits the likelihood of the balanced roles one would like represented on a team.

Team functioning has been complicated by the enormity of the task. The "overwhelming problem" engendered debate about multiple agendas as the group periodically lost its focus, meandering from one issue to another. This approach is probably less a problem with the group and more an indication of the complex and multifaceted nature of the interdisciplinary team-assessment process. However, now that the team has flow-charted the process and worked through the divergent agendas, it does not appear to be as effective and efficient as it might be. In general, there was a recognition (in reflection) that the group got off task from time to time and that some issues were inappropriate for discussion. Data from interviews and process observations suggest that the group is less skilled in shifting from a task orientation to supportive and reinforcing comments.

Evaluation of Outcome and Process

Opinions were positive about interdisciplinary teaming and the CQI process in general. There appears to be a reinvigoration, with enhanced self-satisfaction and feelings of being valued by the organization. References were made to "intrinsic" reward, the "support" for one another, and "growth" in staff. Team members appreciated the opportunity to provide their input and to actually be a part of changing processes that may have been problematic for quite some time.

Recommendations for Effecting Desired Change

1. One department in particular needs to be brought on board to adopt a vision consistent with the agency's interdisciplinary collaboration. Administration needs to reflect on whether it wishes to address or to overlook what many members of the team see quite strongly as the devaluing of interdisciplinary assessments and training by some department directors in the agency.
2. Administration should foster greater dialogue with the departments about the turbulent health care, education, and social system environment and their potential effects on interdisciplinary clinical staff while also listening to their views about the significance of interdisciplinary team work.
3. Recommendations from this CQI team should be considered within a broader context relating to the vision of early childhood intervention services. Over time the team (or subsequent teams) may assume broader missions.
4. Implementation of CQI throughout the agency needs to be accelerated. The strategic plan has set a goal of institutionalizing CQI at all levels; however, some departments have not participated because of a unilateral decision by the department director. In addition, decision making in teams often reverts to a hierarchical model rather than an open model in which all internal customers have the option to participate. Administration is encouraged to survey its own internal customers to gain a greater awareness about how it is perceived in terms of decision making (by hierarchial or partnership). Such examination also can provide insight into organizational threats to deeper implementation of CQI.
5. Although a difficult problem without a clear solution, the organization (top administrators and department directors) needs to consider the time demand required of team members. Their CQI work is in addition to other responsibilities, which are already burdensome. Currently, there is no consideration of these added activities and no reduction in clinical load, other committee work, and technical assistance. Time demands are a significant issue.

Conclusion

CQI is beginning to take root at this agency as members reflect on their early intervention services. This team is firmly committed both to CQI and to interdisciplinary collaboration. For the most part, the group is cohesive, particularly considering the complexity of the issues it is examining and the recent genesis of CQI within the organization. Those who were interviewed are insightful about a broad array of organization and group issues. The group has less insight into each other's feelings, and a minor degree of egocentrism is apparent. For instance, those who are assertive and self-confident seem to be less aware that some group members do not always feel valued. The group is largely effective in its task orientation. However, constrained by its hierarchical organizational context, all group members deferred to department directors for various issues. Some rethinking about increasing opportunities for the direct involvement of other early intervention team members customers is needed.

This team appears to be prepared for another developmental phase. Not only are they positioned to undertake specific tasks now that the broader issues have been delineated, but they also have the degree of commitment, connectedness, compre-hensiveness (*embracing differences and opening dialogue*), confidence in the team leader, and courage to explore themselves as they cultivate self-awareness. The team, its leader, and facilitator have been exemplary models as they embraced "hard think-ing" (cf. Terry, 1993) throughout the organizational development diagnosis. The po-tential is great for substantive organization development and change.

10

Strategies for Effective Program Evaluation: A Critical Factor in Quality Services

The Gretna Family Resource Center advisory board convened to discuss the evaluation of the services at their center. The board members were disappointed with the results. Recommendations were made that were contrary to their previous decisions. One member said, "We needed that information six months ago when we were trying to decide how to resolve these issues." Many of the results presented were not linked to the outcomes that the program was striving for. It was nice information to know but did not tell them how well they were doing. Frustration and defensiveness permeated the atmosphere of the meeting. As the meeting was ending the sentiment of the group was echoed by the chairperson: "How can we have an evaluation that really can help us plan?"

Program evaluation can only be an effective tool for early intervention programs if the findings are used in meaningful ways. Too often the experience of the Gretna Family Resource Center is the norm. The challenge is for programs to use the evaluation information for program decision making and improvement. Patton (1997) labeled this evaluation approach *utilization-focused evaluation,* an evaluation process in which the focus is on its intended use by intended users. Systematic investigation of early intervention efficacy is a complex yet essential process for improving and expanding service delivery for young children and their families. Historically, efficacy studies viewed early childhood intervention as a single entity and asked the question, does early intervention work? Meisels (1992) maintained that this evaluation approach should be abandoned because simple causal models are problematic and provide limited information to guide future practice. More recent conceptualizations of early intervention as a multifaceted, dynamic set of phenomena have broadened our methods for evaluating early intervention programs so that program contexts, processes, and outcomes are examined (Halpern, 1990; Meisels, 1992). Broadening the scope of efficacy investigations results in more useful information for program planners, as evaluators shift from examining general program outcomes to more specific questions that determine what aspects of the program work best under what conditions (Gallagher, 1996). This chapter describes a multivariate evaluation framework, which if implemented effectively will enhance the lives of the children and families being served.

Designing Program Evaluation in Early Intervention Programs

Just as there are guiding principles to clinical practices, there need to be principles that guide program evaluation. It is important for practitioners in the field to recognize that program evaluation efforts are based on best-practice standards as a means of ongoing improvement in programs and practices. The American Evaluation Association (AEA, 1995) suggests five principles:

- Conduct systematic inquiry that is data-based;
- Provide competent services;
- Ensure the integrity and honesty of the evaluation process;
- Respect the people involved in and affected by the evaluation; and
- Be sensitive to the diversity of interests and values of those evaluated.

The Division for Early Childhood Recommended Practices for Program Evaluation (DEC Task Force on Recommended Practices, 1993) included quality indicators that closely parallel AEA principles and can also serve as a useful guide for evaluation efforts. These standards emphasize the importance of (a) serving the needs of stakeholders (e.g., program administrators, service providers, parents–guardians, funding agencies); (b) conducting the evaluation within the constraints of limited resources, time demands, and political subtext of the program; (c) conducting ethical, legal, and responsible program evaluation to protect the rights of children and families; and (d) ensuring the technical adequacy of the evaluation process. These guidelines as well as the AEA principles should provide the foundation for any evaluation conducted in early intervention.

Framework for Evaluation

It is essential to determine the meaning of program evaluation. Patton (1997) offered the following definition:

> Program evaluation is the systematic collection of information about the activities, characteristics, and outcomes of programs to make judgments about the program, improve program effectiveness, and/or inform decisions about future programming. Utilization-focused program evaluation (as opposed to program evaluation in general) is evaluation done for and with specific, intended primary users for specific, intended uses.

This definition suggests that the evaluation process consists of interrelated components that provide program planners with information that can be used for a variety of different purposes. Traditionally, development and implementation of quality evaluation plans consist of two primary components: facilitating program improvement (formative evaluation) and identifying the merit–value of a program (summative evaluation; Johnson & LaMontagne, 1994).

Formative evaluation is improvement-oriented, where the focus is to collect data to enhance the implementation of a program, solve unanticipated problems, and ensure the participants are progressing toward desired outcomes (Patton, 1997). The ultimate goal of formative evaluation is to fine-tune the quality of services, a critical aspect to program development. Goal-related decisions can be evaluated to help program planners assess or reassess program goals and objectives. As the program is implemented, evaluation strategies (e.g., classroom observation, family satisfaction surveys) provide important information that program planners use to make both design-related or implementation changes in their program. For example:

One early intervention program wanted to evaluate its child assessment process used to determine eligibility for the program. This program typically completed children's assessments at the preschool program. The program evaluator conducted a planned focus group with parents in the program to review the program's child assessment process. The families voiced concerns. They believed their children did not perform optimally in this unfamiliar setting. Changes in program design resulted from this feedback, as team members negotiated with families regarding the setting of their child's assessment (i.e., home or center), which enhanced validity of assessment data as well as improved family satisfaction.

Johnson and LaMontagne (1994) suggested that a critical aspect of formative evaluation is monitoring child and family progress toward identified outcomes. Lack of progress may be a red flag that the intervention plans need to be modified. This example further illustrates the purpose of formative evaluation, monitoring progress toward program goals and modifying the program plan as indicated by the data.

Summative evaluation is a judgment-oriented evaluation approach in which the merit, work, or value of the program is the focus. This approach involves selecting criteria of merit and selecting standards for performance to determine program impact on the child, family, and community, cost-effectiveness, and accountability (Scriven, 1996). There are two primary aspects of this component of evaluation: (a) determining if the program is being implemented as designed (process evaluation, also known as treatment fidelity or integrity of the independent variable); and (b) evaluating the identified program outcomes. Program integrity, which is measured through the process evaluation, allows the evaluator to describe the program activities and to attribute program variables to the outcomes. For example:

In designing their Head Start program, the staff decided to adopt a Montessori approach. During the program evaluation, observations of the classroom curriculum revealed major departures from the original Montessori curriculum. Therefore, the evaluation was not assessing the outcome of a Montessori approach. Rather, it evaluated the outcomes attributed to this modified curriculum. This information enlightened the staff, who needed to decide if they wanted to continue with the modified curriculum approach or return to the Montessori model. Information on the effectiveness of the adapted model helped the program planners make this decision. This illustration points to the need to monitor the strategies closely that are used to achieve the program goals. In this situation, the program goals may not have been met because the program was ineffective or it could also be attributed to the inadequate implementation of procedures. Information from well-designed summative evaluation provides data that assists programs in determining whether specific program components should be continued, expanded, or terminated (Patton, 1997).

The Steps to Effective Program Evaluation

In general, there is no one formula that can be applied globally to all programs to determine how to go about program evaluation. Each program's situation is unique, and the plan that emerges must meet the special characteristics of that program. However, Patton (1997) suggested that there is a comprehensive framework that can guide evaluation practice, which includes multiple well-defined steps. These steps are key to successful evaluation. First, it is critical to begin planning early and to *create an inclusive process* that allows for participation by all staff and stakeholders of the service delivery system (Feinberg, Hanft, & Marvin, 1996). Clearly identifying the people who benefit from the evaluation is essential. In early intervention, these stakeholders may include the program staff and administrators, family members, funders, or legislators. To engender commitment to both the kind of evaluation needed and its use, the program evaluator needs to work closely with this group through an interactive process. This process helps programs to *articulate their outcomes* (e.g., parents improve their skills in interacting with their children). The following scenario reflects this process:

The program evaluator met with the Clarion Action Program to begin to define the program evaluation for their newly grant-funded literacy program. After a few minutes, it became clear to the group that although the program activities were defined, the group had not thought about what outcomes they wanted by implementing these activities. For example, they decided to have a summer program for parents and their children that could (a) provide opportunities for parents to learn strategies that promote their children's "joy of reading," (b) allow time for parents to interact with other parents with preschool children, and (c) provide literacy activities for their children. The program evaluator began to ask the staff questions: Did they want parents to improve their interactions with their children? Did they want to increase how much parents read to their child at home? Each outcome would yield a different set of evaluation procedures. This process not only helped the staff to clarify their outcomes but also resulted in the program's modifying their program activities to more directly affect the outcome they identified.

As was done with the Clarion Action Program, the program evaluator needs to ask what results the program planners are anticipating and how they would know if the results were accomplished. The Accreditation Council on Services for People With Disabilities (1995) developed a document that defines quality early intervention programs in terms of family (e.g., families are informed), child (e.g., children develop relationships), and organizational outcomes (e.g., organizations demonstrate a commitment to using and encouraging the use of positive approaches to dealing with children). This document is a useful resource to programs as they begin to identify their outcomes. Outcome clarification is an area in which program planners typically need assistance. Seldom do programs have clearly defined measurable goals. More often, the program has identified service-related goal statements (e.g., to develop a service coordination program that provides support to families) versus outcome-related goals (e.g., parents gain literacy skills as evidenced by increased reading skills). Table 10.1 illustrates common mistakes made by many programs in identifying their program outcomes. When there is inadequate specification in the desired outcomes, it is less likely that they will be achieved.

Once there are clearly defined outcomes, the *program evaluation plan* can be articulated. The challenge for evaluators is to (a) identify the information to be gathered, the measures to be used and information sources (e.g., the child, family, or teachers); (b) develop a management plan (e.g., collecting survey data at the time of program enrollment and six months later); (c) collect data; and (d) analyze and interpret data. In the process of data collection, a variety of different measurement strategies need to

Table 10.1.   Examples of Mistakes in Identifying Program Outcomes

Outcome Examples	Comments
1. Service coordination services will be available to all children and families participating in early intervention.	1. This is a service implementation goal, yet for what outcome?
2. An integrated service system will be developed for children and families.	2. This goal reflects this book's philosophy; however, the terms need to be defined so they can be measured. This goal is a process-related evaluation question. The next step would be to determine the outcomes for the family of such a system.
3. Young children with disabilities will participate in early intervention programs.	3. Program participation is the stated focus. Does program mean the outcome is only the number of children served? The outcome should address what the program wants to accomplish by providing the services (e.g., improved developmental skills).
4. Children will be included in regular preschool/child care programs at least 12 hours per week.	4. This statement is quantitative and specific, but only targets being involved in the program. The extent to which children are socially integrated or other expected outcomes from this service need to be articulated.

be adopted to obtain the information needed efficiently and accurately. *Unobtrusive measures* target existing agency data that are obtained without direct participation of the children and families. For example, if a program was interested in evaluating their neonatal follow-up clinic, hospital discharge records and current health data from the primary care physician provide the information needed with family consent. *Observation data* are based on the systematic documentation of operationally defined behavior. It can focus on quantitative aspects (e.g., frequency) or qualitative aspects (e.g., intensity) of the target behavior (Johnson and LaMontagne, 1994). *Self-report data* can take many forms. Interviews can be conducted on a continuum from unstructured (based on open-ended questions) to structured formats, which are similar to written questionnaires. Interviews can also be conducted on an individual or group basis. Written surveys are a popular and efficient mechanism to collect data. Performance measures use specific norm- or criterion-referenced assessments. This approach can provide quantitative data across multiple points in time.

Patton (1997) suggested identifying measures that can be integrated into the service delivery process. Such an approach is cost-effective and sustains the evaluation because it is built into the program rather then being an added activity. For example:

The Adams Early Head Start Program was committed to enhance parent–child interaction as one of its program components. The program staff and the program evaluator discussed possible measures that could be used to assess if they positively affected the dyadic interaction. Two alternatives were being discussed: Have the parents complete a self-assessment survey or rate videotapes of caregiver–child interactions across two or more data points. The teachers recommended videotaping. They believed that having parents viewing the videotapes could serve as an effective teaching strategy. This idea was warmly received by families.

This type of evaluation can be described as intervention-oriented because it is designed to reinforce and strengthen the program's impact. These strategies help to make the evaluation findings more relevant and useful (Patton, 1997). Collaboration with the program's stakeholders during this aspect of the evaluation is recommended, especially if it results in building their understanding and skills related to the evaluation process. By supporting the skills of the program evaluation planning team (i.e., the program stakeholders) in identification of the evaluation measures, data collection, and interpretation, it potentially can have long-term impact as the team begins to apply these skills to other evaluation activities (Patton, 1997). The final step to evaluation is *effective presentation of findings*. The evaluator must determine creative strategies to translate the findings into simple and understandable presentations. Reporting complex statistical data analysis is typically not recommended. The presentation needs to highlight the important findings, emphasizing clarity and not complexity (Patton, 1997). Providing findings that stakeholders understand enables them to join in a collaborative process of data-based decision making. Different stakeholders bring in varying perspectives that can be invaluable to this process.

There is controversy in the field regarding whose responsibility it is to develop recommendations. Scriven (1996) has advocated that it is the evaluator's responsibility to draw conclusions based on the evaluator's independent judgment. Others suggest that evaluators need to supply the data and the stakeholders are responsible to make the final judgment and recommendations (Stake, 1996). Patton (1997) has suggested that in a utilization evaluation, the program evaluator needs to negotiate with the stakeholders the strategy that would be most useful for their program. Once again, facilitating a discussion with the primary stakeholders regarding their interpretations of the findings can increase their ownership of the evaluation findings and lead to more useful recommendations.

Evaluation of Child- and Family-Related Outcomes

The previous section discussed the process for identifying program outcomes. Typically, program planners need to identify both family and child outcomes. Issues related to identifying these outcomes are addressed in the following section. Table 10.2 illustrates useful measures that can be used in early intervention program evaluation.

Child Outcomes

Most evaluation efforts have focused on outcomes for children, which is appropriate given that concern for the child's development provides the rationale for early intervention and the target of most services (Bailey et al., 1998). A majority of efficacy studies has relied on a restricted range of dependent measures, specifically cognitive outcomes (Bailey & Bricker,

Table 10.2. Selected Measures of Early Intervention Program Evaluation

Program Area	Measures
Child outcomes	Developmental Profiles (Popp, 1992)
Collaboration	Interagency Coordination Questionnaire (Fields, 1992)
Family-centered	FOCAS: Family Orientation of Community and Agency Services (Bailey, 1996)
	Brass Tacks: A Self-Rating of Family-Centered Practices in Early Intervention (McWilliam & Winton, 1991)
	FamPRS (Murphy et al., 1995)
Family empowerment	Family Empowerment Scale (Koren, De Chillo, & Friesen, 1992).
IFSP	IFSP Anchor Guide (Royeen, DeGangi, & Poisson, 1992).
Parent–child interaction	Teaching Skills Inventory (Rosenberg, Robinson, & Beckman, 1984).
	Adult Communication Styles: The Missing Link to Early Language Intervention (MacDonald, & Carroll, 1994).

1985). Bruder (1993) recommended that evaluation and measurement procedures be expanded to calculate the child's attainment of a broader range of intervention goals, such as the child's competence in social interaction and skill in engaging in object play. Other noncognitive effects, such as society variables, can also be targeted (Zigler & Balla, 1982). These outcomes focus on whether individuals meet standards of personal and social responsibility (Grossman, 1983). For young children, targeted areas are related to independence in self-care, communication, and socialization skills. Meisels, Liaw, Dorfman, and Fails (1995) suggested that the method of work sampling data is a powerful substitute for traditional standardized assessments. Bailey et al. (1998) suggested that direct assessment approaches can be augmented with family information. Focus groups consisting of parents–caregivers potentially can provide detailed information about how families perceive the benefits of the program on both the child and their family. Within that discussion, the evaluator can determine if their child's progress was more or less than what would have happened without the services. Child-related societal variables, such as juvenile delinquency, frequently are targeted as longitudinal outcomes, specifically for children who are environmentally at risk. Longitudinal societal markers for success for children with disabilities have not been systematically studied. Perhaps level of independence across areas including daily living or employment may be appropriate targeted outcomes. Program planners and evaluators have had limited discussions regarding the long-term outcomes for children with disabilities, and continued discussion in this area is warranted (Farran, 1990).

Problems in research design evident in early intervention efficacy studies weaken the conclusions that can be drawn (Gallagher, 1993b). Reliable and valid measurement of intervention impact on children is challenging, especially as it relates to child development outcomes. A number of instrumentation problems pertain to the use of standardized assessment scales such as the Bayley Scales of Infant Development-II (Bayley, 1993), especially for young children with disabilities. Normative groups systematically exclude young children with disabilities who are referred for assessments. In addition, standardized assessments have limited capacity to detect child change because they provide a relatively gross summarizing score rather than a measure that reflects small increments of progress that are typical of this population (Bruder, 1993; Epps & Tindal, 1987). Considering the slow and inconsistent rate of development typical of children with disabilities, the magnitude of the treatment effects may be small. If a standardized assessment instrument is used, the data may not reveal change regardless of the success of the intervention (Sheehan & Keogh, 1984).

Meisels and his colleagues (1995) offer a Work Sampling System to document and evaluate child progress–outcomes. This assessment system evaluates and documents children's skills and behaviors across a wide variety of developmental domains across time. It consists of three complementary components: (a) developmental checklists; (b) portfolio samples of child products (e.g., drawings, audiotaped language samples, writing samples), and (c) summary reports of developmental accomplishments across developmental domains. These three sources of data provide information about incremental steps of progress across multiple data sources.

J. D. Turnbull (1993) also suggested that some of the failure to demonstrate the efficacy of early intervention, specifically for children with cerebral palsy, is the inadequacy of child assessment tools. She suggested that new technological devices (e.g., movement-analysis laboratories) will provide the necessary tools to better evaluate the efficacy of programs. Harris (1993) argued that it is not an issue of appropriateness of assessment tools but rather research design that is a mismatch between the intervention (independent variable) and the outcome (dependent variable). In J. D. Turnbull's (1993) review of the literature, half of the 15 group comparisons studied used acquisition of motor developmental milestones on standardized tools as the dependent measure. Those same programs targeted the facilitation of muscle tone, enhancement of postural reactions, and improvement of quality of movement rather than the attainment of developmental milestones as their primary target for intervention.

This program description exemplifies the incongruence between outcomes and treatment goals. Harris (1993) suggested an experimental single-subject design as a useful methodological alternative in determining the efficacy of therapy interventions, especially because of the diversity and variability of the developmental challenges of this population. The focus of this single-subject design is on the formative evaluation of program interventions to define functional relationships between instructional variables and performance (Dunst, 1979). Replicating treatment effects detected using single-subject methodology with different children and settings can enhance the generalizability of findings.

A common methodological weakness in analyzing standardized child data is the lack of appropriate statistical analysis to determine the true developmental effects of early intervention (Marfo & Kysela, 1985). To ameliorate this methodological problem, a number of alternative methods of evaluating child developmental change have been proposed. This issue is particularly salient for early intervention efficacy studies, because often the frequently asked question is how much of the change within these nonrandomly selected groups can be attributed to the intervention (Hauser-Cram & Krauss, 1991). For children with disabilities, the impact on development has been studied using *gain scores*. This change score is calculated by subtracting scores at the time of the pretest from scores at the posttest. In a review of 20 studies, Farran (1990) found that six used gain score methodology (Bailey & Bricker, 1985; Bricker, Bruder, & Bailey, 1982; Bricker & Dow, 1980; Maisto & German, 1979; Rosen-Morris & Sitkei, 1981; Shapiro, Gordon, & Neiditch, 1977). Although those gain scores were obtained by pre–post comparisons of child assessment scores, this alternative still presents significant methodological problems as a result of the absence of control groups (Rosenberg, Robinson, Finkler, & Rose, 1987). Criticisms of gain scores are their low reliability and the relationship between initial status of the child and subsequent change (Hauser-Cram & Krauss, 1991). Hauser-Cram and Krauss (1991) suggested that even with instruments that have high test–retest reliability, the change score may be unreliable because of measurement error. This source of unreliability paired with the measurement at two separate times makes it difficult to identify actual change separate from error. The second problem with change scores is the negative correlation between the initial scores and the change score (i.e., children who have low scores on the pretest tend to demonstrate greater changes than children with high scores who demonstrate less change; Thorndike, 1966).

Indices of change compare preintervention rates of development to those at postintervention by calculating a ratio of developmental gain by months in intervention. In a review of the literature, Farran (1990) concluded that all 10 studies using this type of measurement reported higher rates of development while the children participated in the intervention. Advantages of this approach include its ease of interpretation for both the individual and group and the ability to address change over different intervention periods (Hauser-Cram & Krauss, 1991). Indexes of change methodology are problematic because they presume that development is linear, which is most unlikely for typically developing children and even less likely for children with disabilities (McCall, Appelbaum, & Hogarty, 1973). Statistically, this approach is also troublesome because multiple data points are needed to describe a developmental growth curve with accuracy. To use this approach successfully, one must "collect data from enough children with varying disabilities to construct projected developmental patterns, against which the developmental pattern obtained in programs could be compared" (Farran, 1990, p. 521). Its final limitation is that it can only be used with standardized instruments in which developmental ages can be calculated, which limits its use for those programs that are expanding to evaluate a broader range of program evaluation outcomes.

Family-Related Outcomes

Throughout this book we have emphasized the importance of implementing family-centered intervention. As programs begin to shift from child-centered services to family-centered intervention, it is paramount to expand evaluation efforts to assess subsequent outcomes for families. Examining dimensions of family-related intervention supports a systems approach to evaluation, because children cannot be evaluated independent from their families and the larger society (Barrett, Hampe, & Miller, 1978).

The first step in documenting family outcomes is evaluating the extent to which family-centered practices are implemented. Although a number of instruments were developed to assess family-centered practices, they differ in their degrees of specificity, length, planned uses, and the rigor with which they have been developed and tested (Murphy, Lee, Turnbull, & Turbiville, 1995). Further complicating evaluation efforts is the diversity in the ways programs define and implement the family-centered approach (Murphy et al., 1995). Trivette, Dunst, Allen, and Wall (1993) suggested that practice indicators need to be developed, which provide benchmarks for evaluation that ascertain the extent to which behaviors mirror the intent of family-centered care. In response to this need, DEC developed recommended indicators of quality in programs for infants and young children with delays and their families (DEC, 1993). See chapter 5 for detailed discussion of these indicators of quality.

Recently, the Beach Center on Families and Disability developed the Family Centered Program Rating Scale (FamPRS) to monitor a program's progress in implementing family-centered services and to promote increased understanding of what family-centered practices are (Murphy et al., 1995). This scale was based on defined indicators that reflect the DEC Indicators of Quality: (a) inclusion of families in decision making; (b) services for the entire family, rather than just the child; (c) guidance by family priorities; and (d) respect of families' choices regarding their level of participation. Sample items are described in Table 10.3. Tools such as the FamPRS have utility in program planning, staff development, and program evaluation.

Family perspectives are an important source of data, because quality services are dependent on consumer input. The extent that families have a positive view of the service system and the service providers is based on the family's initial expectations regarding the nature of the encounters with services providers and the extent to which those expectations are met. Three distinct topics are targeted for family input, including the influence of the program on their child's and family's life and the family's view of the providers and special service system (Bailey et al., 1998). These outcomes typically are evaluated by satisfaction surveys. Bailey et al. (1998) recommended that satisfaction measures include information on the (a) amount of service received; (b) quality of services received; (c) degree the services affected the child's development; and (d) extent the IFSP goals were attained. Although it has been argued that the utility of parent satisfaction measures is limited because often high satisfaction ratings are reported, others suggest that such measures provide valuable feedback for program planners (Upshor, 1991). McNaughton (1994) suggested that the helpfulness of satisfaction services can be increased if the tools designed are highly reliable and valid, if they compare parent expectations as a baseline against which outcomes can be judged, and include repeated measures of satisfaction. There are alternatives to these traditional satisfaction surveys. Semistructured interviews help inform programs about family members' views of services and provide information of the dimensions of family–service provider relationships. These data typically cannot be obtained from satisfaction surveys (Bailey et al., 1998). Families also can be asked to evaluate very specific aspects of their child's program, rather than assessing overall satisfaction. They can rank order or cluster practices using a Q-sort methodology (e.g., presenting a list of services that are provided in a program and asking families to sort them according to those services that meet their needs and those that need improving). This strategy allows for program planners to examine specific aspects of their program.

Table 10.3.   Sample Items From the Family-Centered Program Rating Scale

Flexibility and Innovation in Programming
The program gives us information on how to meet other families of children with similar needs.

Providing and Coordinating Responsive Services
Services can change quickly when my family's or child's needs change.

Individualizing Services and Ways of Handling Complaints
There is a comfortable way to work out disagreements between families and staff.

Providing Appropriate and Practical Information
Staff members help my family have a normal life.

Communication Timing and Style
Staff members are friendly and easy to talk to.

Developing and Maintaining Comfortable Relationships
Staff members offer to visit my family in our home.

Building Family–Staff Collaboration
My family is included in all meetings about ourselves and our child.

Respecting the Family as Decision Maker
Staff members give clear and complete information about families' rights.

Respecting the Family Expertise and Strengths
Staff members ask my family's opinions and include us in the process of evaluating our child.

Recognizing the Family's Need for Autonomy
Staff members don't ask my family to repeat information that is already on file.

Building Positive Expectations
Staff members help my family feel we can make a positive difference in our child's life.

Source: Reprinted by permission of the Division for Early Childhood, the Council for Exceptional Children from The family-centered program rating scale: An instrument for program evaluation and change in the *Journal of Early Intervention* by D. L. Murphy, I. M. Lee, A. P. Turnbull, and V. Turbiville. Copyright © 1995.

A challenge for programs is evaluating whether family-centered approaches result in identifiable benefits, either for the child or family. The expected outcomes of high-quality early intervention include the ability of programs to (a) enhance adult–child interaction, (b) strengthen family's capacity to build strong support systems, (c) assist families in gaining skills and competence in accessing services and advocating for their children, and (d) improve their family's overall quality of life. The question becomes, "How can we best evaluate the success of our programs to measure these outcomes?" Approaches to evaluating parent–child interactions are addressed in chapter 6. Strategies include rating interactions based on a number of dimensions (e.g., responsivity, feedback, developmental appropriateness of the activity). An alternative approach involves parent-report scales in which parents' beliefs about their ability to guide and support their children's development effectively is assessed (Koren, De-Chillo, & Friesen, 1992).

Ability to access services can be measured at two different levels: family knowledge of the services system (competence) and family sense of control (empowerment). *Empowerment*, the extent that family members believe they can negotiate the service delivery system and feel a sense of control over the process, is one of the underlying tenets of early intervention. Measurement of empowerment is challenging because it is a subjective construct that can be manifested in many ways (Bailey et al., 1998). Koren and his colleagues (1992) suggested that empowerment consists of at least three related constructs: sense of control over family events, services, and policy. They recommend that all three of these factors be considered when assessing empowerment construct. They developed a parent report measure, Family Empowerment Scale, which reflects these three areas. In addition to evaluating how well families can negotiate the service delivery system, comprehensive evaluation should assess any system barriers that preclude successful access of services. This is important because a family can be both competent and have a strong sense of control, yet system barriers may preclude them from obtaining necessary services.

One of the assumptions based on family systems theory is that early intervention helps families build informal social support systems, which ultimately enhances successful coping (Dunst et al., 1986). A number of scales have been developed to measure social support (e.g., Dunst, Trivette, & Hamby, 1993) and can be used to measure the effects of early intervention. A related area is the degree that intervention addresses the family's identified priorities (e.g., child care, recreation, employment, household tasks; Bailey et al., 1998). Assessing the impact of intervention on the family's and child's quality of life is a formidable challenge. Quality of life can be defined in terms of available resources and opportunities, as well as in terms of physical, economic, and psychological well-being (Bailey et al., 1998). Typically quality of life instruments have been developed for use with adults with disabilities, with few targeted for families. Continued work in this area is needed to develop instruments that can effectively evaluate this construct.

Challenges to Evaluating Early Intervention Programs

Assessing the efficacy of early intervention programs is problematic because the independent variables are frequently not adequately defined or controlled (e.g., Epps & Tindal, 1987). It is difficult to provide operational definitions of early intervention because it encompasses a conglomeration of strategies, with little consistency found among variables. Early intervention varies along many dimensions such as duration, setting, format of intervention, model of provider involvement, family participation, as well as program theoretical orientation. In many evaluation studies, validity is threatened because there is insufficient description of the program data on both the children and families served and the services rendered (Shonkoff et al., 1992). For example, many programs refer to family support or parent education and present limited details that clarify the nature of the intervention or its purpose (Gallagher, 1993b). Yet these outcomes are often compared and attenuate any conclusions drawn. Ambiguous program information and early intervention as a macrovariable leaves many questions about which factors may be influencing outcomes. Without clearly defining the "what" (e.g., dimensions of the family support program), program replication is not possible.

Effects of intervention are best understood with homogeneous populations (Farran, 1990). The heterogeneity of the population served by early intervention programs, therefore, poses challenges to evaluation efforts. Farran (1990) reviewed 42 projects and found that samples included a variety of disabilities. Many studies included a large percentage of children with cerebral palsy, with general developmental delay of unknown etiology as the next most frequently cited category. The diverse and often ambiguous criteria used to classify children also have a significant impact on empirical studies considering the lack of consensus of operationalizing the definitions (Epps & Tindal, 1987). Barrett et al. (1978) delineated at least three factors related to children and their disabilities that need to be controlled in research: (a) age; (b) intelligence, with a sophisticated developmental assessment needed; and (c) severity of disorder, with a need for a standard measurement practice.

It is critical in completing the summative evaluation to develop an evaluation design that controls for threats to internal validity (e.g., history, maturation, testing, instrumentation, regression, selection, mortality, and selection interactions)—that is, variables other than the dependent variable that may be accounting for change in the independent variable. External validity is also important to consider—that is, the generalizability of the results. See D. T. Campbell and Stanley (1963) for a detailed discussion of threats to validity. Evaluation designs attempt to control for these threats by (a) preprogram measures on the identified outcome, (b) nontreatment comparison groups, and (c) random selection of subjects (Johnson & LaMontagne, 1994). A central measurement problem to efficacy research in early intervention is the difficulty of obtaining control groups. Lack of control groups significantly attenuates conclusions that outcomes result from early intervention. Use of control groups is a difficult ethical issue to address, because withholding services otherwise available to children and families is a questionable practice. As a result, early intervention research is typically based on "samples of convenience," which precludes controlling for key variables such as selection of sample and specification of treatment and implementation of pre–post research designs (Gallagher, 1993b).

One alternative method is using those children that are on program waiting lists as the control group. Most program evaluation attempts have resulted in poorly designed studies because of the inability to control the aforementioned variables. Because of these concerns, evaluators look to alternatives to traditional quantitative designs.

Alternative Evaluation Approaches

Many program evaluators find themselves turning to a variety of alternative approaches to evaluate early intervention programs. Qualitative and results mapping methodologies provide the evaluator with additional tools for evaluations. These are addressed in the following.

Qualitative Approaches to Evaluation

In recent years, qualitative approaches, such as ethnographic and case-study methodologies, have gained popularity in early intervention evaluation. Qualitative methods provide rich information that is not possible to achieve with quantitative information. The disadvantage of this approach is the labor-intensive nature of the data analysis of the information sources (e.g., transcripts, anecdotal reports, narratives of observations). Johnson and LaMontagne (1994) have provided specific steps to data analysis of early intervention programs in which the meaning of the communication or content material is objectively and systematically detailed. Often these results are displayed in graphic, matrix, or chart display to help clarify the results (Miles & Huberman, 1984).

Interpreting qualitative data is ongoing throughout the data analysis. Miles and Huberman suggested several steps that prevent misinterpretations. The evaluator should

- Use several measurement techniques (i.e., triangulation). In this sense validity is determined by convergence of different data. For example, a parent's report of his or her sense of competence in parenting is compared to observation and comments from the teacher.
- Critically evaluate the information, with the assumption that data are questionable unless substantial evidence is provided.
- Analyze the data to determine if there are other possible explanations to rule out spurious relationships or to identify if the conclusions drawn are replicated by other parts of the data.

Freel (1995) suggested that the field of ethnography provides an approach to studying new areas of child and family variables by providing a "rich body of contextual information as well as insights into how various environmental factors interweave with and influence the lives of children and families" (p. 7). Qualitative combined with quantitative approaches can provide a holistic approach to evaluation. A case study approach is another alternative research design for early intervention efficacy studies. The examples of two to three families allows for careful analysis of interactive factors that are context-bound and situationally dependent (Gallagher, 1993b). Because of the complexity of the variables studied and the methodological difficulties currently being encountered, qualitative methods may provide a resourceful adjunct to quantitative approaches.

Use of qualitative methods leads to rich portrayals of child and family variables that are not easily measured with traditional tools. For example, Jackson (1995) evaluated whether maternal beliefs about how children develop would affect the mother's interaction with her preschool-aged child. The results of the quantitative data suggested that there was not a direct association between parental beliefs, specifically nurturance and discipline, and subsequent maternal interaction strategies when her child was in a stressful medical situation. Analysis of the qualitative observation narratives revealed the complexity of the relationship among these variables. These observations suggested that the child's reaction (i.e., stress or coping behavior) to the medical situation may have an important impact on how the mother reacted if originally she scored high on nurturance. It appeared that in a majority of the dyadic interactions coded, the mother's behavior fluctuated based on the child's reaction (e.g., low frequency of maternal behavior when the child displayed coping behavior or increased bargaining–criticizing or commanding to cope in response to a distressed child). The qualitative data helped to reveal the potentially powerful influence that child behavior has on the adult, to the extent that it may override the belief system of the mother.

Results Mapping Strategy: An Innovative Evaluation Approach

Results mapping, an innovative evaluation approach developed by Kibel (1999), represents a promising evaluation alternative for early childhood programs. It blends quantitative and qualitative methods to provide a needed bridge between process and outcome forms of evaluation. Most traditional program evaluation frameworks are based explicitly or implicitly on strict causal logic, where it is assumed that one or a few factors in full control of the program can directly produce the target outcome. For programs that aim for one or more long-term outcomes that can be achieved only through a combination of multiple services (e.g., early intervention services) and an active role by the family, Kibel has argued that a very different form of evaluation is needed.

Results mapping bases the analysis and evaluation of multifaceted programs on family success stories (Kibel, 1999). Through these stories, a systematic and comprehensive picture emerges of how program staff interact with clients, with other service providers, and with family and friends of their clients. The stories provide information on how programs contribute to outcomes and how the clients themselves grow and change in response to program inputs and other forces and factors in their lives. The primary use of this information is to ensure the program's supporter that desirable outcomes are happening through the actions of the program, and in sufficient quantity and quality. In addition, the information helps detect program shortfalls that ought to be corrected and pinpoints program strengths and emerging opportunities that can be exploited to increase program contributions toward these outcomes with other clients.

Results mapping is built on many of the same assumptions that underlie effective early intervention. It emphasizes, through the formats used to compile and rate story data, the importance of family self-sufficiency—empowerment, collaborative efforts with other programs and agencies, and the systems approach in dealing with the entire family. Unlike the more traditional methods, this evaluation tool allows programs to evaluate complex, integrated service systems in which multiple efforts contribute in varying degrees to (rather than strictly cause) a range of child and family outcomes. The underlying logic of the evaluation is synchronistic rather than causal. It is assumed that events are linked through connections that overlap and mutually influence one another. In addition, the powerful influences of outside factors beyond the program are anticipated and integrated within the evaluation, as are the contributions of the child and family themselves to the outcomes being sought.

Results mapping methodology includes programs providing stories, which are a narrative account of its best work with current or recent clients. These stories are translated into structured forms (i.e., mapped stories) via a computer program to which coding and scoring conventions are applied. This process leads to fair ratings and accurate measures of the program contributions toward long-term child and family success. Kibel designed the mapping and scoring conventions, as well as related procedures, so that the compiled story data meet acceptable scientific standards. For example, individuals trained in the approach, on hearing the details of a narrative account, map and score that story in precisely the same way (i.e., they demonstrate high intermapper and interrater agreement). And from a relatively small but purposeful sample (e.g., the 15 stories representing the program's most effective work), accurate generalizations can be made to the program overall.

Results mapping is based on a results ladder, which is a hierarchy of levels that individuals, families, or groups pass through on their path to increasing ownership for, and control over, their future. The rungs of the ladder are used to code and score the wide range of activities and outcomes associated with family and child progress. The specific process for coding will be described after the applied example. Included are four action—benefit levels (where program and client interact) and three milestone levels (where clients or family members make personal growth steps for their own benefit). These are described in Table 10.4. The following example illustrates each action level, benefit level, and milestone:

During her prenatal visit, Ms. Jones picked up a flyer in her obstetrician's office, placed there by the program (*action level 1*) that announced a home visitation program for young mothers. She read through the information (*benefit level 1—Received general information via indirect means*) but did not contact the program. At her next clinic visit,

Table 10.4. Descriptions of the Levels, Actions, and Milestones in the Results Mapping Hierarchy

Action Level/Milestone	Description
Level 1	At Level 1, the change agent produces and distributes the public information (ACT1) that reaches the client indirectly as one member of the target audience (LEV1).
Level 2	At Level 2, the change agent motivates, prods, offers advice, and makes referrals (ACT2) to which the client may or may not respond (LEV2).
Level 3	At Level 3, the change agent delivers routine services or helps build client skills (ACT3) that produce short-term client status changes (LEV3).
Milestone 4	At Milestone 4, the client has shifted from passive to active mode. The client has received enough information, prodding, advice, and routine services from other to recognize the need for personal change and has taken first steps in this direction.
Level 5	At Level 5, the change agent plays the role of coach or advisor (ACT5) to the client to support the latter's activities and sustained growth (LEV5).
Milestone 6	At Milestone 6, the client has become more self-sufficient and can point to marked increase in health, positive behavior, or fullness of being.
Milestone 7	At Milestone 7, the client is recognized by self and others as an advanced practitioner in areas associated with the outcome(s) being targeted by the program.

Source: Reprinted by permission of the Plenum Press. From *Successful stories as hard data* by B. Kibel. In press.

the nurse discussed the program with Ms. Jones (*action level 2*). Ms. Jones had an opportunity to ask questions and gather more information about the program. She indicated that she wanted to talk to her mother about the program before calling. Although Ms. Jones had not taken any action, she had received personalized advice and been directed to a course of possible action. (*Benefit level 2—received personalized advice via direct contact.*)

Ms. Jones and her mother discussed the program and decided it might be a helpful resource. Ms. Jones called the program, and a nurse was scheduled for a home visit the following week. The visit took place (*action level 3*). Ms. Jones continued to participate in the four weekly home visits until her baby, Jwanita, was born. This service helped to prepare her for the delivery of her daughter. (*Benefit level 3—Received a routine, short-term service.*)

The next step was critical for Ms. Jones and her daughter. She had to decide if she would continue with the home visitation program. A commitment on Ms. Jones's part would include weekly visits and participation in a monthly play group with other parents and their children. Ms. Jones continued in the program during the next three months and found her confidence as a mother growing. Ms. Jones made adjustments to her life style, including consistently participating actively in both the home visits and play groups. (*Milestone 4—made short-term, positive adjustments on Ms. Jones's own behalf.*)

Over the next six months, the nurse home visitor continued to coach her in a variety of areas including parent–child interaction and health-related areas (*action level 5*). She had gained self-confidence as a mother and consistently played with Jwanita each day. (*Benefit level 5—interacted with coach while assuming increased personal responsibility.*) Ms. Jones was beginning to read parenting books on her own to gain more ideas on ways to help Jwanita grow and develop. Ms. Jones also found that she had established new friendships at the parent group. By the time Ms. Jones had finished the first full year in the program, she was on her way to maintaining positive parenting skills. (*Milestone 6—demonstrates significant gain in skills and confidence, as exhibited in behavior and lifestyle shifts, over an extended period.*)

Ms. Jones, in talking with her nurse, recognized that her community lacked a mentoring program, where young mothers could learn skills to help other young mothers feel competent in caring for their child. She decided to establish such a mentoring program, raised the needed funds, and is now the executive director of the mother-to-mother mentoring program. (*Milestone 7—former client is now a major change agent in the community in support of those with similar needs.*)

A systematic process based on a number of conventions is used to translate loose, narrative accounts into formal, mapped stories, which helps interpret these data. User-friendly, computer software is used to facilitate the mapping and coding. The map-to-map codes and related scores yield a number of descriptive statistics for the mapped story. These include total points earned, number of milestones reached, highest milestone level attained, number of networking points (for hand-offs to other service providers), number of village building points (for services provided by volunteers), highest level of service provided by the program, and points earned for actions taken by clients to benefit others. These varied statistics, as well as the detailed stories themselves, provide a comprehensive profile of the program, highlighting its strengths, its recent progress as an effective program, and simultaneously pinpointing where additional efforts need to be targeted. Kibel (1999) suggested that there is a close tie to results mapping and quality improvement because they both provide a mechanism for feedback with the goal of improving services.

Kibel (1999) has also developed a cost–consequences algorithm that can be used to compute the client benefits and social cost savings of implementing a program. To compute the cost analysis, the program needs an estimate of the market value of services received, the type of negative outcomes that are being averted, and the risk factors associated with the family featured in each story. For example, a program that emphasized adult education can estimate the cost for receiving this training through a private vendor as well as the cost to society in future earnings of an adult not completing a GED. This figure is then used to estimate the fair share of these dollars that the program can rightly take credit for based on the levels of service provided and milestones achieved.

In conclusion, results mapping allows for the complex work done by programs working with families and children to be fully and fairly presented. Armed with these data, a program can meet the wide-ranging requirements for data placed on it by its funders and other stakeholders. It can tell its story through a set of mapped client stories, in ways that should leave little doubt regarding both its contributions and future challenges.

Conclusion

In this time of decreasing resources and the call for outcome-based services, the urgency to have data guide allocation of funds and the direction of early intervention programs becomes paramount. The evaluation process needs to become an integral part of and priority for early intervention programs. Effective evaluation efforts need to blend both quantitative and qualitative approaches to address clearly articulated evaluation questions by ensuring that there are specifically defined independent variables and outcome measures that are matched to the intervention implemented. Clinicians and researchers need to continue to develop assessment tools that are psychometrically sound, ecologically valid, and sensitive to small yet often functional incremental change of both child and family outcomes.

Overall, program evaluation is an important tool for early intervention in its long-range planning process. Many gains made in early intervention typically were achieved because of effective advocacy rather than compelling scientific evidence (Shonkoff, 1992). Although it is a complex and difficult challenge, it is important to ask new questions that will guide evaluation and provide new insights to effective intervention programs in the new century.

Although key ingredients of effective early intervention have been identified, further clarification of the complex, multifaceted interaction of variables is necessary to catapult our understanding, and subsequent program design, to new levels. Lack of meaningful data jeopardizes the potential to refine services and severely attenuates the effects on public policy that well-designed studies can have (Kraus & Jacobs, 1990). The challenge for future researchers is translating the vision for early intervention into "conceptually based research that can be tested in a scientifically rigorous manner" (Shonkoff, 1992, p. 9).

References

Abidin, R. (1986). *Parenting stress index: Manual* (2nd ed.). Charlottesville, VA: Pediatric Psychology.

Able-Boone, H. (1993). Family participation the IFSP process: Family or professional driven? *Infant-Toddler Intervention, 3*(1), 63–72.

Accreditation Council on Services for People With Disabilities. (1995). *Outcome based performance measures.* Landover, MD: Author.

Achenbach, T. M., McConaughy, S. H., & Howell, C. T. (1987). Child/adolescent behavioral and emotional problems: Implications of cross-informant correlations for situational specificity. *Psychological Bulletin, 101,* 213–232.

Advisory Committee on Services for Families With Infants and Toddlers. (1994). *Early Head Start: The statement of the advisory committee on services for families with infants and toddlers.* Washington, DC: U.S. Department of Health and Human Services.

Ainsworth, M. (1969). Object relations, dependency and attachment: A theoretical review of the infant-mother relationship. *Child Development, 40,* 969–1025.

Ainsworth, M., Bell, S., & Stayton, D. (1972). Individual differences in the development of some attachment behaviors. *Merrill-Palmer Quarterly, 18,* 123–143.

Ainsworth, M., Blehar, M., Waters, E., & Wall, J. (1978). *Patterns of attachment.* Hillsdale, NJ: Erlbaum.

Ainsworth, M., & Bowlby, J. (1991). An ethological approach to personality development. *American Psychologist, 46,* 331–341.

Altemeier, W. A., O'Conner, S., Vietze, P. M., Sandler, H. M., & Sherrod, K. B. (1982). Antecedents of child abuse. *Journal of Pediatrics, 100,* 823–829.

American Academy of Pediatrics, Committee on Practice and Ambulatory Medicine. (1988). Recommendations for preventative pediatric health care. *Pediatrics, 81,* 466.

American Association on Mental Retardation. (1992). *Mental retardation: Definition, classification, and systems of supports* (9th ed.). Washington DC: Author.

American Evaluation Association Task Force on Guiding Principles for Evaluators. (1995). Guiding principles for evaluation. *New Directions for Program Evaluation* (Summer), 19–34.

American Psychiatric Association. (1994). *Diagnostic and statistical manual of mental disorders* (4th ed.). Washington, DC: Author.

American Psychological Association. (1990). Ethical principles of psychologists (Amended June 2, 1989). *American Psychologist, 45,* 390–395.

Anderson, G. C., Burroughs, A. K., & Measel, C. P. (1983). Nonnutritive sucking opportunities: A safe and effective treatment for preterm neonates. In T. Field & A. Sostek (Eds.), *Infants born at risk: Physiological, perceptual and cognitive processes* (pp. 129–146). Orlando, FL: Grune & Stratton.

Anderson, P. P., & Fenichel, E. S. (1989). *Serving culturally diverse families of infants and toddlers with disabilities.* Washington, DC: National Center for Clinical Infant Programs.

Anita, S. D., Kreimeyer, K. H., & Eldridge, N. (1994). Promoting social interaction between young children with hearing impairments and their peers. *Exceptional Children, 60,* 262–275.

Annie E. Casey Foundation, and the Center for the Study of Social Policy. (1992). *Kids count data book: State profiles of child well-being.* Washington, DC: Authors.

Appel, F. (1991). From quality assurance to quality improvement: The Joint Commission and the new quality paradigm. *Journal of Quality Assurance, 13*(5), 26–29.

Arcia, E., Serling, J., & Gallagher, J. (1992). Review of state policies to empower families and reach populations typically underserved. Chapel Hill: Carolina Policy Studies Program, University of North Carolina at Chapel Hill.

Aydlett, L. A. (1993). Assessing infant interaction skills in interaction-focused intervention. *Infants and Young Children, 5*(4), 1–7.

Bagnato, S., & Hofkosh, D. (1990). Curriculum-based developmental assessment for infants with special needs: Synchronizing the pediatric early intervention team. In E. Gibbs & D. Teti (Eds.), *Interdisciplinary assessment of infants: A guide for early intervention professionals* (pp. 161–175). Baltimore: Paul H. Brookes.

Bagnato, S. J., Neisworth, J. T., Paget, K. D., & Koraleski, J. (1987). The developmental school psychologist: Professional profile of an emerging early childhood specialist. *Topics in Early Childhood Special Education, 7*, 75–89.

Bailey, D. B., Jr. (1987). Collaborative goal-setting with families: Resolving differences in values and priorities for services. *Topics in Early Childhood Special Education, 11*(3), 59–71.

Bailey, D. B., Jr. (1988). Considerations in developing family goals. In D. B. Bailey & R. J. Simeonsson (Eds.), *Family assessment in early intervention* (pp. 229–249). Columbus, OH: Merrill.

Bailey, D. B., Jr. (1989). Issues and directions in preparing professionals to work with young handicapped children and their families. In J. J. Gallagher, P. L. Trohanis, & R. M. Clifford (Eds.), *Policy implementation and P.L. 99-457* (pp. 97–132). Baltimore: Paul H. Brookes.

Bailey, D. B., Jr. (1991a). Building positive relationships between professionals and families. In M. J. McGonigel, R. K. Kaufmann, & B. H. Johnson (Eds.) *Guidelines and recommended practices for the Individualized Family Service Plan* (2nd ed., pp. 29–38). Bethesda, MD: Association for the Care of Children's Health.

Bailey, D. B., Jr. (1991b). *FOCAS: Family Orientation of Community and Agency Services.* Chapel Hill: University of North Carolina at Chapel Hill.

Bailey, D. B., Jr., & Blasco, P. M. (1990). Parents' perspectives on a written survey of family needs. *Journal of Early Intervention, 14*, 196–203.

Bailey, D. B., Jr., & Bricker, D. (1985). The efficacy of early intervention for severely handicapped infants and young children. *Topics in Early Childhood Special Education, 4*, 30–51.

Bailey, D. B., Jr., & Bricker, D. (1986). A psychometric study of a criterion-referenced assessment instruments designed for infants and young children. *Journal of the Division for Early Childhood, 10*, 124–134.

Bailey, D. B., Jr., Farel, A. M., O'Donnell, K. J., Simeonsson, R. J., & Miller, C. A. (1986). Preparing infant interventionists: Interdepartmental training in special education and maternal and child health. *Journal of the Division for Early Childhood, 11*, 67–77.

Bailey, D. B., Jr., McWilliam, P. J., Darkes, L., Hebbler, K., Simeonsson, R., Spiker, D., & Wagner M. (1998). Family outcomes in early intervention: A framework for program evaluation and efficacy research. *Exceptional Children, 64*(3), 313–328.

Bailey, D. B., Jr., McWilliam, P. J., & Winton, P. J. (1992). Building family-centered practices in early intervention: A team-based model for change. *Infants and Young Children, 5*(1), 73–80.

Bailey, D. B., Jr., Palsha, S. A., & Huntington, G. S. (1990). Preservice preparation of special educators to work with handicapped infants and their families: Current status and training needs. *Journal of Early Intervention, 14*(1), 43–54.

Bailey, D. B., Jr., & Simeonsson, R. J. (1988). *Family assessment in early intervention.* Columbus, OH: Merrill.

Bailey, D. B., Jr., Simeonsson, R. J., Yoder, D. E., & Huntington, G. S. (1990). Preparing professionals to serve infants and toddlers with handicaps and their families: An integrated analysis across eight disciplines. *Exceptional Children, 57*, 26–35.

Bailey, D. B., Jr., & Wolery, M. (1984). *Teaching infants and preschoolers with handicaps.* Columbus, OH: Merrill.

Bailey, D. B., Jr., & Wolery, M. (1989). *Assessing infants and preschoolers with handicaps.* Columbus, OH: Merrill.

Bailey, D. B., Jr., & Wolery, M. (1992). *Teaching infants and preschoolers with disabilities* (2nd ed.). Englewood Cliffs, NJ: Merrill.

Baker, B. L., & Heller, T. L. (1996). Preschool children with externalizing behaviors: Experience of the fathers and mothers. *Journal of Abnormal Child Psychology, 24*, 513–532.

Baldwin, A. L., Baldwin, C., & Cole, R. E. (1990). Stress-resistant families and stress-resistant children. In J. Rolf, A. S. Masten, D. Cicchetti, K. Nueschterlein, & S. Weintraub

(Eds.), Risk and protective factors in the development of psychopathology (pp. 257–280). Cambridge: Cambridge University Press.

Baldwin, D. S., Jeffries, G. W., Jones, V. H., Thorp, E. K., & Walsh, S. A. (1992). Collaborative systems design for Part H of IDEA. Infants and Young Children, 5(1), 12–20.

Barnard, K. E. (1976). NCAST II learners resource manual. Seattle: NCAST Publications.

Barnard, K. E. (1997). Influencing parent–child interactions for children at risk. In M. J. Guralnick (Ed.), The effectiveness of early intervention (pp. 112–145). Baltimore: Paul Brookes.

Barnard, K. E., Bee, H. L., & Hammond, M. A. (1984). Developmental changes in maternal interactions with term and preterm infants. Infant Behavior and Development, 7, 101–113.

Barnard, K. E., & Kelly, J. F. (1990). Assessment of caregiver–child interaction. In S. J. Meisels & J. P. Shonkoff (Eds.), Handbook of early childhood intervention (pp. 278–298). New York: Cambridge University Press.

Barnett, W. S. (1995). Long-term effects of early childhood programs on cognitive and school outcomes. The Future of Children, 5, 25–50.

Barrett, C. L., Hampe, I. E., & Miller, L. C. (1978). Research on child psychotherapy. In S. L. Garfield & A. E. Bergin (Eds.), Handbook of psychotherapy and behavior change: An empirical analysis (2nd ed., pp. 411–435). New York: Wiley.

Barsness, Z. I., Shortell, R. R., Gillies, E. F., Hughes, J. L., O'Brien, D., Bohr, C., Izvi, C., & Kralovec, P. (1993). National survey of hospital quality improvement activities. Hospital and Health Networks, 29, 52–55.

Bayley, N. (1969). Bayley Scales of Infant Development. New York: Psychological Corporation.

Bayley, N. (1993). Bayley Scales of Infant Development (2nd ed.). San Antonio, TX: Psychological Corporation.

Beauchamp, T. L., & Childress, J. F. (1989). Principles of biomedical ethics (3rd ed.). New York: Oxford University Press.

Beauchamp, T., & McCulloch, L. (1984). Medical ethics: The moral responsibility of physicians. Englewood Cliffs, NJ: Prentice-Hall.

Beckman, P. J., & Bristol, M. M. (1991). Establishing family outcomes. Topics in Early Childhood Special Education, 11(3), 19–31.

Beckwith, L. (1990). Adaptive and maladaptive caregiving: Implications for intervention. In S. J. Meisels & J. P. Shonkoff (Eds.), Handbook of early childhood intervention (pp. 53–77). New York: Cambridge University Press.

Beckwith, L., & Cohen, S. E. (1984). Home environment and cognitive competence in preterm children during the first 5 years. In A. W. Gottfried (Ed.), Home environment and early cognitive development (pp. 155–177). New York: Academic Press.

Benn, R. (1993). Conceptualizing eligibility for early intervention services. In D. M. Bryant & M. A. Graham (Eds.), Implementing early intervention: From research to effective practice (pp. 18–45). New York: Guilford Press.

Bennett, T., Watson, A. L., & Raab, M. (1991). Ensuring competence in early intervention personnel through personnel standards and high-quality training. Infants and Young Children, 3(3), 49–58.

Bennis, W. G., Benne, K. D., Chin, R., & Corey, K. E. (1976). The planning of change. New York: Holt, Rinehart, and Winston.

Biro, P., & Daulton, D. (1991). State planning document concerning three related federal initiatives. Chapel Hill, NC: NEC*TAS.

Birtchnell, J. (1988). Depression and family relationships. The study of young, married women on a London housing estate. British Journal of Psychiatry, 153, 758–769.

Bolger, K. E., Patterson, C. J., Thompson, W. W., & Kupersmidt, J. B. (1995). Psychosocial adjustment among children experiencing persistent and intermittent family economic hardship. Child Development, 66, 1107–1129.

Booth, C. L., Barnard, K. E., Mitchell, S. K., & Spieker, S. J. (1987). Successful intervention with multi-problem mothers: Effects on the mother-infant relationship. Infant Mental Health Journal, 8(3), 288–306.

Bornstein, M. H., & Lamb, M. E. (1992). Development in infancy: An introduction. New York: McGraw Hill.

Boros, S. J., Mannel, M. C., Coleman, J. M., Lewallen, P. K., Gordon, M. J., Bing, D. R., & Ophoven, J. P. (1985). Neonatal high-frequency jet ventilation: Four years' experience. *Pediatrics, 75,* 657–663.

Brazelton, T. B. (1984). *Neonatal behavioral assessment scale.* Philadelphia: Lippincott.

Bricker, D., Bruder, M. B., & Bailey, E. (1982). Developmental integration of preschool children. *Analysis and Intervention in Developmental Disabilities, 2,* 207–222.

Bricker, D. D., & Dow, M. G. (1980). Early intervention with the young severely handicapped child. *Journal of the Association for the Severely Handicapped, 5,* 130–142.

Bricker, D., & Slentz, K. (1987). Personnel preparation: Handicapped infants. In M. C. Want, H. J. Walbert, & M. C. Reynolds (Eds.), *Handbook of special education: Research and practice* (Vol. 3, pp. 319–345). New York: Pergamon Press.

Bricker, D., & Veltman, M. (1990). Early intervention programs: Child-focused approaches. In S. J. Meisels & J. P. Shonkoff (Eds.), *Handbook of early childhood intervention* (pp. 373–400). New York: Cambridge University Press.

Bristol, M. M., & Gallagher, J. J. (1982). A family focus for intervention. In C. T. Ram & P. L. Trohanis (Eds.), *Finding and educating high risk and handicapped infants.* Baltimore: University Park Press.

Bromwich, R. (1981). *Working with caregivers and infants: An interactional approach.* Baltimore: University Park Press.

Bronfenbrenner, U. (1975). *The ecology of human development.* Cambridge, MA: Harvard University Press.

Bronicki, G. J., & Turnbull, A. P. (1987). Family–professional interactions. In M. E. Snell (Ed.), *Systematic instruction of persons with severe handicaps* (3rd ed., pp. 9–35). Columbus, OH: Merrill.

Brooks-Gunn, J., & Chase-Lansdale, L. (1991). Teenage childbearing: Effects on children. In R. M. Lerner, A. C. Peterson, & J. Brooks-Gunn (Eds.), *Encyclopedia of adolescence* (pp. 103–106). New York: Garland.

Brooks-Gunn, J., & Furstenberg, F. F. (1986). The children of adolescent mothers: Physical, academic, and psychological outcomes. *Developmental Review, 6,* 224–251.

Brooks-Gunn, J., & Lewis, M. (1982). Maternal responsivity in interactions with handicapped infants. *Child Development, 55,* 782–793.

Brown, C. W., Perry, D. F., & Kurland, S. (1994). Funding policies that affect children: What every early interventionist should know. *Infants and Young Children, 6*(4), 1–12.

Bruder, M. B. (1993). The provision of early intervention and early childhood special education within community early childhood programs: Characteristics of effective service delivery. *Topics in Early Childhood Special Education, 12,* 19–37.

Bruder, M. B. (1998). A collaborative model to increase the capacity of childcare providers to include young children with disabilities. *Journal of Early Intervention, 21*(2), 177–186.

Bruder, M. B., Klosowski, S., & Daguio, C. (1991). A review of personnel standards for Part H of PL 99-457. *Journal of Early Intervention, 15,* 66–79.

Bruder, M. B., & Staff, I. (1998). A comparison of the effects of type and classroom and service characteristics on toddlers with disabilities. *Topics in Early Childhood Special Education, 18*(1), 26–37.

Bruner, J. S. (1975). The ontogenesis of speech acts. *Journal of Child Language, 2,* 1–19.

Bryant, D. M., & Graham, A. (Eds.). (1993). *Implementing early intervention: From research to effective practice.* New York: Guilford Press.

Budd, K. S., McGraw, T. E., Farbisz, R., Murphy, T. B., Hawkins, D., Heilman, N., Werle, M., & Hochstadt, N. J. (1992). Psychosocial concomitants of children's feeding disorders. *Journal of Pediatric Psychology, 17,* 81–94.

Buysee, V., & Bailey, D. B. (1993). Behavioral and developmental outcomes in young children with disabilities in integrated and segregated settings: A review of comparative studies. *Journal of Special Education, 26,* 434–461.

Callahan, S. (1988). The role of emotion in ethical decision making. *Hastings Center Report, 18*(3), 9–14.

Campbell, D. T., & Stanley, J. C. (1963). *Experimental and quasi-experimental designs for research.* Boston: Houghton Mifflin.

Campbell, F. A., & Ramey, C. T. (1994). Effects of early intervention on intellectual and academic achievement: A follow-up study of children from low-income families. *Child Development, 65*(2), 684–698.

Campbell, F. A., & Ramey, C. T. (1995). Cognitive and school outcomes for high-risk African-American students at middle adolescence: Positive effects of early intervention. *American Educational Research Journal, 32*, 743–772.

Capone, A. M., & Divenere, N. (1996). The evolution of a personnel preparation program: Preparation of family-centered practitioners. *Journal of Early Intervention, 20*, 222–231.

Carlson, V., Cicchetti, D., Barnett, D., & Braunwald, K. G. (1989). Finding order in disorganization: Lessons from research on maltreated infants' attachments to their caregivers. In D. Cicchetti & V. Carlson (Eds.), *Child maltreatment: Theory and research on the causes and consequences of child abuse and neglect* (pp. 494–528). New York: Cambridge University Press.

Carmen, S. (1994). Attachment intervention. *Infants and Young Children, 7*(1), 34–41.

Carter, S., Osofsky, J. D., & Hann, D. M. (1991). Speaking for baby: Therapeutic interventions with adolescent mothers and their infants. *Infant Mental Health Journal, 12*, 291–301.

Casto, G., & Lewis, M. (1986). The efficacy of early intervention programs: A meta-analysis. *Exceptional Children, 52*, 417–424.

Cerreto, M. (1986). Developmental issues in chronic illness: Implication and applications. *Topics in Early Childhood Special Education, 3*(4), 23–35.

Chan, S. (1990). Early intervention with culturally diverse families of infants and toddlers with disabilities. *Infants and Young Children, 3*(2), 78–87.

Chinitz, S. P. (1995). Intervention with children with developmental disabilities and attachment disorders. *Developmental and Behavioral Pediatrics, 16*(3), S17–S20.

Chugani, H. T. (1997). Neuroimaging of developmental non-linearity and developmental pathologies. In R. W. Thatcher, G. R. Lyon, J. Rumsey, & N. Krasnegor (Eds.), *Developmental neuroimaging: Mapping the development of brain and behavior* (pp. 187–195). San Diego, CA: Academic Press.

Cicchetti, D., & Lynch, M. (1993). Toward an ecological/transactional model of community violence and child maltreatment: Consequences for children's development. *Psychiatry, 56*, 96–118.

Cicchetti, D., & Toth, S. (1987). The application of a transactional risk model to intervention with multi-risk maltreating families. *Zero to Three, 1*, 1–8.

Cicchetti, D., & Toth, S. (1998). The development of depression in children and adolescents. *American Psychologist, 53*, 221–241.

Cicchetti, D., & Wagner, S. (1993). Alternative assessment strategies for the evaluation of infants and toddlers: An organizational perspective. In S. J. Meisels & J. P. Shonkoff (Eds.), *Handbook of early childhood intervention* (pp. 246–277). New York: Cambridge University Press.

Clarke-Stewart, K. (1973). Interactions between mother and their young children. *Monographs of the Society for Research in Child Development, 38*(6–7, Serial No. 153).

Cohen, A., & Bradford, D. (1990). *Influence without authority.* New York: John Wiley & Sons.

Cohen, S. E., & Parmelee, A. H. (1983). Prediction of five-year Stanford–Binet scores in preterm infants. *Child Development, 54*, 1241–1253.

Cohn, J. F., Matias, R., Tronick, E. Z., Connell, D., & Lyons-Ruth, K. (1986). Face-to-face interactions of depressed mothers and their infants. In E. A. Tronick & T. Field (Eds.), *Maternal depression and infant disturbance. New directions for child development* (pp. 31–46). San Francisco: Jossey-Bass.

Cole, K., Mills, P., & Dale, P. (1989). A comparison of the effects of academic and cognitive curricula for young handicapped children one and two years post program. *Topics in Early Childhood Special Education, 9*, 110–127.

Conner, D. (1993). *Managing at the speed of change: How resilient managers succeed.* New York: Villard Books.

Cooper, C. S., & McEvoy, M. A. (1996). Group friendship activities: An easy way to develop social skills of young children. *Teaching Exceptional Children, 28*(3), 67–69.

Cormier, W. H., & Cormier, L. S. (1979). *Interviewing strategies for helpers: A guide to assessment, treatment, and evaluation.* Monterey, CA: Brooks/Cole.

Counte, M. A., Glandon, D. M., Oleske, D. M., & Hill, J. P. (1992). Total quality management in a health care organization: How are employees affected? *Hospital and Health Services Administration, 37,* 503–518.

Cowen, E. L., Wyman, P. A., Work, W. C., & Parker, G. R. (1990). The Rochester Child Resilience Project: Overview and summary of first year findings. *Development and Psychopathology, 2,* 193–212.

Craig, S. E., & Haggart, A. G. (1994). Including all children: The ADS's challenge to early intervention. *Infants and Young Children, 7*(2), 15–19.

Crittenden, P. M. (1988). Relationships at risk. In J. Belsky & T. Nezworski (Eds.), *Clinical implications of attachment* (pp. 36–167). Hillsdale, NJ: Lawrence Erlbaum Associates.

Crittenden, P. M. (1995). Attachment and risk for psychopathology: The early years. *Developmental and Behavioral Pediatrics, 16*(3), S12–S16.

Crittenden, P. M., & Bonvillian, J. D. (1984). The relationship between maternal risk status and maternal sensitivity. *American Journal of Orthopsychiatry, 54,* 224–235.

Crnic, K. A., & Greenberg, M. T. (1987). Transactional relationships between perceived family style, risk status, and mother–child interactions in two-year olds. *Journal of Pediatric Psychology, 12,* 343–362.

Crnic, K. A., Greenberg, M. T., Ragozin, A., Robinson, N., & Basham, R. (1983). Effects of stress and social support on mothers and premature and full-term infants. *Child Development, 54,* 209–217.

Crockenberg, S., & McCluskey, K. (1986). Changes in maternal behavior during the baby's first year of life. *Child Development, 57,* 746–753.

Crocker, A. C. (1989). The causes of Mental Retardation. *Pediatric Annals, 18,* 623–636.

Cummings, E. M., & Davies, P. T. (1994). Maternal depression and child development. *Journal of Child Psychology and Psychiatry, 35,* 73–112.

Cummings, T. G., & Worley, C. G. (1993). *Organization development and change.* New York: West.

Currie, J., & Thomas, D. (1995). Does Head Start make a difference? *American Economic Review, 85,* 341–364.

Dale, P., & Cole, K. (1988). Comparison of academic and cognitive programs for young handicapped children. *Exceptional Children, 54,* 439–447.

Dalziel, M. M., & Schoonover, S. C. (1992). *Changing ways: A practical tool for implementing change within organizations.* New York: AMACOM.

Danaher, J. (August, 1998). Eligibility policies and practices for young children under Part B of IDEA. *NECT*TAS Notes,* No. 6 (Revised), 1–16.

Danziger, S., & Danziger, S. (1993). Child poverty and public policy: Toward a comprehensive antipoverty agenda. *Daedelus, 122,* 57–87.

Davidson, D. (1998). *Building bridges: Lessons learned in family-centered interprofession collaboration: Year three.* Honolulu: Health and Education Collaboration Project.

Davis, L., Thurman, S. K., & Mauro, L. M. (1995). Meeting the challenges of establishing interdisciplinary preservice preparation for infant personnel. *Infants and Young Children, 8*(2), 65–70.

Dawson, P. (1992). Should the field of early child and family intervention address failure to thrive? *Zero to Three, 12*(5), 20–24.

Dawson, G., Hessl, D., and Frey, K. (1994). Social influence on early developing biological and behavioral systems related to risk for affective disorder. In *Development and Psychopathology* (pp. 759–779). New York: Cambridge University Press.

Deal, A. G., Dunst, C. J., & Trivette, C. M. (1989). A flexible and functional approach to developing Individualized Family Support Plans. *Infants and Young Children, 1*(4), 32–43.

DeGangi, G. A. (1991). Assessment of sensory, emotional, and attentional problems in regulatory disordered infants: Part 1. *Infants and Young Children, 3*(3), 1–9.

DeGangi, G. A., Craft, P., & Castellan, J. (1991). Treatment of sensory, emotional, and attentional problems in regulatory disordered infants: Part 2. *Infants and Young Children, 3*(3), 9–19.

DeGangi, G., Royeen, C. B., & Wietlishbach, S. (1992). How to examine the individualized family service plan process: Preliminary findings and a procedural guide. *Infants and Young Children, 5*(2), 42–56.

DeKlyen, M., Speltz, M. J., & Greenberg, M. T. (1008). Fathering and early onset conduct problems. Positive and negative parenting, father–son attachment, and the marital context. *Clinical Child and Family Psychology Review, 1*(1), 3–21.

Division for Early Childhood. (1991). *Statement of the U.S. Senate Subcommittee on Disability Policy With Respect to Reauthorization of Part H and Amendments to Part B of the IDEA, Regarding Services to Children From Birth to Age Six and Their Families.* Pittsburgh, PA: Author.

Division for Early Childhood. (1993). *DEC recommended practices: Indicators of quality in programs for infants and young children with special needs and their families.* Reston, VA: Author.

Duncan, G., Yeung, W., Brooks-Gunn, J., & Smith, J. (in press). How much does childhood poverty affect the life changes of children? *American Sociological Review.*

Dunst, C. (1979). Program evaluation and the Education for All Handicapped Children Act. *Exceptional Children, 12,* 24–31.

Dunst, C. J. (1985). Rethinking early intervention. *Analysis and Intervention in Developmental Disabilities, 5,* 163–175.

Dunst, C., Lowe, L., & Bartholomew, P. (1990). Contingent social responsiveness, family ecology and infant communicative competence. *National Student Speech Language Hearing Association Journal, 17,* 39–49.

Dunst, C. J., & Snyder, S. W. (1986). A critique of the Utah State University early intervention meta-analysis research. *Exceptional Children, 53,* 269–276.

Dunst, C. J., & Trivette, C. M. (1989). An enablement and empowerment perspective of case management. *Topics in Early Childhood Special Education, 8*(4), 87–102.

Dunst, C. J., Trivette, C. M., & Cross., A. F. (1986). Roles and support networks of mothers and handicapped children. In R. Fewell & P. Vadasy (Eds.), *Families of handicapped children* (pp. 167–172). Austin, TX: ProEd.

Dunst, C. J., Trivette, C. M., & Deal, A. G. (1988). *Enabling and empowering families: Principles and guidelines for practice.* Cambridge, MA: Brookline Books.

Dunst, C. J., Trivette, C. M., Hamby, D., & Pollock, B. (1990). Family systems correlates of the behavior of young children with handicaps. *Journal of Early Intervention, 14*(3), 204–218.

Duwa, S. M., Wells, C., & Lalinde, P. (1993). Creating family-centered programs and policies. In D. M. Bryant & M. A. Graham (Eds.), *Implementing early intervention: From research to effective practice* (pp. 92–123). New York: Guilford Press.

Dworkin, P. H. (1989). British and American recommendations for developmental monitoring: The role of surveillance. *Pediatrics, 84,* 1000–1010.

Early Childhood Training Center. (1995). *A teaching resource on parenting: Educators usage guide.* Lincoln: Nebraska Department of Education.

Eash, M. J., & Lane, J. J. (1985). Evaluation of a model for faculty development: Implications for educational policy. *Educational Evaluation and Policy Analysis, 7*(2), 127–138.

Egeland, B., & Sroufe, L. A. (1981). Attachment and early maltreatment. *Child Development, 52,* 44–52.

Eiserman, W. D., Shisler, L., & Healy, S. (1995). A community assessment of preschool providers' attitudes toward inclusion. *Journal of Early Intervention, 19,* 149–167.

Elder, J. O., & Magrab, P. O. (Eds.). (1985). *Coordinating services to handicapped children: A handbook for interagency collaboration.* Baltimore: Paul H. Brookes.

Elementary and Secondary Education Act. (1965). *United States Statutes at Large.* Washington, DC: U.S. Government Printing Office.

Engelhardt, H. T., Jr. (1986). Ethical issues in aiding the death of young children. In T. A. Mappes & J. S. Zenbaty (Eds.), *Biomedical ethics* (2nd ed., pp. 433–440). New York: McGraw-Hill.

Epps, S. (1991, March). *Training psychologists for family-centered service delivery to at-risk infants and toddlers.* Paper presented at the meeting of the National Association of School Psychologists, Dallas.

Epps, S. (1993). Labeling effects of infant health and parent demographics on nurses' ratings of preterm infant behavior. *Infant Mental Health Journal, 14,* 182–191.

Epps, S. (1995, August). Broadening the scope of practice to the health-care environment. In T. B. Gutkin (Chair), *School psychology and health care: Vital agendas for the future.*

Symposium conducted at the meeting of the American Psychological Association, New York.

Epps, S., & Jackson, B. J. (1991). Professional preparation of psychologists for family-centered service delivery to at-risk infants and toddlers. *School Psychology Review, 20*, 495–506.

Epps, S., & Kroeker, R. (1995). Physician early intervention referral as a function of child age and level of developmental delay. *Mental Retardation, 33*, 104–110.

Epps, S., & Nelson, T. (1991a). *Analysis of professional preparation of psychologists and special educators in early intervention*. Unpublished manuscript.

Epps, S., & Nelson, T. (1991b). *Expertise and professional activities of psychologists and special educators in early intervention*. Unpublished manuscript.

Epps, S., & Nowak, T. A. (1998). Parental perception of neonatal extracorporeal membrane oxygenation. *Children's Health Care. 27,* 215–230.

Epps, S., Thompson, B. J., & Lane, M. P. (1985). *Procedures for incorporating generalization and maintenance programming into interventions for special-education students*. Des Moines, IA: Department of Public Instruction.

Epps, S., & Tindal, G. (1987). The effectiveness of differential programming in serving students with mild handicaps: Placement options and instructional programming. In M. C. Wang, M. C. Reynolds, & H. J. Walberg (Eds.), *Handbook of special education: Research and practice* (pp. 213–248). New York: Pergamon Press.

Erikson, E. H. (1972). Eight ages of man. In C. S. Lavatelli & F. Stendler (Eds.), *Readings in child behavior and child development* (3rd ed., pp. 19–30). New York: Harcourt Brace Jovanovich.

Estrada, P., Arsenio, W., Hess, R., & Holloway, S. (1987). Affective quality of the mother–child relationship: Longitudinal consequences for children's school-relevant cognitive functioning. *Developmental Psychology, 23*, 210–215.

Fabi, B. (1992). Contingency factors in quality circles: A review of empirical evidence. *International Journal of Quality and Reliability Management, 9*(2), 18–33.

Farran, D. C. (1990). Effects of intervention with disadvantaged and disabled children: A decade review. In S. J. Meisels & J. P. Shonkoff (Eds.), *Handbook of early childhood intervention* (pp. 501–540). New York: Cambridge University Press.

Federal Interagency Forum on Child and Family Statistics. (1997). *America's children: Key national indicators of well-being*. Author.

Federal Register. (1992, May 1). *Early intervention program for infants and toddlers with disabilities: Proposed rulemaking* (U.S. Department of Education, 34 CFR Part 303). Washington, DC: U.S. Government Printing Office.

Feinberg, E. A., Hanft, B., & Marvin, N. (1996). Program evaluation and strategic planning in early intervention: General principles and a case example. *Infants and Young Children, 8*(4), 41–48.

Fenichel, E. S., & Eggbeer, L. (1991). Preparing practitioners to work with infants, toddlers, and their families: Four essential elements of training. *Infants and Young Children, 4*(2), 56–62.

Field, T. (1987). Affective and interactive disturbances in infants. In J. D. Osofsky (Ed.), *Handbook of infant development* (pp. 972–1005). New York: Wiley.

Field, T. M., Healy, B., Goldstein, S., & Guthertz, M. (1990). Behavior–state matching and synchrony in mother–infant interactions of nondepressed versus depressed dyads. *Developmental Psychology, 26,* 7–14.

Fields, M. (1992). *Determinants of interagency coordination for the groups implementing the Infants and Toddlers Program in Maryland*. Unpublished doctoral dissertation, Baltimore, Johns Hopkins University.

Fink, D. B. (1991). *In the mainstream—From the beginning?* Wellesley, MA: Wellesley College Center for Research on Women.

Forehand, R., Lautenschlager, G. J., Faust, J., & Graziano, W. G. (1986). Caregiver perceptions and caregiver–child interactions in clinic-referred children: A preliminary investigation of the effects of maternal depressive moods. *Behavior Research and Therapy, 24,* 73–75.

Fowler, M. D. M. (1989). Ethical decision making in clinical practice. *Nursing Clinics of North America, 24,* 955–965.

Fraiberg, S. (1980). *Clinical studies in infant mental health. The first year of life*. New York: Basic Books.

Frank, D. A., & Zeisel, S. H. (1988). Failure to thrive. *Pediatric Clinics of North America, 35,* 1187–1206.

Freedman, D. (1984). Multiethnic/multicultural education: Establishing the foundations. *Social Studies, 5,* 200–202.

Freel, K. S. (1995). Finding complexities and balancing perspectives: Using an ethnographic viewpoint to understand children and their families. *Zero to Three, 16*(3), 3–7.

Friedman, R. M. (1994). Restructuring of systems to emphasize prevention and family support. *Journal of Clinical Child Psychology, 23*(Suppl.), 40–47.

Friedman, S. L., & Sigman, M. D. (Eds.). (1992). *The psychological development of low birthweight children. Annual advances in applied developmental psychology (Vol. 6)*. Norwood, NJ: Ablex.

Friedrich, W. N., & Wheeler, K. K. (1982). The abusing parent revisited: A decade of psychological research. *Journal of Nervous and Mental Disease, 170,* 577–587.

Fuchs, V., & Reklis, D. (1992). America's children: Economic perspectives and policy options. *Science, 55,* 41–46.

Fullan, M. (1982). *The meaning of educational change*. New York: Teachers College Press.

Gaensbauer, T. J., Harmon, R. J., Cytryn, L., & McKnew, D. H. (1984). Social and affective development in infants with a manic-depressive caregiver. *American Journal of Psychiatry, 141,* 223–229.

Gaensbauer, T. J., & Mrazek, D. A. (1981). Differences in the patterning of affective expression in infants. *Journal of the American Academy of Child and Adolescent Psychiatry, 20,* 673–691.

Gallagher, J. F. (1993a). The family as a focus for intervention. In S. J. Meisels & J. P. Shonkoff (Eds.), *Handbook of early childhood intervention* (pp. 540–560). New York: Cambridge University Press.

Gallagher, J. F. (1993b). Policy designed for diversity: New initiatives for children with disabilities. In D. M. Bryant & M. A. Graham (Eds.), *Implementing early intervention: From research to effective practice* (pp. 336–350). New York: Guilford Press.

Gallagher, J. F., Garland, C. W., Kniest, B. A. (1995). *Caring for infants and toddlers with disabilities: A manual for physicians*. Norge, VA: Child Development Resources.

Garbarino, J. (1983). Social support networks. In J. Whittaker & J. Garbarino (Eds.), *Social support networks*. New York: Aldine.

Garland, C. W., & Linder, T. W. (1994). Administrative challenges in early intervention. In. L. J. Johnson, R. J. Gallagher, M. J. LaMontagne, J. B. Jordan, J. J. Gallagher, P. L. Hutinger, & M. B. Karnes (Eds.), *Meeting early intervention challenges: Issues from birth to three* (pp. 133–166). Baltimore: Paul H. Brookes.

Garmezy, N. (1983). Stressors of childhood. In N. Garmezy & M. Rutter (Eds.), *Stress, coping and development* (pp. 43–85). New York: McGraw-Hill.

Gaucher, E. J., & Coffey, R. J. (1993). *Total quality management in health care: From theory to practice*. San Francisco: Jossey-Bass.

George, C., & Main, M. (1979). Social interactions of young abused children: Approach, avoidance, and aggression. *Child Development, 50,* 306–318.

Gersten, R., Woodward, J., & Darch, C. (1986). Direct instruction: A research-based approach to curriculum design and teaching. *Exceptional Children, 53,* 17–31.

Gest, S. D., Neemann, J., Hubbard, J. J., Masten, A. S., & Tellegan, J. (1993). Parenting quality, adversity, and conduct problems in adolescence: Testing process-oriented models of resilience. *Development and psychopathology, 5*(4), 663–682.

Giannino, A., & Tronick, E. (1988). The mutual regulation model: Infant self and interactive regulation. In T. Field, P. McCabe, & N. Schneiderman (Eds.), *Stress and coping* (pp. 86–101). Hillsdale, NJ: Erlbaum.

Gilkerson, L. (1992). Supports for the process of change in "Program Families." *Zero to Three, 12*(3), 19–21.

Girolametto, L., Verbey, M., & Tannock, R. (1994). Improving joint engagement in caregiver–child interaction: An intervention study. *Journal of Early Intervention, 18,* 155–167.

Goldberg, S. (1990). Attachment in infants at risk: Theory, research, and practice. *Infants and Young Children, 2*(4), 11–20.

Goldberg, S., & Simmons, R. (1988). Chronic illness and early development: The caregiver's perspective. *Pediatrics, 15*, 13–20.

Goldberger, J., & Wolfer, J. (1991). An approach for identifying potential threats to development in hospitalized toddlers. *Infants and Young Children, 3*(3), 74–83.

Goldsmith, H., & Campos, J. (1982). Toward a theory of infant temperament. In R. Emde & R. Harmon (Eds.), *The development of attachment and affiliative systems* (pp. 161–189). New York: Plenum Press.

Goodman, S. H., Brogan, D., Lynch, M. E., & Fielding, B. (1993). Social and emotional competence in children of depressed mothers. *Child Development, 64*, 516–531.

Gordon, R. S., Jr. (1989). An operational classification of disease prevention. *Public Health Report, 10*, 403–422.

Gorski, P. A. (1983). Premature infant behavioral and physiological responses to care-giving interventions in the intensive care nursery. In J. D. Call, E. Galenson, & R. L. Tyson (Eds.), *Frontiers of infant psychiatry* (pp. 256–263). New York: Basic Books.

Graziano, A. M. (1992). Treatment for abused children: When is a partial solution acceptable? *Child Abuse and Neglect, 16*, 217–228.

Green, M. (1993). Maternal depression: Bad for children's health. *Contemporary Pediatrics, 11*, 28–36.

Greenberg, M. (1996). *No duty, no floor: The real meaning of 'ending entitlements.'* Washington DC: Center for Law and Social Policy.

Greenberg, M., & Speltz, M. (1988). Attachment and the ontogeny of conduct problems. In J. Belsky & T. Nezworski (Eds.), *Clinical implications of attachment* (pp. 387–435). Hillsdale, NJ: Erlbaum.

Greenspan, S. I. (1990). Infants, mothers, and their interaction: A quantitative clinical approach to developmental assessment. In S. I. Greenspan & G. H. Pollock (Eds.), *The course of life, Vol. I: Infancy* (pp. 503–560). Madison, CT: International Universities Press.

Grossman, H. (1983). *Classification in mental retardation.* Washington, DC: American Association on Mental Deficiency.

Gunnar, M. R. (1996). *Quality of care and the buffering of stress physiology: Its potential in protecting the developing human brain.* St. Paul: University of Minnesota Institute of Child Development.

Guralnick, M. J. (1994). Mother's perceptions of the benefits and drawbacks of early childhood mainstreaming. *Journal of Early Intervention, 18*, 168–183.

Gustavsson, N. S., & Segal, E. A. (1994). Critical issues in child welfare. Thousand Oaks, CA: Sage.

Haas, L. J., & Malouf, J. L. (1989). *Keeping up the good work: A practitioner's guide to mental health ethics.* Sarasota, FL: Professional Resource Exchange.

Hadadian, A. (1996). Attachment relationships and its significance for young children with disabilities. *Infant–Toddler Intervention, 6*(1), 1–15.

Haley, S., Hallenborg, S., & Gans, M. (1989). Functional assessment in young children with neurological impairments. *Topics in Early Childhood Special Education, 9*, 106–126.

Hallam, G. L., & Campbell, D. P. (1992). *Selecting team members: Start with a theory of team effectiveness.* Paper presented at the 7th Annual Meeting of the Society of Industrial and Organizational Psychology, Montreal, Quebec, Canada.

Halpern, R. (1990). Community-based early intervention. In S. J. Meisels & J. P. Shonkoff (Eds.), *Handbook of early childhood intervention* (pp. 469–498). New York: Cambridge University Press.

Halpern, R. (1993). Poverty and infant development. In C. H. Zeanah, Jr. (Ed.), *Handbook of infant mental health* (pp. 73–86). New York: Guilford Press.

Hamblin-Wilson, C., & Thurman, K. (1990). The transition from early intervention to kindergarten: Parental satisfaction and involvement. *Journal of Early Intervention, 14*, 55–61.

Hanft, B. E. (Ed.) (1989). *Family-centered care: An early intervention resource manual.* Rockville, MD: American Occupational Therapy Association.

Hanson, M. J. (1996). Early transactions: The developmental context for infants whose development is atypical. In M. J. Hanson (Ed.), *Atypical infant development* (pp. 3–16). Austin, TX: Pro-Ed.

Hanson, M. J., & Lynch, E. W. (1992). Family diversity: Implications for policy and practice. *Topics in Early Childhood Special Education, 12,* 283–306.

Hanson, M. J., Lynch, E. W., & Wayman, K. I. (1990). Honoring the cultural diversity of families when gathering data. *Topics in Early Childhood Special Education, 10*(1), 112–131.

Hanzlik, J., & Stevenson, M. (1986). Interaction of mothers with their infants who are mentally retarded, retarded with cerebral palsy or non-retarded. *American Journal of Mental Deficiency, 90,* 513–520.

Harbin, G. L., Gallagher, J. J., & Terry, D. V. (1991). Defining the eligible population: Policy issues and challenges. *Journal of Early Intervention, 15,* 13–20.

Harbin, G. L., & McNulty, B. A. (1990). Policy implementation: Perspectives on service coordination and interagency cooperation. In S. J. Meisels & J. P. Shonkoff (Eds.), *Handbook of early childhood intervention* (pp. 700–723). New York: Cambridge University Press.

Hardy, J. B., & Streett, R. (1989). Family support and parenting education in the home: An effective extension of clinic-based preventive health care services for poor children. *Journal of Pediatrics, 115,* 927–931.

Harkness, P. L., Hermansen, K. L., & Mentzel, M. R. (1993). Foiled at every turn: One QI team's battle with resistance. *Quest for quality and productivity in health services: Conference proceedings.* Norcross, GA: Institute of Industrial Engineers.

Harmon, R. J. (1995). Diagnostic thinking about mental health and developmental disorders in infancy and early childhood: A core skill for infant/family professionals. *Zero to Three, 15*(3), 11–15.

Harris, S. R. (1993). Evaluating the effects of early intervention: A mismatch between process and product. *American Journal of Diseases of Children, 147,* 12–13.

Hauser-Cram, P. & Krauss, M. W. (1991). Measuring change in children and families. *Journal of Early Intervention, 15*(3), 288–297.

Hauser-Cram, P., & Shonkoff, J. (1988). Rethinking the assessment of child focused outcomes. In H. Weiss & F. Jacobs (Eds.), *Evaluating family programs* (pp. 73–94). Hawthorne, New York: Aldine.

Hebbeler, K. M., Smith, B. J., & Black, T. (1991). Federal early childhood special education policy: A model for the improvement of services for children with disabilities. *Exceptional Children, 58,* 104–112.

Hersey, P., & Blanchard, K. H. (1988). *Management of organization behavior.* Englewood Cliffs, NJ: Prentice-Hall.

Hobbs, N. (1975). *The future of children.* San Francisco: Jossey-Bass.

Hobbs, N., Dokecki, P. R., Hoover-Dempsey, K. V., Moroney, R. M., Shayne, M. W., & Weeks, K. II. (1984). *Strengthening families.* San Francisco: Jossey-Bass.

Hochstadt, N., & Yost, D. (1992). Newark, NJ: Harwood Academic.

Hofferth, S. (1994). Who enrolls in Head Start: A demographic analysis of Head Start-eligible children. *Early Childhood Research Quarterly, 9,* 243–268.

Hogan, R., Curphy, G. J., & Hogan, J. (1994). What we know about leadership: Effectiveness and personality. *American Psychologist, 49,* 493–504.

Holden, E. W., Willis, D. J., & Corcoran, M. M. (1992). Preventing child maltreatment during the prenatal/perinatal period. In D. Willis, E. W. Holden, & M. Rosenberg (Eds.), *Prevention of child maltreatment: Developmental and ecological perspectives* (pp. 17–46). New York: Wiley-Interscience.

Hollingsworth, D. R., Kotchen, J. M., & Felice, M. E. (1983). Impact of gynecologic age on outcome of adolescent pregnancy. In E. R. McAnarney (Ed.), *Premature adolescent pregnancy and parenthood* (pp. 169–194). New York: Grune & Stratton.

Howes, C., & Hamilton, C. E. (1993). Child care for young children. In B. Spodek (Ed.), *Handbook of research on the education of young children* (pp. 322–336). New York: Macmillan.

Huston, A. C. (1994). Children in poverty: Designing research to affect policy. *Social Policy Report: Society for Research in Child Development, 8*(2), 1–12.

Huttenlocher, P. R. (1984). Synapse elimination and plasticity in developing human cerebral cortex. *American Journal of Mental Deficiency, 88,* 488–496.

Illback, R. J., Cobb, C. T., & Joseph, H. M., Jr. (Eds.). (1997). *Integrated services for children and families: Opportunities for psychological practice.* Washington, DC: American Psychological Association.

Ivey, A. E., Ivey, M. B., & Simek-Downing, L. (1987). *Counseling and psychotherapy: Integrating skills, theory, and practice* (2nd ed.). Englewood Cliffs, NJ: Prentice-Hall.

Jackson, B. J. (1992). *Evaluation of the LB701 Early Intervention Projects: Legislative report.* Unpublished document.

Jackson, B. J., Finkler, D., & Robinson, C. (1992). A case management system for infants with chronic illnesses and developmental disabilities. *Children's Health Care, 21*(4), 224–232.

Jarrett, R. (1995). Growing up poor: The family experiences of socially mobile youth in low-income African American neighborhoods. *Journal of Adolescent Research, 10,* 111–135.

Jeppson, E. S., & Thomas, J. (1995). *Essential allies: Families as advisors.* Bethesda, MD: Institute for Family-Centered Care.

Johns, N., & Harvey, C. (1993). Training for work with parents: Strategies for engaging practitioners who are uninterested or resistant. *Infants and Young Children, 5*(4), 52–57.

Johnson, B. H., Jeppson, E. S., & Redburn, L. (1992). *Caring for children and families: Guidelines for hospitals.* Bethesda, MD: Association for the Care of Children's Health.

Johnson, L. J., & LaMontagne, M. J. (1994). Program evaluation: The key to quality programming. In L. J. Johnson, R. J. Gallagher, & M. J. LaMontagne (Eds.), *Meeting early intervention challenges: Issues from birth to three.* Baltimore: Paul H. Brookes.

Johnstone, B., Frank, R. G., Belar, C., Berk, S., Bieliauskas, L. A., Bigler, E. D., Caplan, B., Elliott, T. R., Glueckauf, R. L., Kaplan, R. M., Kreutzer, J. S., Mateer, C. A., Patterson, D., Puente, A. E., Richards, J. S., Rosenthal, M., Sherer, M., Shewchuk, R., Siegel, L. J., & Sweet, J. J. (1995). Psychology in health care: Future directions. *Professional Psychology: Research and Practice, 26,* 341–365.

Joint Commission on Accreditation of Healthcare Organizations. (1992). *Accreditation manuals for hospitals.* Chicago: Author.

Jordan, A. E., & Meara, N. M. (1990). Ethics and the professional practice of psychologists: The role of virtues and principles. *Professional Psychology, 21,* 107–114.

Kagan, J., Kearsley, R., & Zelazo, P. (1978). *Infancy.* Cambridge, MA: Harvard University Press.

Karraker, K. H., & Lake, M. (1991). Normative stress and coping processes in infancy. In M. Cummings, A. Greene, & K. Karraker (Eds.), *Life-span developmental psychology: Perspectives on stress and coping* (Vol. 1, pp. 85–108). Hillsdale, NJ: Erlbaum.

Katz, K. (1989). Strategies for infant assessment: Implications of PL 99-457. *Topics in Early Childhood Special Education, 9*(3), 99–109.

Katz, L. F., & Gottman, J. M. (1995). *Marital conflict and child adjustment: Father's parenting as a mediator of children's negative peer play.* Paper presented at the biennial meeting of the Society for Research in Child Development, Indianapolis, IN.

Kaufmann, R. K., Hurth, J. L., & McGonigel, M. J. (1991). Identification of families' priorities, concerns, and resources. In M. J. McGonigel, R. K. Kaufmann, & B. H. Johnson (Eds.), *Guidelines and recommended practices for the Individualized Family Service Plan* (2nd ed., pp. 47–54). Bethesda, MD: Association for the Care of Children's Health.

Kazak, A. E., & Marvin, R. S. (1984). Differences, difficulties and adaptation: Stress and social networks in families with a handicapped child. *Family Relations, 33,* 67–77.

Kibel, B. (1999). *Successful stories as hard data.* New York: Plenum Press.

Kjerland, L. (1986). *Early intervention tailor made.* Eagan, MN: Project Dakota.

Klass, C. S. (1997). The home visitor–parent relationship: The linchpin of home visiting. *Zero to Three, 17*(4), 1–9.

Klein, N., & Campbell, P. (1990). Preparing personnel to serve at-risk and disabled infants, toddlers, and preschoolers. In S. Meisels & J. Shonkoff (Eds.), *Handbook of early childhood intervention* (pp. 679–699). New York: Cambridge University Press.

Knitzer, J. (1997). Integrated services for children and families: Lessons and questions. In R. J. Illback, C. T. Cobb, & H. M. Joseph (Eds.), *Integrated services for children and families: Opportunities for psychological practice* (pp. 45–61). Washington, DC: American Psychological Association.

Knollmueller, R. N. (1989). Case management: What's in a name? Nurse-Management Journal, 20(10), 28 10.

Knowles, M. S. (1980). *The modern practice of adult education* (Rev. ed.). Cambridge, MA: Adult Education Company.

Kochanek, T. T. (1991). Translating family policy into early intervention initiatives: Preliminary outcomes and implications. *Infants and Young Children, 3*(4), 12–20.

Kochanek, T. T., & Buka, S. L. (1991). Using biologic and ecologic factors to identify vulnerable infants and toddlers. *Infants and Young Children, 4*(1), 11–25.

Koren, P., DeChillo, N., & Friesen, B. J. (1992). Measuring empowerment in families whose children have emotional disabilities: A brief questionnaire. *Rehabilitation Psychology, 37*, 306–321.

Kram, K. E. (1985). *Mentoring at work: Developmental relationships in organizational life.* Glenview, IL: Scott, Foresman.

Kramer, J. J., & Epps, S. (1991). Expanding professional opportunities and improving the quality of training: A look towards the next generation of school psychologists. *School Psychology Review, 20*, 449–458.

Kraus, M. W., & Jacobs, F. (1990). Family assessment: Purposes and techniques. In S. J. Meisels & J. P. Shonkoff (Eds.), *Handbook of early childhood intervention* (pp. 303–325). New York: Cambridge University Press.

Kubler-Ross, E. (1997). *On children and death.* New York: Touchstone.

Lamb, M. E. (1997). *The role of the father in child development* (3rd ed.). New York: Wiley.

The Lancet. Editorial: Developmental surveillance. (1986). Vol. 1 (8487), 950–952.

Landesman-Dwyer, S., & Butterfield, E. C. (1983). Mental retardation: Developmental issues in cognitive and social adaptation. In M. Lewis (Ed.), *Origins of intelligence: Infancy and early childhood* (2nd ed., pp. 479–519). New York: Plenum Press.

Larson, C. E., & LaFasto, F. M. (1989). *Team work: What must go right / What can go wrong?* Newbury Park, CA: Sage.

Lee, V., Brooks-Gunn, J., Schnur, E., & Liaw, F. (1990). Are Head Start effects sustained: A longitudinal follow-up comparison of disadvantaged children attending Head Start, no preschool, and other preschool programs. *Child Development, 61*, 495–507.

Letourneau, A. (1988). Family focus/family support: Policy and resource issues. *AIMS and Perspectives, 2*(3), 2–3.

Leviton, A., Mueller, M., & Kauffman, C. (1991). *The family-centered catalytic consultation model: Practical applications for professionals.* Baltimore: Kennedy Institute.

Levitt, M., Weber, R., & Clark, M. (1986). Social network relationships as services of maternal support and well-being. *Developmental Psychology, 22*, 310–316.

Levy, J. E., & Kunitz, S. J. (1987). A suicide prevention program for Hopi youth. *Social Science and Medicine, 25*, 931–940.

Lewis, C. (1997). Fathers and preschoolers. In M. E. Lamb (Ed.), *The role of the father in child development* (pp. 121–142). New York: Wiley.

Liaw, F. (1991). *The efficacy of early intervention for low birth weight infants: What works, how, and for whom.* Unpublished doctoral dissertation, University of Michigan, Ann Arbor.

Lieberman, A. F., & Pawl, J. H. (1990). Disorders of attachment and secure base behavior in the second year of life: Conceptual issues and clinical intervention. In M. T. Greenberg, D. Cicchetti, & E. M. Cummings (Eds.), *Attachment in the preschool years* (pp. 375–398). Chicago: University of Chicago Press.

Linder, T. W. (1990). *Transdisciplinary play-based assessment: A functional approach to working with young children.* Baltimore: Paul H. Brookes.

Long, J. G., Lucey, J. F., & Philip, A. G. S. (1980). Noise and hypoxemia in the intensive care nursery. *Pediatrics, 65*, 143–145

Long, J. G., Philip, A. G., & Lucey, J. F. (1980). Excessive handling as a cause of hypoxemia. *Pediatrics, 65*, 203–207.

Lowenthal, B. (1996). Training early interventionists to work with culturally diverse families. *Infant–Toddler Intervention, 6*, 145–152.

Ludlow, B. L. (1994). Using distance education to prepare early intervention personnel. *Infants and Young Children, 7*(1), 51–59.

Lussier, B. J., Crimmins, D. B., & Alberti, D. (1994). Effect of three adult intervention styles on infant engagement. *Journal of Early Intervention, 18*, 12–24.

Lynch, E. W., & Hanson, M. J. (1992). *Developing cross-cultural competence: A guide for working with young children and their families*. Baltimore: Paul H. Brookes.

Lyons-Ruth, K., Alpern, L., & Rapacholi, B. (1993). Disorganized infant attachment classification and maternal psychosocial problems as predictors of hostile–aggressive behavior in the preschool classroom. *Child Development, 64*, 572–585.

Lyons-Ruth, K., Zoll, D., Connell, D., & Grunebaum, H. (1986). The depressed mother and her one-year-old infant: Environmental context, mother–infant interaction and attachment, and infant development. In E. A. Tronick & T. Field (Eds.), *Maternal depression and infant disturbance. New directions for child development* (pp. 61–82). San Francisco: Jossey-Bass.

Maccoby, E. E., & Martin, J. A. (1983). Socialization in the context of the family: Parent–child interaction. In E. M. Hetherington (Ed.), *Handbook of child psychology: Vol. 4, Socialization, personality, and social development* (pp. 469–546). New York: Wiley.

MacDonald, J. D., & Carroll, J. Y. (1994). Adult communication styles: The missing link to early language intervention. *Infant–Toddler Intervention: The Transdisciplinary Journal, 4*, 145–160.

MacMillan, A. (1994). *Primary prevention of child sexual abuse: A critical review. Part II 35*(5), 857–76.

MacMillan, H. L., MacMillan, J. H., & Offord, D. R. (1992). Periodic health examination, 1993 update: Primary prevention of child maltreatment. *Canadian Medical Association Journal, 148*, 151–163.

Mahoney, G., O'Sullivan, P., & Dennebaum, J. (1990a). A national study of mothers' perceptions of family-focused early intervention. *Journal of Early Intervention, 14*, 133–146.

Mahoney, G., O'Sullivan, P., & Dennebaum, J. (1990b). Maternal perceptions of early intervention services: A scale for assessing family-focused intervention. *Topics in Early Childhood Special Education, 10*, 1–15.

Mahoney G., & Powell, A. (1988). Modifying parent–child interaction: Enhancing the development of handicapped children. *Journal of Special Education, 22*, 82–96.

Main, M., Kaplan, N., & Cassidy, J. (1985). Security in infancy, childhood, and adulthood: A move to the level of representation. In I. Bretherton & E. Waters (Eds.), *Growing points of attachment theory and research. Monographs for the Society for Research in Child Development, 50* (1–2), 66–104.

Main, M., & Solomon, J. (1986). Discovery of an insecure-disorganized/disoriented attachment pattern. In T. B. Brazelton & M. W. Yogman (Eds.), *Affective development in infancy* (pp. 95–124). Norwood, NJ: Ablex.

Main, M., & Solomon, J. (1990). Procedures for identifying infants as disorganized/disoriented during the Ainsworth Strange Situation. In M. T. Greenberg, D. Cicchetti, & E. M. Cummings (Eds.), *Attachment in the preschool years: Theory, research and intervention* (pp. 121–160). Chicago: University of Chicago Press.

Maisto, A., & German, M. (1979). Variables related to progress in a parent infant training program for high-risk infants. *Journal of Pediatric Psychology, 4*, 409–419.

Marfo, K., & Kysela, G. M. (1985). Early intervention with mentally handicapped children: A critical appraisal of applied research. *Journal of Pediatric Psychology, 10*, 305–324.

Martin, S. L., Ramey, C. T., & Ramey, S. (1990). The prevention of intellectual impairment in children of impoverished families: Findings of a randomized trial of educational day care. *American Journal of Public Health, 80*(1), 844–847.

Martinez, M. (1987). Dialogues among children and between children and their mothers. *Child Development, 58*, 1035–1043.

Masten, A. S., Best, K. M., & Garmezy, N. (1990). Resilience and development: Contributions from the study of children who overcome adversity. *Developmental Psychopathology, 2*, 425–444.

Masten, A. S., & Coatsworth, J. D. (1998). The development of competence in favorable and unfavorable environments: Lessons from research on successful children. *American Psychologist, 53*, 205–220.

McCall, R., Appelbaum, M., & Hogarty, P. (1973). Developmental changes in mental performance. *Monographs of the Society for Research in Child Development, 42* (3, Serial No. 171).

McCarthy, D. (1972), *McCarthy Scales of Children's Abilities*. New York: Psychological Corporation.

McCollum, J. A., & Maude, S. P. (1994). Issues and emerging practice in preparing educators to be early interventionists. In P. L. Safford, B. Spodek, & O. N. Saracho (Eds.), *Early childhood special education* (pp. 218–241). New York: Teachers College Press.

McCollum, J. A., & Thorp, E. K. (1988). Training of infant specialists: A look to the future. *Infants and Young Children, 1*(2), 55–65.

McCollum, J. A., & Yates, T. J. (1994). Dyad as focus, triad as means: A family-centered approach to supporting caregiver–child interactions. *Infants and Young Children, 6* (4), 54–63.

McCormick, M. C. (1985). The contribution of low birth weight to infant mortality and child morbidity. *New England Journal of Medicine, 312,* 82–90.

McCune, L., Kalmanson, B., Fleck, M., Blazewski, B., & Sillari, J. (1993). An interdisciplinary model of infant assessment. In S. J. Meisels & J. P. Shonkoff (Eds.), *Handbook of early childhood intervention* (pp. 219–243). New York: Cambridge University Press.

McGonigel, M. J., Kaufmann, R. K., & Johnson, B. H. (1991). *Guidelines and recommended practices for the Individualized Family Service Plan* (2nd ed.). Bethesda, MD: Association for the Care of Children's Health.

McLoyd, V. C. (1990). The impact of economic hardship on Black families and children: Psychological distress, parenting, and socioeconomic hardship on Black families and children: Psychological distress, parenting, and socioemotional development. *Child Development, 61,* 311–346.

McLoyd, V. C. (1998). Socioeconomic disadvantage and child development. *American Psychologist, 53,* 185–204.

McNaughton, D. (1994). Measuring parent satisfaction with early childhood intervention programs: Current practice, problems, and future, perspectives. *Topics in Early Childhood Special Education, 14*(1), 26–48.

McNulty, B. A. (1989). Leadership and policy strategies for interagency planning: Meeting the early childhood mandate. In J. J. Gallagher, P. L. Trohanis, & R. M. Clifford (Eds.), *Policy implementation and PL 99-457: Planning for young children with special needs* (pp. 147–167). Baltimore: Paul H. Brookes.

McWilliam, P. J., & Winton, P. (1991). *Brass Tacks: A self-rating of family-centered practices in early intervention. Part #2: Individual interactions with families.* Chapel Hill: University of North Carolina at Chapel Hill, Frank Porter Graham Child Development Center, Carolina Institute for Research on Infant Personnel Preparation.

McWilliam, R. A., & Bailey, D. B. (1995). Effect of classroom structure and disability on engagement. *Topics in Early Childhood Special Education, 15,* 123–148.

McWilliam, R. A., Tocci, L., & Harbin, G. (1995). Services are child-oriented and families like it that way—but why? *Findings: Service utilizations* (pp. 1–5). Chapel Hill, NC: Early Childhood Research Institute.

Meisels, S. (1992). Early intervention: A matter of context. *Zero to Three, 12*(3), 1–6.

Meisels, S. J., & Anastasiow, N. J. (1982). The risks of prediction: Relationships between etiology, handicapping conditions and developmental outcomes. In S. Moore & C. Cooper (Eds.), *The young child: Reviews of research* (Vol. 3, pp. 259–280). Washington, DC: National Association for the Education of Young Children.

Meisels, S. J., Harbin, G., Modigliani, K., & Olson, K. (1988). Formulating optimal state early childhood intervention policies. *Exceptional Children, 55,* 159–165.

Meisels, S. J., Jablon, D. B., Marsden, M. L., Dichtimiller, A. B., Dorfman, J., & Steele, D. M. (1995). *The work sampling system: An overview.* Ann Arbor, MI: Rebus Planning.

Meisels, S. J., Liaw, F., Dorfman, A. B., Falls, R. (1995). The work sampling system: Reliability and validity of a performance assessment for young children. *Early Childhood Research Quarterly, 10*(3), 31–42.

Meisels, S. J., Plunkett, J. W., Pasick, P. L., Stiefel, G. S., & Roloff, D. W. (1987). Effects of severity and chronicity of respiratory illness on cognitive development of preterm infants. *Journal of Pediatric Psychology, 12,* 117–132.

Meisels, S. J., & Wasik, B. A. (1990). Who should be served? Identifying children in need of early intervention. In S. J. Meisels & J. P. Shonkoff (Eds.), *Handbook of early childhood intervention* (pp. 605–632). New York: Cambridge University Press.

Melaville, A. I., & Blank, M. J. (1991). *What it takes: Structuring interagency partnerships to connect children and families with comprehensive services*. Washington, DC: Education and Human Services Consortium.

Miles, M. B., & Huberman, A. M. (1984). Drawing valid meaning from qualitative data: Toward a shared craft. *Educational Research, 13*(5), 20–30.

Miller, C. L., White, R., Whitman, T. L., O'Callaghan, M. F., & Maxwell, S. E. (1995). The effects of cycled versus noncycled lighting on growth and development in preterm infants. *Infant Behavior and Development, 18,* 87–95.

Minuchin, S. (1974). *Families and family therapy*. Cambridge, MA: Harvard University Press.

Morgan, M. L., Guetzloe, E. C., & Swan, W. W. (1991). Leadership for local interagency coordinating councils. *Journal of Early Intervention, 15,* 255–268.

Morris, D. (1982). Attachment and intimacy. In M. Fisher & G. Stricker (Eds.), *Intimacy* (pp. 25–46). New York: Plenum Press.

Mosley, J., & Thomson, E. (1995). Father behavior and child outcomes: The role of race and poverty. In W. Marsiglio (Ed.), *Fatherhood: Contemporary theory, research, and social policy* (pp. 148–165). Thousand Oaks, CA: Sage.

Mrazek, P. J. (1993). Maltreatment and infant development. In C. H. Zeanah, Jr. (Ed.), *Handbook of infant mental health* (pp. 159–172). New York: Guilford Press.

Murphy, D. L., Lee, I. M., Turnbull, A. P., & Turbiville, V. (1995). The family-centered program rating scale: An instrument for program evaluation and change. *Journal of Early Intervention, 19,* 24–42.

Murphy, M. A. (1982). The family with a handicapped child: A review of the literature. *Journal of Developmental and Behavioral Pediatrics, 3,* 73–82.

Murphy, M. J., DeBernado, C. R., & Shoemaker, W. E. (1998). Impact of managed care on independent practice and professional ethics: A survey of independent practitioners. *Professional Psychology: Research and Practice, 29,* 43–51.

Nadler, D. (1987). The effective management of change. In J. Lorsch (Ed.), *Handbook of organizational behavior* (pp. 358–369). Englewood Cliffs, NJ: Prentice-Hall.

Nash, J. K. (1990). PL 99-457: Facilitating family participation on the multidisciplinary team. *Journal of Early Intervention, 14,* 318–326.

National Association for the Education of Young Children. (1984). *Accreditation criteria and procedures of the National Academy of Early Childhood Education: Position statement of the National Academy of Early Childhood Programs*. Washington, DC: Author.

National Association for the Education of Young Children. (1995). *Guidelines for preparation of early childhood professionals*. Washington, DC: Author.

National Association for the Education of Young Children, & National Association of Early Childhood Specialists in State Departments of Education. (1991). Position statement on guidelines for appropriate curriculum content and assessment in programs serving children ages 3 through 8. *Young Children, 46*(3), 21–38.

National Association of School Psychologists. (1984). Principles for professional ethics. In *Professional conduct manual* (pp. 1–17). Stanford, CT: Author.

National Association of State Directors of Special Education. (1997). Developmental delay through age nine: A new option for states. *Liaison Bulletin, 28*(1), 1–8.

National Center for Children in Poverty. (1990). *Five million children*. New York: Author.

National Council on Disability. (1995). *Improving the implementation of the Individuals with Disabilities Education Act: Making schools work for all of America's children*. Washington, DC: Author.

Neisworth, J. T., & Bagnato, S. J. (1988). Assessment in early childhood special education: A typology of dependent measures. In S. L. Odom & M. B. Karnes (Eds.), *Early intervention for infants and children with handicaps: An empirical base* (pp. 23–49). Baltimore: Paul H. Brookes.

Neisworth, J. T., Bagnato, S. J., & Salvia, J. (1995). Neurobehavioral markers for early regulatory disorders. *Infants and Young Children, 8*(1), 8–17.

Nichols, M. P. (1984). *Family therapy: Concepts and methods*. New York: Gardner Press.

Noe, R. A. (1988). Women and mentoring: A review and research agenda. *Academy of Management Review, 13*, 65–78.

Noonan, M. J., & McCormick, L. (1993). *Early intervention in natural environments: Methods and procedures.* Pacific Grove, CA: Brooks/Cole.

Nugent, J. K. (1994). Cross-cultural studies of child development. *Zero to Three*, 1–8.

Odom, S. L., & McEvoy, M. A. (1996). Integration of young children with handicaps and normally developing children. In S. Odom & M. Karnes (Eds.), *Early intervention for infants and children with handicaps: An empirical base* (pp. 241–268). Baltimore: Paul H. Brookes.

Oldershaw, L., Walters, G. D., & Hall, D. K. (1986). Control strategies and noncompliance in abusive mother–child dyads: An observational study. *Child Development, 57*, 722–732.

Olds, D. L. (1990). The prenatal/early infancy project: A strategy for responding to the needs of high-risk mothers and their children. In R. P. Horion (Ed.), *Protecting the children* (pp. 59–87). Binghamton, NY: Haworth Press.

Olds, D. L., Eckenrode, J., Henderson, C. R., Jr., Lotzam, J., Cole, R., Sidora, K., Morris, P., Pettitt, L. M., & Luckey, D. (1997). Long-term effects of home visitation on maternal lifecourse and child abuse and neglect. *Journal of American Medical Association, 278*(8), 637–643.

Olds, D. L., Henderson, C. R., Tatelbaum, R., & Chamberlin, R. (1988). Improving the lifecourse development of socially disadvantaged mothers: A randomized trial of nurse home visitation. *American Journal of Public Health, 8*, 1436–1445.

Olson, J., & Murphy, C. L. (1997). *Teaming.* Moscow, ID: Early Childhood Resources.

Osofsky, J. D., & Eberhart-Wright, A. (1988). Affective exchanges between high risk mothers and infants. *International Journal of Psycho-Analysis, 69*, 221–231.

Osofsky, J. D., & Eberhart-Wright, A. (1992). Risk and protective factors for parents and infants. In G. Suci & S. Robertson (Eds.), *Human development: Future directions in infant development research* (pp. 25–39). New York: Springer-Verlag.

Osofsky, J. D., Hann, D. M., & Peebles, C. (1993). Adolescent parenthood: Risks and opportunities for mothers and infants. In C. H. Zeanah, Jr. (Ed.), *Handbook of infant mental health* (pp. 106–119). New York: Guilford Press.

Pachter, L. M. (1994). Culture and clinical care: Folk illness beliefs and behaviors and their implications for health care delivery. *Journal of the American Medical Association, 271*, 690–694.

Pardes, H., Silverman, M. M., & Wesh, A. (1989). Prevention and the field of mental health: A psychiatric perspective. *Annual Review of Public Health, 10*, 403–422.

Parish, M. L., & Gemmill, D. D. (1993). What makes CQI/TQM a success: A statistical analysis. *Quest for quality and productivity in health services: Conference proceedings.* Norcross, GA: Institute of Industrial Engineers.

Patton, M. Q. (1997). *Utilization-focused evaluation.* (3rd Ed.). London: Sage.

Pearson, J. L., Hunter, A. G., Ensminger, M. E., & Kellam, S. G. (1990). Black grandmothers in multigenerational households: Diversity in family structure and parenting involvement in the Woodlawn Community. *Child Development, 61*, 434–442.

Perrin, J. M., Shayne, M. W., & Bloom, S. R. (1993). *Home and community care for chronically ill children.* New York: Oxford University Press.

Perry, B. D. (1996). Incubated in terror: Neurodevelopmental factors in the 'cycle of violence.' In J. D. Osofsky (Ed.), *Children, Youth and Violence: Searching for Solutions.* New York: Guilford Press.

Peterson, M. L. (1991). Interagency collaboration under Part H: A key to comprehensive, multidisciplinary, coordinated infant/toddler intervention services. *Journal of Early Intervention, 15*, 89–105.

Plunkett, J., Meisels, S., Stieffol, M., Pasick, P., & Roloff, D. (1986). Patterns of attachment among preterm infants of varying biological risk. *Journal of American Academy of Child Psychiatry, 25*, 794–800.

Popp, R. J. (1992). *Family portfolios: Documenting change in parent–child relationships.* Louisville, KY: National Center for Family Literacy.

Poulsen, M. K. (1993). Strategies for building resilience in infants and young children at risk. *Infants and Young Children, 6*(2), 29–40.

Practice Management Information Corporation. (1994). *International classification of diseases* (9th rev.). Los Angeles: Author.

Ragins, B. R. (1989). Barriers to mentoring: The female manager's dilemma. *Human Relations, 42,* 1–22.

Ramey, C. T., Bryant, D. M., Wasik, B. H., Sparling, J. J., Fendt, K. H., & LaVange, L. M. (1992). Infant Health and Development Program for low birth weight, premature infants: Program elements, family participation, and child intelligence. *Pediatrics, 89,* 454–465.

Ramey, C. T., & Campbell, F. A. (1991). Poverty, early childhood education, and academic competence: The Abecedarian experience. In A. C. Huston (Ed.), *Children in poverty: Child development and public policy* (pp. 190–221). New York: Cambridge University Press.

Ramey, C. T., & Ramey, S. L. (1998). Early intervention and early experience. *American Psychologist, 53*(2), 109–120.

Ramey, C. T., Ramey, S. L., Gaines, K., & Blair, C. (1995). Two-generation early intervention programs: A child development perspective. In I. Sigel (Series Ed.) & S. Smith (Vol. Ed.), *Advances in applied developmental psychology: Vol. 9. Two generation programs for families in poverty: A new intervention strategies* (pp. 199–228). Norwood, NJ: Ablex.

Reiss, D. (1981). *The family's construction of reality.* Cambridge, MA: Harvard University Press.

Rescher, N. (1966). *Distributive justice.* Indianapolis, IN: Bobbs-Merrill.

Reynolds, A. (1994). Effects of a preschool plus follow-up intervention for children at risk. *Developmental Psychology, 30,* 787–804.

Robison, S. D. (1992). *Putting the pieces together: Survey of state systems for children in crisis.* Denver: National Conference of State Legislatures.

Rodd, J. (1994). *Leadership in early childhood: The pathway to professionalism.* New York: Teachers College Press.

Rogers, E. M. (1983). *Diffusion of innovations* (3rd ed.). New York: Free Press.

Rogers, S., Herbison, J., Lewis, H., Patone, J., & Reis, K. (1986). An approach for enhancing the symbolic, communicative, and interpersonal functioning of young children with autism or severe emotional handicaps. *Journal of the Division of Early Childhood, 10,* 135–147.

Rosenberg, S., & Robinson, C. (1988). Interactions of parents with their young handicapped children. In S. Odom & M. Karnes (Eds.), *Research in early childhood special education* (pp. 159–177). Baltimore: Paul H. Brookes.

Rosenberg, S., Robinson, C., & Beckman, P. (1984). Teaching Skills Inventory: A measure of parent performance. *Journal of the Division for Early Childhood, 8,* 107–113.

Rosenberg, S., Robinson, C. C., Finkler, D., & Rose, J. S. (1987). An empirical comparison of formulas evaluating early intervention program impact on development. *Exceptional Development, 54,* 213–219.

Rosenkoetter, S. E., Hains, A. H., Fowler, S. A. (1994). *Bridging early services for children with special needs and their families: A practical guide for transition planning.* Baltimore: Paul H. Brookes.

Rosen-Morris, D., & Sitkei, E. G. (1981). Strategies for teaching severely/profoundly handicapped infants and young children. *Journal of the Division for Early Childhood, 4,* 81–93.

Royeen, C. B., DeGangi, G., & Poisson, S. (1992). Development of the individualized family service plan Anchor Guide. *Infants and Young Children, 5*(2), 57–64.

Rule, S., Stowitschek, J. J., Innocenti, M., Striefel, S., Killoran, J., Swezey, K., & Boswell, C. (1987). The Social Integration Project: Analysis of the effects of mainstreaming handicapped children into day care centers. *Education and Treatment of Children, 10,* 175–192.

Rush, D. D., Shelden, M., & Stanfill, L. (1995). Facing the challenges: Implementing a statewide system of inservice training in early intervention. *Infants and Young Children, 7*(4), 55–61.

Sakata, R. T. (1984). Adult education theory and practice. Chapel Hill, NC: Technical Assistance Development System.

Salisbury, C. (1992). Parents as team members. In B. Rainforth, J. York, & C. MacDonald

(Eds.), *Collaborative teams for students with severe disabilities: Integrating therapy and educational services* (pp. 43–66). Baltimore: Paul H. Brookes.

Sameroff, A. J. (1975). Early influences on development. *Merrill-Palmer Quarterly, 21,* 267–294.

Sameroff, A. J. (1986). Environmental context of child development. *Journal of Pediatrics, 109,* 192–200.

Sameroff, A. J. (1987). The social context of development. In N. Eisenberg (Ed.), *Contemporary topics in developmental psychology* (pp. 273–291). New York: Wiley.

Sameroff, A. J., & Emde, R. N. (Eds.). (1989). *Relationship disturbances in early childhood.* New York: Basic Books.

Sameroff, A. J., Seifer, R., Barocas, R., Zax, M., & Greenspan, S. (1987). Intelligence quotient scores of 4-year-old children: Social-environmental risk factors. *Pediatrics, 79,* 343–350.

Sandling, J., Carter, B., Moore, C. A., & Sparks, J. W. (1993). Ethics in neonatal intensive care. In G. B. Merenstein & S. L. Gardner (Eds.), *Handbook of neonatal intensive care* (pp. 609–637). St. Louis, MO: Mosby Year Book.

Schneider-Rosen, K., Braunwald, K. G., Carlson, V., & Cicchetti, D. (1985). Current perspectives in attachment theory: Illustrations from the study of maltreated infants. In I. Bretherton & E. Waters (Eds.), Growing points of attachment theory and research. *Monographs of the Society for Research in Child Development, 50* (1–2, Serial No. 209).

Schwab, W. E. (1991, November). Teaching family-centered care to medical students. *The Medical Home Newsletter,* pp. 2, 4–7.

Scriven, M. (1996). The logic of evaluation and evaluation practice. In D. M. Fournier (Ed.), *Reasoning in evaluation: Inferential links and leaps* (pp. 49–70). San Francisco: Jossey-Bass.

Segal, E. A. (1991). The juvenilization of poverty in the 1980s. *Social Work, 36,* 454–457.

Seitz, V., & Provence, S. (1990). Caregiver-focused models of early intervention. In S. J. Meisels & J. P. Shonkoff (Eds.), *Handbook of early childhood intervention* (pp. 400–426). New York: Cambridge University Press.

Senge, P. M. (1990). *The fifth discipline: The art and practice of the learning organization.* New York: Doubleday.

Senge, P. M., Kleiner, A., Roberts, C., Ross, R. B., & Smith, B. J. (1994). *The fifth discipline fieldbook.* New York: Doubleday.

Sexton, D., Snyder, P., Rheams, T., Garron-Sharp, B., & Perez, J. (1991). Consideration in using written surveys to identify family strengths and needs during the IFSP process. *Topics in Early Childhood Special Education, 11,* 81–91.

Shackelford, J. (1992). State/jurisdiction eligibility definitions for Part H. *NEC*TAS Notes: A Periodic Topical Publication, 5,* 1–11.

Shapiro, L. P., Gordon, R., & Neiditch, C. (1977). Documenting change in young multiply handicapped children in a rehabilitation center. *The Journal of Special Education, 11,* 243–257.

Sheehan, R. (1989). Implications of PL 99-457 for assessment. *Topics in Early Childhood Special Education, 8*(4), 103–115.

Sheehan, R., & Keogh, B. K. (1984). Approaches to evaluation in special education. In B. K. Keogh (Ed.), *Advances in special education* (Vol. 4, pp. 1–20). Greenwich, CT: JAI Press.

Shelton, T. L., Jeppson, E. S., & Johnson, B. H. (1987). *Family-centered care for children with special health care needs.* Washington, DC: U.S. Government Printing Office.

Sherman, A. (1998). *Poverty matters: The cost of child poverty in America.* Washington, DC: Children's Defense Fund.

Shonkoff, J. (1992). Early intervention research: Asking and answering meaningful questions. *Zero to Three, 12*(3), 7–9.

Shonkoff, J., & Hauser-Cram, P. (1987). Early intervention for disabled infants and their families: A quantitative analysis. *Pediatrics, 80,* 650–658.

Shonkoff, J., Hauser-Cram, P., Kraus, M., & Upshur, C. (1992). Development of infants with disabilities and their families. *Monographs of the Society for Research in Child Development, 57* (Serial No. 230).

Shonkoff, J., & Meisels, S. (1991). Defining eligibility for services under Public Law 99-457. *Journal of Early Intervention, 15*(1), 21–25.

Shore, R. (1997). *Rethinking the brain: New insights into early development*. New York: Families and Work Institute.

Short, R. J. (1997). Education and training for integrated practice: Assumptions, components, and issues. In R. J. Illback, C. T. Cobb, & H. M Joseph, Jr. (Eds.), *Integrated services for children and families: Opportunities for psychological practice*. Washington, DC: American Psychological Association.

Shortell, S. M., Buehler, A. C., Levin, D. Z., O'Brien, J. L., & Hughes, F. X. (1995). Assessing the evidence on CQI: Is the glass half empty or half full? *Hospital and Health Service Administration 40*(1), 40–53.

Siegel, B. (1996). Is the emperor wearing clothes? Social policy and the empirical support for full inclusion of children with disabilities in the preschool and early elementary grades. *Social Policy Report: Society for Research in Child Development, X*(2&3), 2–17.

Silber, S. (1989). Family influences on early development. *Topics in Early Childhood Special Education, 8*(4), 1–23.

Silverman, W. (1992). Overtreatment of neonates? A personal retrospective. *Pediatrics, 90*, 971–976.

Simeonsson, R. (1981). *Carolina Record of Individual Behavior.* Unpublished scale, Frank Porter Graham Child Development Center, University of North Carolina, Chapel Hill.

Simeonsson, R. J. (1991). Early intervention eligibility: A prevention perspective. *Infants and Young Children, 3*(4), 48–55.

Slade, A. (1987). A longitudinal study of maternal involvement and symbolic play during the toddler period. *Child Development, 56*, 367–375.

Slentz, K. L., & Bricker, D. (1992). Family-guided assessment for IFSP development: Jumping off the family assessment bandwagon. *Journal of Early Intervention, 16*, 11–19.

Slentz, K., Walker, B., & Bricker, D. (1989). Supporting involvement in early intervention: A role–taking model. In G. Singer & L. Irvin (Eds.), *Support for caregiving families: Enabling positive adaptation to disability* (pp. 221–238). Baltimore: Paul H. Brookes.

Smith, B. J., & Rose, D. F. (1993). *Administrator's policy handbook for preschool mainstreaming*. Cambridge, MA: Brookline Books.

Smith, M. J., & Ryan, A. S. (1987). Chinese-American families of children with developmental disabilities: An exploratory study of reactions to providers. *Mental Retardation, 25*, 345–351.

Smith, S., & Zaslow, M. (1995). Rationale and policy context for two-generation interventions. In I. Sigel (Series Ed.) & S. Smith (Vol. Ed.), *Advances in applied developmental psychology: Vol. 9. Two generation programs for families in poverty: A new intervention strategies* (pp. 122–145). Norwood, NJ: Ablex.

Sonag, J. C., & Schacht, R. (1994). An ethnic comparison of parent participation and information needs in early intervention. *Exceptional Children, 60*, 422–433.

Sorce, J. F., & Emde, R. N. (1981). Mother's presence is not enough. *Developmental Psychology, 17*, 737–745.

Spieker, S. J., & Booth, C. (1988). Maternal antecedents of attachment quality. In J. Belsky & T. Nezworski (Eds.), *Clinical implications of attachment* (pp. 95–135). Hillsdale, NJ: Erlbaum.

Squires, J. K., Nickel, R., & Bricker, D. (1990). Use of parent-completed developmental questionnaires for child-find and screening. *Infants and Young Children, 3*(2), 46–57.

Sroufe, L. A., Egeland, B., & Kreutzer, T. (1993). The fate of early experience following developmental change: Longitudinal approaches to individual adaptation in childhood. *Child Development, 61*, 1363–1373.

Sroufe, L. A., & Fleeson, J. (1986). Attachment and the construction of relationships. In W. W. Hartup & Z. Rubin (Eds.), *Relationships and development* (pp. 34–55). Hillsdale, NJ: Erlbaum.

Stahlman, J. I. (1994). Family and professional collaboration: Issues in early childhood special education. In P. L. Safford, B. Spodek, & O. N. Saracho (Eds.), *Early childhood special education* (pp. 218–241). New York: Teachers College Press.

Stainback, S., & Stainback, W. (1992). *Curriculum consideration in inclusive classrooms: Facilitating learning for all students*. Baltimore: Paul H. Brookes.

Stake, R. E. (1996). *Beyond responsive evaluation: Developments in this decade*. Presented at the Minnesota Evaluation Studies Institute, College of Education and Human Development, University of Minnesota.

State of Delaware. (1993). *Administrative manual: Programs for exceptional children.* Dover, DE: State Board of Education and Department of Public Instruction.

Stayton, V. D., & Karnes, M. B. (1994). Model programs for infants and toddlers with disabilities. In L. J. Johnson, R. J. Gallagher, M. J. LaMontagne, J. B. Jordan, J. J. Gallagher, P. L. Huntinger, & M. B. Karnes (Eds.), *Meeting early intervention challenges: Issues from birth to three* (2nd ed., pp. 13–32). Baltimore: Paul H. Brookes.

Stayton, V. D., & Miller, P. (1993). Personnel competence. In *DEC task force on recommended practices: Indicators of quality in programs for infants and young children with special needs and their families* (pp. 107–117). Reston, VA: Council for Exceptional Children.

Sterm-Bruschweiler, N., & Stern, D. N. (1989). A model for conceptualizing the role of the mother's representational world in various mother–infant therapies. *Infant Mental Health Journal, 10*(3), 142–156.

Stern, D. (1977). *The first relationship: Infant and mother.* Cambridge, MA: Harvard University Press.

Stern, D. (1984). Affect attunement. In J. D. Call, E. Galenson, & R. L. Tyson (Eds.), *Frontiers of infant psychiatry* (pp. 101–122). New York: Basic Books.

Strauss, M. A. (1980). Stress and child abuse. In C. H. Kempe & R. E. Heifer (Eds.), *The battered child* (pp. 86–103). Chicago: University of Chicago Press.

Strong, C. (1984). The neonatologist's duty to patient and parents. *Hastings Center Report, 14*(4), 10–16.

Summers, J. A., Dell'Oliver, C., Turnbull, A. P., Benson, H. A., Santelli, E., Campbell, M., & Siegel-Causey, E. (1991). Examining the Individualized Family Service Plan process: What are family and practitioner preferences? *Topics in Early Childhood Special Education, 10*(1), 78–99.

Swan, W. W., & Morgan, J. L. (1993). *Collaborating for comprehensive services for young children and their families: The local interagency coordinating council.* Baltimore: Paul H. Brookes.

Terkelson, K. G. (1980). Toward a theory of family life cycle. In E. Carter & M. McGoldrick (Eds.), *The family life cycle: A framework of family therapy* (pp. 21–52). New York: Gardner Press.

Terry, R. W. (1993). *Authentic leadership: Courage in action.* San Francisco: Jossey-Bass.

Thomasma, D. C. (1978). Training in medical ethics: An ethical work up. *Forum on Medicine, 1*(9), 33–36.

Thompson, R., & Lamb, M. E. (1983). Security of attachment and stranger sociability in infancy. *Developmental Psychology, 19*, 184–191.

Thorndike, R. L. (1966). Intellectual status and intellectual growth. *Journal of Educational Psychology, 57*, 121–127.

Thorp, E. K., & McCollum, J. A. (1964). Defining the infancy specialization in early childhood special education. In L. J. Johnson, R. J. Gallagher, M. J. LaMontagne, J. B. Jordan, P. L. Hutinger, J. J. Gallagher, & M. B. Karnes (Eds.), *Meeting early intervention challenges: Issues from birth to three* (2nd ed., pp. 167–183). Baltimore: Paul H. Brookes.

Tjossem, T. D. (Ed.). (1976). *Intervention strategies for high risk infants and young children.* Baltimore: University Park Press.

Trad, P. V. (1990). *Infant previewing.* New York: Springer-Verlag.

Trickett, P. K. (1993). Maladaptive development of school-aged, physically abused children: Relationships with the child-rearing context. *Journal of Family Psychology, 7*(1), 134–147.

Trickett, P., Apfel, N., Rosenbaum, L., & Zigler, E. (1982). A five year follow-up of participants in the Yale Child Welfare Research Program. In E. Zigler & E. Gordon (Eds.), *Day care: Scientific and social policy issue* (pp. 200–222). Boston: Auburn House.

Trivette, C. M., Dunst, C. J., Allen, S., & Wall, L. (1993). Family-centeredness of the Children's Health Care Journal. *Children's Health Care Journal, 22*, 241–256.

Trivette, C. M., Dunst, C. J., Hamby, D. W., & LaPointe, N. J. (1996). Key elements of empowerment and their implications for early intervention. *Infant–Toddler Intervention, 6*(1), 59–73.

Tronick, E. Z., & Field, T. (Eds.). (1986). *Maternal depression and infant disturbance: New directions for child development*. San Francisco: Jossey-Bass.

Trout, M., & Foley, G. (1992). Working with families of handicapped infants and toddlers. *Topics in Language Disorders, 10*(1), 57–67.

Turecki, S., & Wernick, S. (1995). *Normal children have problems, too*. New York: Bantam Books.

Turnbull, A. P. (1991). Identifying children's strengths and needs. In M. J. McGonigel, R. K. Kaufmann, & B. H. Johnson (Eds.), *Guidelines and recommended practices for the Individualized Family Service Plan* (2nd ed., pp. 39–46). Bethesda, MD: Association for the Care of Children's Health.

Turnbull, A. P., Strickland, B., & Goldstein, S. (1984). Training professionals and parents in developing and implementing the IEP. In M. L. Henninger & E. M. Nesselroad (Eds.), *Working with parents of handicapped children: A book of readings for school personnel* (pp. 173–194). New York: University Press of America.

Turnbull, A. P., Summers, J. A., & Brotherson, M. J. (1984). *Working with families with disabled members: A family systems approach*. Lawrence: University of Kansas.

Turnbull, A. P., Summers, J. A., & Brotherson, M. J. (1986). Family life cycle: Theoretical and empirical implications and future directions for families with mentally retarded members. In J. J. Gallagher & P. M. Vietze (Eds.), *Families of handicapped persons: Research, programs, and policy issues* (pp. 156–181). Baltimore: Paul H. Brookes.

Turnbull, A. P., & Turnbull, H. R. III (1990). *Families, professionals, and exceptionality: A special partnership*. (2nd ed.). Columbus, OH: Merrill.

Turnbull, J. D. (1993). Early intervention for children with or at risk of cerebral palsy. *American Journal of Diseases of Children, 147*, 54–59.

Turner, R. J., Grindstaff, C. F., & Phillips, N. (1990). Social support and outcome in teenage pregnancy. *Journal of Health and Social Behavior, 31*, 43–57.

Upshur, C. C. (1991). Mothers' and fathers' ratings of the benefits of early intervention services. *Journal of Early Intervention, 15*(4), 345–357.

U.S. Department of Health and Human Services. (1992). *National child abuse and neglect data system: Working paper 1, 1990 summary data component*. DHHS Publication Nol (ACF) 92-30361.

U.S. Department of Health and Human Services (1993). *Creating a 21st Century Head Start: Final report of the Advisory Committee on Head Start quality and expansion*. Author.

U.S. Department of Health and Human Services. (1994). *The statement of the advisory committee on services for families with infants and toddlers: Early Head Start*. Washington, DC: Author.

U.S. Department of Health and Human Services. (1999). *Head Start Fact Sheet*. Washington, DC: U.S. Government Printing Office.

Vadasy, P. F., Fewell, R. R., & Meyer, D. J. (1986). Grandparents of children with special needs: Insights into their experiences and concerns. *Journal of the Division for Early Childhood, 10*, 64–72.

VandenBerg, K. A. (1993). Basic competencies to begin developmental care in the intensive care nursery. *Infants and Young Children, 6*(2), 5–59.

van den Boom, D. (1994). The influence of temperament and mothering on attachment and exploration: An experimental manipulation of sensitive responsiveness among lower-class mothers with irritable infants. *Child Development, 65*, 1457–1477.

Voices for Children in Nebraska. (1997). *Kids Count in Nebraska Report*. Omaha, NE: Author.

Vygotsky, L. (1978). *Mind in society: The development of higher psychological processes*. Cambridge, MA: Harvard University Press.

Waller, A. E., Baker, S. P., & Szocka, A. (1989). Childhood injury deaths: National analysis and geographic variations. *American Journal of Public Health, 79*, 310–315.

Warren, S., & Kaiser, A. (1986). Incidental language teaching: A critical review. *Journal of Speech and Hearing Disorders, 51*, 291–298.

Wasik, B. H., Ramey, C. T., Bryant, D. M., & Sparling, J. J. (1990). A longitudinal study of two early intervention strategies: Project CARE Child Development, *Child Development, 61*, 1682–1696.

Watkins, K. P., & Durant, L., Jr. (1992). *Complete early childhood behavior management guide*. West Nyack, NY: Center for Applied Research in Education.

Weider, S., Drachman, R., & DeLeo, T. (1989). A developmental/relationship inservice training model for public health nurses serving multirisk infants and families. *Zero to Three, 10*(1), 16–20.

Wells, W. M. (1997). Serving families who are hard to reach, maintain, and help through a universal access home visiting program. *Zero to Three, 17*(4), 1–9.

Werner, E. E. (1986). A longitudinal study of perinatal risk. In D. C. Farran & J. D. McKinney (Eds.), *Risk in intellectual and psychosocial development* (pp. 3–28). Orlando, FL: Academic Press.

Werner, E. E., & Smith, R. S. (1992). *Overcoming the odds: High risk children from birth to adulthood*. Ithaca, NY: Cornell University Press.

Wetherby, A. (1986). Ontogeny of communicative functions in autism. *Journal of Autism and Developmental Disorders, 16,* 295–316.

Whitehead, A., Jesien, G., & Ulanski, B. K. (1998). Weaving parents into the fabric of early intervention interdisciplinary training: How to integrate and support family involvement in training. *Infants and Young Children, 10*(3), 44–53.

Winton, P. J. (1988). *The Individualized Family Service Plan: Issues related to the process of developing the product*. Unpublished manuscript. University of North Carolina at Chapel Hill, Frank Porter Graham Child Development Center.

Winton, P. J. (1990). Promoting a normalizing approach to families: Integrating theory with practice. *Topics in Early Childhood Special Education, 10*(2), 90–103.

Winton, P. J. (1993). Early intervention personnel preparation: The past guides the future. *Early Childhood Report, 5*(5), 5.

Winton, P. J. (1996). A model for supporting higher education faculty in their early intervention personnel preparation roles. *Infants and Young Children, 8*(3), 56–67.

Winton, P. J., & Bailey, D. B. (1990). Early intervention training related to family interviewing. *Topics in Early Childhood Special Education, 10*(1), 50–62.

Winton, P. J., McWilliam, P. J., Harrison, T., Owens, A. M., & Bailey, D. B., Jr. (1992). Lessons learned from implementing a team-based model for change. *Infants and Young Children, 5*(1), 49–57.

Winton, P. J., & Turnbull, A. P. (1981). Parent involvement as viewed by parents of preschool handicapped children. *Topics in Early Childhood Special Education, 1,* 11–19.

Wischnowski, M. W., Yates, T. J., & McCollum, J. A. (1996). Program evaluation and strategic planning in early intervention: General principles and a case example. *Infants and Young Children, 8*(4), 49–58.

Wolery, J., & Dyk, L. (1985). The evaluation of two levels of a center-based early intervention project. *Topics of Early Childhood Special Education, 5,* 66–77.

Wolery, J., Holcomb, A., Venn, M. L., Brookfield, J., Huffman, K., Schroeder, C., Martin, C. G., & Fleming, L. A. (1993). Mainstreaming in early childhood programs: Current status and relevant issues. *Young Children, 49,* 78–84.

Wood, D. (1980). Teaching the young child: Some relationships between social interaction, language and thought. In D. R. Olson (Ed.), *The social foundation of language and thought* (pp. 87–99). New York: Norton.

Woody, R. H., LaVoie, J. C., & Epps, S. (1992). *School psychology: A developmental and social systems approach*. Boston: Allyn & Bacon.

Worthington, E. L., Jr. (1987). Changes in supervision as counselors and supervisors gain experience: A review. *Professional Psychology: Research and Practice, 18,* 189–208.

Yarrow, L. J., Rubenstein, J. L., & Pederson, F. A. (1975). *Infant and environment: Early cognitive and motivational development*. New York: Wiley.

Yoder, P. (1990). The theoretical and empirical basis of early amelioration of developmental disabilities: Implications for future research. *Journal of Early Intervention, 14,* 27–42.

Yoder, P., Kaiser, A., & Alpert, C. (1989). *A comparison of didactic and milieu language teaching in small groups of handicapped preschoolers*. Paper presented at the American Speech, Language, Hearing Foundation Conference on Treatment Efficacy, San Antonio, TX.

Zahn-Waxler, C., Iannoti, R. J., Cummings, E. M., & Denham, S. (1990). Antecedents of problem behaviors in children of depressed mothers. *Development and Psychopathology, 2,* 271–291.

Zahn-Waxler, C., Kochanska, G., Krupnick, J., & McKnew, D. (1990). Patterns of guilt in children of depressed and well mothers. *Developmental Psychology, 26,* 51–59.

ZERO TO THREE/National Center for Clinical Infant Programs. (1994). *Diagnostic classification of mental health and developmental disorders of infancy and early childhood.* Arlington, VA: Author.

Zigler, E. (1994). Reshaping early childhood intervention to be a more effective weapon against poverty. *American Journal of Community Psychology, 22*(1), 37–47.

Zigler, E., & Balla, D. (1982). Selecting outcome variables in evaluations of early childhood special education programs. *Topics in Early Childhood Special Education, 1,* 11–22.

Zigler, E., & Styfco, S. J. (1994). Using research and theory to justify and inform Head Start expansion. *Social Policy Report: Society for Research in Child Development, 7* (2), 1–20.

Index

About the Authors

Susan Epps, PhD, MPA, received her Doctor of Philosophy degree from the University of Minnesota and her Master of Public Administration degree from the University of Nebraska at Omaha. She has experience as a classroom teacher, pediatric psychologist, and coordinator of an interdisciplinary early intervention team. She has taught graduate students for many years and mentored interdisciplinary practicum students, doctoral interns, postdoctoral Fellows, and pediatrics and family practice residents and neonatology Fellows. She has consulted with school systems and departments of health and education, provided numerous inservice workshops and grand rounds, and presented at national and international conferences. She also has served on editorial boards of professional journals. As a licensed psychologist, she provides therapeutic supports to young children and their families. Her research publications have focused on developmental disabilities, family experiences in neonatal intensive care, and perceptions of preterm infant behavior.

Barbara J. Jackson, PhD, has her doctorate in psychology and cultural studies, with an emphasis in developmental psychology. During the past 25 years she has worked in the field of early intervention, specializing in work with infants with chronic illness and disabilities and their families. As an assistant professor at the University of Nebraska Medical Center and director of the Department of Education at Munroe Meyer Institute, she supervises interdisciplinary practicum students and teaches classes in early childhood education. Her research has examined the influence of chronic illness on children's coping and has evaluated the impact of early intervention programs on child and family outcomes, specifically Early Intervention, Early Head Start, and Even Start programs. As a member of numerous state task forces, she has contributed to policy development in early childhood.